Ninth Colloquium on Trees in Algebra and Programming

Ninth Colloquium on Trees in Algebra and Programming

5–7 March 1984
Bordeaux, France

Edited by
B. Courcelle
Mathématiques et Informatique, Université de Bordeaux

The right of the University of Cambridge to print and sell all manner of books was granted by Henry VIII in 1534. The University has printed and published continuously since 1584.

CAMBRIDGE UNIVERSITY PRESS
Cambridge
London New York New Rochelle
Melbourne Sydney

Published by the Press Syndicate of the University of Cambridge
The Pitt Building, Trumpington Street, Cambridge CB2 1RP
32 East 57th Street, New York, NY 10022, USA
296 Beaconsfield Parade, Middle Park, Melbourne 3206, Australia

First published 1984

Printed in Great Britain at the University Press, Cambridge

Library of Congress catalogue card number: 84-45246

British Library cataloguing in publication data

Colloquium on Trees in Algebra and Programming
(*9th: 1984: Bordeaux*)
Ninth Colloquium on Trees in Algebra and Programming
1. Electronic digital computers—Programming
I. Title II. Courcelle, B.
001.64'2 QA76.6

ISBN 0 521 26750 1

TABLE OF CONTENTS

FOREWORD

The ninth Colloquium on Trees in Algebra and Programming has been held in Bordeaux on March 5th-7th 1984.

The previous colloquia were held six times in Lille, France, once in Genoa, Italy (in 1981) and once in l'Aquila, Italy (in 1983). The 1985 Colloquium will be held in Berlin, West-Germany.

As the reader will see, the topics cover a wider area of theoretical computer science than one might expect from the title, but trees are of a so frequent use in computer science that there is no discrepancy between the title and the content of this volume.

The program committee consisted of B. Courcelle (Bordeaux), A. Arnold (Poitiers), G. Ausiello (Roma), R. Cori (Bordeaux), M. Dauchet (Lille), M. Dezani-Ciancaglini (Torino), P. Flajolet (Rocquencourt), G. Hotz (Saarbrücken), M. Nivat (Paris), J. Nivergelt (Zurich), J. Thatcher (Yorktown-Heights) who were helped by many colleagues in the difficult task of selecting contributions.

The Colloquium was supported by the European Association for Theoretical Computer Science, the University of Lille, the Institut National de Recherche d'Informatique et d'Automatique,the City of Bordeaux.

I express my gratitude to J.P. Braquelaire, M. Claverie, D. Courcelle, M. Jaubert and A. Polzin who helped me at various stages of the material organization.

The drawing of the program leaflet is due to J.P.Braquelaire.It is based on the letters CAAP abbreviating the French name of the colloquium and reproduces a 15th-century gate of the old city of Bordeaux.

B. Courcelle

CONTRIBUTORS

D. Arquès	Université de Haute Alsace, Mulhouse, France
R. Becker	Dept. of Mathematics, University of Cape Town, South Africa
J.P. Braquelaire	Université de Bordeaux-I, France
N. Dershowitz	Dept. of Computer Science, Urbana, Illinois, USA
J. Engelfriet	Twente University of Technology, The Netherlands
J. Françon	Université de Haute Alsace, Mulhouse, France
M. Gogolla	Abteilung Informatik, Universität Dortmund, West Germany
T. Hayashi	College of General Education, Kyushu University 01, Japan
A. Kanda	Dept. of Computer Science, University of British Columbia, Vancouver, Canada
M. Kaufmann	Universität des Saarlandes, Saarbrücken, West Germany
P. Lescanne	Centre de Recherche en Informatique de Nancy, France
G. Longo	Dipartmento di Informatica, Università di Pisa, Italy
K. Melhorn	Universität des Saarlandes, Saarbrücken, West Germany
S. Miyano	Dept. of Mathematics, Kyushu University 33, Japan
E. Paul	Centre National d'Etudes des Telecommunications, Issy les Moulineaux, France
C. Puech	LRI, Université de Paris-Sud, France
L. Puel	LITP, Université Paris 7, France
J-C. Raoult	LRI, Faculté d'Orsay, France
G. Rozenberg	Institute of Applied Mathematics and Computer Science, University of Leiden, The Netherlands
S. Schach	Dept. of Computer Science, Vanderbilt University, Nashville, USA
M. Soria	Laboratoire de Recherche en Informatique, Université Paris-Sud, France
J-M. Steyaert	Laboratoire de Mathématiques Appliquées, Ecole Polytechnique, Palaiseau, France
K. Theobald	FernUniversität-Gesamthochschule Fachbereich Mathematik & Informatik, Hagen, West Germany
W. Thomas	Lehrstühl fur Informatik II, Aachen, West Germany
E. Timmerman	Laboratoire d'Informatique Fondamentale de Lille, France
H. Vogler	Twente University of Technology, The Netherlands
I. Wegener	FB-20 Informatik, Johann Wolfgang Goethe-Universität, Frankfurt, West Germany
E. Welzl	Institutes for Information Processing, IIG, Technical University of Graz and Austrian Computer Society, Austria
S. Zaks	Dept. of Computer Science, Technion, Haifa, Israel

CONTINUOUS STRUCTURES AND ANALYTIC METHODS IN COMPUTER SCIENCE

G. Longo
Dipartimento di Informatica, Università di Pisa

Abstract. Most of the structures one deals with in Computer Science have a discrete and effective character: (finite) graphs, nets, trees in programming and formal languages, algorithms over finite strings or natural numbers, circuits etc... By continuous structures we mean "smooth" spaces, usually of cardinality not less than continuum, where interesting topological or order properties give some information on, say, classes of functions over them. By discussing results from various areas of Mathematical Computer Science, we stress the role of continuous structures as tools for proving results about discrete or even finite structures. In particular we overview results concerning trees in lambda-calculus, functionals in computability theory, boolean circuits in complexity theory and relate the finitary/combinatorial nature of the problems with their continuous solutions. We mostly focus on the methodology, more than on the technical aspects of the results presented.

§.1 Introduction

In order to outline the purpose of this lecture, it is probably worth mentioning first what we are not going to discuss. We are not simply going to look at the most widely known application of continuous structures in Computer Science. By this we mean the solution of the basic domain equation $X = X \to X$. Scott's solution of this equation, in the early 70's (to within isomorphism, of course; Scott (1972)), and his preliminary work on it, e.g. Scott (1970), set the mathematical basis for the Scott-Strachey approach to programming languages (see Stoy (1978), say). The work done within (or motivated by) denotational semantics by several authors includes, in a rather broad sense, purely mathematical developments (see Gierz et al. (1980)) as well as methods which influenced the actual design of programming languages (e.g. Gordon et al. (1979)). Specific areas are concerned with original applications of Category Theory to the semantics of programming languages (see Plotkin & Smyth (1982) for recent results and references) and computability in abstract structures (see Longo and Martini (1984) for a simple approach and references), just to mention two broadly construed topics.

What is the relation between the equation $X = X \to X$ and continuity properties? The point was to find a model of type-free λ-calculus. This language already was (and more become later) a paradigmatic or stylistic language for functional programming.

Approximation properties suggested the way to find a non-trivial space isomorphic to its own "function space": by allowing only the continuous functions w.r.t. a suitable topology, that isomorphism was made possible without contradicting Cantor's theorem, though obtaining a sufficiently rich function space for the interpretation of all λ-definable functions.

The required approximation properties may be given by the notion of domain as topological space.

1.1 <u>Definition</u>. (i) A poset $(X,\leq)$ is <u>complete</u> if any directed set $Y \subseteq X$ has a l.u.b., $\sqcup Y$.
(ii) Let $(X,\leq)$ be a c.p.o.. $A \subseteq X$ is open in the <u>Scott topology</u> if

(1) $x \in A$ <u>and</u> $x \leq y \Rightarrow y \in A$

(2) $Y \subseteq X$ directed <u>and</u> $\sqcup Y \in A \Rightarrow A \cap Y \neq \emptyset$.

(iii) A c.p.o. $(X,\leq)$ is <u>algebraic</u>, with base X_o, if $\emptyset$ and $\{y \in X / x_o \leq y\}$, for x_o ranging over X_o, form a basis for the Scott topology on $(X,\leq)$. X_o is the set of <u>finite</u> (or algebraic) elements. $(X,\leq)$ is <u>consistently complete</u> if every bounded subset has a l.u.b..
(iv) A <u>domain</u> is a consistently complete algebraic c.p.o., with the Scott topology.

1.2 <u>Remark</u>. Given domains $\underline{X} = (X,X_o,\leq)$ and $\underline{Y} = (Y,Y_o,\leq)$, $f:X \to Y$ is continuous iff $\forall x \in X \;\; f(x) = \sqcup \{f(x_o)/x_o \leq x\}$. The Scott topology on non-trivial domains is T_o, but not T_1. Recent work in denotational semantics has been dealing with stronger separation properties (e.g. metric spaces) or weaker closure properties not necessarily topological.

<u>Examples</u>. The set of partial functions from ω (the natural numbers) to ω, and $P\omega$, the powerset of ω, are domains. ($P\omega$ is also a lattice, of course, and $P\omega_o = \{A : A \subseteq \omega$ <u>and</u> A is finite$\}$).

The category of domains, with continuous maps, is cartesian closed. That is, if $\underline{X}$ and $\underline{Y}$ are domains, then also $\underline{X \times Y}$ and <u>Cont(X,Y)</u>, the continuous functions, are domains, with suitable bases, and they are nicely related (see Mac Lane (1971), Scott (1981), for details).

Most of the research issues mentioned above involve the Category of domains or related structures essentially as foundational tools for Computer Science or, say, analyze the relation between computational and denotational properties of programming languages. More discussion on this matter may be found in several places, see Longo (1984). In the present lecture we would like to motivate the use of continuous structures by their direct applications to results on finite or discrete spaces. Namely, we are going to survey a few results which may be stated in elementary/combinatory terms over discrete or finite structures and which have been proved by using continuous spaces. The mathematical notions used for this investigation are borrowed from (or related to) Mathematical Logic.

Probably a rough analogy with a basic topic in Mathematics may help to understand our methodological viewpoint.

The assertions of number theory deal with integers and are mostly elementary and of a combinatory character. The fundamental theorem of arithmetic, say, proves that any number is the product of a unique finite sequence of primes. In this case the proof is both elementary and simple; the relevance, though, of this old discovery is clear to everybody. Thus more knowledge about properties of prime numbers is surely important; in particular, say, the way they distribute over ω. Gauss, in 1849, first conjectured that, if $p(n)$ denotes the number of primes not exceeding n, then

(G) $$\lim_{n\to\infty} \frac{p(n)\ \log n}{n} = 1 ,$$

that is $p(n)$ is asymptotic to $n/\log n$.

(G) may be clearly stated in elementary formal number theory, Peano Arithmetic, as

$$\forall x\ \exists y\ \forall z (x > o \wedge z > y \rightarrow \left|1 - \frac{p(z)\ \log z}{z}\right| < \frac{1}{x})$$

(G) is known as the Prime Number Theorem. It was first proved by Hadamard and de la Vallée Poussin in 1896 by using Complex Function Theory, i.e. by the strong topological-algebraic properties of the field of complex numbers and the functions over it.

Only much later, in 1949, Selberg and Erdos gave an elementary proof of (G), that is a proof not using properties of functions of complex variables.

This pattern occurred several times in number theory; first an analytic proof, then an elementary argument, with at most a little use of real valued functions.

Usually, as in the case of (G), the elementary proof is more intricate and not simple at all, but it gives a better insight into constructive aspects of the result (y, say, depends uniformly effectively on x, in the formal statement of (G)). The analytic approach, though, may be more transparent, just because the difficulties are scattered over a whole nicely organized theory, such as the theory of complex functions.

Moreover, it may relate the results studied to other problems just because of the unifying power of a large and deep theory. This is exactly what happened with (G), in view of the work done, in order to prove (G), on the Riemann zeta function and the Euler identity by using Fourier series, see Hardy & Wright (1960).

It should be clear, then, that elementary or combinatory does not mean simple (or simpler): it may even mean the opposite, because it is harder to prove something by means of only a few notions, a few tools.

The results below have also been proved by looking at continuous structures. In the first two cases one may even say that "analytic" methods have been used, for elements of domains are described by finite approximations, similarly to approximations by finite expansions of Fourier series in complex function theory. Of course, we do not yet deal with the width and the difficulties of number theory: the Theory of Numbers is the oldest and most basic topic in Mathematics. In Pisa, say, some beautiful results were already obtained by Fibonacci (1202). Mathematical Computer Science is surely not as old as that. Its growth, though, because of the relevance of Computer Science and its applications in every-day life, is much faster.

In <u>§.2</u> below, a (preliminary) fact for the solution of recursive equations between programs is discussed. This is done for a paradigmatic functional language, λ-calculus. The proof uses a non-axiomatizable ("infinitary") consistent extension of λ-calculus and a continuous model. <u>§.3</u> presents an elementary notion of higher type computation. The basic properties of the type structure obtained by this, are proved by an essential use of continuous domains for denotational semantics and generalized computability.

<u>§.4</u> deals with the answer to a question concerning boolean circuits and

their complexity. As a matter of fact, the finitary argument for relating size and depth is based on an analogy to hierarchies of infinite classes of open sets in suitable topological spaces.
References to the eight or more authors, who proved the results in this introductory lecture, are given in the corresponding sections. For the reader's convenience, the few technicalities included decrease with the number of pages.

§.2 Invertible terms in λ-calculus

Terms of λ-calculus are defined by variables, formal application and the binding operator λ. The computation (reduction) rules are axiomatized as follows:

(β) $(\lambda x.M)N \geq [N/x]M$, for N free for x in M, as usual;

(η) $\lambda x.Mx \geq M$, for x not free in M.

The reduction predicate "≥" is reflexive, transitive and substitutive. "=" is the least equivalence relation such that $M \geq M' \Rightarrow M = N$; "=" also is substitutive.

A term is in <u>(β-)normal form</u> (βη-normal form) if no subterm is the LHS of axiom (β) ((β) or (η)).

A term M <u>possesses a (βη-)normal form</u> if, for some M' in (βη-)normal form, one has $\lambda\beta(\eta) \vdash M = M'$. Finally, M is <u>solvable</u> (or has head normal form), if, for some $P_1,\ldots,P_q$, $\vec{x}$ and y, $\lambda\beta \vdash M = \lambda x_1\ldots x_n.y\ P_1\ldots P_q$. M is <u>unsolvable</u>, otherwise.

The paradigmatic role of λ-calculus and Combinatory logic, as functional programming languages, is well known, see Backus (1978).

2.1 <u>The problem.</u> Combinatory Logic and λ-calculus, as type-free applicative languages, have a set of terms which forms a monoid with $I \equiv \lambda x.x$ as identity and composition "o" as application, where $M \circ N = BMN$ for $B = \lambda xyz.x(yz)$. Church proved that the closed terms of λβη-calculus form a recursively presented monoid, with an unsolvable word problem. Note, now, that equations among terms give a standard methods for defining terms, as well as for programs. Equations, though, as well known from algebra, can be more easily solved when working in a group.

Consider, for example, the following definition of the (unknown) term $X : M \circ X = X \circ P$. If M, say, possesses an inverse, M^{-1}, an easy application of Curry's fixed point combinator gives X from $X = M^{-1} \circ X \circ P$, since we obtain an ordinary recursive definition of X.

It is then an important question, raised by Curry & Feys (1958), under what conditions a term in the monoid has an inverse.

2.1.1 Definition. Let T be (an extension of) λ-calculus. M is T-invertible if $\exists N\ T \vdash M \circ N = I$ and $T \vdash N \circ M = I$. (In this case we say that M,N are T-inverse).

Dezani (1976) gives a characterization of invertible terms in λβη-calculus, among those which possess a normal form (for λβ-calculus, the group concides with {I}). This was done by an (implicit) use of the notion below of tree for terms. More recently, Böhm & Dezani (1984), by similar techniques, characterized invertibility w.r.t. a large class of associative combinators, besides composition "∘". By this,more general tools for solving equations are provided.

2.1.2 Definition. (Informal) The Böhm-tree of M is given by:

BT(M) = Ω if M has no head normal form

$$BT(M) = \lambda x_1 \ldots x_n . y \quad \text{if } M =_\beta \lambda x_1 \ldots x_n . y M_1 \ldots M_p$$

$$BT(M_1) \quad \cdots \quad BT(M_p)$$

The definition is informal, since Böhm-trees may be infinite (see Barendregt (1981) for a precise definition). In particular, BT(M) is finite and Ω-free iff M has a normal form.

Thus, there are plenty of interesting terms with infinite Böhm-trees. Take, say the fixed point combinator $Y = \lambda y.(\lambda x.y(xx))(\lambda x.y(xx))$ or the solution of $X = \lambda z.zX$, and a lot more. Since Wadsworth and Hyland's work, Böhm-trees have been a basic tool in the comparison of operational and denotational semantics of λ-calculus (see Barendregt (1981), Longo (1983)).

Roughly, this is because all terms, as all programs, are finite and Böhm-trees "display" their computational (operational) behaviour, which may be infinite (see Longo (1984) for a discussion).

Böhm-trees may be partially ordered by setting Ω, the undefined tree, as the least one and, then, by using induction on the structure of trees. That is, $BT(M) \subseteq BT(N)$ if BT(N) is obtained from BT(M) by replacing Ω is some leaves of BT(M) by some Böhm-tree.

Dezani's result (see 2.2.2, below) uses a difficult combinatory technique, where the finiteness of the Böhm-trees considered has an essential role. The question remained of characterizing all invertible terms, not necessarely with normal form; equations like the example above are perfectly sound also if $BT(M)$ is infinite, for M could still possess an head normal-form.

Bergstra & Klop (1980) fully answered the general questions, by using results in Dezani (1976). Our present interest in the methods used in Bergstra & Klop (1980) relies on the essential application made of infinitary, continuous structures to solve this typically combinatory problem. What's nice is that the characterization in Bergstra & Klop (1980) confirms the result in Dezani (1976), since invertible terms turn out to live only among normal forms. To see this, though, one needs to look also at terms with an infinite computational behaviour.

2.2 <u>The method</u>. Let $\sigma 1,\ldots,\sigma n$ be a permutation of $1,\ldots,n$ and $\vec{z}$ be a finite string of variables.

2.2.1 <u>Definition</u>. (i) The <u>hereditary permutators</u> (HP) is the set of λ-terms defined by:

$$M \in HP \quad \text{if} \quad BT(M) = \begin{array}{c} \lambda z x_1\ldots x_n.z \\ \diagup \qquad \diagdown \\ \lambda\vec{y}_1.x_{\sigma 1} \;\cdots\; \lambda\vec{y}_n.x_{\sigma n} \\ \diagup \;\; \diagdown \qquad \diagup \;\; \diagdown \end{array}$$

and each subtree is the tree of a term in HP.

(ii) The <u>finite hereditary permutators</u> (FHP) are the terms in HP with a finite, Ω-free Böhm-tree.

2.2.2 <u>Theorem</u>. Assume that M has a normal form. Then M is $\beta\eta$-invertible iff $M \in$ FHP.

<u>Proof</u>. Dezani (1976) (see also Bergstra & Klop (1980)). □

2.2.3 <u>Theorem</u>. M is $\beta\eta$-invertible iff $M \in$ FHP.

<u>Proof</u>. Bergstra & Klop (1980) (see also Barendregt (1981)).□

It is clear that in order to prove 2.2.3 from 2.2.2 one only has to show

(0) M $\beta\eta$-invertible $\Rightarrow$ M has a normal form,

since any M in FHP automatically has a normal form.

Bergstra and Klop give two arguments for (0), by embedding λ-

terms into different continuous models, D_∞ and $P\omega$. The discussion below borrows from the presentation in Barendregt (1981) and the authors second proof. It should be clear that we only try to give some transparency, if possible, to what is not immediately transparent from the very technical presentations by the authors, namely the mathematical significance of the methods used.

$P\omega$ may be turned into a model of type-free λ-calculus by a classical recursion theoretic notion of set-theoretic application and by defining abstraction accordingly (see Scott (1976) and Longo (1983), for recent work).

2.2.4 Definition. Let $<,>:\omega^2 \leftrightarrow \omega$ be a coding of pairs (the "little diagonal", say) and $\{e_n\}_{n\in\omega}$ the canonical numbering of the finite subsets of ω. Set then, for $A,B \in P\omega$ and $f \in Cont(P\omega,P\omega)$,

$$A \cdot B = \{m/\exists e_n \subseteq B <n,m>\in A\} \quad \text{and} \quad \underline{\lambda}x.f(x) = \{<n,m>/m \in f(e_n)\}$$

Clearly, $\underline{\lambda}x.f(x) \cdot B = f(B)$, by 1.2, that is $F(A) = \lambda x.A \cdot x$ and $G(f) = \underline{\lambda}x.f(x)$ give a retraction $Cont(P\omega,P\omega) \lhd P\omega$, for $F \circ G(f) = f$. For the given F, G is actually the unique such (see Bruce & Longo (1984) and Longo (1983)). Of course, the cardinality of $P\omega$ is $2^{\aleph_0}$ and its topological structure is the key point for defining the given retraction.

The true equalities between λ-terms in $P\omega$ are characterized by the following theorem.

2.2.5 Theorem. (Hyland) $P\omega \models M = N$ iff $BT(M) = BT(N)$.

Proof. (see Barendregt (1981)). □

We also need to introduce an interesting extension of $\lambda\beta\eta$-calculus, which may be defined in terms of Böhm-trees. The reader who wants to avoid the few technical notions below, at first reading, may skip them, up to comment 2.2.9.

Note first that, once the (possibly infinite) operational behaviour of a λ-term has been displayed by its Böhm-tree, one may also consider infinitary reduction rules (or expansion rules, their inverse operations).

In particular, one may η-expand (possibly infinite) nodes of a tree. Call "$\leq_\eta$" such a (possibly infinitary) rule between trees.

Examples

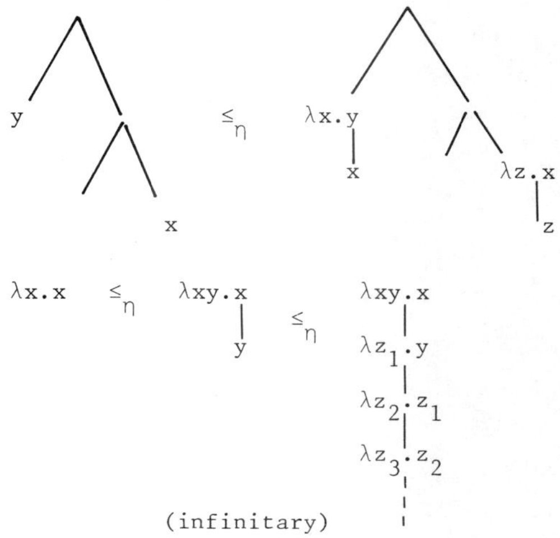

It is easy to see that the last tree is BT(J), for $J = \lambda xy.x(Jy)$.

2.2.6 Definition. Let A,B be Böhm-trees. Define then

(i) $A \overset{\eta}{\subseteq} B$ if $\exists A'\ A \leq_\eta A' \subseteq B$, where $\subseteq$ is defined after 2.1.2,

(ii) $A \overset{\eta}{\subseteq}{}^{\eta} B$ if $\exists A',B'\ A \leq_\eta A' \subseteq B' \geq_\eta B$

(iii) $A =_\eta B$ if $A \overset{\eta}{\subseteq}{}^{\eta} B \overset{\eta}{\subseteq}{}^{\eta} A$

(iv) $H^* = \{M = N / M,N$ are λ-terms and $BT(M) =_\eta BT(N)\}$

H^* is a consistent extension of $\lambda\beta\eta$-calculus. It is actually the largest consistent extension of the theory H, where all unsolvable terms are equated (Barendregt (1981)). Thus H^* is the unique Hilbert-Post completion of H.

2.2.7 Main Lemma Let M,N be H^*-invertible (see def. 2.1.1.). Then for some $n,m \geq 0$, say $n \geq m$, there are permutations π,σ and $M_i (1 \leq i \leq n)$, $N_j (1 \leq j \leq m)$ such that

(i) $\lambda\beta \vdash M = \lambda zx_1 \ldots x_n.z(M_1 x_{\pi 1}) \ldots (M_n x_{\pi n})$,

$\lambda\beta \vdash N = \lambda zy_1 \ldots y_m.z(N_1 y_{\sigma 1}) \ldots (N_m y_{\sigma m})$,

$\pi \circ \sigma = \sigma \circ \pi = id$, and

(ii) $N_i, M_{\sigma i}$, for $1 \leq i \leq m$, and M_i, I, for $m < i \leq n$, are H^*-inverse, modulo some substitution instances.

Notation: $M \in_k$ HP if M is in HP up to level k of BT(M), where the root is level 0 of a tree.

2.2.8 Theorem. If M is $\beta\eta$-invertible, then $M \in$ HP.

Proof. (Sketch) Assume that M,N are $\beta\eta$-inverse. Then M,N are also H^*-inverse, for $\lambda\beta\eta \subseteq H^*$. If we prove

1) $\forall k$ (MH^*-invertible $\Rightarrow M \in_k$ HP),

we are done, by the (informal) inductive definition of HP.

1) above holds for $k = 1$, by (a lot of) combinatory work on BT(M), up to the first two levels (see Dezani (1976), Bergstra & Klop (1980) or Barendregt (1981)).

Assume now (1) for $k > 1$. By 2.2.7,

M,N H^*-inverse $\Rightarrow N_i, M_{\sigma i}$ are H^*-inverse, as in 2.2.7 (ii).

Then, by induction hypothesis, $N_i, M_{\sigma i} \in_k$ HP and, clearly, $M,N \in_{k+1}$ HP. □

2.2.9 Comment Interestingly enough, most of the proof of the Main Lemma may be directly borrowed from Dezani's argument, which never mentions the theory H^*. What is then the use of it? The point is in the induction loading. If one assumes that M and N are $\beta\eta$-inverse, one doesn't get, in general, that $M_i, N_{\sigma i}$, defined as in 2.2.7 (ii), are $\beta\eta$-inverse, but just H^*-inverse (modulo some substitution instances). Thus the argument cannot be iterated inductively. In Dezani (1976) this can be done under the strong assumption that M and N possess a normal form.

Moreover, by the infinitary character of the provable equalities, H^* allows to compare terms with infinite Böhm-trees. Roughly, it is like looking at full decimal expansions of rational numbers, without restricting the attention to numbers with finite expansions (normal forms). The proof, though, works, at finite levels, exactly as for the finitary result and it is then analytically extended to the infinite expansions.

Church original work on λ-conversion used a more restrictive notion of λ-term. Namely, λI-terms are defined similarly to λ-terms, provided that $\lambda x.M$ is a λI-term iff x occurs free in M.

It is easy to see that a λI-term M has a normal form iff all of its subterms have a normal form. By looking at the definition of HP, one may work out the following fact.

2.2.10 Theorem. If $M \in HP$, then $BT(M)$ is Ω-free and there exists a λI-term M' such that $BT(M') = BT(M)$.

Let's now follow stepwise Bergstra and Klop's argument for

(0) If M is $\beta\eta$-invertible, then M has a normal form.

Assume that M,N are $\beta\eta$-inverse and that M has no normal form. Then

(1) There exist λI-terms M',N' s.t. $BT(M') = BT(M)$ and $BT(N') = BT(N)$, by 2.2.10.

(2) $BT(M')$ is infinite, by assumption and 2.2.8+10, and, hence M' has no normal form.

(3) $M' \circ N'$ is a λI-term, for $M' \circ N' \equiv BMN$ where $B \equiv \lambda xyz.x(yz)$, and, hence, it has no normal form, by (2).

(4) $P\omega \models M' = M$ and $P\omega \models N' = N$, by (1) and 2.2.5.

(5) $P\omega \models M' \circ N' = M \circ N$, by (4).

(6) $BT(M' \circ N') = BT(M \circ N)$, by (5) and 2.2.5, again.

(7) $BT(M \circ N)$ is infinite, by (3) and (6), and, hence , $M \circ N$ has no normal form.

The conclusion in (7) is clearly impossible, for $\lambda\beta\eta \vdash M \circ N = I$.

2.2.11 Comment The role of $P\omega$, as continuous model should be clear. It essentially allows to go from (1) to (6), by using 2.2.5. Since BT-equal terms are the same object in $P\omega$ by 2.2.5, one has (4) and, hence, (5) and (6) trivially follow.

It is like looking at a properties of natural numbers by studying them as elements of a more structured continuum they live in, the real or complex field, say. Where does continuity come in, in this case? The proof of 2.2.5 heavily relies on continuity properties of $P\omega$. To see this more closely, one may consult Barendregt (1981) or look at results which distillate the notion of "approximable application" in Longo (1983). This notion relates, in a general setting, the interpretation of formal application to the limit structure of models.

Can one directly go from (1) to (6) by working over Böhm-trees with some smart combinatory technique? This is done is Barendregt (1981; §.18.4), but the continuity argument is important as well. As a matter of fact one has to take the (completion of the) set of Böhm-trees, partially ordered as after 2.1.2, and heavily work with approximation and Scott continuity over this domain.

A final remark on cardinality. It is possible to take a countable model instead of $P\omega$, in the argument above, for $RE \subseteq P\omega$, the set of recursively enumerable sets, is an equationally equivalent sub-model of $P\omega$. That is, by the same notions of application and abstraction, RE yields a model which satisfies the same equalities as $P\omega$. More generally, for any infinite cardinal α, there is an applicative structure of cardinal α which yields lots of different λ-models, including one equationally equivalent to $P\omega$ (see Longo (1983)). The use of RE, though, instead of $P\omega$ would be like looking at rational numbers (or complex numbers with rational coordinates), for the analysis of the behaviour of continuous functions or predicates over the real (or complex) numbers. Those countable subsets are dense and they perfectly determine continuous functions or predicates on the latter sets. Similarly, RE is dense in $P\omega$ w.r.t. the Scott topology (and contains all algebraic elements).

§.3 The Hereditary Partial Effective Functionals

Classical higher type recursion theory deals with total object. As a matter of fact, Gödel and Kreisel's motivation for this topic refers to the analysis of the meaning in constructive mathematics of Peano or Heyting arithmetic (see Kreisel's paper in Heyting (1959)). For Kreisel's "no counterexample" interpretation, say, from $\exists x\ \forall y\ \exists z\ \forall w\ A(x,y,z,w)$ write $\exists F\ \exists G\ \forall f\ \forall g\ A(F(f,g),f(F(f,g)),G(f,g),g(F(f,g),G(f,g)))$, where F,G,f,g are function variables in the due type. Then x and y are effectively recovered from f and g, if F and G are higher type total computable functionals.

In Computer Science, a new branch of mathematical research on these matters has been motivated by the semantics of typed and type free languages, for it is sound to investigate the effectiveness, over semantic domains, of the interpretation of (higher type) programs (see Longo & Martini (1984) for references). In particular, since the work done by Scott in the semantics of programming languages and, in higher type recursion theory, by Ershov, who refers to early research by Scott, there has been a growing interest in partial objects. As a matter of fact, since the 30's, the notion of "partiality" turned out to be essential and helpful in the foundation of recursive function theory. A key point, say, is that the class of partial recursive functions (PR) can be effectively numbered; more precisely, the universal function is also in PR.

By using this idea, in Longo (1982) a direct elementary approach was proposed to higher type partial functionals. In Longo & Moggi (1983) the basic facts are proved and the type structure is compared to extant approaches.

The difference with Scott-Ershov approach (or Hyland's, for total functionals) is that the later first introduces the notion of continuity, possibly in abstract categorical settings, then defines the continuous and computable objects in any type by using PR; while the HPEF are presented by an inductive elementary construction, only based on the notion of partial recursive function. Interestingly enough, the key structural property of the HPEF, which may be expressed in purely elementary terms, could only be proved by using continuous structures. This may be considered a further motivation to the invention of the category of domains.

3.1 <u>The problem</u>. For sets A,B, write $f:A \to B$ if f is a total map from A to B. By setting $\omega^{\perp} = \omega \cup \{\perp\}$, we may write $f:\omega \to \omega^{\perp}$ for any partial number-theoretic function. Integer (pure) types are defined by $n+1:n \to n$ $(n+1:n \to 0)$, for $n \in \omega$.

Let $<,>$ be any effective coding of pairs in ω.

Set $C^{(0)} = \omega$ and $C^{(1)} = PR$. We now define $C^{(n)}$, for all $n > 1$, as the set of <u>hereditary partial effective functionals</u> (HPEF) of integer type n, by induction on n, using a set $C^{(n.5)}$ of maps from $C^{(n-1)}$ to $C^{(n)}$ (functions of "intermediate" type). The maps in $C^{(n)}$ go from $C^{(n-1)}$ to $C^{(n-1)}$. The coding $<,>$ is extended to higher types in one of the several possible ways.

$\lambda xy \,.\, g(x,y)$ is the map $<x,y> \longmapsto g(x,y)$.

3.1.1 <u>Definition</u>. (i) $C^{(n.5)} = \{\phi:C^{(n-1)} \to C^{(n)} / \lambda xy.\phi(x)(y) \in C^{(n)}\}$

(ii) $C^{(n+1)} = \{\tau:C^{(n)} \to C^{(n)} / \forall\phi \in C^{(n.5)} \;\; \tau \circ \phi \in C^{(n.5)}\}$.

In order to see that this definition makes sense, let's check the types.

Assume that $C^{(n-1)}$ and $C^{(n)}$ are given. Consider first $\phi:C^{(n-1)} \to C^{(n)}$ and set $\psi(<x,y>) = \phi(x)(y)$.

Clearly $\psi:C^{(n-1)} \to C^{(n-1)}$. Then $\phi \in C^{(n.5)}$ iff $\psi \in C^{(n)}$.

The following diagram should help in understanding how to define $C^{(n+1)}$, by using $C^{(n.5)}$:

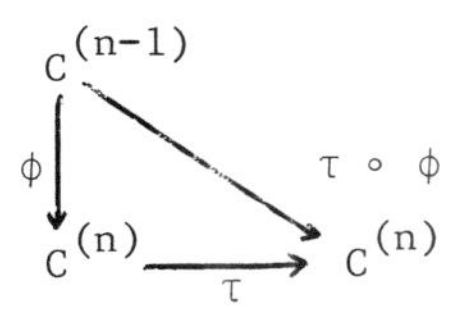

That is, $\tau \in C^{(n+1)}$ iff $\forall\phi \in C^{(n.5)}$ $\tau \circ \phi \in C^{(n.5)}$.

The pure type functionals $\{PC^{(n)}\}_{n\in\omega}$ may be also defined, by the technique above: just substitute $PC^{(n)}$ in the second instance of $C^{(n.5)}$ in the definition of $PC^{(n+1)}$ corresponding to 3.1.1 (ii) (see Longo & Moggi (1983; 3.12)).

In both cases, one only needs to know ω and PR. Apparently, though, it may seem that the full strength of Set Theory is needed in order to define the sets $C^{(n.5)}$ and $C^{(n+1)}$ above. As a matter of fact, a consequence of the results mentioned below is that, for all n, $C^{(n)}$ and $C^{(n.5)}$ are countable and can be effectively numbered.

By this we do not need to look, say, at the set of all functions from $C^{(n-1)}$ to $C^{(n)}$ in order to define $C^{(n.5)}$, but a countable subset would do. A posteriori, this is all expressible in Peano Arithmetic. (Exercise: set $C^{(1)}$ = "the constant functions from ω to ω". What is the cardinality of $C^{(2)}$? And if one takes, as $C^{(1)}$, the primitive recursive functions?).

We want to know, now, what the $C^{(n)}$'s are and how they behave, for $n > 1$. It is easy to see that all acceptable gödel-numberings of $C^{(1)} = PR$ live in $C^{(1.5)}$. It would be nice, say, if one could extend the notion of effective numbering to maps in $C^{(n.5)}$, for $n > 1$. In view of the s-m-n (iteration) theorem, this corresponds to proving the property (P) below, which was conjectured in Longo (1982).

$$\text{(P)} \quad \forall n > 0 \ \ \exists \phi_n \in C^{(n.5)} \ \forall \phi \in C^{(n.5)} \ \exists f_n \in C^{(n)} \ \ \phi = \phi_n \circ f_n .$$

Recall now that for all $f_{n+1} \in C^{(n+1)}$ one has $f_{n+1} \circ \phi_n \in C^{(n.5)}$. Then by (P), for some $f_n \in C^{(n)}$, $f_{n+1} \circ \phi_n = \phi_n \circ f_n$.

By this, HPEF may be visualized in the integer types by the following diagram (bottom-up):

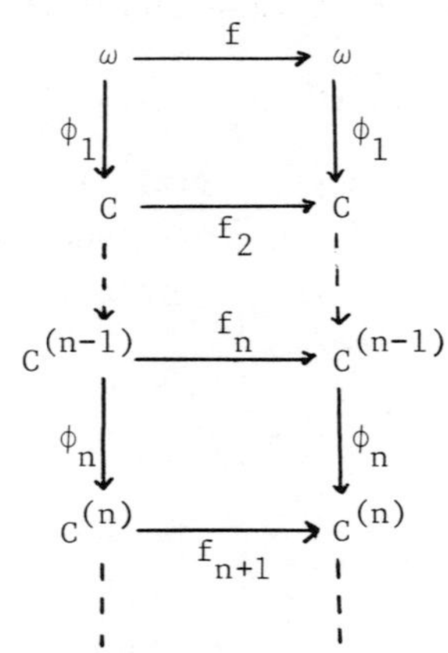

Clearly, in order (P) to hold, ϕ_n has to be onto also, preserving countability at higher types. Again, (P) is elementary and has a combinatory flavour.

3.2 <u>The method</u>. It is hard to look at a proof from "inside". The authors always belive that their proofs are (methodologically) transparent.

In Longo & Moggi (1983), (P) has been proved by an heavy induction loading, proposed by the second author, to be precise, who first pointed out that, by looking only at 3.1.1, the HPEF do not need to be ... well defined. As a matter of fact, $< , >:\omega^2 \leftrightarrow \omega$ is not trivially inherited at higher types. A first sight, one would just set $<f,g>(n) = <f(n),g(n)>$ as a definition for $<,>:C \times C \leftrightarrow C$ and so on. This is clearly wrong, for divergence of f or g cause essential problems. Set then $<f,g>(n) =$ <u>if</u> n is even <u>then</u> $f(\frac{n}{2})$ <u>else</u> $g(\frac{n-1}{2})$.

This is fine for $C^{(1)}$, but doesn't automatically prove that $<\tau,\sigma>(f) = <\tau(f),\sigma(f)>$ defines an (effective) coding of $C^{(n)} \times C^{(n)}$ into $C^{(n)}$, for $n \geq 2$. The proof of this goes inductively together with the proof of (P) and of two more facts, which need a few definitions.

Recall that a numbered set is a pair (D,e) where $e:\omega \to D$ is onto. $f:D \to D'$ is a <u>morphism</u> (of the numbered sets $(D,e),(D',e')$) if $\exists f' \in R \quad f \circ e = e' \circ f'$, where R are the recursive functions.

3.2.2 <u>Definition</u>. (i) Let (D,e) and (D',e') be numbered sets. Define then

(i) $d:\omega \to D$ is an <u>acceptable numbering</u> of D if $\exists f,g \in R \quad e = d \circ g$ and $d = e \circ f$.

(ii) $\phi:D \to D'$ is a <u>relative numbering</u> (of (D',e') w.r.t. (D,e)) if $\phi \circ e$ is an acceptable numbering of (D',e').

(iii) $\phi:D \to D'$ is a <u>principal numbering</u> (of (D',e') w.r.t. (D,e)) if ϕ is a morphism and $\forall\psi \in Mor(D,D') \quad \exists\Theta \in Mor(D,D) \quad \psi = \phi \circ \Theta$

Clearly acceptable, relative and principal numberings are onto maps. In presence of a relative numbering, any principal numbering is also relative. The converse doesn't hold. It is easy to see that, if (D,e) yields (a generalized version of) the recursion theorem and $f:D \to D'$ is a relative numbering, then also D' has the same property (see Longo & Moggi (1983; Intermezzo)).

The other assertion in the inductive proof need notions and

facts from the Category of domains (see 1.1). Let $\underline{X} = (X, X_o, \leq)$ be a countably based domain, with a given numbering $\{x_n\}_{n\in\omega}$ of X_o. Under a few simple decidability conditions for $\{x_n\}_{n\in\omega}$, define $x \in X$ computable if $\{n/x_n \in X_o$ and $x_n \leq x\}$ is r.e. (see Scott (1981) for details). Let X_c be the collection of computable elements. Under these assumptions, call any such domain effective.

Since in Cartesian Closed Categories properties of objects are inherited at higher types, given $\underline{X}$ as above each object in the type structure generated by $\underline{X}$ is an effective domain, with a corresponding notion of computable element. By this the continuous (and computable) partial functionals in the type structure over $\omega^{\perp}$, Ershov nicely related the flat domain with $\perp$ as least element, to the classical Kleene-Kreisel countable functionals (and the Hereditary Effective Operators; see Ershov (1976) for an account). Of course, continuity properties are the key issue in the Category of domains.

Consider now $E = \mathrm{Cont}(\omega, \omega^{\perp})$, where ω is given the discrete topology. Clearly, E is the effective domain of the partial functions and $E_c = PR$.

Set $E^{(n+1)} = \mathrm{Cont}(E^{(n)}, E^{(n)})$.

3.2.3. Theorem. For all $n \geq 1$ one has:

(1) $C^{(n)} = E_c^{(n)}$

(2) $C^{(n)} \times C^{(n)} \cong C^{(n)}$ via $<,>$

(3) $C^{(n.5)} = \mathrm{Cont}(E^{(n-1)}, E^{(n)})_c$

(4) $\exists\phi \in C^{(n.5)}$ principal relative numbering.

Proof. Longo & Moggi (1983). □

Properties (1) - (4) are proved by combined induction. (1) and (3) give the continuity of the HPEF.

More precisely, (2) at type n+1 is obtained from (1) + (2) at type n, by first showing that, in an effective domain, any effective coding of pairs of algebraic elements by algebraic elements is inherited to a corresponding effective coding at the higher type (the function space). (1) + (3) + (4) give (1) at the higher type. (1) + (2), again, prove (3) and so on, with various combinations, to prove the rest.

Note, now, that once proved that each $C^{(n)}$ is a countable set, with the natural numbering of constructive domains, (P) above amounts to say that each $C^{(n.5)}$ contains a principal numbering. In fact, by generalized Myhill-Shepherdson theorem, the continuous and computable functions over the computable elements of effective domains coincide with their morphisms, as numbered sets.

There may be direct arguments for proving (P). In Longo & Moggi (1983), though, it seemed essential to the role of finite approximants (algebraic elements) and their effectiveness properties to deal with the functions in the $C^{(n)}$'s, which are infinite objects.

Properties of effective computations over (possibly) infinite inputs are naturally handled by looking at finite pieces and, then, taking (topological) limits. Apparently, there is no way to escape from this, also when direct (non topological nor limit) definitions are given, as in our case.

Remark. Topological or limit structures are implicit in the definition of the Kleene-Kreisel countable functionals, when given by the "associates" (see Normann (1980)). This is not so for the HPEF, where there is no flavour of continuity nor approximation. Though, as soon as we just want to check if the definition makes sense in any type, finite approximants, that is the algebraic elements of suitable domains, come in. Of course, Myhill-Shepherdson and Kreisel-Lacombe-Shoenfield theorems, and their generalizations, are the key facts to understand this.

Question. Fix C as your prefered set of partial maps from ω to ω. What are, then, the $C^{(n)}$'s defined as in 3.1.1? (Take, say, C equal to the primitive recursive functions or the polynomial time computable functions. The properties of C are naturally inherited at higher types via the intermediate types $C^{(n.5)}$).

§.4 Circuit complexity

By circuits one may compute functions. Actually, boolean circuits form the core of computers, when printed as chips. It is then worth studying the complexity of circuits, e.g. by looking at their size and depth.

4.1 The problem. A boolean circuit is usually described as a finite directed acyclic graph, with input nodes and gates, labelled by $\wedge$ or $\vee$, as other nodes. One node is the output node. The size is given by the number of gates and the depth is the maximum length of a directed path from an input to the output.

One may also define boolean circuits in a more set-theoretic style.

4.1.1 <u>Definition</u>. For $n > 0$, let $\{x_1, \bar{x}_1, \ldots, x_n, \bar{x}_n\}$ be the <u>inputs</u> or <u>litterals</u>. The litterals are $\wedge_o$ $(\vee_o)$-<u>circuits</u>. For $i > 0$, an $\wedge_i$ $(\vee_i)$-<u>circuit</u> is a finite nonempty collection of $\vee_{i-1}$ $(\wedge_{i-1})$-circuits (write <u>i-circuit</u> for a $\wedge_i$-or $\vee_i$-circuit).

A Σ_i-<u>circuit</u> is a $\vee_{i+1}$-circuit. π_i-circuits are defined dually. A $\Sigma_i(\pi_i)$-<u>family</u> is a collection of $\Sigma_i(\pi_i)$-circuits all of whose 1-circuits are uniformly bounded in size (in some n). The <u>depth</u> of an i-circuit is i and the <u>size</u> is the cardinality of its sub-circuits.

Let $I = \{0,1\}$. Clearly, each boolean circuit with n inputs computes a function from I^n to I. A reasonable bound , in the size growth for circuits, is a polynomial growth rate in n. $\Sigma_i(\pi_i)$-families may be considered with this polynomial growth limitation. The question to ask then is how depth and size relate in computing functions. In particular, are there functions computed by polynomial size, depth k+1 circuits which cannot be computed by polynomial size, depth k circuits?

This question does not have an obvious answer since one may expect that a sufficiently large polynomial for the size growth may compensate the little loss in depth.

4.2 <u>The method</u>. In this final example the use of infinitary-continuous structures is indirect. More precisely, the proof in the finitary case is built up by an analogy to the infinitary result. The step towards infinity is made by looking at I^ω instead of I^n, for $n < \omega$. I^ω, of course, is the set of infinite sequences of 0 and 1's.

Infinite circuits are defined similarly as in 4.1.1, by dropping the finitary restrictions. Namely, imputs are from an infinite set $\{x_1, \bar{x}_1, x_2, \bar{x}_2 \ldots\}$ and, at each $\wedge_i$ $(\vee_i)$ level, one may take infinite collections from the level below. We only require that an (infinite) Σ_i-circuit has all of its 1-subcircuits which are finite.

Clearly, each circuit in the present sense defines a function $f: I^\omega \to I$, similarly as finite circuits define functions from I^n to I, for suitable n. $A \subseteq I^\omega$ is <u>defined by</u> a circuit C, if $A = f^{-1}(1)$ for f defined by C.

Definable subsets of I^ω are in a simple relation to a well known σ-algebra of subsets of I^ω as topological space.

4.2.1 Definition. Let X be a topological space.

Define then $\Sigma^0_1 = \{A/A \subseteq X$ and A is open$\}$

$\Pi^0_1 = \{A/A \subseteq X$ and A is closed$\}$,

for $i > 1$, $\Sigma^0_i = \{\bigcup_1^\omega A_n / \forall n < \omega\ \exists j < i\ A_n \in \Pi^0_j\}$

$\Pi^0_i = \{A/\bar{A}$ (the complement of A) is in $\Sigma^0_i\}$.

If X is a countably based complete metric space, then $A \subseteq X$ is Borel if, for some $i < \omega_1$, $A \in \Sigma^0_i$.

Borel sets are extensively used in several areas of Mathematics and in Descriptive Set Theory. Consider now ω and I with the discrete topology.

Note then that I^ω, with the product topology, is a countably based compact metric space (the Cantor space). The distance between $\alpha, \beta \in I^\omega$ is given by $d(\alpha,\beta) = \frac{1}{2^n}$, where n is the least such $\alpha(n) \neq \beta(n)$. Thus the basic open sets are the collections of extensions of finite sequences of 0 and 1's.

Just looking at the definitions, one may easily compare circuits and Borel sets in I^ω, by the following lemma.

4.2.2 Lemma. $A \subseteq I^\omega$ is in Σ^0_i iff it is definable by a Σ_i-circuit.

A classical result for the Borel hierarchy of sets states the non trivial fact that for $i < j$, Σ^0_i is strictly smaller than Σ^0_j.

The proof is usually given by diagonalization (Jech (1978)). Namely, one first shows that for each i, there exist a universal set $\cup$ in Σ^0_i. That is, for every Σ^0_i set A, for some a in the given space, $A = \{x/(x,a) \in \cup\}$. Then, by the usual Cantor-Russell diagonal argument, take $K = \{x/(x,x) \in \cup\} \in \Sigma^0_i$. Clearly, $\bar{K} \in \Sigma^0_{i+1}$, but $\bar{K} \notin \Sigma^0_i$ otherwise, for some k, $\bar{K} = \{x/(x,k) \in \cup\}$ and $k \in K$ iff $k \in \bar{K}$.

In Sipser (1983) a more combinatorial proof is given of the strict inclusion between Σ_i-circuits and Σ_{i+1}-circuits.

4.2.3 Theorem. For all $i > 0$, there exist functions definable by Σ_i-circuits but not by Σ_{i-1}-circuit.

The proof actually gives, for each $p > o$, a function $f_p : I^\omega \to I$ with the required property, at level p, as follows. Let $<,>: \omega^2 \leftrightarrow \omega$ be a pairing function, extended to ω^n in the usual way. Define, for $\alpha \in I^\omega$,

$$f_p(\alpha) = 1 \text{ iff } \exists i_1 \forall i_2 \ldots Q i_p \ \alpha(<i_p,\ldots,i_p>) = 1.$$

For $p = 1$, f_p is clearly Σ_1 definable, but not Σ_0. The basic work is in the inductive step, where, assuming the result for p-1, a Σ_{p-2}-circuit is given for f_{p-1} from a Σ_{p-1}-circuit for f_p. This is done by completing functions constructively defined at finitary levels (Sipser (1983)).

The finitary case deals with circuits, Σ_i-circuits in particular, defined as in 4.1.1.

The input strings, then, and all higher levels of $\wedge$, $\vee$ collections are finite. Since we want to look at polynomial growth rate, the attention is restricted to circuit families whose size is bounded by a polynomial in the number of input variables. Thus a Σ_i-family, say, is a collection of $\vee_{i+1}$-circuits as in 4.1.1, with this polynomial size limitation.

4.2.4 Theorem. For all $i > o$, there exist functions definable by a Σ_i-circuit family but not by a Σ_{i-1}-circuit family.

The proof goes similarly as for 4.2.3. The finitary limitations come in by the finite nature of the counterexamples and by the uniform bounds in their definition. Namely, for $p, m > o$ and $n = m^p$, define $f_p^n: I^n \to I$ as follows:

$$f_p^n(\alpha) = 1 \text{ iff } \exists i_1 < m \ \forall i_2 < m \ldots Q i_p < m \ \alpha(<i_1,\ldots,i_p>) = 1$$

(if n is not a power of m, then f_p^n is everywhere o).

A finitary analogue to the work done for the infinitary statement, in particular in the inductive step, proves that the f_p^n have the required property (Sipser (1983)).

4.2.5 Comment Infinite binary sequences, i.e. the elements of I^ω, are limits of finite sequences in the obvious sense. This is made more precise by taking I^ω with the Cantor topology and by the topological notion of limit: just recall the definition of basic neighbourhood in I^ω.

Thus also in this case one looks at the completion ("take all limits") of a given set of finite objects. Similarly, in §.2 the infinite Böhm-trees considered were limits, w.r.t. the Scott topology, of the finite Böhm-trees used in the original finitary result. In both cases, the finite objects to be extended were clearly provided by the extant result or the problem itself. As for the result sketched in §.3, no explicit hint was given by the problem to the continuous structure which could be used. Myhill-Shepherdson theorem and Scott's work, though, suggested the method and the induction loading.

In the result just presented, the rich topological structure of I^{ω} appears, since the Borel hierarchy theorem is given for (spaces homeomorphic to) countably based complete metric spaces. This is only used for an analogy, though, more than for a rigorous infinitary extension of finitary facts, as in the previous cases.

Proofs as well as conjectures by analogy are fruitfully used in Mathematics. As for the present finite/infinite analogy, applied to circuit complexity, more work may be found in Furst et. al. (1981).

The leading idea in this approach may be extended to the fundamental $P = ?NP$ question in complexity theory, by comparing exponential growth to uncountability (Sipser (1984)). In short, typical NP-complete problems, such as the various satisfiability problems, are decided by deterministic algorithms enumerating and checking all subsets of a given set. The exponential growth arises because the subsets of a set of cardinality n are 2^n.

Analogously, uncountability arises from the powerset operation over infinite sets.

Thus polynomial growth may be related to exponential growth similarly as countability to uncountability. By this analogy Furst et al. (1981) answer a question on the complexity of parity functions. We look forward to seing further applications of this method to the $P = ?NP$ question.

It should be clear that this informal survey is far away from being exhaustive as far as the use of "analytic" methods in Computer Science is concerned. We hope, though, that the examples mentioned could give some motivations for looking at combinatorial facts also in infinitary frameworks or by transporting combinatorial methods on infinite objects, where they are often simpler, to corresponding methods on finite objects.

Acknowledgements

The first part of this lecture was directly inspired by the joint work and a thousand and one discussions with Henk Barendregt.

This work was partly supported by C.N.R. (Comitato per la Matematica).

References

Backus, J. (1978). Can Programming be liberated from the Von Neuman style? A functional style and its Algebra of Programs. CACM, 21,8.

Barendregt, H.P. (1981). The lambda calculus: its syntax and semantics. North-Holland, Amsterdam (revised edition, to appear).

Bergstra, J. & Klop, J.W. (1980). Invertible terms in the lambda-calculus. Theor. Comp. Sci.11, 19-37.

Böhm, C. & Dezani, M. (1983). Combinatory Logic as Monoids. Underground, Rome.

Bruce, K. & Longo, G. (1984). A note on combinatory algebras and their expansions. Theor. Comp. Sci. (to appear).

Curry, H.B. & Feys, R. (1958). Combinatory Logic. North-Holland, Amsterdam.

Dezani, M. (1976). Characterization of normal forms possessing inverse in the λβη-calculus. Theor. Comp. Sci. 2, 323-337.

Ershov, Yu. L. (1976). Model C of partial continuous functionals. In Logic Coll. 76, eds. R. Gandy, M. Hyland. North-Holland, Amsterdam.

Furst, M. , Saxe, J. & Sipser, M. (1981). Parity circuits and the polynomial time hierarchy. 22nd FOCS, 260-270.

Fibonacci, L. (1202). Liber Abaci, Manuscript, Pisa.

Giannini, P. & Longo, G. (1982). Effectively given domains and lambda-calculus semantics. Info. Contr. (to appear).

Gierz, G. et al. (1980). A compendium of Continuous lattices. Springer-Verlag, Berlin.

Gordon, M., Milner R. & Wadsworth C. (1978). Edinburgh LCF. LNCS 78, Springer-Verlag, Berlin.

Hardy, G. & Wright E. (1960). An Introduction to the Theory of Numbers. Oxford.

Heyting, A. (1959). Constructivity in Mathematics. North-Holland.

Jech, T. (1978). Set Theory. Academic Press, London.

Longo, G. (1982). The Hereditary Partial Effective Functionals in any finite type (preliminary note). Forsch. f. Math. ETH, Zürich.

Longo, G. (1983). Set-theoretical models of λ-calculus: theories, expansions, isomorphisms. Ann. Pure Applied Logic (formerely: Ann. Math. Logic), 24, 153-188.

Longo, G. (1984). Proceedings of Math. Found. of Comp. Sci. '84, Prague (invited lecture, in preparation).

Longo, G. & Martini S. (1984). Computability in higher types and the universal domain Pω. Proc. of STACS, LNCS Springer-Verlag (to appear).

Longo, G. & Moggi, E. (1983). The Hereditary Partial Effective functionals and Recursion Theory in Higher Types. J. Symb. Logic (to appear).

Mac Lane, S. (1971). Categories for the working mathematician. Springer-Verlag, Berlin.

Plotkin, G. & Smyth, M.B. (1982). The category-theoretic solution of recursive domain equations. Dept. of Comp. Sci. Edinburgh.

Normann, D. (1980). Recursion on the countable functionals. LNM 811, Springer-Verlag, Berlin.

Scott, D.S. (1970). Outline of a Mathematical Theory of computation. 4th Ann. Princeton conf. on Info. Sci. and Syst..

Scott, D.S. (1972). Continuous lattices, In Toposes, Algebraic Geometry and Logic. LNM 274, Springer-Verlag, Berlin.

Scott, D.S. (1976). Data types as lattices. SIAM J. of Comput., 5, 522-587.

Scott, D.S. (1981) Lectures on a mathematical theory of computation. Oxford Univ. Comp. lab., Tech. monograph PRG-19.

Stoy, J. (1978). Denotational Semantics: the Scott-Strachey approach to Programming Language Theory. Cambridge, Mass.: MIT Press.

Sipser, M. (1983). Borel sets and circuit complexity 15-th STOC, 61-69.

Sipser, M. (1984). On polynomial versus exponential growth. Underground, Boston.

OPTIMAL VLSI-CIRCUITS FOR THE BASIC ARITHMETIC FUNCTIONS*

by
Kurt Mehlhorn
FB 10
Univ. des Saarlandes
66 Saarbrücken
West-Germany

Abstract.

In this paper we review results about the VLSI-complexity of the basic arithmetic functions addition, subtraction, multiplication, and division. In particular, optimal designs for all four operations are surveyed.

INTRODUCTION.

In this paper we will briefly review recent results on the VLSI-complexity of the basic arithmetic functions such as addition and subtraction, multiplication and divison. The paper is organized into two parts:

1. A VLSI Model and Lower Bounds
2. Good Designs

1. A VLSI MODEL AND LOWER BOUNDS

In this section we will do three things: we first set up a model of VLSI computation, then define the relevant complexity measures area, time, and period, and will finally state lower bounds for the basic arithmetic functions.

Our VLSI model is based on Boolean circuits and originates with Thompson's Ph.D thesis [T79]. It was later refined and simplified by several authors [BK81,CM81,LM81, LS81,V80,Y81,MM82]

*This research was supported by the Deutsche Forschungsgemeinschaft, SFB 124, VLSI-Entwurfsmethoden und Parallelität, Teilprojekt B2.

Let $f: B^n \to B^m$, $B = \{0,1\}$ be a Boolean function. A chip for f consists of three structures:

a) The *circuit* Γ: A synchrounous Boolean circuit with feedback and bounded fanin. Formally, this is a directed bipartite graph $\Gamma = (V,E)$ where V is partitioned into a set S of *switches* and a set W of *wires*. Here $S = P \cup G$ where P is a set of *ports* labelled <u>in</u> or <u>out</u> and G is a set of *gates* labelled <u>and</u>, <u>or</u>, <u>nand</u>, or <u>nor</u>. For $s \in W$, if $(s,w) \in E$ then w is called an *output* of s, if $(w,s) \in E$ then w is called an *input* of s. All gates have out-degree 1, all wires have in-degree 1. Each input port has no input and one output. Each output port has one input and no output.

b) The *layout* Λ: The layout maps every vertex in the circuit into a compact connected region in the plane. Furthermore, each point in the region lies inside some Cartesian square of side length $\lambda > 0$ that is completely contained in the region. (This provision models the finite resolution of the fabrication process for VLSI chips.) Each point in the plane belongs to the interior of at most $\nu \geq 2$ regions. (The parameter ν is another fabrication process specific constant representing the number of functional *layers* on the chip. Since $\nu \geq 2$ also non-planar circuits Γ can be laid out.) Two regions touch exactly if the vertices they represent are neighbours in Γ. (We say that regions R_1 and R_2 touch if $R_1 \cap R_2 \neq \phi$ but $R_1^o \cap R_2^o = \phi$, where R_1^o, R_2^o are the interior of R_1 resp. R_2.)

c) The *manual* Δ: The manual is a set of directions for the communication between the chip and its environment. It is an <u>injective</u> mapping $\Delta: \{1,...,n+m\} \to P \times \mathbb{N}$. The intuitive meaning is as follows. If $\Delta(i) = (p,t)$ and $i \leq n$ $(i>n)$ then the i-th input ((n-i)-th output) bit is read (produced) at port p and time $t, t \geq 0$.

After defining all components of the chip we can define the operation of the circuit.
Let $(x_1,...x_n) \in B^n$ and let $(y_1,...y_m) = f(x_1,...x_n)$. A state of the circuit is a mapping from $W \cup P$ (wires and ports) into the set B of boolean values. We start the circuit at time 0 in an arbitrary state. In the t-th cycle, $t \geq 0$, the chip operates as follows

1) if $\Delta(i) = (p,t)$ for some $i \leq n$ then x_i is put on input port p.

2) Each input port puts its value on the wire connected to it

3) Each gate g "reads" the values on all its input wires and computes the Boolean operation given by its label. The resulting value is put on its output wire.

4) if $\Delta(i) = (p,t)$ for some $i > n$ and output port p then the output port "outputs" the value on its input wire. If the chip operates correctly then the value must be y_{i-n}.

We are now ready to define the complexity measures area A, time T and period P.

1) the area A is the area of the smallest rectangle enclosing layout Λ

2) the time T is the maximal t such that $\Delta(i) = (p,t)$ for some i and p.

3) the period P is the minimal distance in time between consecutive problem instances which can be fed into the chip, i.e. if $P = d$ then computations on different inputs can be started at time 0,d,2d,3d,... . The notion of period

corresponds to the fact that hardware can sometimes be pipelined and that pipelined hardware can work on several problem instances at the same time.

We consider the following Boolean functions

Add $(x_1,\ldots,x_n,y_1,\ldots y_n) = (z_0,\ldots z_n)$, i.e. binary number $(z_0,\ldots,z_n)$ is the sum of binary numbers $(x_1,\ldots x_n)$ and $(y_1,\ldots y_n)$

Mul $(x_1,\ldots x_n,y_1,\ldots y_n) = (z_0,\ldots,z_{2n})$, i.e. binary number $(z_0,\ldots z_{2n})$ is the product of binary numbers $(x_1,\ldots,x_n)$ and $(y_1,\ldots y_n)$.

Division is defined similarly. We have

<u>Theorem 1</u>. a) For either Add, Mul or Div : $T \geq \log n$ and $T \geq P$

b) For Add: $AP = \Omega(n + n \log n/T)$

c) For Mul and Div: $A = \Omega(n)$ and $AP^2 = \Omega(N^2)$

<u>Proof</u>. a) $T \geq \log n$ follows from the fact that some outputs of Add and Mul depend on all inputs, and that we restricted our circuits to have bounded fan-in. $T \geq P$ is obvious.

b) We refer the reader to Baudet's paper [B81]

c) We refer the reader to papers by Thompson [T79], Abelson/Andreae [AA80] Brent/Kung [BK81] and Vuillemin [V 80]. □

Theorem 1 defines <u>forbidden</u> regions in the A,P,T-space for addition and multiplication. For example, an adder with $T = O(\log n)$ must satisfy $AP = \Omega(n \log n)$, and a multiplier with $T = O(\log n)$ must satisfy $A = \Omega((n/\log n)^2)$.

We will indicate in the next section that all lower bounds given above are sharp, i.e. can be reached by actual designs.

2. GOOD DESIGNS

The upper bounds are provided by

Theorem 2. a) [BK81] For all $T \geq P$, $\Omega(\log n) \leq T \leq O(N)$ there is a chip for binary addition with $AP = O(n + n \log n/T)$.

b) [LM83,LV83] There is a chip for multiplication with $T = O(\log n)$, $P = O(1)$ and $A = O(n^2)$, i.e. $AP^2 = O(n^2)$.

c) [PM83] For $\Omega(\log n) \leq T \leq O(\sqrt{n})$ there is a chip for binary multiplication with $AT^2 = O(n^2)$

d) [M83] For $\Omega((\log n)^2) \leq T \leq O(\sqrt{n})$ there is a chip for binary division with $AT^2 = O(n^2)$.

Remark 1: a) settles the question of the complexity of binary addition completely. All points on the boundary of the forbidden region can indeed be realized. For multiplication the situation is similar; note that $A = \Omega(n)$, $T = \Omega(\log n)$ and $AT^2 = \Omega(n^2)$ implies that $AT^2 = O(n^2)$ can only be possible for T in the range $[\Omega(\log n), O\sqrt{n})]$. For division, the possibility of AT^2-optimal very fast circuits is left open.

Remark 2: The search for AT^2-optimal multiplication circuits has a short but intensive history. First, there was a sub-optimal $AT^2 = O(n^2 \log^3 n)$ by Brent/Kung [BK81]. Then Preparata/Vuillemin [PV81] proposed a class of AT^2-optimal designs for $\Omega(\log^2 n) \leq T \leq O(\sqrt{n})$, settling the question of "slow" optimal multiplication. In 1982 several groups of researchers (Vuillemin [V83], Becker[B83], Luk/Vuillemin [LV83], Lengauer/Mehlhorn[LM83]) found designs with minimum computation time $T = O(\log n)$. The designs of [LV83,LM83] are AP^2-optimal and are the content of part b). Finally, Preparata/Mehlhorn [PM83] put everything together (this should be interpreted litterally, as all key ideas of their design were used already in one of the previous designs) and settled the problem. The AT^2-optimal circuits for slow division were found shortly afterwards [M83] .

Remark 3: Two of the designs mentioned above were actually implemented. Guibas/Vuillemin [GV82] optimized the design of the optimal adder and implemented it. A layout for an 8 -bit Carry-Lookahead-Adder was generated with the HILL-design system [LM84]. The paper by Luk/Vuillemin [LV 83] describes in detail an implementation of their design.

References

1.[AA80] H. Abelson and P. Andreae, "Information transfer and area-time trade-offs for VLSI multiplication," Communication of the ACM, vol.23, n.1, pp. 20-22, Jan. 1980.

2.[B81] G.M. Baudet, "On the Area Required by VLSI circuits" CMU Conference of VLSI Systems and Computations, 1981, pp. 100-107.

3.[B82] B. Becker, "Schnelle Multiplizierwerke für VLSI-Implementierung," Technical Report, Uni des Saarlandes, 1982.

4.[BK81] R.P Brent and H.T. Kung, "The chip complexity of binary arithmetic," J. Ass. Comp. Mach., vol. 28-pp. 521-534, July 1981.

5.[CM81] B. Chazelle, L. Monier, "A Model of Computation for VLSI with Related Complexity Results", 13th Annual ACM-STOC Conference (1981), pp. 318-325.

*

6.[LM81] T. Lengauer, K. Mehlhorn, "The Complexity of VLSI-Computations", CMU-Conference on VLSI Systems and Computations (1981), pp.89-99

7.[LM83] T. Lengauer, K. Mehlhorn, "VLSI complexity theory, efficient VLSI algorithms and the HILL design system," in "The International Professorship in Computer Science: Algorithmics for VLSI, Ed. Trullemans, Academic Press, to appear.

8.[LM84] T. Lengauer, K. Mehlhorn, "The HILL System: A Design Environment for the Hierarchical Specification, Compaction, and Simulation of Integrated Circuit Layouts, MIT VLSI Confernce, Jan. 1984.

8.[LS81] R.J. Lipton, R. Sedgewick, "Lower Bounds for VLSI", 13th Annual ACM-STOC Conference (1981), pp. 300-307

9.[LV83] W.K. Luk and J.E. Vuillemin, "Recursive implemenation of optimal time VLSI integer multipliers," VLSI83, Trondheim, Norway, September 1983.

10.[M83] K. Mehlhorn, "AT^2-Optimal VLSI-Circuits for Integer Division and Square Rooting", Technischer Bericht 1983.

11.[MM83] K. Mehlhorn, E. Meinecke-Schmidt, "Las Vegas is better than Determinism in VLSI and Distributed Computing," 14th Annual ACM-STOC Conference (1982), pp. 330-337.

12.[PV81] F.P. Preparata, J. Vuillemin, "Area-time optimal VLSI networks for computing integer multiplication and Discrete Fourier Transform", Proceedings of I.C.A.L.P., Haifa, Israel, July 1981, pp. 29-40.

13. [T79] C.D. Thompson, "Area-time complexity for VLSI," Proc. of the 11th Annual ACM Symposium on the Theory of Computing (SIGACT), pp. 81-88, May 1979.

14. [V80] J. Vuillemin: "A Combinatorial Limit to the Computing Power of VLSI Circuits," 21st Annual IEEE-FOCS Symposium (1980), pp 294-300.

15. [V83] J.E. Vuillemin, "A very fast multiplication algorithm for VLSI implementation", Integration, VLSI Journal, vol. 1, n.1, pp. 33-52, 1983.

16. [Y81] A.C. Yao, "The Entropic Limitations on VLSI Computati Computations," 13th Annual ACM-STOC Conference (1981), pp. 308-311.

*17, [GV82] L. Guibas, J. Vuillemin, "on Fast Binary Addition in MOS Technologies", Int. Conf. on Circuits and Computers (1982) 147-150.

LOGICAL ASPECTS IN THE STUDY OF TREE LANGUAGES

Wolfgang Thomas
Lehrstuhl für Informatik II, Büchel 29 - 31, D - 5100 Aachen

Abstract. Making use of model-theoretic concepts and techniques, we study several properties of tree languages: "aperiodic", "star-free", "first-order definable", "chain definable", and "antichain definable". The first three are derived from corresponding properties of word languages (which are equivalent in the word-case but diverge for tree languages). The latter two notions result from definability in monadic second-order logic by restricting the range of the set variables to chains and antichains in trees. We describe the inclusion relations between these properties and present the following characterization results: A tree language is star-free iff it is antichain definable, and a chain definable tree language is aperiodic iff it is first-order definable.

1 INTRODUCTION

Since the concept of a regular tree language emerged in the work of Thatcher & Wright (1968) and Doner (1970), it has been well known that basic notions and results extend in a very direct way from the theory of regular word languages to the case of tree languages. This applies to the step from finite automata to tree automata (in the frontier-to-root version) as well as to the extension of regular expressions to tree language expressions. Also the characterization of regular word languages in terms of monadic second-order logic (as obtained by Büchi (1960) and Elgot (1961)) carries over in rather complete analogy to regular tree languages.

In the present paper we consider other concepts where this parallelism fails. An example of this kind is given by the class of star-free languages which plays a central role in the theory of regular word languages. (A language is star-free if it is defined by a regular expression in which complement but no star is allowed.) It is known by the Theorem of Schützenberger (1965) that a regular word language is star-free iff it is aperiodic (i.e. satisfies a certain "pumping property" to be explained below); and a result of Ladner (1977) says that the star-free languages are also characterized in terms of the first-order theory of linear orders. In section 2 we define canonical extensions of these notions for tree languages and show that both characterizations fail to hold in this case.

The main aim of the paper is to show that the situation is not as unsatisfactory as it appears at this point. Using two further model-theoretic definability notions, the above characterizations are saved in a modified form; and it seems that this reformulation will be useful in clarifying some aspects which are typical for tree languages in comparison with word languages. For this purpose we introduce (in section 3) the following model-theoretic properties of tree languages: chain definability and antichain definability. They result from definability in monadic second-order logic by restricting the range of the set variables to the chains, resp. antichains in a tree. First we settle the inclusion problem for these notions: it is shown that chain definability and antichain definability are incomparable and both located strictly between first-order and monadic second-order definability. Then we present characterization results connecting model-theoretic definability with the properties "star-free" and "aperiodic": A regular tree language is star-free iff it is antichain-definable (which corresponds to Ladner's result mentioned above); and for any chain definable tree language, first-order definability is equivalent to aperiodicity (which corresponds to Schützenberger's Theorem). - Finally we indicate open questions and directions for further work. (Detailed proofs of the present results appear in Thomas (1984).)

2 STAR-FREE REGULAR EXPRESSIONS AND APERIODICITY

We begin by recalling some standard terminology. Let $\Sigma = \Sigma_o \cup \ldots \cup \Sigma_m$ be a ranked alphabet, where each Σ_i is a finite set of i-ary function symbols. Symbols of arity 0 are called constants. A <u>tree</u> over Σ is a (finite) term built up from the symbols in Σ. By T_Σ we denote the set of trees over Σ. A <u>tree language</u> over Σ is a subset of T_Σ.

Given $t, t' \in T_\Sigma$ and $c \in \Sigma_o$ we denote by $t \cdot^c t'$ the tree which results from t when every occurrence of c in t is substituted by t'. For $T, T' \subset T_\Sigma$, the product $T \cdot^c T'$ contains all trees which result from some $t \in T$ by substituting each occurrence of c in t by some $t' \in T'$. This product is associative. Finally, define the iteration operation ^{c} for

$c \in \Sigma_o$ by $T^c = \{c\} \cup T \cup T \cdot^c T \cup \ldots$.

Regular expressions over Σ are introduced here with complement operation: They are built up from $\emptyset$ and the terms $t \in T_{\Sigma_c}$ by means of the binary operations $\cup, \cdot^c$ and the unary operations $\sim$ and ^{c} (where $c \in \Sigma_o$). Any regular expression r over Σ denotes a tree language $T_r \subset T_\Sigma$, using the convention that t denotes $\{t\}$, that $\cdot^c$, ^{c} have their explained meanings, and that $\cup$, $\sim$ denote union and complement w.r.t. T_Σ .

A tree language $T \subset T_\Sigma$ is called regular if, for some $n \geq 0$ and constants $c_1, \ldots, c_n$, T is denoted by a regular expression over $\Sigma \cup \{c_1, \ldots, c_n\}$. We call T star-free if such a regular expression exists in which no iteration occurs.

The regular and the star-free word languages over an alphabet $A = \{a_1, \ldots, a_n\}$ are contained as special cases in this defintion: For this purpose, take $\Sigma = \Sigma_o \cup \Sigma_1$ where $\Sigma_o = \{c\}$ and $\Sigma_1 = \{f_1, \ldots, f_n\}$ and identify a word $a_{i_1} \ldots a_{i_r}$ $(r \geq 0)$ with the corresponding unary tree $f_{i_1}(\ldots f_{i_r}(c)\ldots)$. As mentioned in the Introduction, the class of star-free word languages can be characterized in several quite different ways. By Schützenberger's Theorem, a regular language L is star-free iff the syntactic monoid of L contains only trivial subgroups. An easy argument shows that this condition holds iff L is aperiodic (or noncounting), i.e.

$$\exists n\ \forall u,v,w \in A^*: uv^n w \in L \iff uv^{n+1} w \in L ,$$

or equivalently

$$\exists n\ \forall m,m' \geq n\ \forall u,v,w \in A^*: uv^m w \in L \iff uv^{m'} w \in L .$$

Aperiodicity is a strong "pumping property" of a language. While the standard pumping lemma (for regular languages) states that in long words the repetition of certain segments is not sensitive to L , aperiodicity means that repetitions (when exceeding a certain bound n) of arbitrary segments cannot be distinguished by L .

Let us introduce an aperiodicity notion for tree languages which is related in this way to the pumping lemma for regular tree languages. For this purpose it is convenient to use a restricted concatenation of trees. Consider a fixed alphabet Σ and let $c \notin \Sigma$ be a new constant. Call a tree over $\Sigma \cup \{c\}$ special if it has exactly one occurrence of c . The set of special trees over $\Sigma \cup \{c\}$ is denoted by S_Σ . If $s,s' \in S_\Sigma$ and $t \in T_\Sigma$ we simply write $s \cdot s'$ for $s \cdot^c s'$ and $s \cdot t$ for $s \cdot^c t$. We call $T \subset T_\Sigma$

aperiodic if

$$\exists n\ \forall s_o, s \in S_\Sigma\ \forall t \in T_\Sigma :\ s_o \cdot s^n \cdot t \in T \Leftrightarrow s_o \cdot s^{n+1} \cdot t \in T\ .$$

Remark. As a special case of aperiodic tree languages one obtains the "noncounting context-free parenthesis languages" studied by Crespi-Reghizzi & Guida & Mandrioli (1978): One identifies any word generated by a parenthesis grammar, say with terminal alphabet Σ_o and productions yielding words of length $\leq m$, as a tree over $\Sigma = \Sigma_o \cup \{f_1, \ldots, f_m\}$ where each f_i is i-ary. For instance, (((aab)b)(ab)) corresponds to the tree $f_2(f_2(f_3(a,a,b),b), f_2(a,b))$, or in more readable form to

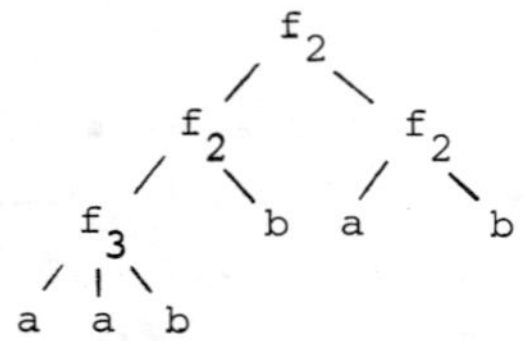

Referring to this identification, it turns out that a parenthesis language is context-free and noncounting iff the corresponding tree language is regular and aperiodic. □

Several results about aperiodic word languages continue to hold for aperiodic tree languages. As a prerequisite one verifies that $(S_\Sigma, \cdot)$ is a monoid (with identity c), and that any regular $T \subset T_\Sigma$ induces a finite submonoid M(T) consisting of classes of special trees given by the equivalence relation

$$s_1 \equiv_T s_2 :\Leftrightarrow \forall s \in S_\Sigma\ \forall t \in T_\Sigma\ (s \cdot s_1 \cdot t \in T \Leftrightarrow s \cdot s_2 \cdot t \in T)\ .$$

The following result is then obtained in exactly the same way as the corresponding theorem for word languages (see e.g. McNaughton & Papert (1971), p.52-53):

Theorem (a) A regular tree language $T \subset T_\Sigma$ is aperiodic iff M(T) contains only trivial subgroups. (b) Aperiodicity is decidable for regular tree languages. □

The concatenation of special trees as used in the aperiodicity definition resembles very much the concatenation of words. While this yields the above theorem in the same way as for word languages, such an analogy fails when tree concatenation in the more general sense is involved (as it appears in regular expressions). In particular, we see that the aperiodic regular tree languages do not coincide with the star-free ones:

<u>Example</u> Let $\Sigma = \{f,a\}$ where a is a constant and f is binary. Denote by cb_n the "comb of height n":

$cb_n =$

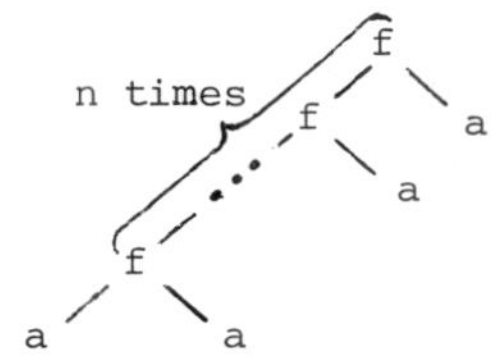

Define $T_o = \{cb_n \mid n \text{ even}\}$. Then T_o is star-free but not aperiodic.

<u>Proof</u> It is immediate that T_o is not aperiodic (take $s = f(c,a)$ in the definition of aperiodicity). We now construct a star-free regular expression over $\Sigma' = \{f,a,c,d\}$ (where c,d are new constants) which denotes T_o . First we see that

$$T_o = \big(f(f(c,d),a) \big)^{c} \cdot^{c} a \cdot^{d} a \quad .$$

The first factor may be rewritten as the union of c with

$$f(c,a) \cdot^{c} \big(f(c,a) \cup f(c,d) \big)^{c} \cdot^{c} f(c,d) - T_{\Sigma'} \cdot^{c} \big(f(f(c,a),a) \cup f(f(c,d),d) \big) \cdot^{c} T_{\Sigma'} \quad .$$

Note that $T_{\Sigma'}$ is star-free (being the complement of $\emptyset$). We are done when $(f(c,a) \cup f(c,d))^{c}$ can be represented without iteration. Indeed, it is equivalent to

$$c \cup \Big(T_d \cdot^{d} \big(f(c,a) \cup f(c,d) \big) - T_d \cdot^{d} \big(f(d,f(d,d)) \cup f(d,c) \big) \cdot^{d} T_{\Sigma'} \Big)$$

where $T_d := T_{\Sigma'} - T_{\Sigma'} \cdot^{d} (a \cup c)$ is the set of trees over Σ' with some d . □

It should be noted that this example shows the failure of the <u>easier</u> part of Schützenberger's Theorem in the case of tree languages. We do not know about the converse, i.e. whether there is a regular tree language which is aperiodic but not star-free.

3 <u>DEFINABILITY IN MONADIC SECOND-ORDER LOGIC</u>

Historically, monadic second-order logic provided the background on which the concept of a regular tree language was formed. Based on earlier work by Büchi (1960) and Elgot (1961), where a close connection was established between finite automata and the weak monadic second-order theory of one successor, Doner (1970) and Thatcher & Wright (1968) extended these results to tree automata and the weak monadic second-order theory of two successors. In all cases, the main motivation was to show the decidability of the respective logical theory. (The weak monadic second-order theory of two successors, for example, consists of all sentences which are true in the full binary tree and can be formulated in a language with symbols for the two successor functions, allowing quantification over the elements and the finite subsets of the tree.) The reference to an infinite structure (the natural numbers, or the full binary tree) was essential for the logical applications, but it causes some complications in formal language theory when one deals soleley with sets of finite words or finite trees. (Namely, quantification usually refers to the whole structure and not to a finite part of it.) It is therefore useful to pursue an idea which seems to have appeared first (for the case of words) in Ladner (1977): Instead of working with a fixed infinite structure in which finite words or trees can be embedded, one associates with any word or tree a separate finite structure. In the case of trees we are led to the following conventions and definitions:

Let $\Sigma = \Sigma_o \cup \ldots \cup \Sigma_m$. As already indicated in the Example of section 2 (where the trees cb_n were considered), any $t \in T_\Sigma$ can be viewed as a finite graph with labels from Σ on its nodes. Let dom(t) be the finite, prefix-closed subset of $\{1,\ldots,m\}^*$ which represents the set of positions of this graph. For example, if $\Sigma = \{f,g,a,b\}$ with binary f, unary g, and constants a,b, we have for $t = f(f(a,b),g(a))$ that dom(t) = $\{\varepsilon,1,2,11,12,21\}$ (where ε is the empty word):

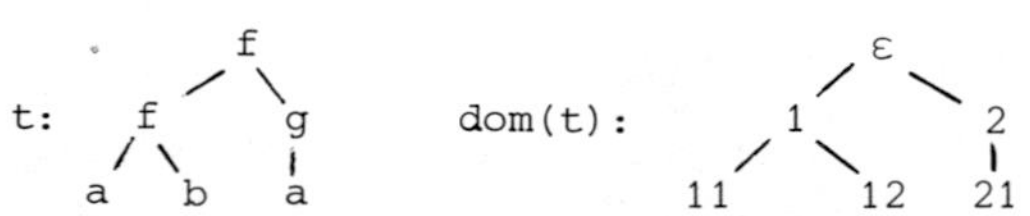

Hence a tree can be represented as a map $t : \mathrm{dom}(t) \to \Sigma$ which associates to any position with i successors a symbol in Σ_i. Given a set of the form dom(t), let $<$ be the partial tree ordering (with minimum ε) and $S_1,\ldots,S_m$ the successor relations (with xS_iy iff $xi = y$) on dom(t). For $t \in T_\Sigma$ and any symbol $\sigma \in \Sigma$ let P_σ be the subset of dom(t) which consists of all positions carrying the symbol σ. We shall identify a tree $t \in T_\Sigma$ with the relational structure

$$t = (\mathrm{dom}(t)\,,\,<\,,\,S_1,\ldots,S_m\,,\,(P_\sigma)_{\sigma\in\Sigma})\ .$$

Properties of trees will be formulated in the corresponding monadic second-order language L_Σ: It includes the symbols $=\,,\,<\,,\,S_1,\ldots,S_m$, a symbol P_σ for each $\sigma\in\Sigma$, variables x,y,... (ranging over positions of a tree), X,Y,... (ranging over sets of positions of a tree), the connectives $\neg\,,\,\wedge\,,\,\vee\,,\,\rightarrow\,,\,\leftrightarrow$, and quantifiers $\exists\,,\,\forall$ (acting on both kinds of variables). The satisfaction relation "$t \models \varphi$" between Σ-trees and L_Σ-sentences is defined in the natural way. For instance, if t is the tree displayed above, we have

$$t \models \exists x\, \exists y\, (xS_1y \ \wedge\ P_fx \ \wedge\ P_fy),$$

$$t \models \forall y (P_by \rightarrow \exists x (P_fx \ \wedge\ xS_2y))\ .$$

For an L_Σ-sentence φ let $T_\varphi = \{t\in T_\Sigma \mid t\models\varphi\}$. We say that $T\subset T_\Sigma$ is <u>monadic second-order definable</u> (m.s.o.d.) if $T = T_\varphi$ for some L_Σ-sentence φ. Similarly, T is <u>first-order definable</u> if there is such a sentence φ in which no set variables occur.

<u>Theorem</u> (essentially Thatcher & Wright (1968), Doner (1970)) A tree language $T\subset T_\Sigma$ is regular iff it is monadic second-order definable. □

The restriction to unary trees yields the corresponding result for word languages, first obtained by Büchi (1960) and Elgot (1961). We state it together with Ladner's theorem (1977), a preliminary version of which was proved in McNaughton & Papert (1971). (In all cases, we identify a word language with a set of unary trees.)

<u>Theorem</u> (a) (Büchi (1960), Elgot (1961)) A word language is regular iff it is monadic second-order definable. (b) (Ladner (1977)) A word language is star-free iff it is first-order definable. □

Now we introduce two restricted versions of monadic second-order definability. If t is a tree, a subset of dom(t) is called a <u>chain</u> if it is linearly ordered by the partial tree ordering $<$, and it is called an <u>antichain</u> if any two distinct elements of it are incomparable w.r.t. $<$. Let us write, for any L_Σ-sentence φ, $t \models^c \varphi$ (resp. $t \models^{ac} \varphi$) if t satisfies φ under the proviso that the set variables in φ range only over the chains (resp. antichains) of dom(t). (When the context admits no ambiguity we sometimes skip the superscripts ^{c} and ^{ac}.) Call $T\subset T_\Sigma$ <u>chain definable</u> (resp. <u>antichain definable</u>) if there is an L_Σ-sentence φ such that $T = \{t \in T_\Sigma \mid t \models^{c} \varphi\}$ (resp. $T = \{t \in T_\Sigma \mid t \models^{ac} \varphi\}$).

The inclusion relations between all these versions of model-theoretic definability are completely described by the following result:

<u>Theorem</u> The classes of first-order, chain, antichain, and monadic second-order definable tree languages are related as shown in the following diagram:

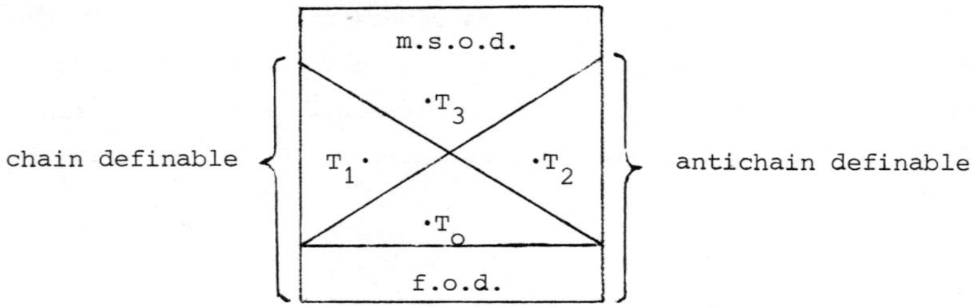

As example languages at the indicated positions one can take the following tree languages (over $\Sigma = \{f, g, a, b\}$ where f is binary, g is unary, and a, b are constants):

$$T_o = \{cb_n \mid n \text{ even}\} \qquad \text{(cf. section 2)}$$

$$T_1 = \{g^n(a) \mid n \text{ even}\}$$

$$T_2 = \{t \in T_{\{f,a,b\}} \mid t \text{ contains an even number of a's}\}$$

$$T_3 = (T_2 \cdot^a T_1) \cdot^b T_1' \text{ , where } T_1' = \{g^n(a) \mid n \text{ odd}\} \text{ .}$$

<u>Remark</u> Note that the claim concerning T_o (together with the result of section 2 that T_o is star-free) implies that Ladner's theorem does not extend to tree languages. □

<u>Proof of Theorem</u> Any f.o.d. tree language is chain definable and antichain definable. In order to show that tree languages of the latter kind are m.s.o.d., apply the fact that quantification over set variables can be relativized to chains or antichains by means of the formulas

$$\text{Chain}(X) : \forall x \forall y (Xx \wedge Xy \rightarrow x < y \vee x = y \vee y < x) \text{ ,}$$

$$\text{Antichain}(X) : \forall x \forall y (Xx \wedge Xy \rightarrow \neg(x < y \vee y < x)) \text{ .}$$

Let us verify the "positive" definability statements for $T_o, \ldots, T_3$. We write $x \leq y$ for $(x = y \vee x < y)$ and use the formulas

$$\text{Root}(x) : \forall y \; x \leq y \text{ ,}$$

$$\text{Frontier}(x) : \neg \exists y \; x < y \text{ .}$$

Then the set of combs cb_n $(n \geqslant o)$ is defined by

$$\forall x(P_f x \vee P_a x) \wedge \forall x \forall y(xS_2 y \rightarrow \text{Frontier}(y)) ,$$

and the set T_o of even combs by the conjunction of this sentence with

$$\exists X(\forall z(\text{Root}(z) \rightarrow \neg Xz) \wedge \forall x \forall y(xS_1 y \rightarrow (Xx \leftrightarrow \neg Xy)) \wedge \forall z(\text{Frontier}(z) \rightarrow \neg Xz) .$$

For antichain definability of T_o one takes the following sentence instead:

$$\exists X(\forall z \forall z'(\text{Root}(z) \wedge zS_2 z' \rightarrow \neg Xz') \wedge \forall x \forall x' \forall y \forall y' (xS_1 y \wedge xS_2 x' \wedge yS_2 y' \rightarrow (Xx' \leftrightarrow \neg Xy')) \wedge \forall z \forall y \forall y' (\text{Frontier}(z) \wedge yS_1 z \wedge yS_2 y' \rightarrow Xy') .$$

The picture indicates sets as required for X in these sentences:

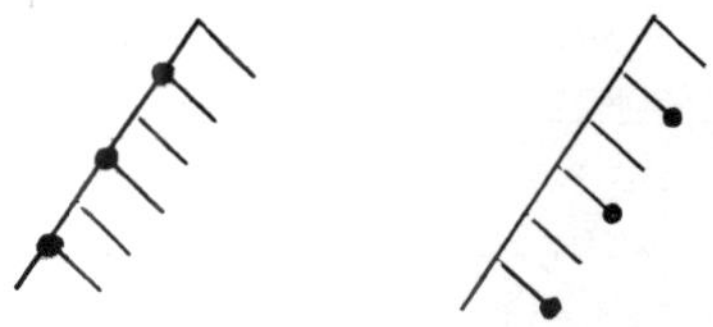

It should be obvious how T_1 can be defined in the same manner using a quantifier over chains.

A similar idea is used for the antichain definability of T_2: We consider the total ordering $\prec$ on a tree defined by

$$x \prec y : x < y \vee \exists z \exists z' \exists z''(zS_1 z' \wedge z' \leqslant x \wedge zS_2 z'' \wedge z'' \leqslant y)$$

and use first-order formulas expressing the following:

$\text{Left}_a(z)$: "z is a $\prec$-minimal position in P_a on the frontier",
$\text{Right}_a(z)$: "z is a $\prec$-maximal position in P_a on the frontier",
$\text{Succ}_a(z,z')$: "z and z' are positions in P_a on the frontier, and no such position is between them w.r.t. $\prec$".

Then T_2 is antichain definable by

$$\exists X(\forall z(\text{Left}_a(z) \rightarrow \neg Xz) \wedge \forall z \forall z'(\text{Succ}_a(z,z') \rightarrow (Xz \leftrightarrow \neg Xz')) \wedge \forall z(\text{Right}_a(z) \rightarrow Xz)) .$$

We leave it to the reader to show that T_3 is m.s.o.d., by combining the definitions of T_1 and T_2 (and using the formulas Chain(X) and Antichain(X) mentioned above).

It remains to be verified that T_o is not f.o.d., T_1 is not antichain definable, T_2 is not chain definable, and T_3 is neither chain nor antichain definable. In the present section we sketch the proof for T_o, T_1. Since T_1 contains only unary trees, it clearly suffices to show that T_1 is not f.o.d. (note that antichain quantification in unary trees is quantification over singletons, which reduces to first-order quantification). But if T_1 were f.o.d., we would obtain an f.o.d. word language which is not aperiodic, contradicting the theorems of Ladner and Schützenberger. - The proof for T_o is similar, using the following intuitively obvious fact which says that sets of combs are essentially word languages: For any $M \subset \mathbb{N}$, the tree language $\{cb_n | n \in M\}$ is f.o.d. iff $\{g^n(a) | n \in M\}$ is f.o.d.. (The proof works by induction over first-order formulas.) Since T_1 was shown above not to be f.o.d., the same applies to T_o. □

4 M-THEORIES AND DECOMPOSITION OF TREES

For a closer analysis of chain and antichain definability it is convenient to alter the monadic second-order language L_Σ slightly: We keep only second-order variables and simulate the use of first-order variables by means of appropriate predicates for sets. More precisely, we eliminate the variables x,y,... from L_Σ and take as nonlogical symbols the following: $\subset$ (for inclusion), Sing (for being a singleton), Empty (for being empty), < and the symbols S_i (for < and the S_i applied to singletons), and the symbols P_σ for all $\sigma \in \Sigma$. The resulting language is denoted L'_Σ. Henceforth, formulas involving first-order variables are used to abbreviate L'_Σ-formulas; e.g., $\exists X \forall x (Xx \rightarrow P_\sigma x)$ stands for $\exists X \forall Y$ (Sing(Y) $\wedge$ $Y \subset X \rightarrow Y \subset P_\sigma$). Clearly the notions "chain definable", "antichain definable", "m.s.o.d." retain their meaning under this change; "f.o.d." becomes "singleton definable".

Fix Σ for the following definitions. For arguments by induction on L'_Σ we admit formulas with free variables. The notation $\varphi(X_1,\dots,X_n)$ indicates that at most $X_1,\dots,X_n$ occur free in φ. Furthermore, we assume an enumeration $X_1, X_2, \dots$ of all variables. If their indices are irrelevant we use $X, Y, Y_1, \dots$ etc. If $\varphi(X_1,\dots,X_n)$ is satisfied in the tree $t \in T_\Sigma$ with $Q_i \subset \mathrm{dom}(t)$ as interpretation for X_i we write $(t, Q_1,\dots,Q_n) \models \varphi(X_1,\dots,X_n)$ or just $(t,\bar{Q}) \models \varphi(\bar{X})$. Note that the n-tuple $\bar{Q}$ defines a partition of each P_σ (where $\sigma \in \Sigma$) into 2^n parts; hence a structure $(t,\bar{Q})$ can be viewed as a tree in $T_{\Sigma(n)}$ where $\Sigma(n)$ results from Σ by taking, for each $\sigma \in \Sigma$, 2^n new symbols instead of σ. A tree language defined by a L'_Σ-formula $\varphi(X_1,\ldots,X_n)$ will be considered as a subset of $T_{\Sigma(n)}$.

An essential notion in the sequel is that of <u>quantifier-depth</u> of a formula φ, written $qd(\varphi)$: It is the maximum number of nested quantifiers in φ. The inductive definition proceeds as follows: $qd(\varphi) = 0$ for quantifier-free φ, $qd(\neg\varphi) = qd(\varphi)$, $qd(\varphi \vee \psi) = \max\{qd(\varphi), qd(\psi)\}$, similarly for the other binary connectives, and $qd(\exists X\varphi) = qd(\forall X\varphi) = qd(\varphi) + 1$. We write, for $\bar{Q} = (Q_1,\ldots,Q_n)$, $\bar{Q}' = (Q'_1,\ldots,Q'_n)$,

$$(t,\bar{Q}) \equiv_m (t',\bar{Q}') \quad \text{iff} \quad (t,\bar{Q}) \models \varphi(\bar{X}) \iff (t',\bar{Q}') \models \varphi(\bar{X})$$
$$\text{for all } \varphi(\bar{X}) \text{ with } qd(\varphi(\bar{X})) \leq m\ .$$

Similarly, $\equiv_m^c$ and $\equiv_m^{ac}$ are defined with $\models^c$, $\models^{ac}$ replacing $\models$.

The equivalence classes of $\equiv_m$ can be represented by finite objects called "m-theories". We give their definition and basic properties without further comments here; a detailed exposition can be found in Rosenstein (1982), p.388ff. Define, for $\bar{Q} = (Q_1,\ldots,Q_n)$ where $Q_i \subset dom(t)$,

$$Th_0(t,\bar{Q}) = \{\varphi(X_1,\ldots,X_n) \mid \varphi \text{ atomic}, (t,\bar{Q}) \models \varphi(\bar{X})\}\ ,$$

$$Th_{m+1}(t,\bar{Q}) = \{Th_m(t,\bar{Q},R) \mid R \subset dom(t)\}.$$

Similarly, $Th_m^c(t,\bar{Q})$ and $Th_m^{ac}(t,\bar{Q})$ are defined: In this case one admits in the inductive step only chains, resp. antichains for R. - All "formally possible" m-theories with n parameters are contained in the set $F_m(n)$, inductively defined by

$$F_0(n) = \text{set of atomic formulas in variables } X_1,\ldots,X_n\ ,$$

$$F_{m+1}(n) = \text{powerset of } F_m(n+1)\ .$$

Clearly each $F_m(n)$ is finite, and we have $Th_m(t,Q_1,\ldots,Q_n) \subset F_m(n)$.

<u>Basic Lemma</u> (a) From $Th_m(t,\bar{Q})$ it can be determined (in an effective way) for any $\varphi(\bar{X})$ with $qd(\varphi(\bar{X})) \leq m$ whether $(t,\bar{Q}) \models \varphi(\bar{X})$ or not.
(b) For any $\tau \subset F_m(n)$ there is a formula $\varphi_\tau(\bar{X})$ of quantifier-depth m such that for all $(t,\bar{Q})$ we have $(t,\bar{Q}) \models \varphi_\tau(\bar{X})$ iff $Th_m(t,\bar{Q}) = \tau$.
(c) $Th_m(t,\bar{Q}) = Th_m(t',\bar{Q}')$ iff $(t,\bar{Q}) \equiv_m (t',\bar{Q}')$. Moreover, $(t,\bar{Q}) \equiv_{m+1} (t',\bar{Q}')$ holds iff

$$\forall Q \subset dom(t)\ \exists Q' \subset dom(t') :\ (t,\bar{Q},Q) \equiv_m (t',\bar{Q}',Q') \text{ and}$$

$$\forall Q' \subset dom(t')\ \exists Q \subset dom(t) :\ (t,\bar{Q},Q) \equiv_m (t',\bar{Q}',Q')\ .$$

(d) Any L'_Σ-formula $\varphi(\bar{X})$ of quantifier-depth m is equivalent (over models in $T_{\Sigma(n)}$) to the disjunction

$$\bigvee\{\varphi_\tau(\bar{X}) \mid \tau \subset F_m(n), \exists(t,\bar{Q}) : (t,\bar{Q}) \models \varphi(\bar{X}) \text{ and } Th_m(t,\bar{Q}) = \tau\} .$$

(e) All statements hold for Th_m^c, resp. Th_m^{ac} if $\models$ is replaced by $\models^c$, $\models^{ac}$ and $\equiv_m$ by $\equiv_m^c$, $\equiv_m^{ac}$ respectively. □

The use of m-theories is a standard method in the model theory of linear orderings. An important property of m-theories in that context is that the m-theory of a concatentation of two orderings can be computed from the m-theories of the constituents (cf., e.g., Rosenstein (1982), p.392). A corresponding result for trees is proved similarly (we omit the inductive proof which is tedious but not difficult):

<u>First Decomposition Lemma</u> Let $s \in T_{\Sigma \cup \{c\}}$ be a special tree and $t \in T_\Sigma$. Assume $\bar{Q}$ is an n-tuple of subsets of dom(s·t), and $\bar{Q}_s, \bar{Q}_t$ are the corresponding n-tuples of subsets of dom(s), dom(t) respectively. Then $Th_m(s \cdot t, \bar{Q})$ is determined by $Th_m(s, \bar{Q}_s)$ and $Th_m(t, \bar{Q}_t)$ (moreover, can be computed effectively from these two m-theories). - Similarly for Th_m^c and Th_m^{ac}. □

Let us apply this lemma to show that the tree language T_2 of the preceding section (containing all trees over {f,a,b} with an even number of a's) is not chain definable. We have to verify the following claim:

$$(*) \quad \forall m \geq 1 \; \exists t_m \in T_2 \; \exists t'_m \notin T_2 : t_m \equiv_m^c t'_m .$$

(Then formulas of arbitrary quantifier-depth cannot define T_2 w.r.t. $\models^c$, and hence T_2 is not chain definable.) For the definition of t_m, t'_m and the proof of (*) we proceed by induction: By direct inspection (of the possible formulas $\exists X \varphi(X)$ with φ quantifier-free) one sees that $f(f(f(a,a),b),b) \equiv_1^c f(f(f(a,a),a),b)$; so as t_1 we take the left-hand tree and as t'_1 the right-hand tree.

Assume $t_m \in T_2$, $t'_m \notin T_2$ are given with $t_m \equiv_m^c t'_m$. Let $cb_k(i)$, resp. $cb_k(i,j)$ be the tree which results from the comb cb_k by substituting c for a at the right successor of the i-th f-symbol, resp. of the i-th and the j-th f-symbol. Consider the m-theories $Th_{m+1}^c(cb_k(i) \cdot^a t_m)$ for $0 < i \leq m$. By finiteness of $F_{m+1}(0)$ there is k and $i_1 < i_2$ such that the corresponding (m+1)-theories coincide:

$$(+) \quad cb_k(i_2) \cdot^a t_m \equiv_{m+1}^c cb_k(i_1) \cdot^a t_m .$$

Define

$$t_{m+1} = cb_k(i_1,i_2) \cdot^a t_m \cdot^c t'_m \quad ,$$
$$t'_{m+1} = cb_k(i_1) \cdot^a t_m \cdot^c t'_m \quad .$$

t_{m+1}: 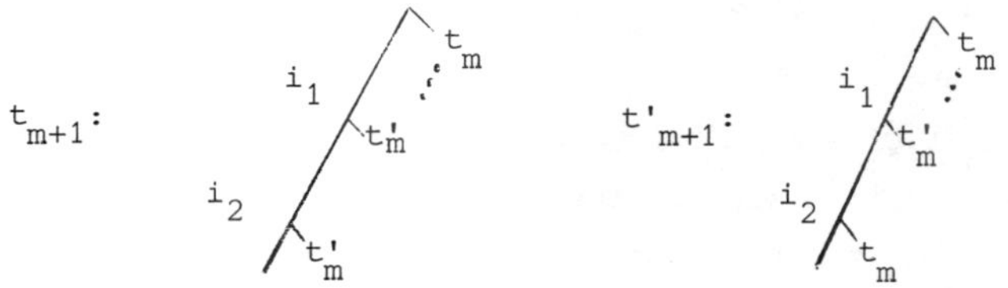

Clearly $t_{m+1} \in T_2$, $t'_{m+1} \notin T_2$. We use (c) of the basic lemma to prove $t_{m+1} \equiv^c_{m+1} t'_{m+1}$; namely we show: For any chain Q in dom(t_{m+1}) there is a chain Q' in dom(t'_{m+1}) such that $(t_{m+1},Q) \equiv^c_m (t'_{m+1},Q')$. (The converse direction is similar.) Since the given Q is a chain, it is the union of two chains Q_o, Q_1 where Q_1 is the Q-part in at most one (!) of the subtrees $t^{(')}_m$ and Q_o is the part up to (and including the root of) this subtree. If Q_1 is not contained in the subtree t'_m at position i_2, we pick as Q' in t'_{m+1} exactly the same elements as given by Q. Replace the tree $t^{(')}_m$ at position i_2 in t_{m+1}, t'_{m+1} by c, thus obtaining the isomorphic special trees s,s'. Then $(s,Q) \equiv^c_m (s',Q')$. But also $(t_m,\emptyset) \equiv^c_m (t'_m,\emptyset)$ by $t_m \equiv^c_m t'_m$ and the definition of m-theory for L'_Σ. Hence the first decomposition lemma yields $(t_{m+1},Q) \equiv^c_m (t'_{m+1},Q')$ as required. Assume now that Q_1 intersects the subtree t'_m at position i_2. By (+) we pick Q'_o such that $(cb_k(i_2) \cdot^a t_m, Q_o) \equiv^c_m (cb_k(i_1) \cdot^a t_m, Q'_o)$. In the first of these trees, use the decomposition lemma (as above) to replace the subtree t_m at position i_1 by t'_m and still preserve $\equiv^c_m$-equivalence. Call the resulting trees (s,Q_o) and (s',Q'_o). Choose Q'_1 in t'_m exactly as given by Q_1 to obtain $(t'_m,Q_1) \equiv^c_m (t'_m,Q'_1)$ and set $Q' = Q'_o \cup Q'_1$. The decomposition lemma, applied to (s,Q_o), (t'_m,Q_1) and (s',Q'_o), (t'_m,Q'_1) yields $(t_{m+1},Q) \equiv^c_m (t'_{m+1},Q')$. □

For the general analysis of antichain definability we need a more refined decomposition result than the previous lemma. For this purpose we shall generalize the notion of quantifier-depth. We define, for a sequence $\bar{m} = (m_1,\ldots,m_k)$ of positive integers, the set of <u>$\bar{m}$-formulas</u> by induction on k: If $\bar{m}$ is empty, it is the set of quantifier-free formulas, and for a sequence $(m,\bar{m})$, an $(m,\bar{m})$-formula is a boolean combination of formulas $\exists Y_1 \ldots \exists Y_m\ (Y_1 \subset Y_m \wedge \ldots \wedge Y_{m-1} \subset Y_m \wedge \varphi)$ where φ is an $\bar{m}$-formula. Up to equivalence, the formulas of quantifier-depth k are the $\bar{m}$-formulas where $\bar{m} = (1,\dots,1)$ and this sequence is of length k. The $\bar{m}$-theories are defined in analogy to the m-theories, by induction on the length of $\bar{m}$:

$$Th_{\emptyset}(t,\bar{Q}) = Th_o(t,\bar{Q}) ,$$

$$Th_{(m,\bar{m})}(t,\bar{Q}) = \{Th_{\bar{m}}(t,\bar{Q},\bar{R}) \mid \bar{R} = (R_1,\dots,R_m) , \\ R_1,\dots,R_{m-1} \subset R_m \subset dom(t)\} .$$

Similarly, $Th^c_{\bar{m}}(t,\bar{Q})$ and $Th^{ac}_{\bar{m}}(t,\bar{Q})$ are defined (where the R_i are chains resp. antichains): note that e.g. in the latter case the union of the R_i in the induction step has to be an antichain. The analogue of the basic lemma holds unaltered for these $\bar{m}$-theories.

The step from m to $\bar{m}$ is essential for a proof of a decomposition result where a tree is not just splitted into two subtrees but into finitely many subtrees, resulting from a given tree t by separating all subtrees beginning at some antichain in t. (This is similar to the "grafting process" appearing in Rabin (1972) and Gurevich & Shelah (1983).)

We need some notation in order to describe this decomposition. Let $(t,\bar{Q})$ be given, $R \subset dom(t)$, $r \in dom(t)$; then $(t,\bar{Q})^{R]}$ is defined to be the substructure of $(t,\bar{Q})$ over $dom(t) - \{p \mid p > q$ for some $q \in R\}$, similarly $(t,\bar{Q})^{[r}$ the substructure over $\{p \mid p = r$ or $p > r\}$. The corresponding relativizations of formulas $\varphi(\bar{X},Y)$, $\varphi(\bar{X},y)$ are denoted $\varphi(\bar{X},Y)^{Y]}$ and $\varphi(\bar{X},y)^{[y}$. For example, $\varphi(\bar{X},Y)^{Y]}$ expresses that φ holds on the domain consisting of all elements which are not > some Y-element. Thus

$$(t,\bar{Q},R) \models \varphi(\bar{X},Y)^{Y]} \quad \text{iff} \quad (t,\bar{Q},R)^{R]} \models \varphi(\bar{X},Y) ,$$

$$(t,\bar{Q},r) \models \varphi(\bar{X},y)^{[y} \quad \text{iff} \quad (t,Q,r)^{[r} \models \varphi(\bar{X},y) .$$

(Recall that strictly speaking $\varphi(\bar{X},y)^{[y}$ stands for a formula $\varphi(\bar{X},Y)^{[Y}$ in which $Sing(Y)$ is required; similarly r stands for $\{r\}$.)

The following lemma is a variant of the composition theorem in Gurevich & Shelah (1983).

<u>Second Decomposition Lemma</u> For given n and a sequence $(m,\bar{m})$ let $\tau_1,\dots,\tau_l$ be an enumeration of the $\bar{m}$-theories $\tau \subset F_{\bar{m}}(n+1)$. There exists a sequence $\bar{n}$ of same length as $\bar{m}$ such that: For any $(t,Q_1,\dots,Q_n)$ and any m-tuple $\bar{R} = (R_1,\dots,R_{m-1},R)$ of antichains in $dom(t)$ with $R_1,\dots,R_{m-1} \subset R$, the $\bar{m}$-theory $Th_{\bar{m}}(t,\bar{Q},\bar{R})$ is determined by (and computable from) $Th_{\bar{n}}(t,\bar{Q},\bar{R},\bar{S})^{R]}$ where $\bar{S} = (S_1,\dots,S_l)$ is given by $S_i = \{r \in R \mid Th_{\bar{m}}(t,\bar{Q},r)^{[r} = \tau_i\}$. Similarly for theories $Th^c_{\bar{m}}$, $Th^c_{\bar{n}}$, resp. $Th^{ac}_{\bar{m}}$, $Th^{ac}_{\bar{n}}$.

In the sequel the quantified variables range over antichains. For an application of the lemma consider an $(m,\bar{m})$-formula $\psi(\bar{X}) = \exists Y_1 \ldots \exists Y_m (Y_1 \subset Y_m \wedge \ldots \wedge Y_{m-1} \subset Y_m \wedge \varphi(\bar{X},\bar{Y}))$. By (d) of the basic lemma (for $\bar{m}$-theories), $\psi(\bar{X})$ is equivalent to a disjunction of formulas $\exists Y_1 \ldots \exists Y_m$ $(Y_1 \subset Y_m \wedge \ldots \wedge Y_{m-1} \subset Y_m \wedge \varphi_\tau(\bar{X},\bar{Y}))$. The second decomposition lemma allows to split each φ_τ into a disjunction where each disjunction member describes one of the $\bar{n}$-theories which determine φ_τ to hold. Hence we have

Corollary An $(m,\bar{m})$-formula $\exists Y_1 \ldots \exists Y_m (Y_1 \subset Y_m \wedge \ldots \wedge Y_{m-1} \subset Y_m \wedge \varphi(\bar{X},\bar{Y}))$ is equivalent to a disjunction of formulas

$$(*) \quad \exists Y_1 \ldots \exists Y_m \exists Z_1 \ldots \exists Z_l (\text{"}Z_1,\ldots,Z_l \text{ partition of } Y_m\text{"}$$
$$\wedge\ \varphi_{\tau_o}(\bar{X},\bar{Y},\bar{Z})^{Y_m]} \wedge \bigwedge_{i=1}^{l} \forall z (Zz_i \leftrightarrow \varphi_{\tau_i}(\bar{X},z)^{[z})$$

where τ_o is an $\bar{n}$-theory, $\bar{n}$ of same length as $\bar{m}$, and $\tau_1,\ldots,\tau_l$ are $\bar{m}$-theories.

5 CHARACTERIZATION RESULTS

Using the preceding Corollary we can now outline the proofs of the characterization theorems announced in the Introduction.

Theorem A tree language is star-free iff it is antichain definable.

Proof The easier direction (from left to right) is shown by induction on star-free regular expressions (over some alphabet $\Sigma \cup \{c_1,\ldots,c_n\}$). Clearly $\emptyset$ and any $\{t\}$ is antichain definable (by a contradictory sentence, resp. a first-order sentence characterizing t). The induction steps concerning $\sim, \cup$ are obvious (by means of the connectives $\neg, \vee$). Let $r = r' \cdot^c r''$ and assume that $T_{r'}, T_{r''}$ are antichain definable by the sentences φ', φ'' respectively. We denote by $\varphi(Y/P)$ the formula which results from φ by substituting Y for the occurrences of P. Then T_r is antichain definable by

$$\exists Y (\varphi'(Y/P_c)^{Y]} \wedge \forall y (Yy \rightarrow \varphi''^{[y})) \ .$$

Conversely, we show by induction on the length of $\bar{m}$ that for any $\bar{m}$-formula $\varphi(X_1,\ldots,X_n)$ the tree language $T_\varphi \subset T_{\Sigma(n)}$ is star-free. If $\bar{m}$ is empty, we deal with quantifier-free φ. It suffices to consider the atomic case, i.e. formulas of the form $X \subset Y$, $Sing(X)$, $Empty(X)$, $X < Y$, XS_iY where X indicates a variable or some P_σ. In the first case we have

$T_\varphi = T_{\Sigma'}$ for some subset Σ' of $\Sigma(n)$. Hence as the corresponding regular expression we take the intersection over $\sigma \in \Sigma(n) - \Sigma'$ of expressions r_σ which exclude the occurrence of the respective σ. - For $\varphi = \mathrm{Sing}(X)$, T_φ contains all $\Sigma(n)$-trees in which there is exactly one occurrence of a symbol in a certain set $\Sigma' \subset \Sigma(n)$ (determined by the variable X). Since the boolean operations are available, we may assume $|\Sigma'| = 1$, say $\Sigma' = \{f\}$ with binary f. If T_c denotes the trees with some c, T_φ is defined by

$$T_c \cdot^c f(c,c) \cdot^c T_{\Sigma(n)} - (T_{\Sigma(n)} \cdot^c f(c,c) \cdot^c T_{\Sigma(n)} \cdot^c f(c,c) \cdot^c T_{\Sigma(n)}).$$

The formulas $X < Y$, XS_iY are treated similarly.

The induction step is obvious for the propositional connectives. Consider a sequence $(m,\bar{m})$ of length k+1 and an $(m,\bar{m})$-formula $\psi = \exists Y_1 \ldots \exists Y_m (Y_1 \subset Y_m \wedge \ldots \wedge Y_{m-1} \subset Y_m \wedge \varphi(\bar{X},Y))$. By the preceding Corollary we obtain an equivalent disjunction of formulas of the form (*). Since $\bar{m}$ and $\bar{n}$ are of length k, the induction hypothesis applies; hence there are star-free regular expressions $r_o, r_1, \ldots, r_l$ defining the same tree languages as $\varphi_{\tau_o}, \ldots, \varphi_{\tau_l}$. W.l.o.g. we may assume that Z_i corresponds to a constant c_i. The required regular expression can then be taken as

$r_o \cdot^{c_1} r_1 \cdot^{c_2} \ldots \cdot^{c_l} r_l$. □

<u>Theorem</u> A chain-definable tree language is aperiodic iff it is first-order definable.

<u>Proof</u> The aperiodicity proof for a f.o.d. tree language follows the pattern of the corresponding proof for star-free word languages (as given, e.g., in Lemma 1 of Meyer (1969)) and is omitted here.

For the converse direction, we use induction on the quantifier-depth of formulas. The only nontrivial step concerns the quantifier over chains. Assume, as induction hypothesis, that for any $\psi(\bar{X})$ with $qd(\psi(\bar{X})) \leq m$ there is an equivalent first-order formula $\psi'(\bar{X})$ provided T_ψ is aperiodic. Consider $\varphi = \exists Y\, \varphi_o(\bar{X},Y)$ where $qd(\varphi_o(\bar{X},Y)) \leq m$, and assume T_φ is aperiodic. Let $(t,\bar{Q},R)$ be a tree satisfying $\varphi_o(\bar{X},Y)$ with chain R. The elements r' in dom(t) whose predecessor is less than or equal to the maximal R-element (w.r.t. the partial tree ordering $<$) but which themselves are not less than or equal to the maximal R-element, form an antichain R' which we call the "hull of R". By the second decomposition lemma, $\exists Y\, \varphi_o(\bar{X},Y)$ is equivalent to a disjunction of formulas of the form

$$\text{(+)}\quad \begin{array}{l}\exists Y\exists Y'\ \exists Z_1\ldots\exists Z_l\ (\text{"}Y' = \text{hull of } Y\text{"} \wedge \text{"}Z_1,\ldots,Z_l \text{ partition of } Y'\text{"}\\ \quad \wedge\ \varphi_\tau(\bar{X},Y,Y',\bar{Z})^{Y']} \wedge \bigwedge_{i=1}^{l} \forall z(Z_i z \leftrightarrow \varphi_{\tau_i}(\bar{X},z)^{[z})) \end{array}$$

where the τ_i are m-theories (and hence φ_{τ_i} of quantifier-depth $\leqslant m$), and τ is some $\bar{n}$-theory. Since T_φ is aperiodic, we can assume that only those quantifiers $\exists Z_i$ are needed such that φ_{τ_i} describes a tree language which is aperiodic (the other Z_i must be interpreted by the empty set in any tree model of φ). By induction hypothesis these φ_{τ_i} can be written as first-order formulas ψ_i. We can rewrite (+) in the following form:

$$\text{(++)}\quad \begin{array}{l}\exists y\exists Y'\ \exists Z_1\ldots\exists Z_l\ (\text{"}Y' = \text{hull of the path up to } y\text{"}\\ \qquad \wedge\ \text{"}Z_1,\ldots,Z_l \text{ partition of } Y'\text{"}\\ \qquad \wedge\ \exists Y(\varphi_\tau(\bar{X},Y,Y',\bar{Z})^{Y']} \wedge \text{"}Y \subset \text{path up to } y\text{"})\\ \qquad \wedge \bigwedge_{i=1}^{l} \forall z(Z_i z \leftrightarrow \psi_i(\bar{X},z))\end{array}$$

where Y ranges over chains and $Y', Z_1,\ldots,Z_l$ range over antichains. Let $\chi(\bar{X},Y',\bar{Z},y)$ be the formula in the third line of (++). We eliminate the use of the chain quantifier by invoking Schützenberger's Theorem for word languages. Satisfaction of χ in a model $(t,\bar{Q},R',\bar{S},r)$ depends only on the substructure of this model consisting of the path leading to r together with its hull. Any such substructure can be coded by a word whose length is equal to the length of the path up to r, taken over a sufficiently large alphabet for storing all information about the hull along this path and the predicates $\bar{Q},R',\bar{S}$. (We skip the details of such a coding.) It turns out that those words which correspond to substructures satisfying χ form a m.s.o.d. word language L. Moreover, L is aperiodic (since a counterexample to aperiodicity of L could be used, by "decoding" into trees, to show that T_φ is not aperiodic, contrary to assumption). Hence, using Schützenberger's Theorem, L is f.o.d. It follows that also the corresponding set of paths with hull is f.o.d., which implies that χ can be written as a first-order formula χ'. The Z_i can be eliminated by means of the corresponding $\psi_i(\bar{X},z)$ (e.g., for $Z_i \subset P_\sigma$ write $\forall z(\psi_i(\bar{X},z) \rightarrow P_\sigma z)$. Similarly, Y' can be eliminated by means of its definition in terms of y : $Y'z \leftrightarrow \neg z \leqslant y \wedge$ "(predecessor of z) $\leqslant y$". Altogether we obtain a first-order formula equivalent to (++). □

To close the discussion of chain definability, we add a remark on a connection with the <u>deterministic root-to-frontier tree automata</u>

as defined in Thatcher (1973). It is known that the tree languages recognized by these automata form a proper subclass of the regular tree languages. Since this class is not a boolean algebra, let us consider boolean combinations of such languages, which we call "boolean deterministic". It can be shown that every boolean deterministic tree language is chain definable (using the fact that the state of a deterministic root-to-frontier tree automaton at a certain point of a tree depends only on the path from the root to this point). Hence the boolean deterministic tree languages do not exhaust the regular tree languages. There are even f.o.d. tree languages which are not boolean deterministic ; an example is provided by the trees over $\Sigma = \{f,a,b\}$ in which at least two a's occur. On the other hand, the tree language T_1 of section 3 shows that there are boolean deterministic languages which are not f.o.d..

6 CONCLUDING REMARKS

The present results suggest several problems. Let us first mention that (except for the result on aperiodicity in section 2) the decision problem for all classes of tree languages considered here remains open. A related problem asks whether there are characterizations of the f.o.d., resp. chain definable, resp. antichain definable tree languages in terms of properties of tree automata (possibly minimal tree automata).

By refining the conditions on logical formulas it is possible to impose a still finer structure on the class of regular tree languages. For instance, one may classify by prefix types of defining formulas. In the case of word languages, such a classification was considered in Thomas (1982) ; it turned out that Σ_n-prefixes of first-order formulas characterize just the n-th level of the so-called dot-depth hierarchy. Considering tree languages, one should also obtain hierarchies in this way for all kinds of restricted quantifiers (f.o., chain, antichain), whereas it is known that for full monadic second-order quantifiers a reduction to a purely existential prefix is always possible.

It would also be interesting to look at analogues of other notions which are familiar from the theory of regular word languages and are known to be characterized in logical terms, such as "definite", "locally testable", or "piecewise testable" (cf. Eilenberg (1976), Pin (1984), Thomas (1982)).

Finally it should be mentioned that the definability concepts studied in this paper extend without any change also to sets of infinite trees (or sets in which both finite and infinite trees occur). This is quite different from the situation for automata, where the step from finite to infinite trees requires the invention of new acceptance conditions (which is often a subtle and difficult issue). For sets of infinite trees, the inclusion result of section 3 holds without change; however, the status of first-order, chain, and antichain definability in connection with other formalisms (e.g., automata or grammars) remains to be clarified.

REFERENCES

Büchi, J.R. (1960). Weak second-order arithmetic and finite automata, Z. math. Logik Grundlagen Math. 6, 66-92.

Crespi-Reghizzi, S. & Guida, G. & Mandrioli, D. (1978). Noncounting Context-free languages, J. Assoc. Comput. Mach. 25, 571-580.

Doner, J.E. (1970). Tree acceptors and some of their applications, J. Comput. System Sci. 4, 406-451.

Eilenberg, S. (1976). "Automata, Languages, and Machines", Vol. B, Academic Press, New York.

Elgot, C.C. (1961). Decision problems of finite automata design and related arithmetics, Trans. Amer. Math. Soc. 98, 21-52.

Gurevich, Y. & Shelah, S. (1983). Rabin's uniformization problem, J. Symbolic Logic 48 (1983), 1105-1119.

Ladner, R.E. (1977). Application of model-theoretic games to discrete linear orders and finite automata, Inform.Contr. 33, 281-303.

McNaughton, S. & Papert, S. (1971). "Counter-free Automata", MIT-Press, Cambridge, Mass., 1971.

Meyer, A.R. (1969). A note on star-free events, J. Assoc. Comput. Mach. 16, 220-225.

Pin, J.E. (1984). "Variétés de langages formels", Masson, Paris.

Rabin, M.O. (1972). Automata on infinite objects and Church's problem", Amer. Math. Soc., Providence, R.I.

Rosenstein, J.G. (1982). "Linear orderings", Academic Press, New York.

Schützenberger, M.P. (1965). On monoids having only trivial subgroups, Inform. Contr. 8, 190-194.

Thatcher, J.W. (1973). Tree automata: An informal survey, in: Currents of the Theory of Computing (A.V. Aho, Ed.), Prentice-Hall, Englewood Cliffs, N.J.

Thatcher, J.W. & Wright, J.B. (1968). Generalized finite automata theory with an application to a decision problem of second-order logic, Math. Systems Theory 2, 57-81.

Thomas, W. (1982). Classifying regular events in symbolic logic, J. Comput. System Sci. 25, 360-376.

Thomas, W. (1984). Definability of tree languages by chains and antichains, in preparation.

ARBRES BIEN ETIQUETES ET FRACTIONS MULTICONTINUES

D. ARQUÈS
Université de Haute Alsace, Mulhouse, France
J. FRANÇON
Université de Haute Alsace, Mulhouse, France

RESUME. Cori et Vauquelin ont montré récemment que les cartes planaires "sont" des arbres bien étiquetés. Dans cette note on montre que la série génératrice des arbres bien étiquetés, comptés par nombre de sommets, est développable en fraction multicontinue, notion qui généralise celle de fraction continue. Des propriétés des réduites de cette fraction sont données.

ABSTRACT. Cori and Vauquelin have shown that planar maps "are" well labeled trees. In this note it is shown that the generating series of rooted well labeled trees, counted by number of nodes, has a multicontinued fraction expansion (a generalization of a continued fraction). Properties of the convergents of this fraction are given.

1. INTRODUCTION

Cori et Vauquelin ont introduit la notion d'arbre bien étiqueté et montré son intérêt pour l'étude des cartes planaires [1] . L'objet de cette note est de montrer que la série génératrice des arbres bien étiquetés, comptés par nombre de sommets d'étiquette donnée, est développable en fraction multicontinue (notion qui généralise celle de fraction continue) et d'en donner des propriétés. La méthode suivie ici est celle de De Bruijn, Knuth et Rice [2], que Flajolet [3] a considérablement développée. De nouveaux problèmes concernant les cartes planaires se posent alors d'eux-mêmes. Se pose aussi immédiatement la question de savoir quelles propriétés des fractions continues se généralisent aux fractions multicontinues.

La section 2 pose les définitions et montre comment on peut développer en fraction multicontinue la série génératrice des arbres bien étiquetés dénombrés par nombre de sommets d'étiquette donnée. La section 3 donne un résultat d'énumération relatif aux réduites de la fraction multicontinue. La section 4 généralise aux fractions multicontinues deux résultats classiques sur les polynômes des réduites d'une fraction continue. Enfin la section 5 énonce de nombreux problèmes ouverts.

2. UN DEVELOPPEMENT EN FRACTION MULTICONTINUE

Définissons tout d'abord un arbre bien étiqueté. Pour i entier naturel, un arbre i-bien étiqueté est un arbre planaire enraciné dont tout sommet porte pour étiquette un entier naturel de façon que (1) si j est l'étiquette d'un sommet alors celle de son père est soit j, soit j-1, soit j+1 et (2) l'étiquette de la racine est i. Un arbre bien étiqueté est un arbre 0-bien étiqueté (donc enraciné). Dans notre terminologie tous les arbres sont enracinés.

Une variable classique définie sur les arbres enracinés est celle de hauteur. La hauteur d'un sommet d'un arbre vaut 1 de plus que celle de son père, celle de la racine étant 0 ; la hauteur d'un arbre est le maximum des hauteurs de ses sommets.

Notons $B^{\leqslant h}_{i;n_o,n_1\dots}$ le nombre d'arbres i-bien étiquetés de hauteur inférieure ou égale à h et ayant n_o (resp. $n_1,\dots$) sommets d'étiquette 0 (resp. 1,...), pour h, n_o, $n_1,\dots$ entiers donnés. Il est clair que les entiers n_j sont nuls pour tout $j > i+h$. Notons $B^{\leqslant h}_i(z_o,z_1,\dots)$ la série génératrice correspondante, c'est-à-dire

$$B^{\leqslant h}_i(z_o,z_1,\dots) = \sum_{n_o\geqslant 0,n_1\geqslant 0,\dots} B^{\leqslant h}_{i;n_o,n_1,\dots}\, z_o^{n_o} z_1^{n_1} \dots$$

et $B_i(z_o,z_1,\dots)$ la série des arbres i-bien étiquetés sans restriction de hauteur. Nous allons étendre un raisonnement très classique sur les arbres pour obtenir une expression de la série $B^{\leqslant h}_i$.

Considérons les arbres i-bien étiquetés de hauteur inférieure ou égale à h > 0 donné et ayant k fils, k donné. Un tel arbre est, à sa racine près, un k-uple d'arbres de hauteur inférieure ou égale à h-1 et ces arbres sont soit i, soit i-1, soit i+1-bien étiquetés (sauf si i = 0, auquel cas ils sont soit 0, soit 1-bien étiquetés). La série génératrice de ces arbres s'écrit donc

$$z_i(B_{i-1}^{\leqslant h-1} + B_i^{\leqslant h-1} + B_{i+1}^{\leqslant h-1})^k .$$

En sommant sur $k \geqslant 0$ on obtient

$$B_i^{\leqslant h} = \frac{z_i}{1 - [B_{i-1}^{\leqslant h-1} + B_i^{\leqslant h-1} + B_{i+1}^{\leqslant h-1}]}$$

avec $B_i^{\leqslant -1} = 0$ pour tout $i \geqslant 0$ et $B_{-1}^{\leqslant h} = 0$ pour tout h.
On peut énoncer :

THEOREME 1 - <u>La série génératrice des arbres bien étiquetés de hauteur inférieure ou égale à h, entier naturel donné, est une fraction rationnelle qui s'écrit sous la forme</u>

$$B_o^{\leqslant h}(z_o, z_1, \dots, z_h) = \frac{z_o}{1 - B_o^{\leqslant h-1} - B_1^{\leqslant h-1}}$$

<u>où</u> $$B_i^{\leqslant h} = \frac{z_i}{1 - B_{i-1}^{\leqslant h-1} - B_i^{\leqslant h-1} - B_{i+1}^{\leqslant h-1}}$$

<u>pour tout</u> $i \geqslant 1$ <u>et</u> $h \geqslant 0$, <u>avec</u> $B_i^{\leqslant -1} = 0$ <u>pour tout</u> $i \geqslant 0$.

<u>La série génératrice des arbres bien étiquetés peut s'écrire sous la forme</u>

$$B_o = \frac{z_o}{1 - B_o - B_1}$$

où $$B_i = \frac{z_i}{1 - B_{i-1} - B_i - B_{i+1}}$$ pour tout $i \geqslant 1$.

Nous appelons fraction multicontinue la fraction développant B_o par itération à partir des expressions du théorème précédent, c'est-à-dire la fraction

$$\cfrac{z_o}{1 - \cfrac{z_o}{1 - \cfrac{z_o}{1- \dots} - \cfrac{z_1}{1- \dots}} - \cfrac{z_1}{1 - \cfrac{z_o}{1- \dots} - \cfrac{z_1}{1- \dots} - \cfrac{z_2}{1- \dots}}}$$

une telle fraction ne semble pas avoir été considérée jusqu'à présent dans la littérature. Aux deux sections suivantes nous étudions les réduites de cette fraction.

3. UNE PROPRIETE DES REDUITES

Considérons les fractions rationnelles exprimant B_o^h, h entier naturel, par le théorème 1. Ainsi on a

$$B_o^{\leqslant o} = z_o$$

$$B_o^{\leqslant 1} = \frac{z_o}{1 - z_o - z_1}$$

$$B_o^{\leqslant 2} = \cfrac{z_o}{1 - \cfrac{z_o}{1 - z_o - z_1} - \cfrac{z_1}{1 - z_o - z_1 - z_2}}$$

$$B_o^{\leqslant 3} = \cfrac{z_o}{1 - \cfrac{z_o}{1 - \cfrac{z_o}{1-z_o-z_1} - \cfrac{z_1}{1-z_o-z_1-z_2}} - \cfrac{z_1}{1 - \cfrac{z_o}{1-z_o-z_1} - \cfrac{z_1}{1-z_o-z_1-z_2} - \cfrac{z_2}{1-z_1-z_2-z_3}}}$$

On peut schématiser la structure de la fraction $B_o^{\leqslant h}$ par un arbre planaire enraciné A_h dont tout sommet porte une étiquette z_i, i entier naturel, tel que

(i) la racine est étiquetée par z_o ;
(ii) si z_o est l'étiquette d'un sommet non feuille alors ce sommet a deux fils, celui de gauche étant étiqueté par z_o, celui de droite par z_1 ;
(iii) si z_i, $i > 0$, est l'étiquette d'un sommet non feuille alors ce sommet a trois fils, celui de gauche étant étiqueté par z_{i-1}, celui du milieu par z_i et celui de droite par z_{i+1} ;
(iv) toutes les feuilles sont de hauteur h.

THEOREME 2 - Le nombre $M_{h,i}$ de feuilles d'étiquette z_i, $i \geqslant 0$, dans l'arbre A_h est égal au nombre de facteurs gauches de mots de Motzkin sur l'alphabet $\{x,\bar{x},p\}$ de longueur h et dont le nombre d'occurrences de x surpasse de i le nombre d'occurrences de $\bar{x}$.

Avant de prouver ce théorème, définissons les mots de Motzkin et rappelons une propriété des nombres $M_{h,i}$. Un mot w sur l'alphabet $\{x,\bar{x},p\}$ est dit de Motzkin si le nombre d'occurrences de x dans w est égal au nombre d'occurrences de $\bar{x}$ dans w et si dans tout facteur gauche de w le nombre d'occurrences de x n'est pas inférieur au nombre d'occurrences de $\bar{x}$. On montre aisément que les nombres $M_{h,i}$ de facteurs gauches de mots de Motzkin, de longueur h et dont le nombre d'occurrences de x surpasse de i le nombre d'occurrences de $\bar{x}$, vérifient les relations

$$M_{h,i} = M_{h-1,i-1} + M_{h-1,i} + M_{h-1,i+1} \qquad h > 0,\ i \geqslant 0$$

$$M_{o,o} = 1 \text{ et } M_{h,i} = 0 \text{ pour tout } i \text{ négatif.}$$

Les entiers $M_{h,o}$ sont connus sous le nom de nombres de Motzkin dont on trouvera dans [3] des propriétés.

Preuve du théorème 2 - A toute feuille f de A_h associons le mot $\varphi(f) = w_1w_2 \ldots w_h$ ainsi défini. Soit $s_o, s_1, \ldots, s_h$ la suite des sommets sur le chemin allant de la racine à ladite feuille (s_o est donc la racine et s_h la feuille f) dans A_h. On pose, pour $i = 1,2, \ldots, h$, $w_i = x$ (resp. $\bar{x}, p$) si l'étiquette de s_i est supérieure (resp. égale, inférieure) à l'étiquette de s_{i-1}. La condition de bon étiquettage implique que $\varphi(f)$ est un facteur gauche de mot de Motzkin sur l'alphabet $\{x,\bar{x},p\}$ et que l'étiquette de f est z_j si et seulement si le nombre d'occurrences de x dans $\varphi(f)$ surpasse de j le nombre d'occurrences de $\bar{x}$. De plus on vérifie aisément la bijectivité de φ.

4. POLYNOMES DES REDUITES

Soit $A = (X,U)$ un arbre planaire enraciné de racine s_o, X ensemble des sommets et U ensemble des arcs.

On note $\bar{A} = (\bar{X},\bar{U})$, l'arbre obtenu en adjoignant à A un sommet noté s_{-1} et l'arc (s_{-1},s_o). Le sommet s_{-1} est la racine de l'arborescence $\bar{A}$. On appelle niveau d'un sommet de A, la longueur (en nombre d'arcs) du chemin unique joignant s_o à ce sommet. On range les sommets par niveaux $\mathcal{N}_o = \{s_o\}$, $\mathcal{N}_n$ ensemble des sommets de niveau n. On note s_n l'élément courant de l'ensemble $\mathcal{N}_n$, et u_n l'élément générique de l'ensemble U_n des arcs de U ayant leur origine dans $\mathcal{N}_n$. On pose $\mathcal{N}_{-1} = \{s_{-1}\}$ et $U_{-1} = \{(s_{-1},s_o)\}$. Soit $\bar{A}_n = (\bigcup_{i=-1}^{n} \mathcal{N}_i, \bigcup_{i=-1}^{n-1} U_i)$ l'arbre constitué par les (n+2) premiers niveaux de $\bar{A}$.

On note $\mathcal{C}_n$ (resp. $\tilde{\mathcal{C}}_n$), l'ensemble des couplages c sur $\bar{A}_n$ contenant (resp. ne contenant pas) l'arc (s_{-1},s_o). Etant donné un alphabet $\mathcal{A} = \{\alpha_u, u \in \bar{U}\}$ et un couplage c sur $\bar{A}_n$, on note $\Lambda_c = \prod_{u \in c} \alpha_u$ (=1 si c est vide), élément de l'algèbre $\mathbf{Z}[\mathcal{A}]$ des polynômes formels à coefficients dans $\mathbf{Z}$ en les variables commutatives α_u, $u \in \bar{U}$.

Définition - La fraction multicontinue $F_{A,\mathcal{A}}$ dont le $n^{\text{ième}}$-approximant est défini pour $n \geqslant 0$ par

$$F_n = \cfrac{\alpha_{(s_{-1},s_o)}}{1 + \displaystyle\sum_{s_1 \varepsilon \mathcal{N}_1} \cfrac{\alpha_{(s_o,s_1)}}{1 + \displaystyle\sum_{\substack{s_2 \varepsilon \mathcal{N}_2 \\ (s_1,s_2)\varepsilon U_1}} \cfrac{\alpha_{(s_1,s_2)}}{\ddots \cfrac{}{1 + \displaystyle\sum_{\substack{s_n \varepsilon \mathcal{N}_n \\ (s_{n-1},s_n)\varepsilon U_{n-1}}} \alpha_{(s_{n-1},s_n)}}}}}$$

est dite associée à l'arbre A et à l'alphabet $\mathcal{A}$.

Exemple 1 - Considérons l'arbre A de racine s_o étiqueté 0 et tel que tout sommet étiqueté i à trois successeurs étiquetés i-1, i, i+1 si $i \geqslant 1$ et deux successeurs étiquetés 0 et 1 si i = 0. On peut considérer cet arbre A comme la limite pour h infini de l'arbre A_h de la section 3. On note e l'application qui à un sommet s de l'arbre associe son étiquette e(s).

L'image de $F_{A,\mathcal{A}}$ par le morphisme qui envoie $\alpha_{(s,s')}$ sur $-z_{e(s')}$ n'est autre que $-B_o$, où $B_o(z_o,z_1,z_2,\dots)$ est la série génératrice des arbres 0-bien étiquetés.

Exemple 2 - Considérons l'arbre "filiforme" B, c'est-à-dire l'arbre dont tout sommet a un seul fils. L'image de $F_{B,\mathcal{A}}$ par le morphisme qui envoie $\alpha(s,s')$ sur $-z_k$, où k est la hauteur du sommet s est la fraction continue

$$\cfrac{-z_o}{1 - \cfrac{z_1}{1 - \cfrac{z_2}{1- \dots}}}$$

Les deux théorèmes de cette section généralisent aux fractions multicontinues deux résultats classiques pour les fractions continues. En effet, quand on les applique à l'arbre filiforme de l'exemple 2 ci-dessus, on obtient respectivement l'interprétation d'Euler-Mindig des polynômes des réduites et la relation de récurrence de Wallis (dite aussi "à trois termes") de ces mêmes polynômes.

THEOREME 3 - Les $n^{\text{ièmes}}$ numérateur P_n et dénominateur Q_n de la fraction multicontinue $F_{A,\mathcal{A}}$ sont les polynômes de $\mathbf{Z}[\mathcal{A}]$ définis par

$$F_n = \frac{P_n}{Q_n} .$$

On a les égalités $P_n = \sum_{c\in\mathcal{C}_n} \Lambda_c$, $Q_n = \sum_{c\in\tilde{\mathcal{C}}_n} \Lambda_c$.

Preuve - Elle se fait par récurrence.

. Le résultat est évident pour n = 1 ; $F_1 = \frac{P_1}{Q_1}$, $P_1 = \alpha_{(s_1,s_o)}$ et $Q_1 = 1 + \sum_{s_1\in\mathcal{M}_1} \alpha_{(s_o,s_1)}$.

. Supposons le résultat vrai à l'ordre n.

La réduite F_{n+1} de $F_{A,\mathcal{A}}$ peut être considérée comme réduite d'ordre n de la fraction $F_{A,\mathcal{A}'}$ où $\mathcal{A}' = \{\alpha'_u,\ u \in \bar{U}\}$ est défini par

$$\alpha'_u = \alpha_u \text{ pour } u \in U_i \text{ et } -1 \leqslant i \leqslant n-2$$

$$\alpha'_{(s_{n-1},s_n)} = \alpha_{(s_{n-1},s_n)} / [1 + \sum_{(s_n,s_{n+1})\in U_n} \alpha_{(s_n,s_{n+1})}]$$

$$\text{pour } (s_{n-1},s_n) \in U_{n-1} .$$

En appliquant l'hypothèse de récurrence, on obtient (on note f(u) et i(u) les extrémités finales et initiales de l'arc u), $F_{n+1} = P/Q$ avec

$$P = \sum_{c\in\mathcal{C}_n} \prod_{\substack{u\in c \\ u\notin U_{n-1}}} \alpha_u \cdot \prod_{u\in c\cap U_{n-1}} [\alpha_u/(1 + \sum_{\substack{v\in U_n \\ f(u)=i(v)}} \alpha_v)]$$

$$Q = \sum_{c\in\tilde{\mathcal{C}}_n} \prod_{\substack{u\in c \\ u\notin U_{n-1}}} \alpha_u \cdot \prod_{u\in c\cap U_{n-1}} [\alpha_u/(1 + \sum_{\substack{v\in U_n \\ f(u)=i(v)}} \alpha_v)] \quad ;$$

d'où $$P \cdot \prod_{u\in U_{n-1}} \Big(1+\sum_{\substack{v\in U_n\\ f(u)=i(v)}} \alpha_v\Big) = \sum_{c\in\mathcal{C}_n} \prod_{u\in c} \alpha_u \prod_{\substack{u\in U_{n-1}\\ u\notin c}} \Big(1+\sum_{\substack{v\in U_n\\ f(u)=i(v)}} \alpha_v\Big)$$

$$= \sum_{c\in\mathcal{C}_{n+1}} \prod_{u\in c} \alpha_u = \sum_{c\in\mathcal{C}_{n+1}} \Lambda_c .$$

De même $$Q \cdot \prod_{u\in U_{n-1}} \Big(1+\sum_{\substack{v\in U_n\\ f(u)=i(v)}} \alpha_v\Big) = \sum_{c\in\tilde{\mathcal{C}}_{n+1}} \Lambda_c ,$$ d'où le résultat.

Pour $k \geqslant 0$, les couplages sans rupture sur le sous graphe $\left(\bigcup_{i=k}^{n+1} \mathcal{N}_i, \bigcup_{i=k}^{n} U_i\right)$ de $\overline{A}_{n+1}$, sont les couplages c tels que $c \cap U_i$ soit non vide pour tout i dans $\{k,\ldots,n\}$.

On note $S_{k,n+1}$ l'ensemble de ces couplages et $R_{k,n+1}$ le polynôme de $\mathbb{Z}[\alpha]$ défini par $R_{k,n+1} = \sum_{c\in S_{k,n+1}} \Lambda_c$.

THEOREME 4 - <u>Les polynômes P_n et Q_n vérifient les relations de récurrence</u>

$$Q_{n+1} = \sum_{i=-1}^{n} R_{i+1,n+1}\, Q_i \; , \quad Q_{-1} = 1$$

$$P_{n+1} = \sum_{i=0}^{n} R_{i+1,n+1}\, P_i \; , \quad P_o = \alpha_{(s_{-1}, s_o)} .$$

<u>Preuve</u> - Les deux égalités de l'énoncé sont la traduction en termes de polynômes des égalités ensemblistes, sur les couplages, suivantes

$$\tilde{\mathcal{C}}_{n+1} = \bigcup_{i=-1}^{n} \tilde{\mathcal{C}}_i \times S_{i+1,n+1}$$

(où $\tilde{\mathcal{C}}_i \times S_{i+1,n+1}$ est l'ensemble des couplages obtenus en réunissant un couplage de $\tilde{\mathcal{C}}_i$ et un couplage de $S_{i+1,n+1}$)

$$\mathcal{C}_{n+1} = \bigcup_{i=0}^{n} \mathcal{C}_i \times S_{i+1,n+1}$$

où les réunions sont disjointes.

5. PROBLEMES

Etant donné le rôle essentiel joué par la hauteur dans le théorème 1, la première question qui se pose d'elle-même est comment caractériser une variable sur les cartes planaires qui corresponde à la hauteur d'arbre dans la bijection de Cori et Vauquelin (ou bien dans une autre bijection à trouver). On peut espérer qu'une telle variable éclairerait d'un jour nouveau la combinatoire des cartes planaires.

Une série de problèmes se posent dans le même esprit. En effet, certaines familles d'arbres bien étiquetés peuvent être étudiées facilement par la méthode introduite ici ; quelles sont alors les familles de cartes planaires correspondantes ? Par exemple, considérons les arbres i-bien étiquetés tels que l'étiquette de tout sommet est différente de celle de son père. Soit C_i leur série génératrice. On a

$$C_i = \frac{z_i}{1 - C_{i-1} - C_{i+1}} \quad \text{pour } i \geqslant 0 \text{ et } C_{-1} = 0$$

De façon plus générale, il est souvent facile d'exprimer sur la fraction multicontinue une contrainte imposée aux étiquettes des sommets quand cette contrainte ne dépend que de la hauteur du sommet.

D'autre part, nous ne savons rien sur les polynômes R du théorème 4, même si on se contente de dénombrer les arbres bien étiquetés par nombre de sommets, c'est-à-dire si on pose $z_i = z$ pour tout i. En ce qui concerne les polynômes des réduites, nous ne connaissons ni leurs degrés ni leurs coefficients, sauf pour les premières valeurs obtenues par calcul direct

$$B_o^{\leqslant o}(z) = z$$

$$B_o^{\leqslant 1}(z) = \frac{z}{1 - 2z}$$

$$B_o^{\leqslant 2}(z) = \cfrac{z}{1 - \cfrac{z}{1-2z} - \cfrac{z}{1-3z}} = \frac{z(1-2z)(1-3z)}{1 - 7z + 11z^2} = \frac{z(1-5z+6z^2)}{1 - 7z + 11z^2}$$

$$B_o^{\leqslant 3}(z) = \cfrac{z}{1 - \cfrac{z}{1 - \cfrac{z}{1-2z} - \cfrac{z}{1-3z}} - \cfrac{z}{1 - \cfrac{z}{1-2z} - \cfrac{z}{1-3z}}}$$

$$= \frac{z(1-15z+80z^2-179z^3+143z^4)}{1-17z+105z^2-290z^3+353z^4-144z^5}$$

Cependant, on montre facilement que

$$B_h^{\leqslant h}(z) = \frac{T_{h-1}(z)}{T_h(z)}$$

où T_h est un polynôme de degré $\lceil \frac{h}{2} \rceil$. En fait les polynômes T_h $(\frac{z}{3})$ sont des Tchebycheff, comme onpeut le voir dans [2] ou [3].

REMERCIEMENTS - Les auteurs remercient Philippe FLAJOLET de leur avoir indiqué la relation entre le théorème 3 et l'interprétation d'Euler-Mindig des polynômes des réduites.

REFERENCES

[1] R. CORI et B. VAUQUELIN, Planar maps are well labeled trees, Canadian J. of Math. 33 (1981) 1023-1042.

[2] N.G. de BRUIJN, D.E. KNUTH et S.O. RICE, The average height of planted plane trees, in Graph THeory and Computing, R.C. READ ed., Academic Press, New York (1972) pp. 15-22.

[3] P. FLAJOLET, Combinatorial aspects of continued fractions, Discrete Math. 32 (1980) 125-161.

A BOTTOM-UP ALGORITHM FOR WEIGHT- AND HEIGHT-BOUNDED MINIMAL PARTITION OF TREES

R I Becker
Department of Mathematics, University of Cape Town,
7700 Rondebosch, South Africa.

S R Schach
Department of Computer Science, Vanderbilt University,
Nashville, TN 37235.

Abstract. Let $T = (V,E)$ be a rooted tree with n edges. We associate a non-negative weight $w(v)$ with each vertex v in V. A q-partition of T into q connected components $T_1,\ldots,T_q$ is obtained by deleting $k = q-1$ edges of T, $1 \leq q \leq n$. Let $w(T_i)$ denote the sum of the weights of the vertices in T_i. The height of T_i is denoted by $h(T_i)$.

The following problem is considered: Given $W,H > 0$, find a q-partition satisfying

$$w(T_i) \leq W, \quad \text{height } (T_i) \leq H \qquad (1 \leq i \leq q)$$

for which q is a minimum.

A bottom-up polynomial time algorithm is given for this problem which has complexity $O(Hn)$, or independently of H, $O(\text{height}(T)n)$.

1 INTRODUCTION

Let $T = (V,E)$ be a rooted tree with n edges. We associate a non-negative weight $w(v)$ with each vertex v in V. A q-partition of T into q connected components $T_1,\ldots,T_q$ is obtained by deleting $k = q-1$ edges of $T, 1 \leq k \leq n$. The weight $w(T_i)$ of a component T_i is the sum of the weights of the vertices in T_i. The height of T_i is denoted by $h(T_i)$. We regard the partition as being accomplished by assigning k cuts to edges of T. We will consider the following problem:

1.1 Minimal Weight- and Height-bounded Partition:

Given $W, H > 0$, find a q-partition satisfying

$$w(T_i) \leq W, \quad h(T_i) \leq H \qquad (1 \leq i \leq q)$$

for which q is a minimum.

Several related problems have been considered in the literature. We will give a short account of these. Problems 2 to 6 below are formulated in terms of unrooted trees. Problem 7 (like problem 1) involves the heights of components, and is therefore defined for a rooted tree.

1.2 Minimal Weight-bounded Partition:

Given $W > 0$, find a q-partition satisfying

$$w(T_i) \leq W \qquad (1 \leq i \leq q)$$

for which q is a minimum.

Problem 2 was considered in Kundu and Misra (1977) where a linear algorithm was given.

1.3 Minimal Diameter-bounded Partition:

Find a q-partition satisfying

$$\text{diameter } (T_i) \leq D \qquad (1 \leq i \leq q)$$

for which q is a minimum.

Farley, Hedetniemi and Proskurowski (1981) considered this problem and once again gave a linear algorithm. The two solutions of problems 2 and 3 both employ similar bottom-up procedures. A more general problem for larger classes of weighting functions is considered in Becker and Schach (1983).

A different class of optimization problems are the following:

1.4 Max-min Partition:

Given $q > 0$, find a q-partition such that

$$\min_{1 \leq i \leq q} w(T_i) \text{ is a maximum.}$$

1.4 Min-max Partition:

Given $q > 0$, find a q-partition such that

$$\max_{1 \leq i \leq q} w(T_i) \text{ is a minimum.}$$

Problem 4 was treated in Perl and Schach (1981), where an algorithm with complexity $O(Rk^2 + nk)$ was obtained using a top-down procedure known as a "shifting algorithm" (R denotes the radius of the tree). Problem 5 was solved in Becker, Perl and Schach (1982a); an implementation of complexity $O(Rk^2 + nk)$ was given (1982b). Subsequent to this, Perl and Vishkin (1982) gave an implementation with complexity $O(Rk(k + \lg d) + n)$, where d denotes the maximum degree of the tree.

The case of more general weighting functions was considered in Becker and Perl (1983). Problem 4 and 5 can also be solved using the bottom-up procedure of Kundu and Misra (1977) together with binary search, but the complexity then depends on the weights (Becker et al (1982a), Perl and Schach (1981)).

Suppose now that a weighting function s is defined by associating a non-negative size $s(v)$ with each vertex v in V, and define $s(T_i)$ as the sum of $s(v)$ for v in T_i. This leads to the problem

1.6 <u>Size Constrained Min-max Partition</u>:

Given $S > 0$, find a q-partition such that

$$s(T_i) \leq S \qquad (1 \leq i \leq q)$$

and such that $\max_{1 \leq i \leq q} w(T_i)$ is a minimum.

A further problem is

1.7 <u>Height Constrained Min-max Partition</u>:

Given $H > 0$, find a q-partition such that

$$h(T_i) \leq H \qquad (1 \leq i \leq q)$$

and such that $\max_{1 \leq i \leq q} w(T_i)$ is a minimum.

These latter two problems were treated in Agasi, Becker and Perl (1982). It was shown that 6 is NP-complete, while 7 can be solved by a polynomial algorithm, using a top-down shifting procedure similar to those used in solving 4 and 5, but very much more complicated. The complexity is $O(h_T nq^2)$, where h_T denotes the height of tree T.

In the present paper we present a polynomial algorithm for solving problem 1, using a bottom-up approach of the type employed by Kundu and Misra (1977) in solving problem 2. However, the additional requirement of the height constraint in our problem leads to an algorithm which is more involved than the original algorithm, although simpler than that of Agasi et al (1982). In our algorithm, cuts may have to be shifted to a brother edge in order to ensure that both constraints are satisfied. An important role in both algorithms is played by a similar procedure which ensure that a component satisfies the height constraint, if this is at all possible. The complexity of the new algorithm is $O(Hn)$, or independently of H, $O(h_T n)$.

Section 2 contains definitions. In section 3 we present the algorithm and section 4 gives an extended example. In section 5 the complexity of the algorithm is discussed.

We omit here the correctness proof, which will be published elsewhere, as well as certain minor improvements in the algorithm which just add to its complication.

2 DEFINITIONS

Suppose throughout that we are given a rooted tree T, to each of whose vertices is assigned a non-negative weight $w(v)$. The weight of a component is the sum of the weights of its vertices. The height of a tree rooted at r is the maximum of the number of edges in a path having one end at r. A component is said to be height-bounded if its height is $\leq H$. A component is said to be valid if it is height-bounded and its weight is $\leq W$. We use the usual terminology of Graph Theory (see Harary (1969)).

Many non-standard terms that we use are self-explanatory; when in doubt consult Becker et al (1982a). We list some of these: incident to, incident from, head(e) = vertex of e farthest from the root, tail(e), father(e), brother(e), son, down component, up component. Given a partition of a (sub)tree rooted at v, the component containing v is termed the top component.

A subtree T' of T is a partial (complete) subtree of T rooted at a vertex v if v is the root of T' and T' contains one (every) son of v together with all the latter's descendants. Such a partial subtree with initial edge e is denoted by $PS(e)$, while the complete subtree rooted at v is denoted by $CS(v)$.

A partition of T is said to be an algorithm partition if it is a partition found by the H-W Algorithm described in the next section. A partition is said to be optimal if it is a valid partition having a minimum number of cuts.

3 THE ALGORITHM

We state the algorithm, and give a short informal account of its method of operation.

H-W Algorithm

Scan the tree bottom-up level by level. Let v be the vertex currently being scanned. Let v have sons $w_1, \ldots, w_r$, and let e_i denote (v, w_i), $1 \leq i \leq r$.

1. For $i := 1$ to r do:

If the height of the down component of w_i is H, then call procedure $B(e_i, ANS_i)$. If ANS_i = FAIL, then place a cut on e_i.

2. While the weight of the down component of v is $> W$ do: Place a cut on a vacant son edge of v with heaviest down component.

Procedure B(e, ANS)

Let w = head (e) .
Untick any ticked cuts, unmark any marked edges.

A. For each vertex u in CS(w) distant H from w do: By performing a side shift if necessary, ensure that the lowest possible unticked cut lies on the path from u to w . If no such unticked cut exists, then go to F , else tick this cut and mark its edge and all descendant edges in the tree.

B. Scan the subtree of unmarked edges of CS(w) bottom up level by level. Side shift each cut c to a vacant brother edge if this will increase the weight of the down component of c .

C. With the exception of cuts bounding the top component, restore all cuts side shifted in A or B to their original position.

D. If the weight of the top component is $> W$, then go to F .

E. (Success) Let ANS : = SUCCEED . Return.

F. (Failure) Let ANS : = FAIL . Restore all cuts shifted in A or B to their original positions. Return.

Overview the operation of the algorithm

After each vertex v has been processed by the algorithm (i.e. at the end of step 2 after processing v), the top component of CS(v) has minimum weight over all valid partitions of CS(v) .

In processing v , a cut may apparently be needed on $e_i = (v,w_i)$ due to the top component of $PS(e_i)$ violating the height constraint. Procedure B is then called to determine whether it is possible to side shift the cuts below w_i in such a way that a height-bounded partition of $PS(e_i)$ is obtained which still satisfies the weight constraint in this subtree. So at the end of step 1 of the algorithm, all cuts needed on son edges of v due to height constraint violations have been placed. Step 2 then places cuts on son edges of v until the top component satisfies the weight constraint.

Procedure B operates as follows: In step A the lowest possible cuts are placed on paths from w to leaves so that the length of the path satisfies the height constraint. There must be cuts on the paths at these positions or possibly higher up, if validity is to be ensured. If it is not possible to block all long paths, then step A transfers control to step F which returns procedure value FAIL. If all such paths can be blocked, then at step B the procedure side shifts cuts above the blocking (or ticked) cuts so that the top component has minimal weight. If this weight satisfies the weight constraint then the procedure returns SUCCEED, and step 1 of the algorithm does not place a cut on this edge. However, if the top component has resultant weight > W , the procedure restores the old partition, returns FAIL, and step 1 of the algorithm places a cut on the top edge.

4. A WORKED EXAMPLE

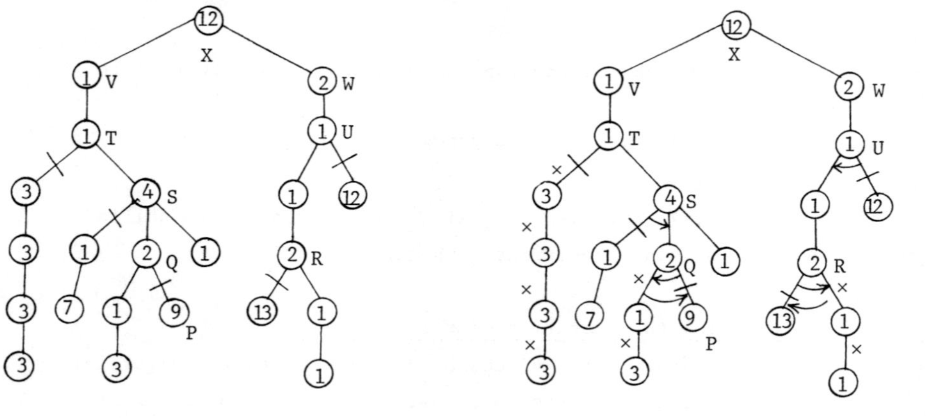

(a) (b)

Figure 1: Tree to be partitioned into components with weight ≤ 14, height ≤ 4 (W = 14, H = 4).

(a) Configuration after vertices at heights 0 through 4 have been processed.

(b) Processing vertices V and W .

Figure 1(a) shows a rooted tree which is to be partitioned into components with weight ≤ 14 , height ≤ 4 (W = 14, H = 4) after the vertices at heights 0 through 4 have been processed. At step 2 of the algorithm cuts are placed in turn below vertices Q, R, S, T and U to ensure that the weight bound is satisfied.

The first time that a path of length > 4 is encountered is when the vertices of height 5 (V and W) are processed. First consider vertex V . As can be seen in Figure 1(b), there are two paths of length 5 below V , so procedure B is called. The first path is already blocked by the cut below T , so at step A that cut is ticked, and the edge on which it lies and the edges below that marked (with an in Figure 1(b)). Turning now to the second path, it is possible to block it by side shifting the cut below Q . The cut is then ticked, and the appropriate two edges marked. This concludes the operations of step A of procedure B. At step B, the cut below S is side shifted to maximize its down component, whereupon the shifted cut below Q is restored (at step C) to its position before procedure B was called. Procedure B then returns the value SUCCEED.

Turning now to vertex W , the cut below R is side shifted and ticked at step A. The cut below U is side shifted at step B. The cut below R is then restored at step C. Again procedure B returns SUCCEED, but thereafter, at step 2 of the algorithm, a cut is placed below W .

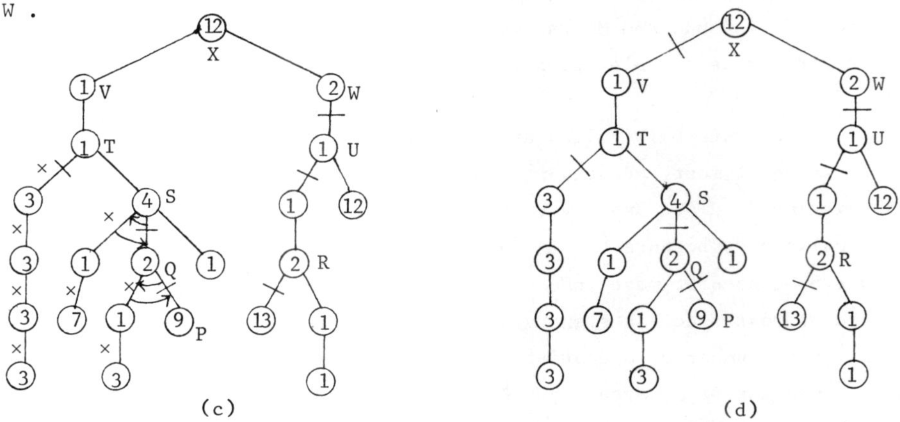

Figure 1: (continued) Tree to be partitioned into components with weight ≤ 14 , height ≤ 4 (W = 14, H = 4).

(c) Processing vertex X .

(d) Final configuration.

Figure 1(c) shows the configuration when vertex X is processed by the algorithm. At step A, the cut below T is ticked as before, and the edge on which the cut lies and the edges below it are marked. Then the cuts below S and Q are side shifted in turn and ticked, and the appropriate edges marked. However, after side shifting the cut below Q there are insufficient unticked cuts to block the path (P,Q,S,T,V,X). Accordingly, the side shifted cuts below S and Q are replaced, procedure B returns FAIL, and a cut is placed below X by step 1 of the algorithm. The final configuration is shown in Figure 1(d).

5. COMPLEXITY ANALYSIS

Complexity of the H - W Algorithm

We will show informally the following:

There is an implementation of the H - W Algorithm with complexity $O(Hn)$, where $n = |V|$, if $h_T > H$, and complexity $O(n)$ if $h_T \leq H$.

We will not discuss the details of the data structures necessary, but similar structures to those in the implementations in Becker, Perl and Schach (1982b), and Perl and Vishkin (1982) are needed.

The assignment of cuts in step 2 of the algorithm can be made in time linear in the number of sons of v being processed, by making use of the linear median-finding algorithm Aho et al (1976) (similarly to the method of Kundu and Misra (1977)). Each vertex is processed once by the algorithm as a whole, so step 2 leads to $O(n)$ operations in total.

Procedure B is called at most once for each edge, so there are $|E| = n$ calls at most. Procedure B need work only with the portion of CS(v) distant $\leq H+1$ from v. So each vertex is processed in at most $(H+1)$ calls of procedure B. In each call of procedure B, cuts on marked edges are processed at most once (in step A), and unmarked edges are processed at most once (in step B). Performing step A can easily be done using a linear number of operations. The assignment in step B of the cuts on son edges of a vertex y to those son edges of y with heaviest down components can be done in linear time as follows: Suppose that there are m cuts on son edges of y. Find the son edge with m'th heaviest down component in linear time using the linear k-median finding algorithm Aho et al (1976); let the weight of this down component be denoted by W_m . Place as many cuts as possible on son edges of y with down components $> W_m$, and then place the remaining cuts on son edges with down component equal to W_m . Restoring cuts to their previous positions in steps C or F requires time linear in the number of cuts on edges of subtrees of height $(H+1)$. Thus each vertex in a single call of procedure B requires a linear number of operations to process. So the total number of operations needed to process a single vertex in <u>all</u> calls of procedure B is $O(Hn)$. The total complexity is therefore $O(Hn)$ if $h_T > H$.

By including a (linear time) check to see whether $h_T \leq H$, we deduce the following results:

(a) In the (trivial) case of $h_T \leq H$, procedure B is never called, and the algorithm has complexity $O(n)$, as in Kundu and Misra (1977).

(b) Otherwise, the algorithm has complexity $O(Hn)$, or, since $H < h_T$ in this case, complexity $O(h_T n)$.

(c) Combining these two results, we see that in all cases the number of operations is $O(h_T n)$, i.e. we have a polynomial algorithm.

REFERENCES

Agasi, E., Becker, R.I. and Perl, Y. (1982). A shifting algorithm for constrained min-max partition of trees. Research Report 010, Department of Mathematics, University of Cape Town. (Submitted).

Aho, A.V., Hopcroft, J.E. and Ullman, J.D. (1976). The Design and Analysis of Computer Algorithms. Addison-Wesley, Reading, Mass.

Becker, R.I., Perl, Y. and Schach, S.R. (1982a). A shifting algorithm for min-max tree partitioning. J. ACM. 29, 58-67.

Becker, R.I., Perl, Y. and Schach, S.R. (1982b). An efficient implementation of an algorithm for min-max tree partitioning. Quaest. Informaticae 2, 27-30.

Becker, R.I. and Perl, Y. (1983). Shifting algorithms for tree partitioning with general weighting functions. J. Algorithms, 4, 101-120.

Becker, R.I. and Schach, S.R. (1983). Bottom-up algorithms for tree partitioning with general weighting functions. In preparation.

Farley, A., Hedetniemi, S. and Proskurowski, A. (1981). Partitioning trees: matching, domination and maximum diameter. Intern. J. Comp. Inf. Sci. 10, 55-61.

Harary, F. (1969). Graph Theory. Addison-Wesley, Reading, Mass.

Kundu, S. and Misra, J. (1977). A linear tree-partitioning algorithm. SIAM J. Computing 6, 131-134.

Perl, Y. and Schach, S.R. (1981). Max-min tree-partitioning. J. ACM 28, 5-15.

Perl, Y. and Snir, N. (1982). Circuit partitioning with size and connection constraints. Proc. Sixteenth Annual Conf. on Information Science and Systems. Princeton, 80-84.

Perl, Y. and Vishkin, V. (1982). Junction tree structure with application to a shifting algorithm. IBM Research Report RC 9405, Yorktown Heights, New York.

GRAPHS AND RATIONAL EXPRESSIONS DENOTING REGULAR TREES

by J.P. Braquelaire
Université de Bordeaux-I
Cours de la libération
33405 Talence, France.

Introduction.

The concept of program scheme is essential for theoritical studies on programming langages : formalization of control structures and the corresponding equivalences on programs, program transformations, proof methods for program correctness. In the case of iterative programs, an infinite regular tree can be associated with the program scheme which represents all its possible computation sequences. This is the main reason of the importance of regular trees apart from their theoretical interest (another one concerns first-order unification, see Courcelle [8]).

An iterative program scheme can be defined in two very different ways, corresponding to two styles of programming : by a graph, i.e. a flowchart ("unstructured") and by an expression, defined in a "structured way" by a context-free grammar. The same two types of definitions exist for the representation of regular trees.

Our aim is to investigate the relations between them, since both representations by graphs and by rational expressions are important. Each of them has its own advantages :

- for graphs, the existence of unique minimal graph, the definition of the flow of control as a path in the graph, the fact that the graph and the tree it defines are of same nature (both of they are graphs), and that there is no need for indices for exits,
- for expressions the semantics is defined in parallel with the syntax; formal manipulation (for program transformations) is easier with expressions than with graphs. As we shall see, there exist many types of expressions for regular trees. They introduce iteration operators either with bound variables (raising problems of renaming) or with multiple levels of exits that behave in a rather little intuitive way. They have been investigated for studying the semantics of EXEL program schemes (Cousineau [12]), program structuration (Jacob[23], Kosaraju [25]).

Another motivation for studying the relations between graphs and expressions denoting regular trees is the need of expressions denoting graphical objects that we felt when working on the system SIGMA, an interactive graphic system for manipulation of trees and graphs (Braquelaire, Courcelle [4]). In this system, expressions are used in order to input the manipulated objects when the system is running.

Our research was motivated by the following two problems :

- to find an algorithm for constructing an expression of minimal star-height from another expression that denotes a regular tree or a graph. This problem splits into two problems which are :
- to build an expression of minimal star-height that denotes a regular tree; it has been solved in Braquelaire, Courcelle [5],
- to build an expression of minimal star-height that denotes a graph (which is "structured" in some sense); it is solved in this paper.
- to find a class of expressions in bijection with graphs, as a convenient way to represent them. This is the problem we consider here.

The graphs we shall consider are very close to program schemes, and their characteristics are the followings :
- each node is labeled by a symbol with a rank and has a number of successors equal to the rank of its label,
- the set of arcs having a same source node is ordered,
- there exists a distinguished node called pointed node such that there is a path from this node to each other node in the graph. These graphs are l. o. p. graphs (labeled ordered pointed). We define the equivalence of two graphs by the equality of their unfolded graphs, i.e. the tree of all the paths starting from the pointed nodes. This equivalence coincides with the equivalence of the corresponding program schemes.

In order to make these graphs closer to iterative programs schemes, we divide the set A of the arcs into two disjoint sets A_S and A_L which form respectively the skeleton and the set of links, and such that the arcs of A_S form a spanning tree of the graph, with root being the pointed node. For example, the two graphs of figure 1 are two partitions of a same l.o.p. graph.

The purpose of a such partition is to distinguish in the scheme the arcs which denote sequential transfer to the next instruction from those which denote jumps. The skeleton is an indication of the sequential structure of the program, when the links may be seen as corresponding to goto's or do-repeat statements.

These considerations lead us to define a subclass of these graphs, namely the family of quasi-trees, which correspond to structured programs. A quasi-tree is a partitioned graph each link of which is such that its target is an ancestor (with respect to the skeleton) of its source. Arcs which verify this property are called back-edges. In the previous example, the arc with target P and source Q is a back-edge.

The quasi-trees has been investigated under different forms, reducible flow graphs [Hetch, Ullman 20], arborescent systems [Cousineau 10], stratified expansions [Jacob 23], ... It is classical that every graph has an equivalent quasi-tree; it can be obtained by a graph rewriting system. Moreover, a l.o.p graph is a quasi-tree if and only if there exists a single way to partition its arcs. We shall consider quasi-trees, which by reason of their structuration, can be denoted by rational expressions.

We shall use rational expressions defined with operators of iteration and composition. The value of a rational expression is a regular tree that can be defined by induction on the structure of the rational expression. A quasi-tree can be associated in a natural way to a rational expression, also by induction on the structure of the rational expression. It is closer to the flowchart, and represents its abstract syntax.

There exists a natural bijection between a restricted family of rational expressions (defined without composition operator) and the quasi-trees which can be seen as "graphs of abstract syntax" for these expressions, in the sense that they represent them without using bound variables, giving an intrinsic representations of expressions. We shall give various "normal forms" for rational expressions, which can be obtained by rewriting systems, corresponding to certain types of program transformations. We construct a bijection between a sub-family of rational expressions called reduced rational expressions and the quasi-trees supplied with a certain mapping, called structure. We show the existence of a minimal structure, and the bijection between structured quasi-trees and reduced rational expressions gives us a mean to solve the minimal star-height problem for quasi-trees.

We shall not give here all the proofs; the reader will refer to Braquelaire [4] for complete proofs.

-1- Graphs and rational expressions

We first recall some notations : F is a finite ranked alphabet, $\rho(f)$ is the rank of a symbol f of F, F_i is the set of symbols of rank i, V is an infinite set of variables and we consider $M^{\infty}(F,V)$, the set of infinite trees on $F \cup V$ (Courcelle [8]). We denote by PS(S) the power-set of a set S, by $|S|$ the cardinal of S, and by $f \restriction D$ the restriction of a mapping f to a domain D.

(1.1) Definition : E(F,V) is the set of rational expressions (r.e.) inductively defined as follows :

(i) $v \in V \cup F_0$ is a r.e.

(ii) $f(e_1,\dots,e_k)$ is a r.e. if $f \in F_k$ and $e_1,\dots,e_k$ are r.e.'s

(iii) $*_x(e)$ is a r.e. if $x \in V$ and if e is a r.e.

(iv) $e_0 \cdot_\sigma (e_1, \ldots, e_k)$ is a r.e. if $e_0, \ldots, e_k$ are r.e.'s and if σ is a sequence $(v_1, \ldots, v_k)$ of distinct variables of V.

We shall denote by $\sigma(i)$ the ith element of σ $(1 \leqslant i \leqslant k)$, and by $E_0(F,V)$ the set of restricted rational expressions (r.r.e.), i.e. the subset of $E(F,V)$ consisting of r.e.'s built without rule (iv). It is well-known that these expressions denote the regular trees. The tree val(e) associated with e, called the value of e, can be defined inductively, interpreting the $*$ operator as tree iteration, and the $\cdot_\sigma$ operator as tree substitution. For example, the r.e. $*_x(f(a,x))$ denotes the tree $f(a,x)$ iterated with respect to the variable x, i.e. the tree $f(a, f(a, f(a, \ldots)))$.

It is possible to represent a r.e. by a graph which is also a finite representation of the tree. The r.e. $*_x(f(x,a))$ may be associated with the graph 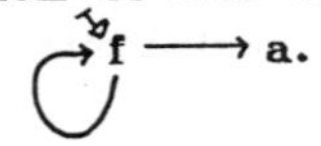

This provides a finite representation which does not need to use bound variables. The set of graphs definable by r.e.'s is a subset of the set of the labeled ordered pointed graphs (l.o.p) defined as follows :

(1.2) Definition : A labeled ordered pointed graph (l.o.p.) is a triple <G, r, eti> satisfying the following conditions :

- G is a directed graph (each arc has a source and a target),
- r is a node of G (the pointed node or the root) such that for each node n of G $(n \neq r)$, there exists a path $(r=n_0, n_1, \ldots, n_k=n)$ in G with r as origin and n as extremity (i.e there exists an arc of source n_{i-1} and target n_i for every i, $1 \leqslant i \leqslant k$),
- for each node n of G, the set $Iss_G(n)$ of arcs with n as source is ordered,
- eti : Nod(G) $\longrightarrow$ $F \cup V$, where Nod(G) is the set of nodes of G, is a mapping such that for each node n of G, $\rho(eti(n)) = |Iss_G(n)|$.

We shall denote by $n_1 \xrightarrow{k} n_2$ an arc with n_1 for source, n_2 for target, and which is the kth element of $Iss_G(n_1)$.

We now consider l.o.p graphs for which the set of arcs is the disjoint union of two sets A_S and A_L called respectively the skeleton and the set of links, and such that the arcs of the skeleton constitute a spanning tree of the graph. We can intuitively say that these graphs are generally unstructured. For example, in the partitioned l.o.p. graph of figure-2, the link $g \xrightarrow{1} h$ may be seen as a goto statement when the link $g \xrightarrow{2} f$ may be seen as a do-repeat statement. The graphs definable by rational expressions are those that correspond to structured program schemes, i.e. without transversal links. We call them quasi-trees, and define them as follows :

(1.3) <u>Definition</u> : A <u>quasi-tree</u> is a l.o.p graph G such that the set of arcs is the disjoint union of two sets A_S and A_L, where A_S forms a spanning tree of G, and every arc in A_L has a target which either is equal to its source, or is an ancestor of its source, with respect to the spanning tree.

The links in a quasi-tree are called <u>back-edge,</u> and we call <u>strict path</u> a path the arcs of which belong to the skeleton A_S, and <u>branch</u> a maximal strict path. We denote by QT(F,V) the set of quasi-trees built on F∪V.

We can construct all the quasi-trees by using two operators that we can informally define as follows :

- if $f \in F_K$ and $Q_1,\dots,Q_k$ are quasi-trees, then $f(Q_1,\dots,Q_k)$ is the quasi-tree of figure-3,
- if Q is a quasi-tree with <u>leaves</u> (i.e. nodes without successors) labeled by the variable v, then $\underline{iter}_v(Q)$ is the quasi-tree obtained by replacing each arc with a leaf labeled by v as target by an arc with the same source and the root of Q as target (see figure-4).

So we can associate a quasi-tree with a r.r.e. by interpreting the operator $*_x$ as $\underline{iter}_x$. In order to find the value of a r.e. built with the $\cdot_\sigma$ operator, we need a third operator which realizes substitution of quasi-trees; we denote by $Q_0[Q_1/v_1,\dots,Q_k/v_k]$ the quasi-tree obtained by substituting for each leaf labeled by v_i the quasi-tree Q_i for $1 \leqslant i \leqslant k$. We denote by <u>qval</u>(e) the quasi-tree denoted by e, and we say that <u>qval</u>(e) is the <u>q-value</u> of e.

<u>Remark</u> : The quasi-tree obtained by unfolding all the paths starting from the root in a quasi-tree <u>qval</u>(e) is also the tree we associate directly with the expression e.

It is clear that different r.e.'s can describe a same quasi-tree, as for example $*_x(*_y(f(x,y)))$ and $*_z(f(z,z))\cdot_{(u)}(g(u))$ which both denote

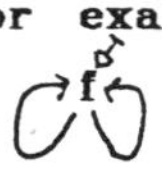 .

We denote by <u>Var</u>(Q) the set of variables appearing in a quasi-tree Q, and by FV(e) the set of variables having a free occurence in a r.e. e. In general we have : Var(val(e))⊂FV(e)). We shall now give various canonical forms of r.e.'s in order to eliminate unnecessary parts of r.e.'s. We shall first give the following lemmas :

(1.4) <u>Lemma</u> : <u>If</u> $v \notin$ <u>Var</u>(<u>qval</u>(e)) <u>then</u> <u>qval</u>($*_v$(e))=<u>qval</u>(e)

We denote by $e[v/w]$ the result of substitution in e of v for each free occurence of w (this includes a renaming of bound variables in order to avoid collisions of variables).

(1.5) Lemma : $\underline{qval}(*_v(*_w(e))) = \underline{qval}(*_w(*_v(e))) = \underline{qval}(*_v(e[v/w]))$

In consequence we have $\underline{qval}(*_v(*_v(e))) = \underline{qval}(*_v(e))$.

(1.6) Lemma : If σ is the sequence $(v_1,\dots,v_k)$, if v is a variable different of v_i, for $1\leq i\leq k$, and if $e_1,\dots,e_k$ are r.e.'s such that $v\notin \underline{Var}(\underline{qval}(e_i))$ for $1\leq i\leq k$, then $\underline{qval}(*_v(e\cdot_\sigma(e_1,\dots,e_k))) = \underline{qval}(*_v(e)\cdot_\sigma(e_1,\dots,e_k))$.

(1.7) Definition : A simplified r.e. is a r.e. of one of the following forms :

(i) $e\in V\cup F_0$

(ii) $e= f(e_1,\dots,e_k)$ where $e_1,\dots,e_k$ are simplified r.e.

(iii) $e= *_v(e')$ if $v\in\underline{Var}(\underline{qval}(e'))$, and if e' is a simplified r.e.

(iv) $e= e_0\cdot_\sigma(e_1,\dots,e_k)$ if $\sigma(i)\in\underline{Var}(\underline{qval}(e_0))$ for $1\leq i\leq k$ and if $e_0,\dots,e_k$ are simplified r.e.'s.

We denote by SE(F,V) the set of simplified r.e.'s.

(1.8) Lemma : If e is a simplified r.e., then $\underline{FV}(e)=\underline{Var}(\underline{qval}(e))$.

We can get a simplified r.e. e' from a r.e. e by using the following rewriting system :

SE1 : $e_0\cdot_\sigma(e_1,\dots,e_k) \longrightarrow e_0\cdot_{\sigma'}(e_1,\dots,e_{i-1},e_{i+1},\dots,e_k)$ if $\sigma=(v_1,\dots,v_k)$, $\sigma'=(v_1,\dots,v_{i-1},v_{i+1},\dots,v_k)$ and if $v_i\notin\underline{Var}(\underline{qval}(e_0))$

SE2 : $*_v(e_0) \longrightarrow e_0$ if $v\notin\underline{Var}(\underline{qval}(e_0))$

It can be shown that this system is confluent and noetherian, and that the canonical form of a r.e. e is an equivalent simplified r.e. e'. (The equivalence follows from lemma-1.4). We denote by simp(e) the simplified r.e. obtained from a r.e. e.

(1.9) Lemma : If e is a r.e., simp(e) is a simplified r.e. with the same q-value.

We now want to get r.e.'s that cannot be transformed by suppression of * operators without changing the q-value. For example the r.e. $*_x(*_y(f(x,y,z)))$ may be simplified into $*_x(f(x,x,z))$, and $*_x(*_y(f(x,y))\cdot_x(g(x,z)))\cdot_z(h(y)))$ into $*_u((f(x,u)\cdot_x(g(u,z)))\cdot_z(h(y)))$. One remarks that in this second example, we need to rename occurences of the bound variables x and y in u in order to avoid conflicts. This is one of the purposes of quasi-trees to allow a representation which avoid these conflicts.

(1.10) Definition : A r.e. is strongly simplified if it is simplified and if each of its subexpression of the form $*_v(e)$ verifies $\underline{first}(e) \neq *$, where first is defined as follows :

(i) $\underline{first}(e) = e$ if $e \in V \cup F_0$

(ii) $\underline{first}(f(e_1, \ldots, e_k)) = f$

(iii) $\underline{first}(*_v(e)) = *$

(iv) $\underline{first}(e_0 \cdot_\sigma (e_1, \ldots, e_k)) = \underline{first}(e_0)$

We denote by SSE(F,V) the set of strongly simplified r.e. and by $SSE_0(F,V)$ the set of strongly simplified r.r.e.'s.

(1.11) Definition : For each variable v belonging to V, we define the operator q_v on SE(F,V)−V by :

(i) $q_v(a) = a$ if $a \in F_0$

(ii) $q_v(f(e_1, \ldots, e_k)) = f(e_1, \ldots, e_k)$

(iii) $q_v(*_w(e)) = q_v(e)[v/w]$

(iv) $q_v(e_0 \cdot_\sigma (e_1, \ldots, e_k)) = q_v(e_0) \cdot_\sigma (e_1, \ldots, e_k)$

We can now define the operator ssimp, using the operator q_v, and which produce a strongly simplified r.e. from a simplified r.e. (this operator can be defined inductively, but the recursive definition is much more easier to use).

(1.12) Definition : We denote by ssimp the operator defined as follows :

(i) $\underline{ssimp}(e) = e$ if $e \in V \cup F_0$

(ii) $\underline{ssimp}(f(e_1, \ldots, e_k)) = f(\underline{ssimp}(e_1), \ldots, \underline{ssimp}(e_k))$

(iii) $\underline{ssimp}(*_v(e)) = *_v(\underline{ssimp}(e))$ if $\underline{first}(e) \neq *$

$= *_v(\underline{ssimp}(q_v(e)))$ if $\underline{first}(e) = *$

(iv) $\underline{ssimp}(e_0 \cdot_\sigma (e_1, \ldots, e_k)) = \underline{ssimp}(e_0) \cdot_\sigma (\underline{ssimp}(e_1), \ldots, \underline{ssimp}(e_k))$

With the help of lemma-1.5 it can be shown :

(1.13) Proposition : if e is a simplified r.e., ssimp(e) is defined and is a strongly simplified r.e. with the same q-value.

This new simplification corresponds for program schemes to the elimination of useless nested loops.

There exists a one to one correspondence between strongly simplified r.e.e.'s and quasi-trees. We show on an example how to form a r.r.e. from a quasi-tree. Let Q and Q_0 be the quasi-trees of figure 5 and 6; we form $Q = \underline{iter}_y(Q_0)$ and $Q_0 = f(y, Q_1)$, with $Q_1 = \underline{iter}_z(g(z,x,y))$, and we finally get $e = *_y(f(y, *_z(g(z,x,y))))$ which verifies $\underline{qval}(e) = Q$. This

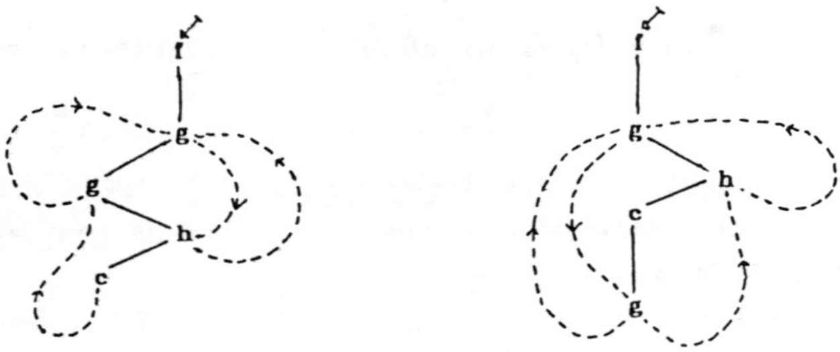

- Figure 1 -

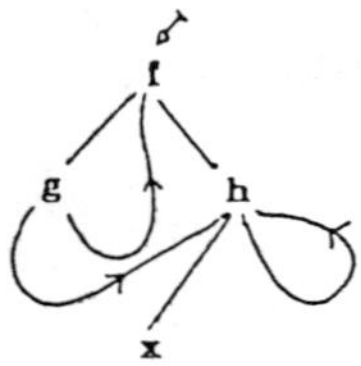

- Figure 2 -

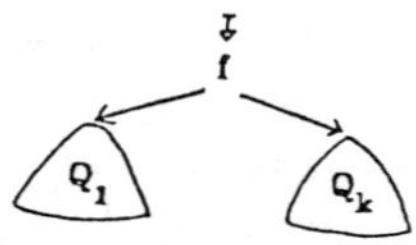

- Figure 3 -

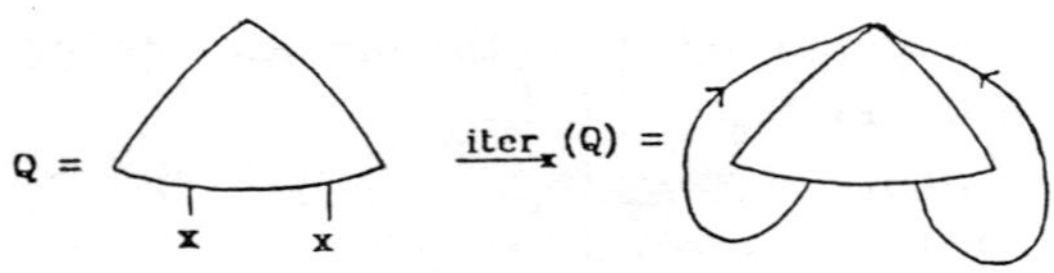

- Figure 4 -

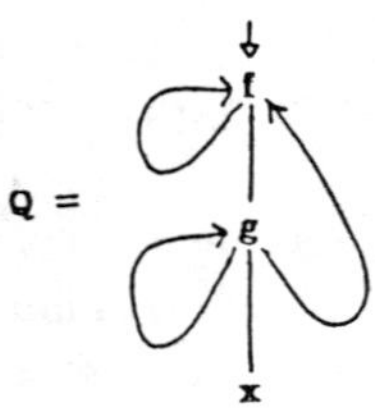

- Figure 5 -

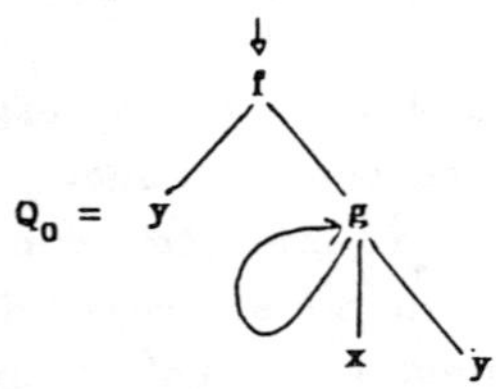

- Figure 6 -

operator denoted by $\underline{exp_0}$ can be easily formalized, and we show that $\underline{exp_0}(Q)$ is a strongly simplified r.r.e. for all quasi-tree Q, that $\underline{exp_0 \circ qval}$ is the identity on $SSE_0(F,V)$ and that $\underline{qval \circ exp_0}$ the identity on QT(F,V).

We now define a third canonical form which is the result of an ordering of the $\cdot_\sigma$ composition operators. The r.e. $e_0 \cdot_\sigma (e_1,\ldots,e_k)$ may be seen as a scheme e_0 with k outputs labeled by $\sigma(1), \ldots, \sigma(k)$, these outputs being associated with the schemes $e_1,\ldots,e_k$ with respect to the e_i's.

(1.14) Definition : A r.e. e is normal if it is strongly simplified, if each sub-expression of e of the form $*_v(e')$ verifies $e'=f(e_1,\ldots,e_k)$, and if each sub-expression of the form $e_0 \cdot_\sigma (e_1,\ldots,e_k)$ verifies $e_0= *_v(e')$ or $e_0=f(e'_1,\ldots,e'_k)$.

If e is a strongly simplified r.e., we can get an equivalent normal r.e. by a rewriting system.
rewriting system.

(1.15) Definition : One defined the system NRM by if $e_0,\ldots,e_p,e'_1,\ldots,e'_q$ are r.e.'s:

NRM1: $(e_0 \cdot_\sigma (e_1,\ldots,e_p)) \cdot_\tau (e'_1,\ldots,e'_q) \longrightarrow \underline{simp}(e_0 \cdot_{\sigma'} (e''_1,\ldots,e''_p,e'_{j_1},\ldots,e'_{j_r}))$
with $e''_i=e_i \cdot_\tau (e'_1,\ldots,e'_q)$, and if $\tau-\sigma=(\tau(j_1),\ldots,\tau(j_r))$
then $\sigma'=(\sigma(1),\ldots,\sigma(p),\tau(j_1),\ldots,\tau(j_r))$

NRM2 : $f(e_1,\ldots,e_p) \cdot_\sigma (e'_1,\ldots,e'_q) \longrightarrow f(e''_1,\ldots,e''_p)$
avec $e''_i= \underline{simp}(e_i \cdot_\sigma (e'_1,\ldots,e'_q))$,

NRM3 : $v \cdot_\sigma (e_1,\ldots,e_k) \longrightarrow e_i$ if $v=\sigma(i)$.

Since we define these rules without simp's operator, a simplified r.e. can be rewriting into a non simplified r.e.; for example the simplified r.e. $f(x,y) \cdot_{(x,y)} (a,b)$ would be rewriting by NRM2 into $f(x \cdot_{(x,y)} (a,b), y \cdot_{(x,y)} (a,b))$ (the which is simplifiable in $f(x \cdot_x (a), y \cdot_y (b))$). If we represent the r.e.'s $f(e_1,\ldots,e_k)$ and $e_0 \cdot_\sigma (e_1,\ldots,e_k)$ by the schemes of figures 7 and 8, we can illustrate the rules NRM1 and NRM2 by figure 9. It can be proove that NRM is Church-Rosser and Noetherian, and we denote by norm(e) the canonical form of a r.e. e by NRM. We have :

Remark : The NRM system produces strongly normal r.e, i.e. such that each sub-expression of the form $e_0 \cdot_\sigma (e_1,\ldots,e_k)$ verifies $e_0=*_v(e')$.

(1.16) Lemma : If e is a strongly simplified r.e., then norm(e) is a normal r.e. with the same q-value.

We finally define a last canonical form, the reduced r.e. :

(1.17) Definition : A r.e. is reduced if

(i) it is normal,

(ii) if $e_0 \cdot \sigma(e_1, \ldots, e_k)$ is a sub-expression of e, then $e_i \notin V$ for $1 \leq i \leq k$,

(iii) if $e_0 \cdot \sigma(e_1, \ldots, e_k)$ is a sub-expression of e, then for all i, $1 \leq i \leq k$, the variable $\sigma(i)$ has a unique free occurence in e_0.

We can get a reduced r.e. from a normal r.e. by using the following rewriting system :

RD1 : $e_0 \cdot \sigma(e_1, \ldots, e_{j-1}, v, e_{j+1}, \ldots, e_k) \longrightarrow e'_0 \cdot \sigma' (e_1, \ldots, e_{j-1}, e_{j+1}, \ldots, e_k)$
for $v \in V$, $e'_0 = e_0[v/\sigma(j)]$, and $\sigma' = (\sigma(1), \ldots, \sigma(j-1), \sigma(j+1), \ldots, \sigma(k))$.

RD2 : $e_0 \cdot \sigma(e_1, \ldots, e_k) \longrightarrow e'_0 \cdot \sigma' (e_1, \ldots, e_k, e_{k+1})$,
if there exist two free occurences of $\sigma(i)$ in e_0, for some i, $1 \leq i \leq k$, if e'_0 is the result of the renaming of only one of these occurence v does not appear in $e_0 \cdot \sigma(e_1, \ldots, e_k)$, and with $e_{k+1} = e_i$ and $\sigma' = (\sigma(1), \ldots, \sigma(k), v)$.

The interest of the reduced form is the existence of a bijection between reduced r.e.'s and quasi-trees supplied with a certain mapping, called structure, defined on the set on their nodes. This allows a graphical representation for the general rational expressions. In the second part of this paper, we shall study the properties of these structured quasi-trees and give the bijection.

-2- Structured quasi-trees.

(2.1) Definition : A structure of a quasi-tree Q with root r is a mapping $p : \underline{Nod}(Q) \longrightarrow PS(\underline{Nod}(Q))$ verifying :

(i) $p(n) = \emptyset$ if and only if $\underline{lab}(n) \in V$, and if $n' \in p(n)$ then there exists a strict path from n to n' such that all the nodes of this path belong to $p(n)$,

(ii) for every nodes n_1, n_2 of Q, if $p(n_1) \cap p(n_2) \neq \emptyset$, then either $p(n_1) \subset p(n_2)$, or $p(n_2) \subset p(n_1)$ (inclusions are stricts),

(iii) if $n_1 \xrightarrow{k} n_2$ is a back-edge of Q, then $n_1 \in p(n_2)$.

We say that <Q, p> is a structured quasi-tree if p is a structure of the quasi-tree Q, and we denote by $QT^s(F,V)$ the set of structured quasi-trees belonging to $QT(F,V)$.

Condition (i) forbids nestings (see figure-10) and condition (ii) overlapping (see figure-11); condition (iii) guarantees that no back-edge can have its target in a box where it has not its source. This idea of structured trees implicitely appears in [Jacob 23].

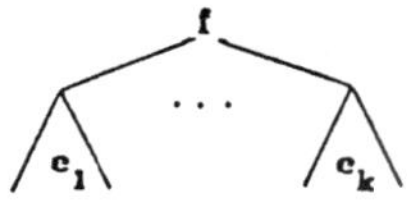

- Figure 7 -

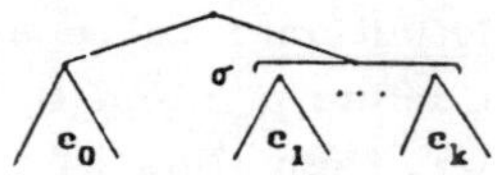

- Figure 8 -

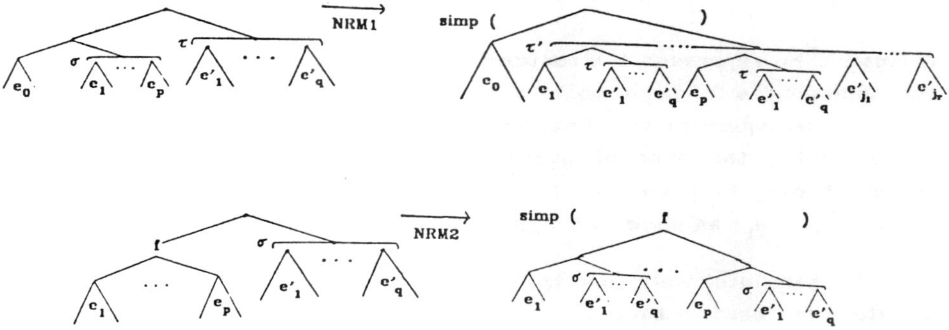

- Figure 9 -

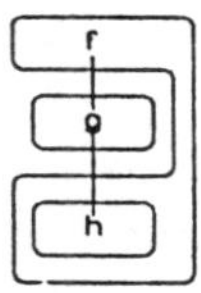

- Figure 10 -

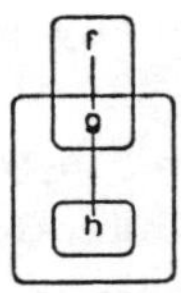

- Figure 11 -

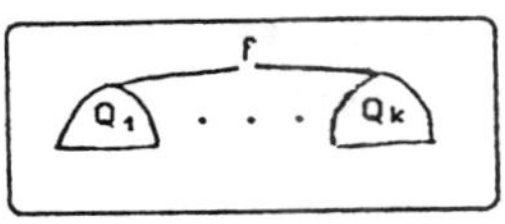

- Figure 12 -

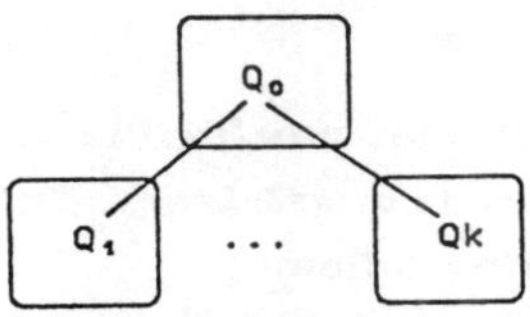

- Figure 13 -

(2.2) Definition : Let e be a r.e. of q-value Q, and let r be the root of Q. We define p_e : Nod(Q) ⟶ PS(Nod(Q)) by :

(i) if $e \in V \cup F_0$ then Nod(Q) = {r} and $p_e(r)=N_f(r)$

(ii) if $e=f(e_1,\dots,e_k)$ then $p_e(r) = N_f(r)$, and $p_e(n) = p_{e_i}(n)$ if $n \in$ Nod(qval(e_i))

(iii) if $e=*_x(e')$, then Nod(Q)=Nod(qval(e')), and $p_e(n)=p_{e'}(n)$ for all n in Nod(Q).

(iv) if $e=e_0 \cdot_\sigma (e_1,\dots,e_k)$ then $p_e(n)=p_{e_i}(n)$ if $n \in$ Nod(qval(e_i))

where $N_F(n)$ is the set of the strict descendants of n labeled in F.

Example : We represent a structure by boxes drawn on the quasi-tree; a box including a node n that is the ancestor of all the other nodes $n_1,\dots,n_k$ belonging to this box, means that $p(n)=\{n,n_1,\dots,n_k\}$. Let e be a r.e. and r the root of qval(e); if e is of th form $f(e_1,\dots,e_k)$ we represent p(r) as shown on figure-12, and if e is of the re-12, form $e=e_0 \cdot_\sigma (e_1,\dots,e_k)$ as shown on figure 13.

We can intuitively see that the p_e fonction shows where the $\cdot_\sigma$ operators are used in the r.e. e.

(2.3) Lemma : If e is a reduced r.e., p_e is a structure of qval(e).

Proof : we examine the four cases of definition (2.1)

- Case i : immediate.
- Case ii : $e = f(e_1,\dots,e_k)$. If e is reduced, so are $e_1,\dots,e_k$, and by induction p_{e_i} is a structure of qval(e_i) for $1 \leqslant i \leqslant k$. We have to show that $p_e(r)=N_f(r)$ verifies the three conditions of definition (2.1). Condition (i) is trivially verified. We have $p(s) \subset p(r)$ for all s of qval(e), and then (ii) follows. Finally we have (iii) since back-edges of qval(e) are in the qval(e_i)'s.
- Case iii : $e = *_x(e')$. Since e is reduced, $x \in FV(e')$ and $e'=f(e_1,\dots,e_k)$. By induction, $p_{e'}$ is a structure of qval(e'). We have to show that $p_{e'}$ is also a structure of qval(e). It suffices to verify (2.1.iii) condition. If b is a back-edge of qval(e) which does not belong to qval(e'), it has r for target. Since $p_e(r)= p_{e'}(r)= S_f(r)$, the source of b belongs to $p_e(r)$.
- Case iv : $e = e_0 \cdot_\sigma (e_1,\dots,e_k)$. Since $e_0 \neq e'_0 \cdot_\sigma (e_1,\dots e_k)$, justifications directly follows from induction hypothesis. □

We can now define the operator exp which associates a r.e. with a structured quasi-tree. This operators uses both ↾ and $\setminus_\sigma$ operators defined as follows :

(2.4) *Definition* : Let Q be a quasi-tree; if n is a node of Q, $Q\restriction n$ is the quasi-tree obtained when taking n as root and forgetting the unreachable nodes from n and the corresponding arcs. If Σ is a sequence $(n_1,\dots,n_k)$ of nodes of Q and $\sigma=(v_1,\dots,v_k)$ a sequence of distinct variables, $Q\backslash_\sigma\Sigma$ is the quasi-tree obtained when replacing each node n_i by a new node labeled by σ_i, and forgetting the successors of n_i, the nodes which become unreachable from the root, and the corresponding arcs.

(2.5) *Lemma* : *Let* Q *be a quasi-tree,* $\Sigma=(n_1,\dots,n_k)$ *a sequence of nodes of* Q *and* $\sigma=(n_1,\dots,n_k)$ *a sequence of variables such that* :

(i) *there are not two nodes of* Σ *on a same branch of* Q,

(ii) *for each node* n_i , $1\leqslant i\leqslant n$, *there is no path from* n_i *to a strict ancestor of* n_i,

(iii) *none of the variables of* σ *appears in* Q,

then, $Q=Q\backslash_\sigma\Sigma[Q\restriction n_1/v_1,\dots,Q\restriction n_k/v_k]$

(2.6) *Definition* : Let <Q,p> be a structured quasi-tree with root r. The r.e. $\underline{exp}(Q,p)$ is defined as follows :

(i) if $\underline{Nod}(Q)=\{r\}$, then $\underline{exp}(Q,p)=\underline{lab}(r)$,

(ii) if $Q=f(Q_1,\dots,Q_k)$ and for all node $n\neq r$ of Q, $p(n)\subset p(r)$ then $\underline{exp}(Q,p)=f(e_1,\dots,e_k)$, with $e_i=\underline{exp}(Q_i,p\restriction\underline{Nod}(Q_i))$, for $1\leqslant i\leqslant k$,

(iii) if $Q=\underline{iter}_x(Q')$, with $Q'=f(Q_1,\dots,Q_k)$, $x\in\underline{Var}(Q')$, and for all node n of Q, $p(n)\subset p(r)$, then $e=*_x(\underline{exp}(Q',p))$,

(iv) if there exists $n\in Q$, $p(n)\not\subset p(r)$, then let $\Sigma=(s_1,\dots,s_k)$ be the sequence of Q's nodes which are strict successors of a p(r)'s node, which do not belong to p(r) and which are labeled in F. Let $\sigma=(v_1,\dots,v_k)$ be distinct variables which do not belong to Var(Q). We form :

$$\underline{exp}(Q,p)=\underline{exp}(Q_0,p_0)\cdot_\sigma(\underline{exp}(Q_1,p_1),\dots,\underline{exp}(Q_k,p_k))$$

with $Q_0 = Q\backslash_\sigma\Sigma$

$Q_i = Q\restriction s_i$ for $1\leqslant i\leqslant k$

$p_i = p\restriction\underline{Nod}(Q_i)$ for $0\leqslant i\leqslant k$.

(2.7) *Theorem* : *The structured quasi-trees are in bijection with the reduced rational expressions.*

We have $RE(F,V) \underset{\underline{exp}}{\overset{f}{\rightleftarrows}} QT^s(F,V)$ where $f(e)=\langle\underline{qval}(e),p_e\rangle$.

This theorem is a consequence of the two following propositions :

(2.8) Proposition : If <Q, p> is a structured quasi-tree then $\exp(Q,p)$ is a reduced r.e. e such that : $qval(e)= Q$ and $p_e= p$.

Proof : We do an induction on the structure of Q.

- Case 1 : Q is a unique node without arcs : immediate.

- Case 2 : $Q = f(Q_1,\dots,Q_k)$ and $p(n)\subset p(r)$ for all node n of Q. Since none of the back-edges of Q has r for target, $p_i=p\restriction Nod(Q_i)$ is a structure of Q_i for $1\leqslant i\leqslant k$. By induction we have $e_i=\exp(Q_i,p_i)$ with $qval(e_i)=Q_i$ and $p_{e_i}=p_i$. It follows $qval(e)=Q$. For all node $n\in Nod(Q_i)$, $p_e(n)= p_{e_i}(n)= p_i(n)= p(n)$. Finally, $p_e(r)= N_f(r)= p(r)$, and the e_i's being reduced, so is e.

- Case 3 : $Q=iter_x(f(Q_1,\dots,Q_k)$ and $p(n)\subset p(r)$ for all node n of Q: immediate.

- Case 4: there exists n such that $p(n) \not\subset p(r)$; we consider Σ and σ as in 2.7.iv; for each node n_i of Σ, we denote by Q_i the quasi-tree $Q\restriction s_i$, and by p_i the mapping $p\restriction Nod(Q_i)$. The condition 2.1.iii garantees the equality of the sets of descendants and strict descendants of n_i for $1\leqslant i\leqslant k$; furthermore we have $p(n)\cap p(r)=\emptyset$ for all descendant n of a node n_i. It follows that p_i is a structure of Q_i.

Let $e_i=\exp(Q_i,p_i)$ for $1\leqslant i\leqslant k$. We have by induction $p_{e_i}=p_i$ and $qval(e_i)=Q_i$, the e_i's being reduced. It follows that $qval(\exp(Q,p))= qval(e_0\cdot_\sigma(e_1,\dots,e_k)= Q\backslash_\sigma\Sigma[Q_1/\sigma(1),\dots,Q_k/\sigma(k)]= Q$ (Lemme 2.6) and if $s\in qval(e_i)$ then $p_e(s)= p_{e_i}(s)= p_i(s)= p(s)$.

Finally, $p_0(s)\subset p_0(r)$ for $s\in Nod(Q_0)$, and so $\exp(Q_0,p_0)\neq e'_0\cdot_\tau(e'_1,\dots,e'_k)$. Each node of Σ is labeled by a distinct variable, and $e_i\notin V$ for every i, $1\leqslant i\leqslant k$, anf the r.e. e is so reduced. □

(2.9) Corollary : If p and p' are two structures of a same quasi-tree Q, the expressions $\exp(Q,p)$ and $\exp(Q,p')$ have the same q-value.

(2.10) Proposition : If e is a reduced r.e., then <$qval(e), p_e$> is a structured quasi-tree such that $\exp(qval(e),p_e)=e$

Proof : We know from lemma (2.3) that p_e is a structure of $qval(e)$. Let us examine the different cases for e :

- case 1 : $e\in V\cup F_0$, immediate.

- case 2 : $e=f(e_1,\dots,e_k)$: $qval(e)= f(qval(e_1),\dots,qval(e_k))$ and $p_e(r)= N_f(r)$ from wich $p_e(n)\subset p_e(r)$ for all node n of $qval(e)$. It follows $\exp(qval(e),p_e)=$
$f(\exp(qval(e_1,p_1),\dots,qval(e_k,p_k)))= f(e_1,\dots,e_k)$ (by induction).

- case 3 : $e=*_x(f(e_1,\dots,e_k))$: let $e'=f(e_1,\dots,e_k)$; we have $qval(e)= iter_x(qval(e'))$ and $p_e=p_{e'}$ from which by induction $\exp(qval(e'),p_{e'})= e'$ and $\exp(qval(e),p_e)= *_x(e')$.

- <u>case 4</u> : $e=e_0\cdot_\sigma(e_1,\ldots,e_k)$: let $Q_i=\underline{qval}(e_i)$, r_i be the root of Q_i, for $1\leqslant i\leqslant k$. The sequence Σ is exactly $(r_1,\ldots,r_k)$. Let $\tau=(v_1,\ldots,v_k)$ be a sequence of distinct variables which does not belong to Q. We have :
$\underline{exp}(\underline{qval}(e),p_e)=\underline{exp}(Q'_0,p_0)\cdot_\tau(\underline{exp}(Q'_1,p'_1),\ldots,\underline{exp}(Q'_k,p'_k))$
with $Q'_0 = \underline{qval}(e)\setminus_\tau\Sigma = Q_0[\tau(1)/\sigma(1),\ldots,\tau(k)/\sigma(k)]$,
$Q'_i= \underline{qval}(e)\restriction r_i = qval(e_i) = Q_i$,
$p'_i= p\restriction\underline{Nod}(Q'_i) = p_i$.
By induction $\underline{exp}(\underline{qval}(e_i),p_i)=e_i$, hence $\underline{exp}(\underline{qval}(e),p_e)=$
$e_0[\sigma(1)/\tau(1)]\ldots[\sigma(k)/\tau(k)]\cdot_\tau(e_1,\ldots,e_k)= e_0\cdot_\sigma(e_1,\ldots,e_k)$. □

We have the following commutative diagram :

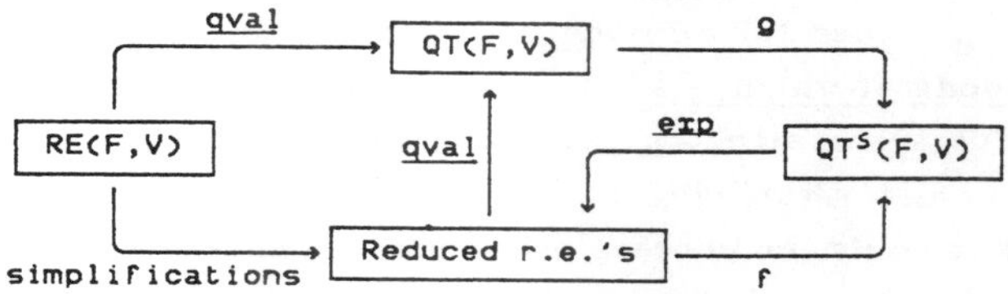

with $f(e)= \langle\underline{qval}(e),p_e\rangle$ and $g(Q)= \langle Q,p_Q\rangle$, where p_Q is a canonical structure associated with Q that we define in the next part.

-3- <u>Minimal structures and star-height of a quasi-tree.</u>

(3.1) <u>Definition</u> : Let Q be a quasi-tree, and p, p' two structures of Q; we say that $p<_Q p'$ if :

(i) $p(s)\subseteq p'(s)$ for all s in Q

(ii) there exists a node s_0 for which the inclusion is strict.

(3.2) <u>Proposition</u> : <u>Each quasi-tree</u> Q <u>has a unique minimal structure</u> p_Q <u>for the order</u> $<_Q$.

In order to prove this proposition, we now establish the two following lemmas :

(3.3) <u>Lemma</u> : <u>If</u> $\langle Q,p\rangle$ <u>is a structured quasi-tree,</u> <u>and if</u> n' <u>is a is a strict descendant of a node</u> n <u>such that there exists in</u> Q <u>a path each node of</u> <u>which is a strict descendant of</u> n, <u>and going from</u> n' <u>to</u> n, <u>then</u> $n'\in p(n)$.

<u>Proof</u> : We do the proof by induction on the length of the path c from n' to n.

- If $|c|=1$, there exists a back-edge $n'\longrightarrow n$ and $n'\in p(n)$ (2.1-iii).
- Let us assume that the property is true for all path of length

lower or equal to m and let $c = (n' \xrightarrow{k_1} n_1 \ldots \xrightarrow{k_m} n_m \xrightarrow{k_{m+1}} n)$ be a path of length m+1 each node of which is a strict descendant of n. The path $(n_1 \xrightarrow{k_2} n_2 \ldots \xrightarrow{k_m} n_m \xrightarrow{k_{m+1}} n)$, which length is m, is going from n_1 to n. Each of the nodes $n_1, \ldots, n_m$ is a strict descendant of n, and so by induction $n_1 \in p(n)$. We have to consider two cases :

- <u>case 1</u> : if n_1 is a strict successor of n', condition (2.1-i) implies $n' \in p(n)$.

- <u>case 2</u> : if n' is a strict successor n'_1, then $n' \xrightarrow{k_1} n_1$ is a back-edge, and $n' \in p(n_1)$. We have $n_1 \in p(n) \cap p(n_1)$, and we cannot have $p(n) \subset p(n_1)$, then the condition (2.1-ii) implies $n' \in p(n)$. □

(3.4) <u>Lemma</u> : <u>If</u> <Q,p> <u>is a structured quasi-tree and if</u> p <u>is a minimal structure for</u> $<_Q$, <u>then for all node</u> n' <u>of</u> p(n), <u>there exists a path from</u> n' <u>to</u> n, <u>each node of which is a strict descendant of</u> n.

<u>Proof</u> : Let us assume that p is a structure of Q such that there exists two nodes n and n' verifying $n' \in p(n)$ and such that there is no path from n' to n only composed of strict descendants of n. (We only consider paths the node of which are strict descendants of n). Let u be the extremity of a path starting at n' which is the nearest of n, and u_0 its predecessor. We have :

$$n = n_0 \text{ — } n_1 \ldots \text{ — } n_m = u_0 \text{ — } u \text{ — } \ldots \text{ — } n'$$

where $(n_0 \ldots n_m)$ is the strict path from n to u_0. We construct p': <u>Som</u>(Q) $\longrightarrow$ <u>Part</u>(<u>Nod</u>(Q)) by

$p'(n') = p(n')$ if $n' \notin \{n_0, \ldots, n_m\}$

$p'(n_i) = p(n_i) - \{\text{strict successors of } u\}$ for $1 \leqslant i \leqslant n$. We now show that p' is a structure of Q.

- <u>condition i</u> : the condition is clearly true for the nodes $n_0, \ldots, n_m$, and the result follows.

- <u>condition ii</u> : we first consider two nodes n_i and n_j of $\{n_0, \ldots, n_m\}$. Let us assume that n_j is a strict descendant of n_i: if $p(n_i) \cap p(n_j) = \emptyset$ then $p'(n_i) \cap p'(n_j) = \emptyset$, and if $p(n_j) \subset p(n_i)$ then $p'(n_j) \subset p'(n_i)$. In the both cases, (ii) is verified.

Let us now consider a node n" that does not belong to $\{n_0, \ldots, n_m\}$: $p'(n'') = p(n')$ only includes strict descendants of n", and on the contrary, $p(n_i)$ does not contain any. Hence we have $p'(n'') \cap p'(n_i) = \emptyset$ for all i, $1 \leqslant i \leqslant n$.

- <u>Condition iii</u> : since u is the extremity of a path starting at s' which is the nearest of n, there is no back-edge having its source into the strict descendants of u and its target into $\{n_0, \ldots, n_m\}$. Otherwise we have $p' <_Q p$, whence p is not a minimal structure of Q. □

We can now prove proposition (3.2). It is clear that there exists a minimal structure; Let us assume there exist two minimal structures p and p', and let n be a node of Q. If $p(n)=\emptyset$ then $\underline{lab}(n)\in V$, and $p'(n)=\emptyset$, hence $p(n)=p'(n)$, and if $p(n)\neq\emptyset$, then $p'(n)\neq\emptyset$ et $n\in p(n)\cap p'(n)$. Let n' be a node of p(n). Since p is minimal, there exists a path from n' to n, each node of which is a strict descendant of n (lemma 3.4), hence $n'\in p'(n)$ (lemma 3.3) and $p(n)\subset p\,(n)$. By symmetry we have $p'(n)\subset p(n)$ and so $p=p'$. □

(3.5) Definition : The star-heigt h(Q) of a quasi-tree Q is the minimal star-height of a r.e. with q-value Q, where the star-height h(e) of a r.e. e is defined as follows :

$h(e) = 0$ if $e\in F_0\cup V$

$= \max\{ h(e_1),\dots,h(e_k) \}$ if $e=f(e_1,\dots,e_k)$ or $e=e_{1}\cdot_{\sigma}(e_2,\dots,e_k)$

$= 1 + h(e)$ if $e = *_v(e')$.

One can read the star-height of a quasi-tree on its minimal structure; It is the length of the largest sequence of nested structures associated with targets of back-edges.

(3.6) Definition : If <Q,p> is a structured quasi-tree, we denote by H(Q,p) the length k of the largest sequence of nodes $n_1,\dots,n_k$ such that :

(i) $p(n_1)\supset p(n_2)\supset \dots \supset p(n_k)$

(ii) $n_i \in T(Q)$ for $1\leqslant i\leqslant k$.

where T(Q) is the set of nodes which are the target of back-edges in Q.

For example, if <Q,p> is the quasi-tree of figure 14, H(Q,p)=3.

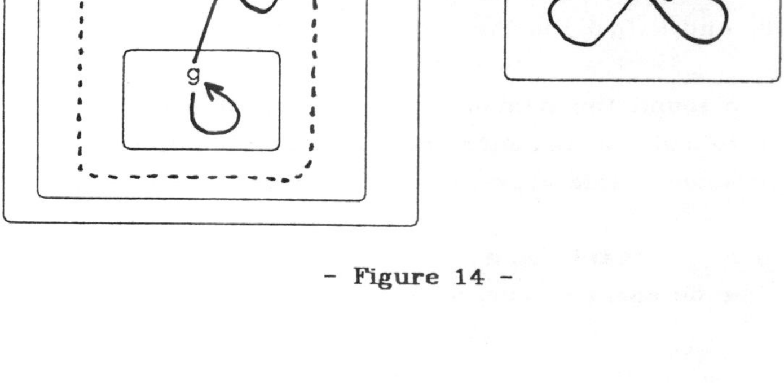

- Figure 14 -

(3.7) <u>Lemma</u> : <u>If</u> e <u>is a reduced r.e. then</u> $h(e)=H(\underline{qval}(e), p_e)$.

<u>Proof</u> : We do the proof by induction on the structure of e.

- <u>Case 1</u> : $e = v \in V$, then $h(e) = 0 = H(v, p_v)$
- <u>Case 2</u> : $e = a \in F_0$, then $h(e)=0$ and $\underline{qval}(e)$ is a node r labeled by a, which does not belong to T(Q), and so $H(Q, p_e)=H(a, p_a)=0$.
- <u>Case 3</u> : $e=f(e_1, \ldots, e_k)$; the root of $\underline{qval}(e)$ is a node r labeled by f, which does not belong to T(Q). Hence $H(\underline{qval}(e), p_e)= \underline{max}\,\{H(\underline{qval}(e_1), p_{e_1}), \ldots, H(\underline{qval}(e_k), p_{e_k})\} = \underline{max}\,\{h(e_1), \ldots, h(e_k)\} = h(e)$.
- <u>Case 4</u> : $e=*_x(e_0)$ with $e_0=f(e_1, \ldots, e_k)$. The quasi-trees $Q=\underline{qval}(e)$ and $Q_0=\underline{qval}(e_0)$ have the same root r labeled by f. We have $p_e=p_{e_0}$ and $p_e(n) \subset p_e(r)$ for all node n of Q. Moreover $r \in T(Q)$ and $r \notin T(Q_0)$, hence $H(Q, p_e)= 1+H(Q_0, p_{e_0})= 1+h(e_0)= h(e)$.
- <u>Case 5</u> : $e= e_0 \cdot_\sigma (e_1, \ldots, e_k)$ with $e_0 \neq e'_0 \cdot_\tau (e'_1, \ldots, e'_l)$; let $Q_i=\underline{qval}(e_i)$ for $1 \leqslant i \leqslant k$. We have $p_e(s)=p_{e_i}(s)$ if $s \in \underline{Nod}(Q_i)$. Since the sets $\underline{Nod}(Q_i)$ are pairwise disjoint, we have $H(\underline{qval}(e), p_e)= \underline{max}\,\{H(Q_0, p_{e_0}), \ldots, H(Q_k, p_{e_k})\} = \underline{max}\,\{h(e_0), \ldots, h(e_k)\} = h(e)$. □

(3.8) <u>Lemme</u> : <u>If</u> Q <u>is a quasi-tree and</u> p_1, p_2 <u>two structures of</u> Q <u>such that</u> $p_1 <_Q p_2$ <u>then</u> $H(Q, p_1) \leqslant H(Q, p_2)$.

<u>Proof</u> : We have $p_1(n) \subset p_2(n)$ for all node n of Q. Let $n_1, \ldots, n_k$ be a maximal sequence of nodes of T(Q) verifying $p_1(n_1) \supset \ldots \supset p_1(n_k)$. We have $H(Q, p_1)=k$. Moreover, $p_1(n_1) \subset p_2(n_1)$, and so $p_2(n_1) \supset p_1(n_2) \supset \ldots \supset p_1(n_k)$. The node n_2 is a strict successor of n_1, hence we have either $p_2(n_1) \supset p_2(n_2)$, or $p_2(n_1) \cap p_2(n_2)=\emptyset$. But $p_1(n_1) \subset p_1(n_2) \subset p_2(n_2)$, and $p_1(n_1) \subset p_2(n_1)$, hence $p_2(n_1) \cap p_2(n_2) \neq \emptyset$. It follows $p_2(n_1) \supset p_2(n_2) \supset p_1(n_3) \supset \ldots \supset p_1(n_k)$ and since the sequence is finite, we can repeat the constuction and we get $p_2(n_1) \supset p_2(n_2) \supset p_2(n_3) \supset \ldots \supset p_2(n_k)$ hence $H(Q, p_2) \geqslant H(Q, p_1)$. □

(3.9) <u>Theorem</u> : <u>The star-height of a quasi-tree</u> Q <u>is</u> $H(Q, p_Q)$.

<u>Proof</u> : We have $p_Q <_Q p$ for all structure p of Q. Let e be a r.e. denoting Q, then $h(e)= H(Q, p_e)$ by lemma-3.7, $H(Q, p_e) \geqslant H(Q, P_Q)$ by lemma-3.8, and $H(Q, p_Q)$ is the star-height of $exp(Q, p_Q)$. □

It easy to found the minimal structure p_Q of a given quasi-tree Q. This allows us to build a canonical minimal r.e. denoting the quasi-tree, i.e. a given flowchart. This expression is the reduced r.e. $\underline{exp}(Q, p_Q)$.

<u>Acknowledgement</u> : I thank Bruno Courcelle for the hints he gave to me and for the time he spent to correct my poor english style.

References.

[1] S.Bloom, C.Elgot, The existence and construction of free iterative theories J.Comput.System Sci.12(1976) pp.305-318.

[2] S.Bloom, S.Ginali, J.Rutledge, Scalar and vector iteration, J.Comput. System sci. 14 (1977) pp.251-256.

[3] J.P.Braquelaire, Représentation des arbres infinis réguliers par des graphes et des expressions rationnelles, Thèse de 3ème cycle, Université Bordeaux-I, 1983.

[4] J.P.Braquelaire, B.Courcelle, Notice d'utilisation du système SIGMA, Research report AAI 8205, Université de Bordeaux-I.

[5] J.P.Braquelaire, B.Courcelle, The solutions of two star-height problems for regular trees, Research report AAI 8306, to appear in Theor. Comput. Sci.

[6] P.Casteran, Structures de controle: définitions opérationnelles et algébriques, Thèse de 3eme cycle, Université Paris-7, 1979.

[7] B.Courcelle, A representation of trees by languages, Theor.Comput. Sci.6(1978)255-279 and 7(1978) pp.25-55.

[8] B.Courcelle, Fundamental properties of infinite trees, Theor.Comput.Sci. 25(1983) pp.95-169.

[9] B.Courcelle, G.Khan, J.Vuillemin, Algorithmes d'équivalence et de réduction à des expressions minimales dans une classe d'équations récursives simples, 2nd Int. Coll. on Automata, Langages and Programming, Saarbrucken 1974, L.N.C.S. 14, pp.200-213.

[10] G.Cousineau, Les arbres à feuilles indicées: un cadre algébrique pour l'étude des structures de controle, Thèse d'état, Université de Paris-VII (1977).

[11] G.Cousineau, La programmation en Exel, Revue technique de Thompson-CSF 10 (1978) pp.209-234 et 11 (1979) pp.13-35.

[12] G.Cousineau, An algebraic definition for control structures, Theor.Comput. Sci.12(1980)175-192.

[13] J.Darlington, R.M.Burstall, A system wich automatically improves programs, Acta Informatica 6 (1976), pp.41-60.

[14] C.Elgot, Structured progamming with and without GOTO statements, IEEE Trans. on Software engineering, SE-2 (1976) 41-54.

[15] C.Elgot, S.Bloom, R.Tindell, The algebraic structure of rooted trees, J.Comput.System Sci.16(1978)362-399.

[16] P.Enjalbert, Systèmes de déductions pour les arbres et les schémas de programmes, RAIRO Informatique théorique 14 (1980) pp.247-278 and 15 (1981) pp.3-21.

[17] S.Ginali, Regular trees and the free iterative theory, J.Comput.Sci. 18(1979) pp.228-242.

[18] J.Goguen, J.Thatcher, E.Wagner, J.Wright, Initial algebra semantics and the continuous algebras, J.Assoc. Comput. Mach. 24 (1977) pp.68-95

[19] K.Hashiguchi, N.Honda, Homomorphisms that preserve star-height, Information and Control, Vol.30, n.3 (1976).

[20] M.S.Hetch, J.D.Ullman, Characterizations of reducible flow graphs, J.Assoc. Comput. Mach., Vol.21, n.3 (1974), pp.367-375.

[21] G.Huet, Confluent reductions:abstract properties and applications to term rewriting systems, J.Assoc.Comput.Mach. 27(1980) pp.797-821.

[22] K.Indermark, Complexity of infinite trees, 10-th colloque ICALP, Barcelone, Jul. 1983, L.N.C.S. Vol.154, pp.347-360.

[23] G.Jacob, Calcul du rang des arbres infinis réguliers, Proc.CAAP'81, Lec.Notes Comput.Sci. Vol.112, Springer 1981, pp.238-254.

[24] T.Kasai, Translatability of Flowcharts into While Programs, J.Comput. System Sci., 9 (1974), pp.177-195.

[25] S.Rao Kosaraju, Analysis of structured programs, J.Comput. System Sci. 9 (1974), pp232-255.

[26] B.Mont-Reynaud, Removing trivial assignments from programs, Research Report.

[27] M.Nivat, On the interpretation of recursive polyadic program schemes, Symposia Mathematica 15, Academic Press, (1975) pp.255-281.

[28] L.Nolin, G.Ruggiu, A formalization of EXEL, Proc. of ACM Symp. on principles of Programming Langages, Boston, 1973.

[29] B.Rosen, Program Equivalence and context-free grammars, J.Compt. System Sci. (1975) pp.358-374.

PATTERNS IN TREES

Nachum Dershowitz
Department of Mathematics and Computer Science
Bar-Ilan University, Ramat-Gan, Israël
on leave from University of Illinois,
Department of Computer Science, Urbana,
Illinois 61801, USA +

and

Shmuel Zaks
M.I.T., Laboratory of Computer Science
Cambridge, MA 02 139, USA *
on leave from Department of Computer Science,
Technion, Haïfa, Israël

ABSTRACT
A very general enumeration formula for occurrences of patterns in the class of ordered trees is presented, and its wide usefulness is demonstrated.

1. INTRODUCTION

An ordered or (plane-planted) tree is a tree in which the order of the outgoing edges of each node is significant. We denote by T_n the class of trees of n edges. For example, there are 5 trees in T_3:

T_3:

The number of trees in T_n is the well-known Catalan number $\frac{1}{n+1}\binom{2n}{n}$.

We are interested in enumerating occurrences of multisets of patterns in classes of ordered trees. In the proof of our main result we adapt the Cycle Lemma, presented in Section 2. Patterns and their occurrences are presented in Section 3. Our main result is discussed in Section 4, and its applications are the subject of Section 5.

+ supported in part by NSF grant MCS-8109831

* supported by NSF grant MCS-8302391

2. THE CYCLE LEMMA

A sequence $p_1, p_2, \ldots, p_\ell$ of boxes and circles is called <u>k-dominating</u> if for every position i, $1 \leqslant i \leqslant \ell$, the number of boxes in $p_1, p_2 \ldots p_i$ is more than k times the number of circles (k is a positive integer). For example, the sequence □ □ □ □ □ ○ ○ □ □ □ ○ is 2-dominating; the sequence □ □ □ □ ○ ○ □ □ ○ is 1-dominating (or just <u>dominating</u>) but not 2-dominating; the sequences ○ □ □ □ □ ○ ○ □ □ and □ □ ○ ○ □ □ ○ □ □ are not even 1-dominating.

The following lemma has been rediscovered many times. Though it is not difficult to prove, it is a powerful tool in enumeration arguments.

<u>Cycle Lemma</u> (Dvoretzky and Motzkin [1947]): For any sequence $p_1 p_2 \ldots p_{m+n}$ of m boxes and n circles, $m \geqslant kn$, there exist exactly $m-kn$ cyclic permutations $p_j p_{j+1} \ldots p_{m+n}\, p_1 \ldots p_{j-1}$, $1 \leqslant j \leqslant m+n$, that are k-dominating.

For example, of the nine cyclic permutations of the sequence ○ □ □ □ □ ○ ○ □ □ of six boxes and three circles, only three are dominating: □ □ ○ □ □ □ □ ○ ○ , □ □ □ □ ○ ○ □ □ ○ and □ □ □ ○ ○ □ □ ○ □ . None are 2-dominating. As a special case of this lemma, if $m = n+1$, then there is a unique dominating permutation. For proofs see Raney [1960] or Dershowitz and Zaks [1983] , for example.

3. PATTERNS AND THEIR OCCURRENCES

A <u>pattern</u> is like a tree except that some of its nodes are designated <u>open slots</u> and some of its edges are designated <u>closed slots</u> and do not end in nodes. For example, the pattern

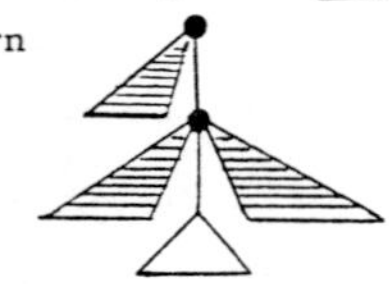

occurs wherever a node has a grandchild through its youngest child. Slots in a pattern represent arbitrary trees and are depicted as triangles; closed slots as shaded triangles hanging off a node; open slots as unshaded triangles hanging off an edge. An open slot 'matches' any subtree, including the empty tree (consisting of a single node), while a closed slot acts like a variable number of open slots and 'matches' any number (including zero) of edges along with the subtrees (= open slots) below them. (Thus, there is no reason in having adjacent closed slots in a pattern.) For example, the above pattern occurs five times in the class T_3 (see figure in Section 1): twice in the first tree (once at the root and once at its child), twice in the second (once for each of the two grandchildren), and once in the fourth.

Precise definitions of patterns and their occurrences follow : A <u>pattern</u> is said to <u>occur</u> at a subtree of an ordered tree according to the following rules:

1) The <u>leaf</u> pattern

occurs at the empty subtree

2) The <u>closed slot</u> pattern

occurs at all subtrees.

3) The <u>open slot</u> pattern

occurs at all unary nodes.

4) If p' and p'' are patterns occurring at subtrees s' and s'', respectively, then the <u>adjoined pattern</u>

P = 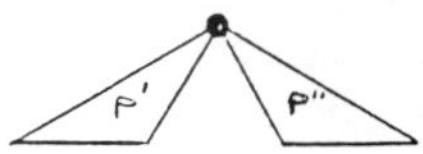

occurs at the subtree

s = 

If there is more than one way of partitioning s into s' and s" so that p' occurs at s' and p" at s", then they give rise to multiple occurrences of p at s. Thus, if s can be divided in k ways into s_1' and s_1'', s_2' and s_2'', ..., s_k' and s_k'', and p' occurs m_i times at s_i' and p'' n_i times at s_i'', then p occurs $m_1n_1 + m_2n_2 + \ldots + m_k n_k$ times at s.

5) If the pattern p occurs n times at a subtree s, then the <u>extended</u> pattern

occurs n times at the tree

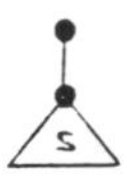

.

6) It follows that if $p_1, p_2, \ldots, p_k$ are patterns occurring $n_1, n_2, \ldots, n_k$ times at subtrees s_1, $s_2, \ldots,$ s_k, respectively, then the composite pattern

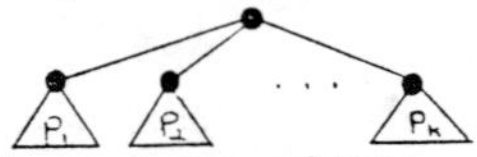

occurs $n_1 \cdot n_2 \cdot \ldots \cdot n_k$ times at the subtree

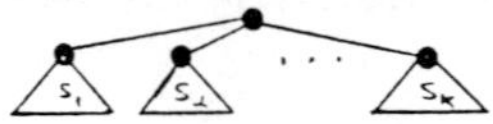

For example, the pattern

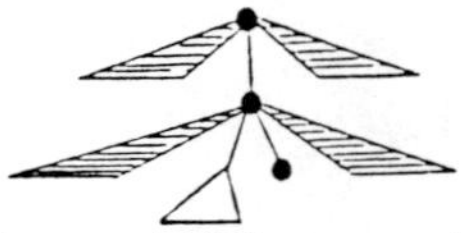

occurs at any node that has a childless grandchild with an older sibling. It occurs four times in the tree

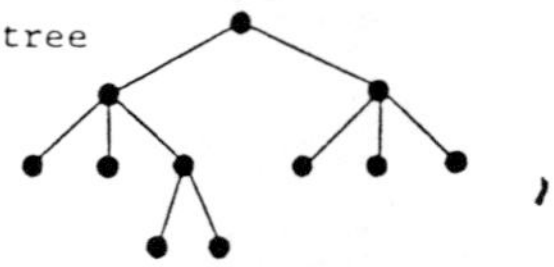

three times at the root and once at its oldest child.

Let p_1, p_2, ..., p_k be distinct patterns. The multiset m containing n_1 copies of p_1, n_2 copies of $p_2, \ldots,$ n_k copies of p_k, is denoted by $m = \{n_1 * p_1, n_2 * p_2, \ldots, n_k * p_k\}$. Let T be an ordered tree with vertex set V. The multiset m of patterns is said to occur in the tree if each of its individual patterns occurs, and the (non-slot) nodes of the occurrences are disjoint. For example, the pattern

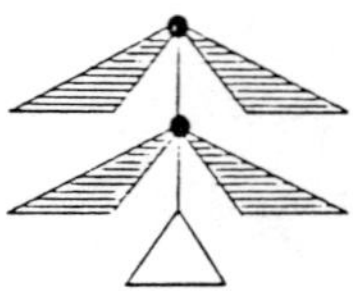

matches any grandparent-grandchild relation between two nodes. The multiset of two such patterns occurs six times among the four trees

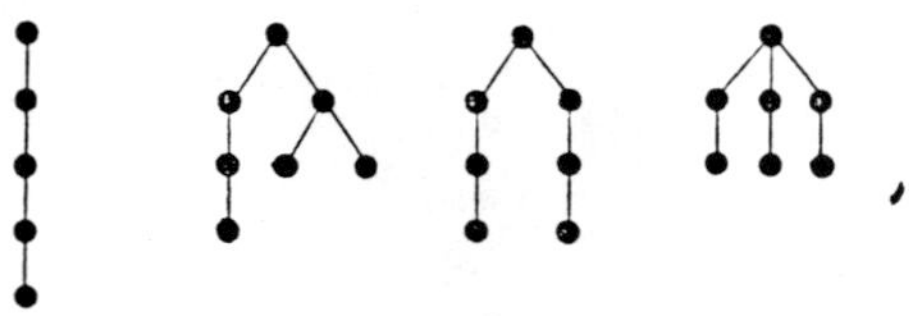

once in the first tree, twice in the second, and three times in the third. It does not occur in the fourth tree at all, since any two such relations share the grandparent node.

4. ENUMERATION

Our main result is the following enumeration formula for occurrences of a multiset of patterns in the class of ordered trees with a given number of edges:

Theorem. The total number of occurrences of a multiset $\{n_0{*}p_0, n_1{*}p_1, \ldots, n_k{*}p_k\}$ of patterns among all ordered trees with n edges is

$$\frac{1}{n-e+d+1}\binom{n-e+d+1}{n_0,\ n_1,\ldots,n_k}\binom{2n-m-2e+s}{n-e},$$

where e is the total number of edges in the patterns (excluding slots), s is the total number of (open and closed) slots, d is the number of open slots, and $m = \sum n_i \leqslant n-e+d+1$ is the total number of patterns. By the second factor in the formula, we intend the multinomial coefficient

$$\frac{(n-e+d+1)!}{n_0!n_1!\ldots n_k!(n-e+d+1-\sum n_i)!}.$$

For example, the number of occurrences of the multiset of patterns

(three leaves, two nodes of degree at least two, and one leaf below level one) in the class T_8 of 1430 ordered trees with eight edges is (n=8, k=2, $n_0=3$, $n_1=2$, $n_2=1$, m=6, e=6, s=10, d=4)

$$\frac{1}{7}\binom{7}{3,2,1}\binom{8}{2} = 1680.$$

Proof: The m given patterns include m + e-d nodes. That leaves (n+1)-(m+e-d) of the nodes in a tree unrestricted, for each of which we add single closed slot patterns

The (s-d) + (n+1) - (m + e-d) = n + 1-m-e + s closed slots we now have can each be replaced with an open slot pattern of the form

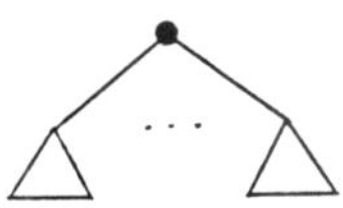

containing among themselves the n−e edges unaccounted for in the given patterns, in $\binom{(n+1-m-e+s)+(n-e)-1}{n-e} = \binom{2n-m-2e+s}{n-e}$ ways. The $m+(n+1)-(m+e-d)=n-e+d+1$ patterns can be placed on a cycle in

$$\frac{1}{n-e+d+1}\binom{n-e+d+1}{n_0,\ n_1,\ \ldots,n_k} \qquad \text{ways.}$$

Such a cycle of patterns corresponds to a unique tree. To see this, we adapt the Cycle Lemma. There are (n−e) + d open slots among the n+1−e+d patterns. Thus there must be at least one slotless pattern p that is followed by a pattern q with slots. Hanging p on the leftmost slot in q and removing p from the cycle leaves a cycle with one less pattern and one less slot. Continuing in this manner until no slots remain, we end up with a single (slotless) tree. Since filling one slot does not affect the filling of another, the resultant tree in unique.

Each possible arrangement of patterns on the cycle yields a different occurrence. Since only open slots are filled, the patterns do not share nodes. □

The above theorem generalizes

- (Harary, Prins, and Tutte [1964]) the Catalan number

  $$\frac{1}{n+1}\binom{2n}{n}$$

  for unrestricted ordered trees with n edges ($k=-1$, $m=e=s=d=0$);
- (Cayley [1859]) the Catalan number

  $$\frac{1}{2r+1}\binom{2r+1}{r}$$

  for unrestricted binary trees with r binary nodes and hence r+1 leaves ($n=2r$, $k=1$, $n_0=r$, $n_1=r+1$, $m=2r+1$, $e=d=s=2r$) ;
- (Tutte [1964]) the multinomial formula

  $$\frac{1}{n+1}\binom{n+1}{n_0 n_1,\ldots,n_n}$$

  for enumerating trees with n_i nodes of degree i and a total of n edges ($k=n$, $m=n+1$, $e=s=d=n$);
- (Flajolet and Steyaert [1980]) the binomial formula

  $$\binom{2n-2e+s-1}{n-e}$$

  for occurrences of a single pattern (with no closed slots and no leaves) among all ordered trees with n edges ($k=0$, $m=1$).

5. APPLICATIONS

This theorem has wide applicability. We give here some representative illustrations.

Example 1. The number of ordered trees with n edges and exactly ℓ leaves is equal to the number of occurrences of the patterns

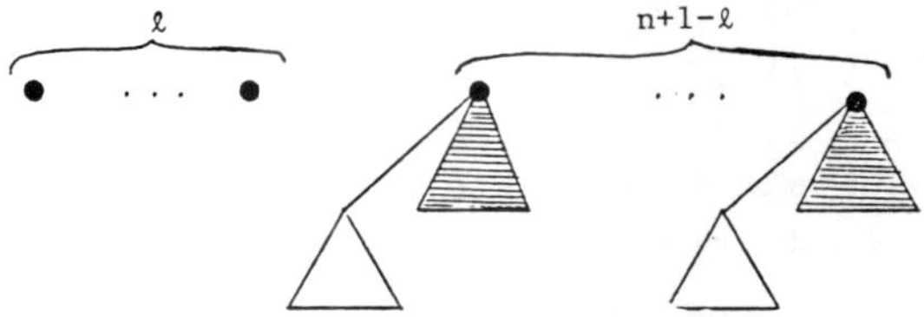

(ℓ leaves and $n+1-\ell$ nodes of degree at least one), since there can be only one occurrence per tree. By letting $k=1$, $n_0=\ell$, $n_1=n+1-\ell$, $m=n+1$, $e=n+1-\ell$, $d=n+1-\ell$, and $s=2(n+1-\ell)$ in the theorem, we get

$$\frac{1}{n+1}\binom{n+1}{\ell,\, n+1-\ell}\binom{n-1}{\ell-1} = \frac{1}{n+1}\binom{n+1}{\ell}\binom{n-1}{\ell-1}.$$

These "common knowledge" numbers appear in Narayana [1959] in the context of ballots and in Riordan [1968] in reference to a communication problem. See also Dershowitz and Zaks [1980], where these numbers are found using the Cycle Lemma.

Example 2. The number of left children having right leaves among all binary trees with r internal nodes is equal to the number of occurrences of the patterns

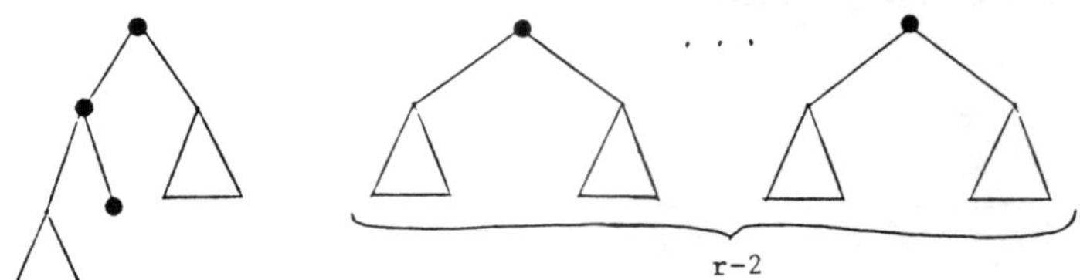

(a left child with a right leaf and the remaining r-2 nodes). By letting $n=2r$, $k=1$, $n_0=1$, $n_1=r-2$, $m=r-1$, $e=2r$, $d=2r-2$, and $s=2r-2$ in the theorem, we get

$$\frac{1}{2r-1}\binom{2r-1}{1,\, r-2}\binom{r-1}{0} = \binom{2r-2}{r}.$$

This formula is derived in Brinck and Foo [1981] using generating functions. See also Gouyou-Beauchamps [1975].

Example 3. The number of ordered trees with n edges, ℓ leaves, and no unary nodes is equal to the number of occurrences of the patterns

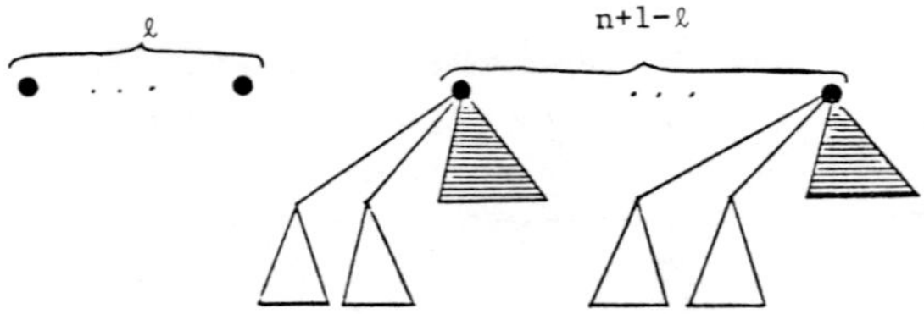

(ℓ leaves and $n+1-\ell$ nodes with at least two edges). By letting $k=1$, $n_0=\ell$, $n_1=n+1-\ell$, $m=n+1$, $e=2(n+1-\ell)$, $d=2(n+1-\ell)$, and $s=3(n+1-\ell)$ in the theorem, we get

$$\frac{1}{n+1}\binom{n+1}{\ell}\binom{\ell-2}{n-\ell}.$$

Summing this for all n, we get

$$\frac{1}{\ell}\sum_{n}\binom{\ell-2}{n-\ell}\binom{n}{\ell-1}$$

for any given number of leaves ℓ. These numbers were investigated by Schröder [1870]; their relation to polygon partitions is discussed in Motzkin [1948]; their relation to trees appears in Knuth [1968]. See also Donaghey [1977,1980], Donaghey and Shapiro [1977], and Rogers and Shapiro [1977].

Example 4. The number of ternary trees with r internal nodes and a leaf ℓ levels directly below the root may be determined in the following manner: Let the pattern p be

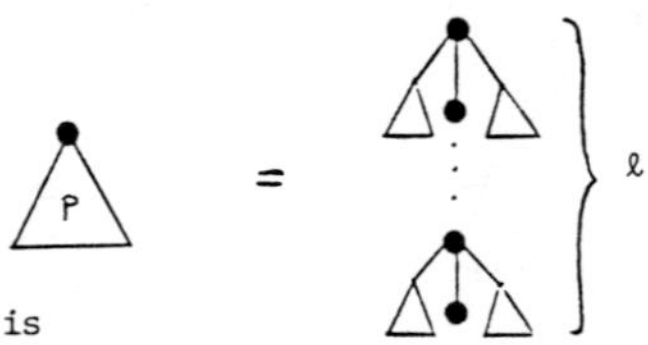

The desired number is

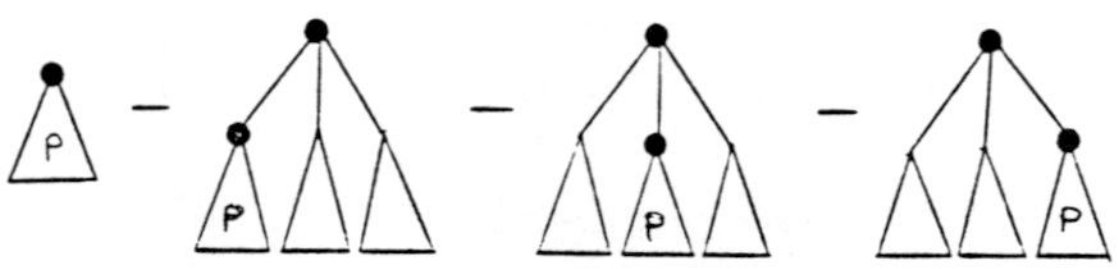

(a leaf directly beneath a node, but not beneath a non-root node), where each pattern denotes the number of times it occurs in the class of r-node ternary trees. By letting $n=3r$, $k=1$, $n_0=1$, $n_1=r-\ell$, $m=r-\ell+1$, $e=3r$, and $d=s=3r-\ell$ in the theorem, we get

$$\frac{1}{3r-\ell+1}\binom{3r-\ell+1}{1,r-\ell}\binom{3r-1}{0}=\binom{3r-\ell}{r-\ell}$$

for the pattern p; by letting n=3r, k=1, n_0=1, n_1=r-ℓ-1, m=r-ℓ, e=3r, and d=s= 3r-ℓ-1 in the theorem, we get

$$\frac{1}{3r-\ell}\binom{3r-\ell}{1,r-\ell-1}\binom{3r-2}{0}=\binom{3r-\ell-1}{r-\ell-1}$$

for each of the excluded patterns. Thus, the desired number of occurrences is

$$\binom{3r-\ell}{r-\ell}-3\binom{3r-\ell-1}{r-\ell-1}=\frac{2\ell}{3r-\ell}\binom{3r-\ell}{r-\ell}.$$

This is the same as the number of ordered forests of 2ℓ ternary trees with a total of r-ℓ internal nodes. Similarly, it can be shown that the number of ℓ tree forests of t-ary trees with a total of r internal nodes (of degree t) is

$$\frac{\ell}{tr+\ell}\binom{tr+\ell}{r}.$$

REFERENCES

1. K. Brinck and N. Y. Foo [1981], "Analysis of algorithms on threaded trees," Comp. J., Vol. 24, no. 2, pp. 148-155.
2. A. Cayley [1859], "On analytical forms called trees," Phil. Mag., Vol. 20, pp. 374-378. Also in Collected Math. Papers, Vol. 4, pp. 112-115.
3. N. Dershowitz and S. Zaks [1980], "Enumerations of ordered trees," Discrete Math., Vol. 31, no. 1, pp. 9-28.
4. N. Dershowitz and S. Zaks [1983], "The Cycle Lemma and some applications," submitted.
5. R. Donaghey [1977], "Restricted plane tree representations of four Motzkin-Catalan equations," J. Combinatorial Theory (B), Vol. 22, pp. 114-121.
6. R. Donaghey [1980], "Automorphisms on Catalan trees and bracketings," J. Combinatorial Theory (B), Vol. 29, pp. 75-90.
7. R. Donaghey and L. W. Shapiro [1977], "Motzkin numbers," J. Combinatorial Theory (A), Vol. 23, pp. 291-301.
8. A. Dvoretzky and Th. Motzkin [1947], "A problem of arrangements," Duke Math. J., Vol. 14, pp. 305-313.
9. Ph. Flajolet and J. M. Steyaert [1980], "On the analysis of tree-matching algorithms," Proc. 7th Intl. Conf. Automata, Languages and Programming, Amsterdam, pp. 208-220.

10. D. Gouyou-Beauchamps [1975], "Deux propriétés combinatoires du langage de Łukasiewicz," R.A.I.R.O., Vol. 3, pp. 13-24.

11. F. Harary, G. Prins, and W. T. Tutte [1964], "The number of plane trees," Indagationes Math., Vol. 26, pp. 319-329.

12. D. E. Knuth [1968], The Art of Computer Programming, Vol. 1: "Fundamental algorithms," Addison-Wesley, Reading, MA.

13. Th. Motzkin [1948], "Relations between hypersurface cross ratios and a combinatorial formula for partititons of a polygon, for permanent preponderance, and for non-associative products," Bull. Amer. Math. Soc., Vol. 54, pp. 352-360.

14. T. V. Narayana [1959], "A partial order and its applications to probability," Sankhya 21, pp. 91-98.

15. G. M. Raney [1960], "Functional composition patterns and power series reversion," Transactions of the AMS, Vol. 94, pp. 441-451.

16. J. Riordan [1968], Combinatorial Identities, Wiley, New York.

17. D. G. Rogers and L. W. Shapiro [1977], "Some correspondences involving the Schröder numbers and relations," Lecture Notes in Mathematics 686, pp. 267-274.

18. E. Schröder [1870], "Vier combinatorische Probleme," Zeit. fur Math. und Physik, Vol. 15, pp. 361-376.

19. W. T. Tutte [1964], "The number of planted plane trees with a given partition," Amer. Math. Monthly, Vol. 71, pp. 272-277.

REGULAR CHARACTERIZATIONS OF MACRO TREE TRANSDUCERS

Joost Engelfriet and Heiko Vogler*
Twente University of Technology, P.O. Box 217,
7500 AE Enschede, The Netherlands

Abstract. It is well known that the languages defined by OI macro grammars, indexed grammars, and nested stack automata (equivalently, 1-way pushdown^2 automata) are the same. Generalizing this to tree transducers we show that OI macro tree transducers, indexed tree transducers, and pushdown^2 tree transducers induce the same translation class. In fact, we prove this characterization for D-transducers instead of tree transducers, where D is any storage type and a D-transducer translates storage-configurations of D into trees (or strings). From this general result we obtain the "classical" one by taking the trivial storage type, and the characterization of the macro tree transducer by taking the storage type of trees.

1 INTRODUCTION

A macro tree transducer [E4,CF,EV1] combines the capabilities of a top-down tree transducer [Ro,Th,E1] and of a context-free tree grammar [Fi,ES]. It generalizes the syntax-directed translations [AU1,AU2,Vo] by allowing context to be handled. In particular, viewing the attribute grammar of [Kn] schematically, i.e., as a tree transducer [EF,CM,CF], the total deterministic macro tree transducer can simulate the attribute grammar [CF,Fr,E5,E4]. In fact, a macro tree transducer is a first modest approach to model denotational semantics of programming languages [Go]; it models at least the features of denotational semantics needed to simulate attribute grammars (cf.[Ma]).

In the framework of program scheme theory the macro tree transducer can be viewed as a system of recursive function procedures with parameters [CF,E5,EV1]: every function procedure possesses one "syntactic" parameter the actual value of which is (a subtree of) an input tree, and moreover some "semantic" or context parameters, keeping context

* The work of the second author has been supported by the Netherlands Organization for the Advancement of Pure Research (Z.W.O.)

information for the current value of the syntactic parameter. Context information is built up out of (basic) operation symbols and recursive calls of function procedures. This situation of nested recursive calls is closely related to the nesting of nonterminals in context-free tree grammars [ES] and in level 2-schemes [Da]. Hence, as usual, we can distinguish between two evaluation strategies: inside-out (IO) and outside-in (OI). In this paper we are only interested in the OI case.

Considering a system of recursive function procedures with parameters it should be clear that its evaluation proceeds in a "highly non-sequential" way: at a given moment of evaluation, several recursive calls may occur, which may even be nested. The purpose of this paper is to provide two "more sequential" types of transducers equivalent with macro tree transducers. These transducers are called "regular" in the sense that they have no context parameters. (Note that a regular transducer has still one syntactic parameter). We proceed in two steps.

First, we remove the context parameters from the states (i.e., function procedures) of the macro tree transducer, thereby avoiding the nesting of states. This is achieved by associating with every state a pushdown which keeps the information of its context parameters until the computation starting in this state is finished. Thus we obtain a, still recursive, regular transducer called indexed tree transducer, equivalent with the macro tree transducer (see Theorem 1, Theorem 2, and Theorem 5(a)). This equivalence (and the idea of the construction) can be compared with the equivalence of OI macro grammars and indexed grammars [Fi], and of OI context-free grammars and pushdown tree automata [Gu].

Second, we start with the tree-to-string version of the indexed tree transducer and remove the recursion. The construction involved extends the usual technique of implementing a context-free grammar on a pushdown. Hence, we obtain an iterative (i.e., non-recursive) regular transducer called pushdown^2 tree transducer, equivalent with the macro tree-to-string transducer (see Theorem 3, Theorem 4, and Theorem 5(b)). The pushdown^2 tree transducer is a sequential machine which reads a tree as input, uses a pushdown of pushdowns [Gr,Ms,PDS,DG,E7] as additional memory, and produces an output string. (Note that the checking-tree pushdown transducer, which in this context we would call a pushdown tree transducer, characterizes the top-down tree-to-string transducer [ERS]). In [E5] a nested stack [A1] instead of a pushdown of pushdowns is suggested as additional memory to obtain a machine model of the macro tree transducer. This suggestion is worked out in [EV2] by showing that a nested stack and a pushdown[2] are "equivalent" storage types (see also [E7]).

Apart from the usual nondeterministic case we consider in this paper in particular the total deterministic case (i.e., for every input tree exactly one output tree is computed), which is relevant to the semantics of context-free languages.

So far we have mentioned several transducers and grammars and have already given some intuitive ideas about their connections, but supposedly the reader is already lost in this "jungle" of concepts. To bring more light into this jungle and to build precisely but in an understandable way the connecting roads, we set up the mentioned concepts in one unifying framework by adopting the general philosophy of Scott (cf.[Sc]) of distinguishing between programs and machines (i.e., control and datatype). This approach, in which the control is an iterative, sequential program, can be generalized to any kind of control: here we take well known objects from (tree) language theory such as regular tree grammars, context-free grammars, macro grammars, etc. These grammars may act on the elements of a datatype by associating one such element with each (occurrence of a) nonterminal; taking regular (string) grammars we reobtain the "classical" programs. Since a context-free (tree) grammar may be viewed as a recursive control and a datatype is similar to the storage of an automaton (its elements can be tested and transformed), such "grammars with datatype" may be viewed as recursive automata (recursive transducers).

Of course, in this paper we are interested in special storage types: we will view the input trees of macro tree transducers as a storage type (denoted by TR) which has trees as storage configurations; the label of a root of a tree can be tested and a specified subtree can be selected. In this way the macro tree transducer can be viewed as a context-free tree grammar with storage type TR. Furthermore, for the implementation of "recursion with parameters", we are interested in an operator P on storage types constructing pushdowns of elements of a given storage type [Gr,E7]. Viewing tree grammars as programs over a storage type D, we obtain D-transducers, each providing a translation from D-storage configurations to output trees. To profit from the clarity and power of the general approach, we prove all our results for the macro D-transducer which generalizes the macro tree transducer: it works on configurations of an arbitrary storage type D rather than on (input) trees of TR.

The results of this paper are taken from [E6] and [EV2]. [E6] contains the basic ideas (such as the general approach described above) and results on the context-free (string), regular (string), and regular tree case. [EV2] contains all main results of this paper as described in the introduction (the context-free tree, the macro (string) case).

2 STORAGE TYPES AND D-TRANSDUCERS

In this section we provide the basic notions of storage type [Sc], pushdown of a storage type [Gr], macro D-transducer, and its induced translation.

A storage type D is a tuple (C,I,P,F,m), where C is the non-empty set of (D-)configurations, I is the set of initial configuration sets (i.e., I is a set of subsets of C), P and F are sets of predicate and instruction symbols, respectively. Every $p \in P$ and $f \in F$ is interpreted by the meaning function m as a total function $m(p)\colon C \to \{true,false\}$ and $m(f)\colon C \to C \cup \{\perp\}$ (where $\perp$ stands for "undefined), respectively. We extend m to the set $(P \cup \overline{P})^*$ of tests of D, where $\overline{P}=\{\overline{p} \mid p \in P\}$, as follows: for every $c \in C$ and $q_1,q_2 \in (P \cup \overline{P})^*$, $m(\overline{p})(c)$ = not $m(p)(c)$, $m(q_1q_2)(c)$ = $m(q_1)(c)$ and $m(q_2)(c)$, and $m(\lambda)(c)$ = true for the empty string λ.

We use the following notations from tree language theory. For a ranked alphabet Σ, Σ_k denotes the set of symbols of rank k. The rank of a symbol σ is indicated as a superscript, like $\sigma^{(k)}$. T_Σ denotes the set of all trees over Σ: if $\sigma \in \Sigma$ and $(t_1,\ldots,t_k) \in T_\Sigma$ with $k \geq 0$, then $(t_1,\ldots,t_k) \in T_\Sigma$. For a set Y, $T_\Sigma(Y)=T_{\Sigma \cup Y}$, where every element of Y has rank 0.

As a storage type of special interest we consider the tree storage type, denoted by TR. A configuration of TR is a tree over an infinite, fixed, ranked alphabet Σ_∞; $\{T_\Sigma \mid \Sigma$ is a finite subset of $\Sigma_\infty\}$ is the set of initial configuration sets; for every $\sigma \in \Sigma_\infty$, root=σ is a predicate, testing whether the root of a tree over Σ_∞ is labelled σ, i.e., $m(root{=}\sigma)(t)$=true iff $t = \sigma(t_1,\ldots,t_k)$ where $\sigma \in \Sigma_\infty$ for some $k \geq 0$ and $t_1,\ldots,t_k \in T_{\Sigma_\infty}$; with the instructions sel_n for every $n \geq 1$, subtrees can be selected from a tree $t = \sigma(t_1,\ldots,t_k)$, i.e., $m(sel_n)(t) = t_n$ if $n \leq k$, otherwise $m(sel_n)(t) = \perp$.

To implement recursion with parameters we need the concept of pushdown. Since we want to put configurations of an arbitrary storage type on the pushdown, we define for every storage type D = (C,I,P,F,m) the pushdown of D, denoted by P(D), as the storage type (C′,I′,P′,F′,m′), where $C' = (\Gamma \times C)^+$ and Γ is a fixed, infinite pushdown alphabet, $I' = \{ \{Z_0\} \times C_0 | C_0 \in I\}$ for a fixed initial pushdown symbol Z_0 (in fact, we identify (Z_0,c) and c, for every $c \in C$; in that sense $I' = I$), $P' = \{top{=}\gamma | \gamma \in \Gamma\} \cup \{test(p) | p \in P\}$, $F' = \{pop\} \cup \{push(\gamma,f) | \gamma \in \Gamma,\ f \in F\} \cup \{stay(\gamma) | \gamma \in \Gamma\}$, and m' interprets predicate and instruction symbols as follows. For every $\gamma \in \Gamma$, $c \in C$, and $\zeta \in C' \cup \{\bot\}$,

$$m'(top{=}\delta)((\gamma,c)\zeta) = (\delta{=}\gamma)$$

$$m'(test(p))((\gamma,c)\zeta) = m(p)(c)$$

$$m'(pop)((\gamma,c)\zeta) = \begin{cases} \zeta & \text{if } \zeta \in C' \\ \bot & \text{otherwise} \end{cases}$$

$$m'(push(\delta,f))((\gamma,c)\zeta) = \begin{cases} (\delta,m(f)(c))(\gamma,c)\zeta & \text{if } m(f)(c) \in C \\ & \text{otherwise} \end{cases}$$

$$m'(stay(\delta))((\gamma,c)\zeta) = (\delta,c)\zeta.$$

Remarks: (i) This pushdown operator can be iterated, i.e., $P^0(D) = D$, $P^{n+1}(D) = P(P^n(D))$. (ii) There is no empty pushdown in $P(D)$. (iii) For a test $q \in (P \cup \overline{P})^*$ we define $test(q) \in (P' \cup \overline{P'})^*$ as follows: $test(\overline{p}) = \overline{test(p)}$, $test(q_1q_2) = test(q_1)test(q_2)$ and $test(\lambda) = \lambda$. (iv) $P(TR)$ is equivalent to the "tree-walking" storage type of the checking-tree pushdown transducer of [ERS].

We also mention the <u>trivial storage type</u> D_0 which has one configuration, no predicates and one instruction id, which is the identity on C. We denote $P(D_0)$ by P: the ordinary pushdown.

Now we are ready to define the concept of D-transducer. Let X be a modifier taken from the set {context-free tree, macro, regular tree, context-free, regular} which we also abbreviate by {CFT, MAC, RT, CF, REG}. We assume the reader to be familiar with the corresponding notions of X grammar (note in particular that a regular tree grammar is a context-free tree grammar in which every nonterminal has rank 0). Let $D = (C,I,P,F,m)$ be a storage type.

An <u>X(D)-transducer</u> K is a tuple (N,C_0,Δ,S,R), where N, Δ, and $S \in N$ are the (possibly ranked) alphabet of nonterminals, the alphabet of terminals, and the initial nonterminal of a usual X grammar, respectively, $C_0 \in I$ is the set of initial configurations, and R is a finite set of rules whose form is determined in the following way. If u --> v is a rule of an X grammar, then a rule of R has the form u --> <u>if</u> q <u>then</u> v', where $q \in (P \cup \overline{P})^*$ and v' is obtained from v by replacing every occurrence of a nonterminal B by B(f) for some $f \in F$. Then v′ is also called the right-hand side tree (or string) of the rule.

As an example, since A --> aBCB is a possible rule of a context-free grammar, A --> <u>if</u> q <u>then</u> $aB(f_1)C(f_2)B(f_2)$ is a possible rule of a CF(D)-transducer.

K is <u>deterministic</u> iff for every $c \in C$: if u --> <u>if</u> q_1 <u>then</u> v_1 and u --> <u>if</u> q_2 <u>then</u> v_2 are rules in R with the same left-hand sides, then $m(q_1)(c)$ = false or $m(q_2)(c)$ = false.

From the transducer point of view the nonterminals of K are also called states and the terminals are called output symbols.

Now we define for an X(D)-transducer K the derivation relation $\Rightarrow_K$. For this purpose, we associate with K an (infinite) X grammar G=G(K) in which two pieces of information are encoded in the nonterminals: a nonterminal of K and a configuration of D. Then we can define $\Rightarrow_K$ by means of the derivation relation of G. (For the case X = CFT and D = TR cf. [EV1] section 3.2.) Formally, let $K=(N,C_0,\Delta,S,R)$ be an X(D)-transducer with a storage type D = (C,I,P,F,m). We associate with K the (possibly infinite) X grammar $G = (N',\Delta,S',R')$, where $N'= \{\langle A,c\rangle \mid A \in N,\ c \in C\cup\{\bot\}\}$ and the ranks carry over from the nonterminals of K, S′ is any element of N′(S′ is irrelevant), and R′ is obtained as follows. If u --> <u>if</u> q <u>then</u> v is a rule in R, then for every $c \in C$ for which m(q)(c) = true, the rule u(c) --> v(c) is in R′, where u(c) is obtained from u by replacing its nonterminal A by $\langle A,c\rangle$ and v(c) is obtained from v by replacing every B(f) by $\langle B,m(f)(c)\rangle$. (Note that N′ and R′ may be infinite.) Then we can define the <u>derivation relation $\Rightarrow_K$ of K</u> by $\Rightarrow_K \; = \; \Rightarrow_G$, where $\Rightarrow_G$ is the usual derivation relation for X grammars. For $X \in \{MAC, CFT\}$ we choose the OI derivation relation.

The <u>translation induced by K</u>, denoted by T(K), is the relation $\{(c,w) \mid \langle S,c\rangle \overset{*}{\Rightarrow}_K w$, w contains only symbols of Δ, and $c \in C\}$. K is <u>total</u> iff the domain of T(K) is C_0. Note that, e.g., a CFT(D)-transducer translates D-configurations into trees (and not vice versa!).

The <u>translation class</u> of X(D)-transducers is denoted by X(D). Total deterministic X(D)-transducers are indicated by D ; for example, the translation class of total deterministic RT(TR)-transducers is denoted by D_tRT(TR).

The following list should give an impression about the expressive power of the general D-transducer approach. For a classical concept at the left the equivalent D-transducer is provided at the right;

for the transducers at the left our notion of determinism is the usual one, but not for the automata at the left; for the automata, the corresponding X(D)-transducer should be viewed as a (nondeterministic) acceptor of its range (for the connection between transducers and (checking) acceptors in general, see [E3]).

X grammar	$X(D_0)$-transducer
indexed grammar [A2]	CF(P)-transducer
restricted pushdown tree automaton [Gu]	RT(P)-transducer
top-down tree-to-string transducer [ERS]	CF(TR)-transducer
checking-tree pushdown transducer [ERS]	REG(P(TR))-transducer
top-down tree transducer [Ro,Th,E1]	RT(TR)-transducer
macro tree transducer [E4,CF,EV1]	CFT(TR)-transducer
macro tree-to-string transducer [EV2]	MAC(TR)-transducer
1-way D automaton	REG(D)-transducer

The sequence of flags attached to a nonterminal of an indexed grammar behaves just as a pushdown (cf. [Gu]); therefore the indexed grammar is equivalent to the CF(P)-transducer. For that reason we may call the RT(P)-transducer an indexed tree grammar, and the RT(P(TR))-transducer an <u>indexed tree transducer</u> (each nonterminal has a pushdown of trees attached to it). We will call the REG(P^2(TR))-transducer a <u>pushdown^2 tree transducer</u>.

We are in particular interested in the macro tree transducer, i.e., the CFT(TR)-transducer. To support the readers understanding of the introduced terminology and notations we provide an easy example.

<u>Example</u>. Let K be the CFT(TR)-transducer $(\{S^{(0)}, A^{(1)}\}, T_\Sigma, \{b^{(1)}, a^{(0)}\}, S, R)$ where Σ is the ranked alphabet $\{\sigma^{(1)}, \alpha^{(0)}\}$ and R contains the rules

S --> <u>if</u> root=σ <u>then</u> A(sel_1)(A(sel_1)(a))

S --> <u>if</u> root=α <u>then</u> b(a)

A(y) --> <u>if</u> root=σ <u>then</u> A(sel_1)(A(sel_1)(y))

A(y) --> <u>if</u> root=α <u>then</u> b(y).

Then K can derive:

$$\langle S,\sigma(\sigma(\alpha))\rangle \Longrightarrow \langle A,\sigma(\alpha)\rangle(\langle A,\sigma(\alpha)\rangle(a))$$
$$\Longrightarrow \langle A,\alpha\rangle(\langle A,\alpha\rangle(\langle A,\sigma(\alpha)\rangle(a))) \Longrightarrow b(\langle A,\alpha\rangle(\langle A,\sigma(\alpha)\rangle(a)))$$
$$\Longrightarrow b(b(\langle A,\sigma(\alpha)\rangle(a))) \Longrightarrow b(b(\langle A,\alpha\rangle(\langle A,\alpha\rangle(a))))$$
$$\Longrightarrow b(b(b(\langle A,\alpha\rangle(a)))) \Longrightarrow b(b(b(b(a)))).$$

Clearly, $T(K) = \{(\sigma^n\alpha^m, b\ a) \mid n\geq 0,\ m=2^n\}$. Thus, K is total and deterministic.

3 GENERAL RESULTS

Here we characterize the translation classes CFT(D) and MAC(D) in terms of regular transducers, viz. by RT(P(D))-transducers and $REG(P^2(D))$-transducers, respectively. In view of the relevance to the semantics of context-free languages we also consider the total deterministic case. First, we realize a translation in CFT(D) via an RT(P(D))-transducer by putting whatever is nested under a nonterminal on a pushdown, to be kept until the computation starting with that nonterminal is finished.

Lemma 1 $CFT(D) \subseteq RT(P(D))$, $MAC(D) \subseteq CF(P(D))$, and determinism is preserved in both inclusions.

Proof Let $K = (N, C_0, \Delta, S, R)$ be a CFT(D)-transducer. The application of a rule of K is simulated by an RT(P(D))-transducer L by pushing the right-hand side tree of the applied rule on the pushdown of L and work it through with a special control nonterminal $Q \notin N$ from the root to the frontier. This means that we need all well-bracketed subexpressions of right-hand side trees (viewed as expressions) of rules of K as pushdown symbols. Denote this set of subexpressions by SUB. The set of rules of L is constructed as follows.

(i) If $A(y_1,\dots,y_k) \to$ if q then t is a rule of K, then $A \to$ if test(q) then Q(stay(t)) is a rule of L.

(ii) For every $\delta \in \Delta_k$, $k \geq 0$, and $t_1,\dots,t_k \in$ SUB, the rule $Q \to$ if top = $\delta(t_1,\dots,t_k)$ then $\delta(Q(\text{stay}(t_1)),\dots,Q(\text{stay}(t_k)))$ is in L.

(iii) For every $A \in N_k$, $k \geq 0$, $f \in F$, and $t_1,\dots,t_k \in$ SUB, the rules $Q \to$ if top = $A(f)(t_1,\dots,t_k)$ then $P_{A(f)}(\text{stay}((t_1,\dots,t_k)))$ and $P_{A(f)} \to$ if λ then $A(\text{push}(Z_0,f))$ are in L.

(iv) For every $(t_1,\dots,t_k) \in$ SUB and every parameter y_j, $1 \leq j \leq k$, the rules $Q \to$ if top = y_j then P_j(pop) and $P_j \to$ if top = $(t_1,\dots,t_k)$ then $Q(\text{stay}(t_j))$ are in L.

Note that $P_{A(f)}$ and P_j are (auxiliary) nonterminals of L.

The following statement proves the construction to be correct.

For every $A \in N_k$, $k \geq 0$, $c \in C$, and $t \in T_\Delta(\{y_1,\dots,y_k\})$, $\langle A,c\rangle(y_1,\dots,y_k) \overset{*}{\Rightarrow}_K t$ iff $\langle A,(Z_0,c)\rangle \overset{*}{\Rightarrow}_L t'$ with no push instruction leading to $\perp$, where t′ is obtained from t by

replacing every y_j by $\langle P_j, \perp\rangle$.
It is easy to see that the second inclusion of this Lemma also holds and that determinism is preserved. □

Next, we prove the converse result by viewing a pushdown associated with a nonterminal as a parameter of that nonterminal. Since we do not know in advance in which nonterminal the considered pushdown is popped, we use the technique of [Ro], Theorem 7, and prepare as much copies of a parameter as there are nonterminals. Just as for the simulation of a checking-tree pushdown transducer by a top-down tree transducer [ERS] we need a small extension of the CFT(D)-transducer concept (denoted by CFT_{ext}) to simulate a RT(P(D))-transducer. This extension is defined in the proof.

<u>Lemma 2</u> $RT(P(D)) \subseteq CFT_{ext}(D)$, $CF(P(D)) \subseteq MAC_{ext}(D)$, and determinism is preserved in both inclusions.

<u>Proof</u> Let L be a RT(P(D))-transducer with $N = \{A_1, \ldots, A_r\}$ for some $r \geq 1$ and $S = A_1$. W.l.o.g. we can assume that in every pushdown occurring in a computation of L, Z_0 is the pushdown symbol of the bottom square. Combining a nonterminal A_j of L with a pushdown symbol γ which occurs in L (these are finitely many) we obtain the nonterminal $[A_j, \gamma]$ for the desired $CFT_{ext}(D)$-transducer K. ($[A_j, \gamma]$ has rank r, if $\gamma \neq Z_0$; $[A_j, Z_0]$ has rank 0). We construct K in such a way that the following statement holds.

For every $A_j \in N$, $\gamma \in \Gamma$, $c \in C$, $t \in T_\Delta(N(\perp))$ with $N(\perp) = \{\langle A_j, \perp\rangle \mid A_j \in N\}$,
$\langle A_j, (\gamma, c)\rangle \overset{*}{\Longrightarrow}_L t$ with no push instruction leading to $\perp$ iff
$\langle [A_j, \gamma], c\rangle (y_1, \ldots, y_r) \overset{*}{\Longrightarrow}_K t'$, where t' is obtained from t by replacing every $\langle A_k, \perp\rangle$ by y_k.

The rules of K are as follows.
If A_j --> <u>if</u> top=γ test(q) <u>then</u> t is a rule of L (we may assume that all rules are of this form), then $[A_j, \gamma](y_1, \ldots, y_r)$ --> <u>if</u> q <u>then</u> t′ is a rule of K, where t′ is obtained from t by replacing

- $A_k(\text{push}(\delta, f))$ by $[A_k, \delta](f)([A_1, \gamma](id)(\overline{y}), \ldots, [A_r, \gamma](id)(\overline{y}))$
  where $\overline{y}$ abbreviates $y_1, \ldots, y_r$ and id denotes an instructionsymbol which is interpreted as the identity on C
- $A_k(\text{pop})$ by y_k
- $A_k(\text{stay}(\delta))$ by $[A_k, \delta](id)(y_1, \ldots, y_r)$.

(For $\gamma = Z_0$ we may assume that no $A_k(\text{pop})$ occurs in t, and we drop

$(y_1,\ldots,y_r)$ from the rule.)

In an extended CFT(D)-transducer, such as K, we allow the right-hand side trees of rules to have $A(id)(y_1,\ldots,y_k)$ as subtrees, where A is a nonterminal and k is the rank of the left-hand side nonterminal. Note that if D contains an identity, then $CFT_{ext}(D) = CFT(D)$. As in Lemma 1 it is an easy observation that the second inclusion holds and determinism is preserved. □

<u>Theorem 1</u> $CFT_{ext}(D) = RT(P(D))$, $MAC_{ext}(D) = CF(P(D))$, and determinism is preserved in both cases.

If D contains an identity, then "ext" can be dropped.

<u>Proof</u> Lemma 1 also holds for the extended concept. We only have to enrich our construction a bit by adding

(v) for every $A \in N_k$, $k \geq 0$, the rule
$Q \dashrightarrow$ <u>if</u> top $= A(id)(y_1,\ldots,y_k)$ <u>then</u> $A(stay(Z_0))$ is in L. □

Note that D_0 contains an identity. Thus, for $D = D_0$, Theorem 1 states the equivalence of OI context-free tree grammars and (restricted) pushdown tree automata [Gu], and of OI macro grammars and indexed grammars [Fi], respectively. Note that TR does not contain an identity. However, in the total deterministic case, we can get rid of the extension in general. We only cite the result.

<u>Theorem 2</u> $D_tCFT(D) = D_tRT(P(D))$ and $D_tMAC(D) = D_tCF(P(D))$.

Theorem 2 generalizes the result in [Fr] that all (noncircular) attribute grammars can be simulated by total deterministic macro tree transducers (cf. also [CF,E5]): Every noncircular attribute grammar (AG) can easily be simulated by a total deterministic indexed tree transducer (assuming that, in TR, also every set of derivation trees of a context-free grammar is an initial configuration set); the attributes of the AG are the nonterminals of the transducer and the semantic rules of the AG its rules. Thus, using the previous result, $AG \subseteq D_tRT(P(TR)) = D_tCFT(TR)$.

Now we turn to the characterization of MAC(D) in terms of $REG(P^2(D))$-transducers. First we mention a result, which is the analogue of Theorem 1 for monadic trees, i.e., for strings. We only need the non-extended case.

Proposition 1   If D contains an identity, then $CF(D) = REG(P(D))$.

Theorem 3 $MAC_{ext}(D) = CF(P(D)) = REG(P^2(D))$,
and if D contains an identity, then "ext" can be dropped.

Proof Follows from Theorem 1 and Proposition 1. Note that the identity on P(D)-configurations can be simulated by testing the finitely many possible pushdown symbols on top of the pushdown, and then use the stay-instruction with the actual pushdown symbol. □

For $D = D_0$, Theorem 3 states the equivalence of OI macro grammars, indexed grammars, and 1-way pushdown^2 automata (which are equivalent with 1-way nested stack automata), see [A1,PDS,DG].

Unfortunately, in Proposition 1 determinism is only preserved in one direction (that of Lemma 1) and generally not in the other direction. As in the classical triple construction, the simulation of a REG(P(D))-transducer by a CF(D)-transducer involves the guessing of the return nonterminal by nondeterminism. Hence, we need a more powerful device to simulate a D_tREG(P(D))-transducer deterministically. For this purpose we enrich a storage type with look-ahead, as follows.

For a storage type $D = (C,I,P,F,m)$, the associated look-ahead storage type $D_{LA} = (C,I,P',F,m')$ is given by $P' = P \cup \{\langle A,H\rangle \mid A$ is a nonterminal of a CF(D)-transducer $H\}$ and, for $d \in P \cup F$, $m'(d) = m(d)$, and for every $c \in C$, $m'(\langle A,H\rangle)(c) =$ true iff there is a $w \in \Delta^*$ such that $\langle A,c\rangle \overset{*}{\Longrightarrow}_H w$, where Δ is the terminal alphabet of H. $\langle A,H\rangle$ is called a look-ahead predicate symbol and H is called the look-ahead transducer of $\langle A,H\rangle$.

Note that, for D = TR, this corresponds to the notion of regular look-ahead [E2,EV1], because a CF(TR)-transducer is a top-down tree(-to-string) transducer the domain of which is a regular tree language.

Proposition 2 $D_tCF(D) \subseteq D_tREG(P(D)) \subseteq D_tCF(D_{LA})$.

Proof Add look-ahead tests to the nondeterministic CF(D)-transducer K obtained by the application of the usual triple construction to a D_tREG(P(D))-transducer (using K itself as look-ahead transducer). The look-ahead test computes the correct return nonterminal and thus determines which rule is appropriate. □

Of course, if $D_tCF(D_{LA}) \subseteq D_tCF(D)$, then in Proposition 2 equality holds. This condition can be expressed entirely on the level of storage types using the reflexive and transitive simulation-relation $\leq$. Roughly speaking, for two storage types D_1 and D_2, $D_1 \leq D_2$ (in words: D_1 is simulated by D_2) means that there is a representation mapping from D_1-configurations to D_2-configurations and for every predicate and instruction of D_1, say s, there is a deterministic flowchart (using the predicates and instructions of D_2) imitating the meaning of s on the represented D_1-configurations (for details and motivation see [Ho,E7,EV2].

<u>Corollary 1</u> (i) If $D_{LA} \leq D$, then $D_tCF(D) = D_t REG(P(D))$.
(ii) If $P(D)_{LA} \leq P(D)$,
then $D_tMAC(D) = D_tCF(P(D)) = D_tREG(P^2(D))$.

<u>Proof</u> (i) Follows from Proposition 2 and the general fact: if $D_1 \leq D_2$, then $X(D_1) \subseteq X(D_2)$. (ii) Follows from Theorem 2 and application of (i) to P(D). □

The hypothesis in Corollary 1(ii) can be weakened by the use of the following result (note that, obivously, $P(D_{LA}) \leq P(D)_{LA}$).

<u>Lemma 3</u> $P(D)_{LA} \leq P(D_{LA})$.

<u>Proof</u> We only give a rough idea of the construction. Let <A,H> be a look-ahead predicate symbol in $P(D)_{LA}$, where $H = (N, C_0, \Delta, S, R)$ is the look-ahead CF(P(D))-transducer. Let $c' = (\gamma,c)\zeta$ be a P(D)-configuration. The main idea to simulate the test <A,H> on c', i.e., to decide whether there is a $w \in \Delta^*$ such that $\langle A,c'\rangle \overset{*}{\Longrightarrow}_H w$, is to cut the derivation of H into two parts: the first part contains those derivation steps which are executed until (γ,c) is popped. Defining (for every $M \subseteq N$) the set $L(A,\gamma,M)$ of D-configurations c for which such a "successful" derivation exists (with "final" nonterminals in M), membership of $L(A,\gamma,M)$ can be decided by a look-ahead test on D-configurations. For the construction of the look-ahead CF(D)-transducer we use the facts that $L(A,\gamma,M) \in$ dom (CF(P(D))) and dom(CF(P(D))) = dom(CF(D)), where dom(X(D)) is the class of domains of X(D)-transducers. The proof of this equation is too involved to explain (see [EV2]).

The second part contains those steps which derive terminal strings from the restpushdown ζ. Knowing, for all nonterminals $B \in M$, whether $\langle B,\zeta\rangle$ derives a terminal string in H, is clearly equivalent to knowing the truth value of the look-ahead predicates <B,H> applied to ζ. To have this knowledge available, we put these truth-values as auxiliary information on the pushdown (i.e., added to γ); this is the involved representation function. With each push-instruction this information can be computed: if push(δ,f) is applied to c′, the values of the look-ahead predicates applied to c′ can be obtained as described above and added to δ.□

The construction in Lemma 3 uses the same technique as the construction of the predicting machine for a deterministic pushdown automaton and a finite automaton (cf.[HU], section 12.3). As immediate consequence of Lemma 3 we can sharpen Corollary 1(ii).

Theorem 4 If $P(D_{LA}) \leq P(D)$, then $D_tMAC(D) = D_tCF(P(D)) = D_tREG(P^2(D))$.

4 APPLICATION TO THE STORAGE TYPE TR

Of course, all results of section 3 are true in particular for the storage type TR. Moreover, we can even improve now the situation of Theorem 4: the involved condition holds for the tree storage type.

Lemma 4 $P(TR_{LA}) \leq P(TR)$.

Proof The proof is analogues to that of Theorem 4.7 in [ERS], where it is shown that a checking-tree pushdown transducer can handle regular look-ahead deterministically by backtracking. □

Collecting the results of this paper for the storage type TR we obtain the desired regular characterizations of macro tree(-to-string) tranducers by indexed tree transducers and pushdown^2 tree transducers.

Theorem 5 (a) tree translation:

$CFT_{ext}(TR) = RT(P(TR))$ and $D_tCFT(TR) = D_tRT(P(TR))$

(b) tree-to-string translation:

$MAC_{ext}(TR) = CF(P(TR)) = REG(P^2(TR))$ and

$D_tMAC(TR) = D_tCF(P(TR)) = D_tREG(P^2(TR))$.

We note that the tree-walking pushdown transducer defined in [Ka] to simulate attribute grammars (viewed as tree-to-string transducers) is a special case of the $D_tREG(P^2(TR))$-transducer. This fits with the fact that $AG \subseteq D_tRT(P(TR))$ and hence tree-to-string $AG \subseteq D_tCF(P(TR)) = D_tREG(P^2(TR))$.

Finally, we mention that in [EV2] the concept of D-transducers is exploited to provide a regular characterization of compositions of D_tCFT(TR)-transducers in terms of iterated pushdown tree transducers (cf.[DG,E7]), viz., for every $n \geq 1$, $D_t\mathrm{CFT(TR)}^n = D_t\mathrm{RT}(P^n(\mathrm{TR}))$ and $yD_t\mathrm{CFT(TR)}^n = D_t\mathrm{CF}(P^n(\mathrm{TR})) = D_t\mathrm{REG}(P^{n+1}(\mathrm{TR}))$, where the n-fold composition of relation(classe)s is defined as usual and $yD_t\mathrm{CFT(TR)}^n$ is $D_t\mathrm{CFT(TR)}^{n-1}$ composed with D_tMAC(TR). The D-transducer approach allows us to give an inductive proof of these results. As an example, to prove that $D_t\mathrm{CF}(P^n(\mathrm{TR})) = D_t\mathrm{REG}(P^{n+1}(\mathrm{TR}))$, it suffices, by Corollary 1(ii), to show that $P^n(\mathrm{TR})_{LA} \leq P^n(\mathrm{TR})$. Using Lemma 3 and the obvious fact that, if $D_1 \leq D_2$ then $P(D_1) \leq P(D_2)$, we can prove by induction: $P^n(D)_{LA} \leq P^n(D_{LA})$. Then Lemma 4 yields the desired result.

REFERENCES

[A1] A.V. Aho; Nested stack automata; JACM 16 (1969), 383-406.

[A2] A.V. Aho; Indexed grammars, an extension of context-free grammars, JACM 15 (1968), 647-671.

[AU1] A.V. Aho, J.D. Ullman; Translations on a context-free grammar; Inf. and Contr. 19 (1971), 439-475.

[AU2] A.V. Aho, J.D. Ullman; "The Theory of Parsing, Translation, and Compiling Vol. I, II, Prentice Hall, Englewood Cliffs, N.J. 1973.

[CM] L.M. Chirica, D.E. Martin; An order algebraic definition of Knuthian semantics; Math. Syst. Theory 13 (1979), 1-27.

[CF] B. Courcelle, P. Franchi-Zannettacci; Attribute grammars and recursive program schemes I, II; TCS 17 (1982), 163-191, TCS 17 (1982), 235-257.

[Da] W. Damm; The IO- and OI- hierarchies, TCS 20 (1982), 95-206.

[DG] W. Damm, A. Goerdt; An automata-theoretic characterization of the OI-hierarchy; Proc. of the 9-th ICALP, Aarhus, 1982, pp. 141-153.

[E1] J. Engelfriet; Bottom-up and top-down tree transformations - a comparison; Math. Syst. Theory 9 (1975), 198-231.

[E2] J. Engelfriet; Top-down tree transducers with regular look-ahead; Math. Syst. Theory 10 (1977), 289-303.

[E3] J. Engelfriet; Two-way automata and checking automata; Math. Centre Tracts 108 (1979), 1-69.

[E4] J. Engelfriet; Some open questions and recent results on tree transducers and tree languages; in: "Formal language theory; perspectives and open problems", (R.V. Book, Ed.), New York, Academic Press, 1980.

[E5] J. Engelfriet; Tree transducers and syntax-directed semantics; TW-Memorandum Nr. 363 (1981), Twente University of Technology; also: Proc. 7th CAAP, March 1982, Lille, pp. 82-107.

[E6] J. Engelfriet; Recursive automata, (1982) unpublished notes.

[E7] J. Engelfriet; Iterated pushdown automata and complexity classes; Proc. 15th STOC, April 1983 (Boston), 365-373.

[EF] J. Engelfriet, G. Filè; The formal power of one-visit attribute grammars; Acta Informatica 16 (1981), 275-302.

[ERS] J. Engelfriet, G. Rozenberg, G. Slutzki; Tree transducers, L-systems, and two-way machines; JCSS 20 (1980), 150-202.

[ES] J. Engelfriet, E.M. Schmidt; IO and OI; JCSS 15 (1977), 328-353 and JCSS 16 (1978), 67-99.

[EV1] J. Engelfriet, H. Vogler; Macro tree transducers; Inf-Memorandum Nr. 7 (1982), Twente University of Technology.

[EV2] J. Engelfriet, H. Vogler; Machine characterizations of macro tree transducers: an application of grammars with datatypes; in preparation.

[Fi] M.J. Fischer; Grammars with macro-like productions; Ph.D. thesis Harvard University, 1968.

[Fr] P. Franchi-Zannettacci; Attributs sematiques et schemas de programmes; Thèse d'Etat, Univ. de Bordeaux, 1982.

[Go] M.J.C. Gordon; "The denotational description of programming languages, an introduction"; Springer-Verlag, New York, 1979.

[Gr] S.A. Greibach; Full AFLs and nested iterated substitution; Inf. and Contr. 16 (1970), 7-35.

[Gu] I. Guessarian; Pushdown tree automata; Math. Syst. Theory 16 (1983), 237-263.

[Ho] C.A.R. Hoare; Proof of correctness of data representations; Acta Informatica 1 (1972), 271-281.

[HU] J.E. Hopcroft, J.D. Ullman; "Formal languages and their relation to automata"; Addison-Wesley Publ. Comp. (1969).

[Ka] T. Kamimura; Tree automata and attribute grammars; Proc. 10th ICALP, LNCS 154, Springer-Verlag, 1983, pp. 374-384.

[Kn] D.E. Knuth; Semantics of context-free languages; Math. Syst. Theory 2 (1968), 127-145; correction: Math. Syst.Theory 5 (1971), 95-96.

[Ma] B. Mayoh; Attribute grammars and mathematical semantics; SIAM J. Comp. 10 (1981), 503-518.

[Ms] A.N. Maslov; Multi-level stack automata; Probl. of Inf. Transm. 12 (1976), 38-43.

[PDS] R. Parchmann, J. Duske, J. Specht; On deterministic indexed languages, Inf. and Contr. 45 (1980), 48-67.

[Ro] W.C. Rounds; Mappings and grammars on trees; Math. Syst. Theory 4 (1970), 257-287.

[Sc] D. Scott; Some definitional suggestions for automata theory; JCSS 1 (1967), 187-212.

[Th] J.W. Thatcher; Generalized^2 sequential machine maps; JCSS 4 (1970), 339-367.

[Vo] H. Vogler; Berechnungsmodelle syntaxgesteuerter Übersetzungen; Diplomarbeit, RWTH Aachen, April 1981.

HISTOIRES DE FILES DE PRIORITE AVEC FUSIONS

Jean FRANCON

ISEA, Université de Haute-Alsace, 4 Rue des Frères Lumière, 68093 MULHOUSE Cédex, FRANCE.

Claude PUECH

ERA 452 du CNRS, "Al Khowarizmi", LRI, Université de Paris-Sud, Bat 490, 91405 ORSAY Cédex, FRANCE; et Ecole Normale Supérieure, 1 Rue Maurice Arnoux, 92120 MONTROUGE. FRANCE.

Resumé: *L'étude du comportement dynamique de structures de données sous l'effet de suites d'opérations (adjonction, suppression d'une clé, ...), peut se ramener à des dénombrements de chemins ou de classes de permutations. Nous abordons ici, sur l'exemple des files de priorité, l'étude de l'évolution de fichiers soumis à des opérations plus "générales", pouvant porter sur plusieurs clés (il s'agit de modéliser, par exemple, la fusion de fichiers séquentiels triés). Les problèmes de dénombrement associés aux "Files de Priorité avec Fusions" sont résolus par des méthodes algébriques.*

Abstract: *The evolution of dynamic data structures under sequences of operations is usually studied under the hypothesis that the basic operations (insertions, deletions) are performed on single keys. We deal here with a more general case for Priority Queues: deletions are, as usual, deletions of the key of minimal priority but several insertions can be combined in a merging of the file with a batch of keys. The analyses of the evolutions of the queues involve counting paths and classes of permutations. These counting problems are solved by "algebraic" methods.*

1 INTRODUCTION.

Une *file de priorité avec fusions* est un ensemble de données, structuré d'une certaine façon, sur lequel les opérations autorisées sont:

(i) la *suppression* , notée $S_{\min}$, de la † clé de valeur minimale (ou de plus haute priorité),

(ii) la *fusion* , notée F, avec le fichier existant, d'un ensemble fini ou *lot* de clés (distinctes des clés du fichier).

---

† ***la*** clé, car on suppose que les clé présentes à un instant donné dans un un fichier sont distinctes, leurs valeurs étant prises dans un ensemble ordonné dense.

Comme on le verra de manière plus précise plus loin, certaines contraintes peuvent être, éventuellement imposées sur ces opérations. On étudie les files de priorité avec fusions d'un point de vue *dynamique* , c'est-à-dire que l'on considère leur évolution sous l'effet de suites d'opérations. Ainsi la suite (avec une notation évidente):

$$F(1.3,2.5)S_{\min}F(0.9,8.4)F(3.2)S_{\min}S_{\min}F(1.3)S_{\min}S_{\min}S_{\min}$$

est une suite possible d'opérations sur une file de priorité avec fusions , initialement vide (revenant d'ailleurs à une file vide), dont les clés sont des nombres réels.

L'objectif informatique d'une telle étude est de calculer le "coût" de telles suites à partir du coût de chaque opération, ces coûts dépendant de la façon dont les files sont structurées (c'est-à-dire des "structures de données" utilisées pour les implanter en machine) et des algorithmes réalisant les opérations. Un tel calcul permet de déterminer les structures de données et les algorithmes les plus économiques prenant en compte les deux opérations globalement, au lieu de se contenter, comme souvent, d'une structure de données "bonne" pour une opération et "pas trop mauvaise" pour l'autre.

Cette approche dynamique de l'étude des structures de données et des algorithmes a été introduite dans [Fr78]. Elle a été développée dans plusieurs travaux: [Fr 79], [Fl 79], [Fl 80], [FFV 80], [FF 80], [CFFPV 80], [Ch 81], [FPV 82] (on pourra se reporter à [FlP 81] pour un panorama des résultats obtenus). Dans tous ces travaux, toutes les opérations ne portent que sur une seule clé. Dans le présent travail nous étudions des types de fichiers aux comportements plus complexes, puisque l'opération de fusion porte sur un ensemble de clés. D'un point de vue informatique, il s'agit de modéliser l'évolution de fichiers soumis à des réorganisations périodiques, ces réorganisations pouvant mettre en jeu des lots groupés de clés, ces lots ayant pu, par exemple, subir un prétraitement hors-ligne.

Comme dans les travaux précédents rappelés ci-dessus, nous définissons - c'est l'objet de la section suivante - la notion d'histoire, une histoire représentant une classe de suites d'opérations, qui permet de formuler le problème informatique en un problème de Combinatoire. Puis, à la section 3, nous présentons une approche "algébrique" de ce problème de dénombrement, approche qui permet, dans tous les cas étudiés, d'obtenir une expression "simple" de la série géneratrice, d'où l'on peut déduire les cardinaux des ensembles d'histoires qui nous intéressent: certains de ces dénombrements font intervenir les nombres de Schroeder et les nombres de Stirling 2-associés. Enfin, à la section 4, nous montrons comment, dans le cas des files de priorité avec adjonctions par lots, (c'est-à-dire le cas particulier des files avec fusions dans lequel on interdit deux fusions consécutives) on peut obtenir les dénombrements par des méthodes de combinatoire géométrique, en mettant en bijection les histoires étudiées et certaines classes de fonctions sous-excédentes (fonctions f de $[1..n]$ dans lui-même telles que $f(i)\leq i$ pour tout i); ces méthodes (qui ne semblent pas se géneraliser) permettent d'obtenir, dans ce cas particulier, d'autres dénombrements qui conduisent à des évaluations précises des coûts unitaires d'opérations, pour des implantations sous forme de listes simples des files de priorité (ces derniers résultats, qui sont développés dans [FrP 83], sont seulement résumés, de manière à les situer par rapport à ceux obtenus, ici, par l'approche algébrique).

2 LA NOTION D'HISTOIRE DE FILE DE PRIORITE AVEC FUSION.

Revenons tout d'abord sur la notion de suite d'opérations valide pour une file de priorité avec fusion. La suite d'opérations:

$$F(1.3,2.5)S_{min}F(0.9,8.4)F(3.2)S_{min}S_{min}F(1.3)S_{min}S_{min}S_{min}$$

valide pour une file de priorité avec fusion est à bien distinguer de la suite

$$A(1.3)A(2.5)S_{min}A(0.9)A(8.4)A(3.2)S_{min}S_{min}A(1.3)S_{min}S_{min}S_{min}$$

valide pour une file de priorité classique. La suite des états intermédiaires de la file pour la première suite est incluse dans la suite des états intermédiaires de la deuxième; la différence essentielle apparaît au niveau de l'ensemble des évolutions possibles d'un fichier: les nombres de façons de passer d'un fichier de taille p à un fichier de taille $p+q$, par une fusion avec un lot de q clés, dans le premier cas, par q adjonctions consécutives, dans l'autre, sont différents: dans le cas d'une fusion, il y a

$$\binom{p+q}{q}$$

façons d'interclasser les p clés du fichier avec les q clés du lot; par contre, si l'on opère clé par clé, par adjonctions succéssives, le nombre de cas possibles est:

$$(p+1)(p+2)\cdots(p+q)$$

($p+1$ est le nombre de façons d'adjoindre la première clé aux p clés présentes dans le fichier, $p+2$ le nombre de façons d'adjoindre alors la deuxième clé aux $p+2$ présentes ...).

Le nombre d'évolutions possibles est donc $q!$ fois plus grand dans le cas des files de priorité classiques; ainsi, en particulier, il y a une seule fusion possible d'un lot de q clés avec un fichier vide, alors qu'il y a $q!$ façons de créer un fichier de taille q à partir du fichier vide par adjonctions successives.

Employant la même terminologie que pour les histoires "classiques", nous dirons que le *nombre de possibilités* d'une fusion d'un fichier de taille p avec un lot de q clés est $\binom{p+q}{q}$; le nombre de possibilités de suppression est, lui, toujours égal à 1, puisque seul le minimum peut être supprimé.

Si les seules opérations effectuées sur les clés d'un fichier sont des comparaisons de clés, deux suites d'opérations mettant en jeu des clés différentes mais isomorphes du point de vue de l'ordre ont le même "coût" (en nombres de comparaisons par exemple). C'est pourquoi, comme dans le cas "classique", nous n'étudierons pas les suites d'opérations elles-même mais des représentants canoniques des classes d'équivalence de ces suites modulo le morphisme d'ordre.

On passe d'une suite d'opérations à l'histoire associée en remplaçant chaque clé d'un lot qu'on fusionne par son rang (compté conventionnellement à partir de 0) dans l'ensemble des clés du fichier *après* qu'ait été effectuée la fusion.

Ainsi l'histoire associée à la suite:

$$F(1.3,2.5)S_{\min}F(0.9,8.4)F(3.2)S_{\min}S_{\min}F(4.1)S_{\min}S_{\min}S_{\min}$$

est:

$$F(0,1)SF(0,2)F(2)SSF(0)SSS$$

(pour simplifier $S(0)$ est noté S)

La suite des opérations (les fusions étant indicées par la taille des lots sur lesquelles elles portent):

$$F_2SF_2F_1SSF_1SSS$$

est appelée *schéma* de l'histoire, la suite des rangs

(0,1) (0) (0,2) (2) (0) (0) (0) (0) (0) (0)

sa *valuation*.

Il sera utile, dans la Section 4 en particulier, d'utiliser une représentation géométrique des histoires par des "chemins" dans le plan. L'histoire ci-dessus est alors representée comme indiqué sur la figure 1.

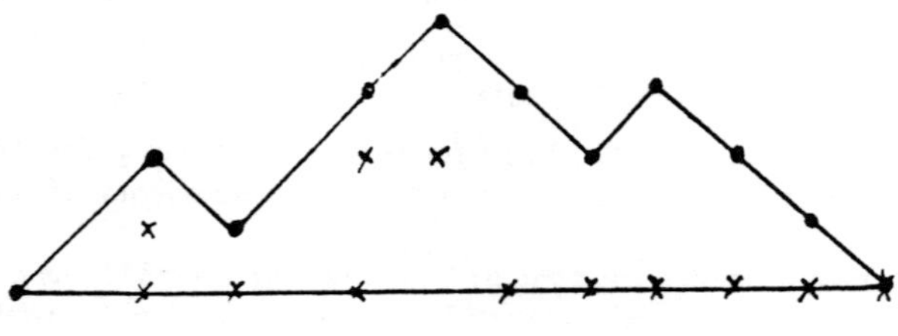

Figure 1

Le contour supérieur représente le schéma de l'histoire. Une suppression est representée par un segment "descendant" de longueur 1, une fusion d'un lot de p clés par un segment "ascendant" de longueur p.

Les croix traduisent les valuations des adjonctions de l'histoire; la valuation d'une adjonction se marque à la fin de l'adjonction par des croix ayant pour "altitudes" les rangs apparaissant dans la valuation de l'adjonction.

Dans la suite, nous parlerons de *Files de Priorité avec Fusions Quelconques* lorsqu'aucune contrainte n'est imposée sur les opérations de base: Suppression du minimum et Fusion.

Mais nous nous intéresserons aussi à des cas où des contraintes existent.

Ces contraintes peuvent porter sur la *taille* des lots que l'on fusionne: par exemple, si l'on impose que les lots soient de taille 1, on retrouve le type *File de Priorité* "classique", comme cas particulier des Files de Priorité avec Fusions.

Les contraintes peuvent aussi être des contraintes de *succession;* c'est ainsi que, dans [FrP 83], nous nous sommes intéressés au cas où l'on interdit deux fusions consécutives (cas de mises à jour pèriodiques de fichiers par fusion avec un fichier, ou lot, unique prétraité), type que nous avons appelé *Files de Priorité avec Adjonctions par Lots*.

3 UNE APPROCHE ALGEBRIQUE DU PROBLEME DE DENOMBREMENT D'HISTOIRES.

Nous appelons *niveau initial* d'une histoire le nombre de clés présentes dans le fichier dans l'état initial (ou *taille* du fichier initial), définissons de manière analogue le *niveau final* , et appelons *longueur* de l' histoire le nombre total de clés qu'elle met en jeu, chaque clé étant comptée autant de fois qu'une opération porte sur elle (une suppression S porte sur une clé, une fusion F^q porte sur q clés, et est dite de longueur q); par exemple, l'histoire:

$$F(0,1)SF(0,2)F(2)SSF(0)SSS$$

de niveaux initial et final nuls est une histoire de longueur 12.

Pour des raisons de commodité, qui apparaitront dans la suite, nous considérons l'ensemble $\mathbf{H}_{k,l;m,n}$ des histoires de niveau initial k, de niveau final l, formées de m suppressions et n fusions, ***et telles que la dernière opération soit une suppression.*** Notre but, ici, est de calculer le nombre $H_{k,l;m,n}$ de ces histoires.

Le premier résultat que nous allons prouver est un résultat valable pour un type de données plus géneral que celui des files de priorité avec fusions , plus géneral au sens suivant:

i) Le nombre de possibilités d'une fusion d'un fichier de taille p et d'un lot de q clés n'est plus supposé égal à $\binom{p+q}{q}$; on suppose seulement donné $f_{j,k;p}$, le nombre de façons de passer de niveau j à niveau k par p fusions consécutives.

ii) une suppression ne porte plus nécessairement sur la clé de valeur minimale du fichier; on note σ_p le nombre de possibilités de suppression à niveau p.

Soit

$$H_{k,l}(x,y) = \sum_{m,n} H_{k,l;m,n} x^m y^n$$

la série géneratrice des histoires suivant leurs nombres d'adjonctions et de suppressions; soit, d'autre part,

$$f_{j,k}(y) = \sum_p f_{j,k;p} y^p$$

la série génératrice associée aux $f_{j,k;p}$.

Les $H_{k,l}$ vérifient la propriété:

Proprieté 1: *Sous les hypothèses ci-dessus, les polynômes $H_{k,l}$ vérifient les relations de récurrence:*

$$H_{k,l}(x,y) = x\sigma_{l+1}\sum_{j=0}^{l+1} H_{k,j}(x,y) f_{j,l+1}(y) \quad \textit{pour tout} \quad k\geq 0, l\geq 0 \quad \textit{avec} \quad k\neq l$$

$$H_{k,k}(x,y) = 1 + x\sigma_{k+1}\sum_{j=0}^{k+1} H_{k,j}(x,y) f_{j,k+1}(y) \quad \textit{pour tout} \quad k\geq 0.$$

Démonstration: Une histoire h de $\mathbf{H}_{k,l;m,n}$ peut (voir Figure 2) se décomposer selon le niveau de fin de l'avant-dernière suppression, en une histoire de la famille des $\mathbf{H}_{k,l;m,n-1}$ (avec m et l convenablement choisis), suivie par une suite (éventuellement vide) de fusions consécutives, suivie par la suppression qui termine h.

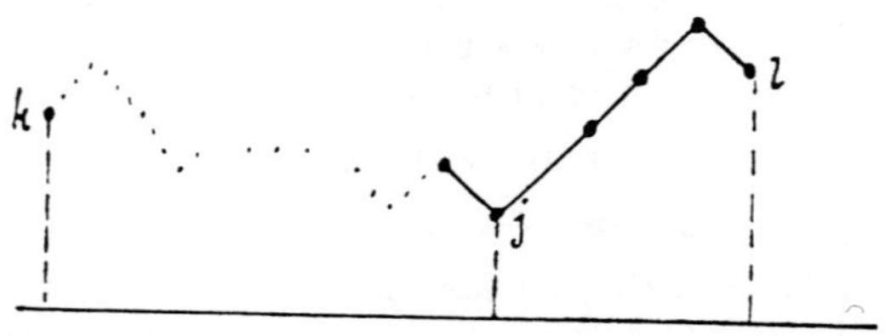

Figure 2

Cette décomposition se traduit par les récurrences suivantes:

$$H_{k,l;m,n} = \sum_{j=0}^{l+1} \sum_{p=1}^{l+1-j} H_{k,j;m-p,n-1} f_{j,l+1;p}\sigma_{l+1}$$

pour tout $l\geq 0, k\geq 0$ avec $l\neq k$ ou $l=k$ et $(m,n)\neq(0,0)$

et:

$$H_{k,k;0,0} = 1 \quad \text{pour tout} \quad k\geq 0$$

D'où les récurrences sur les polynômes générateurs.

Pour k fixé, on peut écrire l'ensemble des relations de récurrence, qui forme un système linéaire, sous la forme matricielle suivante:

$$[I-xM(y)]\widetilde{H}_k = \widetilde{\delta}_{k+1}$$

avec

$$M(y) = \begin{pmatrix} \sigma_1 f_{0,1}(y) & \sigma_1 & 0 & 0 & 0 & \cdots \\ \sigma_2 f_{0,2}(y) & \sigma_2 f_{1,2}(y) & \sigma_2 & 0 & 0 & \cdots \\ \sigma_3 f_{0,3}(y) & \sigma_3 f_{1,3}(y) & \sigma_3 f_{1,3}(y) & \sigma_3 & 0 & \cdots \\ \cdots & \cdots & \cdots & \cdots & \cdots & \cdots \\ \cdots & \cdots & \cdots & \cdots & \cdots & \cdots \\ \cdots & \cdots & \cdots & \cdots & \cdots & \cdots \end{pmatrix}$$

$$\widetilde{H}_k = (H_{k,0} H_{k,1} \cdots H_{k,k} \cdots)^t$$

$\widetilde{\delta}_{k+1}$ vecteur colonne dont tous les élements sont nuls, sauf le $k+1$-ème, égal à 1.

On en déduit:

Corollaire: *Le nombre $H_{k,l;m,n}$ d'histoires, partant du niveau k, se terminant (par une suppression) au niveau l, formées de m fusions et n suppressions est égal au coefficient de y^m dans le polynôme en y qui se trouve sur la ligne $l+1$ et la colonne $k+1$ de la matrice $M^n(y)$*

Démonstration: Ce corollaire traduit l'égalité formelle entre le polynôme $H_{k,l}(x,y)$ et l'élément qui se trouve sur la ligne $l+1$ et la colonne $k+1$ de $[I-xM(y)]^{-1} = \sum x^n M^n(y)$

Dans le cas général envisagé plus haut, il semble difficile d'obtenir plus que le corollaire ci-dessus. Par contre, dans le cas des files de priorité avec fusions, le fait que le nombre de possibilités de fusion d'un fichier de taille p et d'un lot de q clés soit égal à $\binom{p+q}{q}$ induit sur les $f_{j,k}(y)$ la relation:

$$f_{j,k}(y) = \binom{k}{j} f_{0,k-j}(y)$$

qui permet de factoriser les séries génératrices associées aux éléments de $M(y)^n$, et donc, d'obtenir des expressions utiles pour les dénombrements.

Comme σ_i est, dans le cas des files de priorité avec fusions, égal à 1, la matrice $M(y)$ s'écrit, dans ce cas:

$$M(y) = \begin{pmatrix} f_{0,1}(y) & 1 & 0 & 0 & 0 & \cdots \\ f_{0,2}(y) & 2f_{0,1}(y) & 1 & 0 & 0 & \cdots \\ f_{0,3}(y) & 3f_{0,2}(y) & 3f_{0,1}(y) & 1 & 0 & \cdots \\ \cdots & \cdots & \cdots & \cdots & \cdots & \cdots \\ \cdots & \cdots & \cdots & \cdots & \cdots & \cdots \\ \cdots & \cdots & \cdots & \cdots & \cdots & \cdots \end{pmatrix}$$

(l'élément se trouvant en ligne i et colonne j vaut:

$$m_{ij}(y) = \binom{i}{j-1} f_{0,i-j+1}(y) \quad)$$

Donc, l'élement (i,j) de $M^2(y)$vaut:

$$m_{ij}^{(2)}(y) = \sum_k m_{ik}(y) m_{kj}(y) = \sum_k \binom{i}{k-1} f_{0,i-k+1}(y) \binom{k}{j-1} f_{0,k-j+1}(y)$$

On en déduit que:

$$\sum_{i,j} m_{ij}^{(2)}(y) \frac{u^i}{i!} v^{j-1} = \sum_{i,j,k} f_{0,i-k+1}(y) \frac{u^{i-k+1}}{(i-k+1)!} . k u^{k-1} \frac{f_{0,k-j+1}(y)}{(k-j+1)!} \frac{v^{j-1}}{(j-1)!}$$

est le produit de Cauchy de

$$B(y,u) = \sum_i f_{0,i}(y) \frac{u^i}{i!}$$

et de

$$\frac{\partial}{\partial u}[B(y,u) e^{uv}] = \sum_k \left[\sum_j \frac{f_{0,k-j}(y)}{(k-j)!} \frac{v^j}{j!} \right] . k u^{k-1}$$

Ainsi:

$$\sum_{i,j} m_{ij}^{(2)}(y) \frac{u^i}{i!} v^{j-1} = B(y,u) . \frac{\partial}{\partial u}[B(y,u) e^{uv}]$$

En tenant compte de:

$$\sum m_{ij}^{(n)}(y) \frac{u^i}{i!} v^{j-1} = \sum f_{0,i-k+1}(y) \frac{u^{i-k+1}}{(i-k+1)!} . m_{kj}^{(n-1)}(y) \frac{u^{k-1}}{(k-1)!} v^{j-1}$$

(qui est une conséquence de $m_{ij}^{(n)}(y) = \sum_k m_{ik}(y) m_{kj}^{(n-1)}(y)$), on démontre sans peine, par récurrence, le

Théorème 1: *La série génératrice triple des histoires de files de priorité avec fusions contenant n suppressions:*

$$H_n(u,v,y) = \sum_{k,l;m,n} H_{k,l;m,n} \frac{u^{l+1}}{(l+1)!} v^k y^m$$

se calcule à partir de la série génératrice:

$$B(y,u) = \sum_i f_{0,i}(y) \frac{u^i}{i!} = \sum_{i,p} f_{0,i;p} \frac{u^i}{i!} y^p$$

(où $f_{0,i;p}$ est le nombre de façons, pour le type considéré, de créer un fichier de taille i à partir d'un fichier vide, par p fusions consécutives) par la formule:

$$H_n(u,v,y) = B(y,u) \frac{\partial}{\partial u}[B(y,u) \frac{\partial}{\partial u}[\cdots B(y,u) \frac{\partial}{\partial u}[B(y,u) e^{uv}]] \cdots]$$

(où la fonction B apparaît n fois)

En extrayant des termes particuliers de la série, on en déduit:

Corollaire 1: *Le nombre d'histoires de files de priorité avec fusions partant du niveau 0 et se terminant au niveau 0 par une suppression, formées de m fusions et n suppressions est égal au coefficient de* $\frac{u^{k+1}}{(k+1)!}y^m$ *dans:*

$$B(y,u)\frac{\partial}{\partial u}[B(y,u)\frac{\partial}{\partial u}[\cdots B(y,u)\frac{\partial}{\partial u}[B(y,u)]]\cdots]$$

Corollaire 2: *Le nombre d'histoires de files de priorité avec fusions partant du niveau k et se terminant au niveau 0, formées de m fusions et n suppressions est égal au coefficient de* $v^k y^m$ *dans:*

$$\frac{\partial}{\partial u}[B(y,u)\frac{\partial}{\partial u}[B(y,u)\frac{\partial}{\partial u}[\cdots B(y,u)\frac{\partial}{\partial u}[B(y,u)e^{uv}]]\cdots]$$

évalué en $u=0$ *(où* $B(y,u)$ *apparaît n fois).*

Corollaire 3: *Le nombre d'histoires de files de priorité avec fusions partant du niveau 0 et revenant au niveau 0, formées de m fusions et n suppressions est égal au coefficient de* y^m *dans:*

$$\frac{\partial}{\partial u}[B(y,u)\frac{\partial}{\partial u}[B(y,u)\frac{\partial}{\partial u}[\cdots B(y,u)\frac{\partial}{\partial u}[B(y,u)e^{uv}]]\cdots]$$

évalué en $u=0$ *(où* $B(y,u)$ *apparaît n fois).*

Etudions maintenant ce que donnent les résultats ci-dessus dans le cas particulier des files de priorité, des files de priorité avec adjonctions par lots et des files de priorité avec fusions quelconques. La valeur de la série $B(y,u)$ associée à chacun de ces types est donnée dans le

Lemme: *i) Dans le cas des files de priorité:*

$$B(y,u) = \frac{1}{1-yu}$$

ii) Dans le cas de files de priorité avec adjonctions par lots:

$$B(y,u) = 1+y(e^u-1)$$

iii) Dans le cas des files de priorité avec fusions quelconques:

$$B(y,u) = \frac{1}{1-y(e^u-1)}$$

Démonstration: i) Dans le cas des files de priorité, la taille des lots que l'on fusionne ne peut qu'être égale à 1, donc (en tenant compte de l'ordre des fusions):

$f_{0,p;p} = p!$

$f_{0,i;p} = 0$ sinon

$f_{0,i}(y) = p!\, y^p$

et

$$B(y,u) = \sum p! y^p \frac{u^p}{p!} = \sum y^p u^p = \frac{1}{1-yu}$$

ii) Dans le cas des files de priorité avec adjonctions par lot, on interdit deux fusions consécutives, donc:

$f_{0,i;p} = 1$ si $p=1$ et $i \neq 0$

$f_{0,i;p} = 0$ sinon

$f_{0,i}(y) = y$ si $i \neq 0$

$f_{0,0}(y) = 1$

et

$$B(y,u) = 1 + \sum_{i \geq 1} y \frac{u^i}{i!} = 1 + y(e^u - 1)$$

iii) Dans le cas des files de priorité avec fusions quelconques, passer du niveau 0 au niveau i par p fusions consécutives est équivalent à choisir une partition des i clés en p "blocs", qui seront les lots (on sait que ça peut se faire de $S_{i,p}$ façons, où $S_{i,p}$ est un nombre de Stirling de seconde espèce), puis à interclasser les lots. Donc:

$f_{0,i;p} = p!\, S_{i,p}$ si $i \neq 0$

$f_{0,0;p} = 0$

$f_{0,i}(y) = \sum p!\, S_{i,p} y^p$ si $i \neq 0$

$f_{0,i}(y) = 0$

et

$$B(y,u) = 1 + \sum_{p \geq 1, i \geq 1} p!\, S_{i,p}\, y^p \frac{u^i}{i!} = \frac{1}{1 - y(e^u - 1)}$$

puisque la série géneratrice exponentielle des Stirling de seconde espèce est:

$$\sum_i S_{i,p} \frac{u^i}{i!} = \frac{(e^u - 1)^p}{p!}$$

(cf [Co 74] p. 206)

A partir des corollaires 1, 2, 3 et des valeurs de B données dans le lemme ci-dessus, on peut dénombrer les histoires. Les résultats obtenus sont résumés dans les propositions suivantes (les résultats de la proposition 1 sont "classiques", cf [Fr 79]; ceux de la proposition 2 peuvent être prouvés de manière géométrique, cf [FrP 83] et la section 4; enfin, le résultat de la proposition 3 est plus difficile; c'est lui qui a motivé le présent travail):

Proposition 1: *Pour les files de priorité classiques:*

$$H_{0,0;n,n} = 1.3.5....(2n-1)$$

$$H_{0,k;m,n} = \frac{(m+n)!}{n!2^n}$$

$$H_{k,0;m,n} = \frac{(m+n)!}{k!n!2^n}$$

(il s'agit d'histoires de longueur $2n$ dans le premier cas, de longueur $m+n$ dans les autres).

Proposition 2: *Pour les files de priorité avec adjonctions par lots:*

$$H_{0,0;m,n} = A(n,m)$$

(où $A(n,m)$ sont les nombres eulériens (cf [Co 74] p. 51)).

De plus, le nombre d'histoires partant du niveau 0, revenant au niveau 0 et possédant n suppressions vaut:

$$H_{0,0;\bullet,n} = n!$$

Proposition 3: *Pour les files de priorité avec fusions quelconques:*

$$H_{0,0;m,n} = S_2(m+n,m)$$

(où les $S_2(n,k)$ sont les nombres de Stirling 2-associés de seconde espèce).

De plus, le nombre d'histoires partant du niveau 0, revenant au niveau 0, et possédant n suppressions est égal au $n+1$ -ième nombre de Schroeder:

$$H_{0,0;\bullet,n} = Schr_{n+1}$$

(Rappelons, cf [Co 74] p. 222, que les nombres de Stirling 2-associés de seconde espèce dénombrent les partitions de $[n]$ en k blocs sans singletons; leur série génératrice double est:

$$\sum_{n,k} S_2(n,k)x^k \frac{z^n}{n!} = e^{x(e^z-z-1)}$$

Par ailleurs, les nombres de Schroeder Sch_n, dont la série génératrice exponentielle $\varphi(x) = \sum Sch_n \frac{x^n}{n!}$ vérifie l'équation:

$$e^{\varphi}-2\varphi-1+x = 0,$$

dénombrent les arbres sans sommet de degré 1, ayant n feuilles étiquetées, ou, de manière équivalente, les systèmes de Schroeder à k emboitements).

Donnons seulement la démonstration de la proposition 3. Il est facile de démontrer, par récurrence sur le nombre de dérivations, que:

$$\frac{\partial}{\partial u}[B(y,u)\frac{\partial}{\partial u}[B(y,u)\frac{\partial}{\partial u}[\cdots B(y,u)\frac{\partial}{\partial u}[B(y,u)]]\cdots] = \sum_k \alpha_{n,k} y^k e^k B^{n+k}(y,u)$$

où les $\alpha_{n,k}$ vérifient la relation de récurrence:

$$\alpha_{n,k} = k\,\alpha_{n-1,k} + (n+k-1)\alpha_{n-1,k-1}$$

avec les conditions initiales:

$\alpha_{n,1} = 1$ pour tout $n \geq 1$

$\alpha_{n,k} = 0$ si $n < k$

D'aprés [Co 74] p. 222, les $\alpha_{n,k}$ sont donc des nombres de Stirling 2-associés de seconde espèce; plus précisément:

$$\alpha_{n,k} = S_2(n+k,k)$$

La deuxième partie de la proposition résulte de ce que:

$$Sch_n = \sum_{k=0}^{n-1} S_2(n+k,k+1)$$

(cf [Co 74] p. 224; cette égalité traduit la décomposition, suivant leur nombre de sommets internes, des arbres sans sommet de degré 1 dont les n feuilles sont étiquetées)

4 LE CAS DES FILES DE PRIORITE AVEC ADJONCTIONS PAR LOTS: UNE APPROCHE GEOMETRIQUE DU PROBLEME DE DENOMBREMENT.

Dans le cas des files de priorité avec adjonctions par lots, une approche géométrique, fondée sur la bijection décrite au paragraphe 4.1. permet de prouver de manière différente certains des résultats obtenus à la section 3 dans ce cas particulier, et d'en obtenir de nouveaux.

Pour l'approche géométrique, il s'est averé fructueux de considérer non pas l'ensemble $\mathbf{H}_{k,l;n,m}$ mais l'ensemble $\mathbf{H}_{k,l;/n/}$ des histoires de niveau initial k, de niveau final l, de *longueur* n (nous noterons $H_{k,l;/n/}$ le nombre de ces histoires). L'ensemble $\mathbf{H}_{0,0;/n/}$ des histoires de longueur n, de niveaux initial et final nuls sera souvent consideré, et noté, pour simplifier $\mathbf{H}_n$ (son cardinal étant noté H_n).

4.1 Une bijection fondamentale.

Soit $\mathbf{E}_n$ l'ensemble des "fonctions sous-excédentes" de $[1..n]$ dans lui-même, c'est-à-dire l'ensemble des fonctions f, définies sur $[1..n]$, telles que $f(i) \leq i$ pour tout i de $[1..n]$; une telle fonction peut être représentée graphiquement comme sur la figure 3.

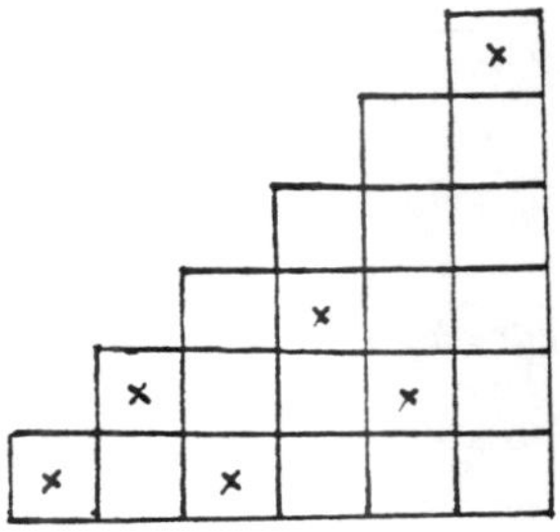

Figure 3

(On a représenté l'élément de $\mathbf{E}_6$ défini par $f(1)=1, f(2)=2, f(3)=1, f(4)=3, f(5)=2, f(6)=6$). Pour cette raison nous appellerons "escaliers de taille n" les élements de $\mathbf{E}_n$.

Considérons l'application ϑ de $\mathbf{H}_{2n}$ dans $\mathbf{E}_n$ définie de la manière suivante: étant donnée une histoire h de $\mathbf{H}_{2n}$ on numérote les débuts des suppressions, dans l'ordre des "temps croissants", par $1,2, \cdots, n$ (comme l'on part du fichier vide pour revenir au fichier vide, il y a exactement n suppressions); à cette histoirc on associc l'cscalicr dc taillc n construit commc suit: à partir dc $i=n$, ct en décroissant jusqu'à $i=1$, on place dans l'horizontale d'altitude i autant de croix qu'il y en a dans l'histoire sur la verticale du début de suppression numerotée i; ces croix sont placées en respectant leurs positions sur cette verticale: on considère comme inutilisables les cases au-dessus desquelles on a déjà placé une croix; il reste alors un nombre de cases utilisables égal au niveau (ou altitude) du début de suppression consideré; en supposant les cases utilisables numerotées de droite à gauche à partir de 0, on place une croix dans la case j si et seulement si il y a une croix d'altitude i dans l'histoire sur la verticale considerée. Cette construction est illustrée sur la figure 4, où, pour mieux faire comprendre la construction, on a hachuré sur l'escalier les cases non utilisables.

Montrons maintenant comment passer d'un escalier à une histoire: dans chaque marche horizontale (en partant du niveau n et en décroissant jusqu'au niveau 1) on "pousse" les croix, s'il y en a, de manière à ce qu'elles forment un "bloc"; ce bloc doit être placé le plus à droite possible sur la marche et tel qu'aucune des croix du bloc ne se trouve à la verticale de croix de blocs déjà placées (dans les marches situées au dessus); on trace alors le "contour limite" des blocs comme indiqué en gras sur la figure 5. Ce contour définit le schéma de l'histoire: chaque portion horizontale correspond à une adjonction; sa longueur détermine le nombre de clés sur lesquelles elle porte; chaque portion verticale

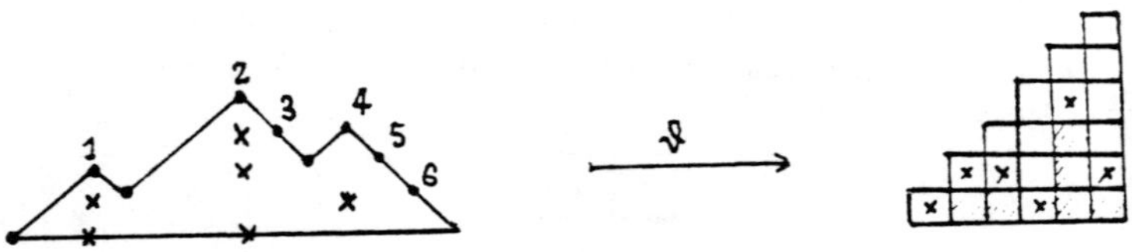

Figure 4

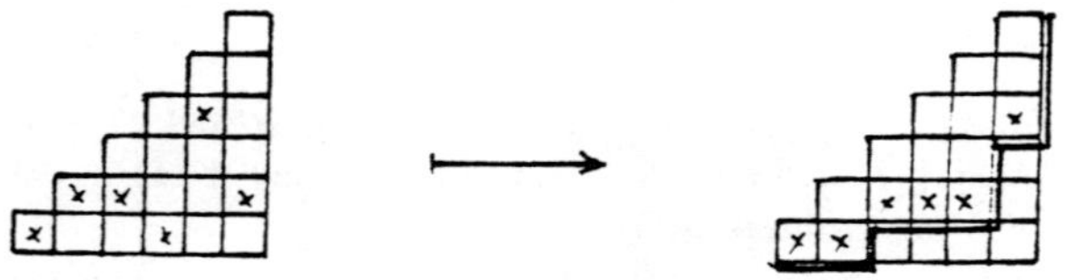

Figure 5

(de longueur 1) correspond à une suppression; on rajoute de plus une suppression à la fin (voir la figure 6).

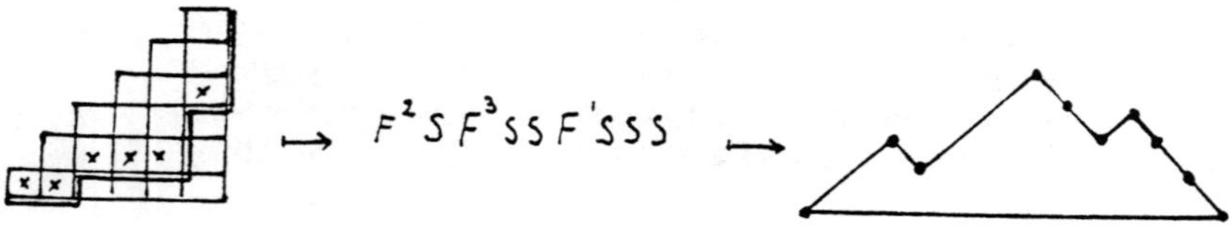

Figure 6

En numérotant les débuts de suppressions comme indiqué dans la définition de ϑ, et en plaçant des croix sur les verticales de ces débuts par la procédure inverse de celle utilisée dans la définition de ϑ, on obtient la valuation de l'histoire construite à partir de l'escalier (voir la figure 7).

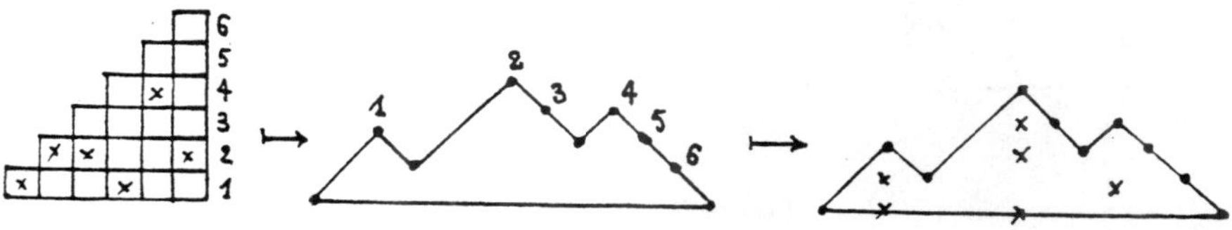

Figure 7

Il est facile de montrer que l'application φ que nous venons de définir de $\mathbf{E}_n$ dans $\mathbf{H}_{2n}$ est l'inverse de ϑ, et de prouver le:

Théorème 2: *ϑ est une bijection de* H_{2n} *sur* $\mathbf{E}_n$.

4.2 Quelques conséquences de la bijection fondamentale.

Le théorème précédent a plusieurs corollaires qui permettent de dénombrer des familles particulières d'histoires. Nous allons seulement énoncer, sous forme de propositions, quelques uns des corollaires et esquisser certaines preuves renvoyant à [FrP 83] pour plus de détails.

Proposition 4: *On a:* $H_{2n} = n!$

(il s'agit d'une conséquence immédiate du théorème)

Comme le nombre de possibilités d'une suppression est 1, il est clair, qu'il y a bijection entre $\mathbf{H}_{0,k;n}$ et l'ensemble des histoires de $\mathbf{H}_{n+k}$ qui se terminent par k suppressions (voir la figure 8).

Or, on peut montrer que, par l'application ϑ les histoires de $\mathbf{H}_{n+k}$ qui se terminent par k suppressions ont pour images les escaliers dont les $k-1$ dernières marches ne portent pas de croix. On en déduit la:

Proposition 5: *On a:*

$$H_{0,k;n} = \left(\frac{n-k}{2}+1\right)^k \left(\frac{n-k}{2}\right)!$$

Figure 8

De même, il y a bijection entre $\mathbf{H}_{k,0;n}$ et l'ensemble des histoires de $\mathbf{H}_{n+k+2}$ qui commencent par une adjonction de longueur $k+1$, et par l'application ϑ les histoires de $\mathbf{H}_{n+k+2}$ commençant par une adjonction de longueur k ont pour images les escaliers dont la première marche porte $k+1$ croix. On en déduit:

Proposition 6:

$$H_{k,0;n} = s_{\frac{n+k}{2}+1,k+1}$$

Par ailleurs, la distribution du nombre d'adjonctions dans les histoires de $\mathbf{H}_{2n}$ est donnée par le résultat suivant:

Proposition 7: *Le nombre d'histoires de* $\mathbf{H}_{2n}$ *possédant* k *adjonctions est égal au nombre eulérien* $A(n,k)$.

En utilisant les dénombrements obtenus jusqu'ici on peut obtenir le nombre de fusions (adjonctions par lot) à niveau donné, ainsi que le nombre de suppressions à niveau donné, paramètres qui jouent un rôle essentiel dans l'évaluation du coût moyen d'une opération pour une implantation donnée.

Les histoires que nous considérerons sont de niveaux initial et final nuls, c'est à dire sont des histoires de $\mathbf{H}_{2n}$.

Une histoire de longueur $2n$ possédant une suppression de niveau initial k au "temps" i peut se décomposer en une histoire quelconque de $\mathbf{H}_{0,k;i}$ suivie par une suppression puis par une histoire quelconque de $\mathbf{H}_{k-1,0;2n-i-1}$. On en déduit la proposition:

Proposition 8: *Le nombre total de "suppressions à niveau k" (c'est-à-dire de niveau initial k) dans les histoires de* H_{2n} *vaut:*

$$\alpha_{n,k} = \sum_{j=0}^{n-k} (j+1)^k j! s_{n-j,k}.$$

A partir de cette expression, et en utilisant la série géneratrice double:

$$\alpha(t,z) = \sum_{n,k} \alpha_{n,k} t^k \frac{z^n}{n!}$$

on démontre la

Proposition 9: *La distribution des niveaux initiaux de suppressions dans les histoires de* H_{2n} *a pour moyenne:*

$$\mu_n = \frac{n+3}{4}$$

et pour variance:

$$V_n = \frac{(n-1)(5n^2+35n+144)}{432n} - \frac{1}{3n}(\overline{H}_n - 1)$$

Pour ce qui est des fusions, on démontre:

Proposition 10: *Le nombre total de l-adjonctions à niveau k dans* H_{2n} *vaut:*

$$\beta_{k,l;n} = \sum_{j=0}^{n-l-k} j^k j! s_{n-j,k+l}.$$

En d'autres termes, le nombre total d'adjonctions de niveau initial k, et de niveau final h vaut:

$$\gamma_{k,h;n} = \sum_{j=0}^{n-k} j^k j! s_{n-j,h}$$

De plus, le nombre total d'adjonctions à niveau k dans H_{2n} vaut:

$$\xi_{n,k} = \sum_{j=1}^{n-k-1} j^k j!(n-j) s_{n-j,k+1} + \delta_{0k} n!$$

où δ_{0k} vaut 1 si $k=0$, 0 sinon.

Enfin, le nombre total d'adjonctions de niveau final k dans H_{2n} vaut:

$$\eta_{n,k} = \sum_{j=0}^{n-k} j![(j+1)^k - j^k] s_{n-j,k}$$

On en déduit la

Proposition 11: *La distribution des niveaux initiaux d'adjonction dans les histoires de* H_{2n} *a pour moyenne:*

$$\mu_n = \frac{(n-1)(n-2)(5n+3)}{18n(n+1)}$$

et pour variance:

$$V_n = \frac{(n-2)(11n^5+271n^4+373n^3+185n^2-48n+72)}{1296n^2(n+1)^2} - \frac{2}{3(n+1)}(\overline{H}_n - \frac{3}{2})$$

(où $\overline{H}_n$ *est le n ième nombre harmonique).*

La distribution des niveaux finaux d'adjonction dans les histoires de H_{2n} *a pour moyenne:*

$$\mu_n = \frac{5n^3+24n^2+n+6}{18n(n+1)}$$

et pour variance:

$$V_n = \frac{(n-1)(11n^5+116n^4+811n^3+1690n^2-24n+144)}{1296n^2(n+1)^2} - \frac{2}{3(n+1)}(\overline{H}_n - 1)$$

Le profil d'une histoire, c'est à dire la distribution du nombre d'opérations à niveau donné, donne des indications sur l'évolution, au cours du temps, de la taille du fichier sur lequel portent les opérations.

Proposition 12: *Au cours des histoires de* H_{2n}, *le fichier sur lequel portent les opérations a pour taille moyenne:*

$$\mu_n = \frac{14n^3 + 15n^2 + +n+6}{18n(3n+1)}$$

La distribution des tailles a pour variance:

$$V_n = \frac{125n^6+1053n^5+8501n^4+2379n^3+14n^2+168n-144}{1296n^2(3n+1)^2} - \frac{4}{3(3n+1)}\overline{H}_n$$

Les dénombrements effectués permettent de comparer les coûts de suites d'opérations pour diverses implantations des files de priorité avec adjonctions par lot. Ainsi, par exemple, en tenant compte des coûts de fusions et de suppressions, on démontre:

Proposition 13: *Le coût moyen d'une opération d'une histoire de* H_{2n} *est:*
- *égal à* $\frac{n(n+1)}{2(3n+1)}$ *si la file est implantée sous forme de liste non triée*

- *inférieur à* $\frac{5n^3+24n^2+n+6}{18n(3n+1)}$ *si elle est implantée sous forme triée.*

Ainsi l'implantation liste triée est pres de deux fois plus efficace que l' implantation liste non triée, pour n grand.

Si l'on veut un critère asymptotiquement indépendant de n on peut rapporter ces coûts moyens à la taille moyenne d'une histoire de $\mathbf{H}_{2n}$, ce qui donne pour coût "intrinsèque" (asymptotique) d'une opération:

$\frac{9}{14} = 0.64$ si la file est implantée sous forme non triée

$\frac{5}{14} = 0.36$ si la file est implantée sous forme triée.

Réferences.

[Ch 81] CHENO L.: Profils limites d'histoires sur les dictionnaires et les files de priorité; application aux files binomiales, Thèse de Troisième Cycle, Orsay, (1981).

[CFFPV 80] CHENO L.,FLAJOLET P., FRANCON J., PUECH C., VUILLEMIN J.: Dynamic data structures: finite files, limiting profiles and variance analysis, in 18th Allerton Conf., Monticello, Ill., (1980), pp. 223-232.

[Co 74] COMTET L.: "Advanced Combinatorics", Reidel, (1974).

[Fl 79] FLAJOLET P.: Analyse d'algorithmes de manipulation d'arbres et de fichiers, Thèse d'Etat, Orsay, (1979); et *Cahiers du BURO*, 34-35, (1981), pp. 1-209.

[Fl 80] FLAJOLET P.: Combinatorial aspects of continued fractions, *Discrete Math.* , 32, (1980), pp. 125-161.

[FF 80] FLAJOLET P., FRANCON J.: Histoires de fichiers en réservoir borné, in 3 èmes Journées Algorithmiques, Nice, (1980).

[FFV 80] FLAJOLET P., FRANCON J., VUILLEMIN J.: Sequence of operations analysis for dynamic data structures, *Journal of Algorithms* , 1, (1980), pp. 111-141.

[FlP 81] FLAJOLET P., PUECH C.: Analyse de structures de données dynamiques et histoires de fichiers, *Questiio* , v.5, 1, (1981), pp.31-47.

[FlPV] FLAJOLET P., PUECH C., VUILLEMIN J.: The analysis of simple list structures, Rapport INRIA, (1983).

[Fr 78] FRANCON J.: Histoires de fichiers, *RAIRO Info. Théor.* , 12, (1978), pp. 49-67.

[Fr 79] FRANCON J.: Combinatoire des structures de données, Thèse d'Etat, Strasbourg, (1979).

[FrP 83] FRANCON J., PUECH C.: Permutations et files de priorité, Rapport LRI, (1983).

[Kn 68-73] KNUTH D.: "The Art of Computer Programming", Addison-Wesley, v.1-3, (1968-1973).

[Vu 80] VUILLEMIN J.: A unifying look at data structures, *CACM* , v.23, 4, (1980), pp.229-239.

PARTIALLY ORDERED SORTS IN ALGEBRAIC SPECIFICATIONS

Martin Gogolla
Abteilung Informatik, Universität Dortmund
Postfach 500500, D-4600 Dortmund 50

Abstract

Conventional algebraic specification techniques cannot express relationships between sorts formally. The approach presented here puts more structure into the specification by allowing a partial ordering on the set of sorts to describe that one sort is a subsort of another sort. This concept implies that one function can occur more than one time in the signature with different domains and codomains. The initial algebra semantics of our equational specifications with a partial ordering on the set of sorts are studied.

Key words

Abstract data type, algebraic specification, initial algebra semantics, equation, subsort, partial ordering, overloading, error and exception handling.

1. Introduction

Algebraic specification of data types is regarded today as an instrument of great promise for program developement. The first papers in this field [LZ 74 , Gu 75] date from the middle seventies and a large amount of work has been done since then. The mathematical foundations of this specification method [ADJ 78 , Eh 79 , WPPDB 80 , Li 82] as well as precise concepts of implementation and parametrization [EKMP 80 , EKTWW 81 , SW 82] have been studied and led to the developement of specification languages.
But by conventional algebraic specifications, relationships between sorts cannot be expressed formally. For example it is impossible to point out clearly in a specification that the natural numbers are included in the integers, which again are included in the rationals. In our approach this can be done straightforward. The set of sorts is classified by a partial ordering, which expresses that one sort is a subsort of another sort. This concept implies that one function can occur more than one time in the signature with different domains and codomains or - for short - that functions are overloaded. The main results are theorems concerning initial models in the spirit of [ADJ 78] and a method to treat errors in abstract data types.

The idea of structuring the set of sorts by a partial ordering can al= ready be found in [Go 78], but there are some difficulties with that approach. For example the usual relationship between the concepts of morphism and congruence - in the sense that a morphism induces a con= gruence and vice versa - is not valid there. Apart from this, the basic notions of signature, algebra and congruence and the philosophy of error and exception handling are different here. In [Go 78] disjoint ok and error subsorts are wanted, whereas we only introduce an ok sub= sort representing the ok values [GDLE 82]. Similar problems of struc= turing the set of sorts are also discussed in [Gu 83 , Bi 83] and the concept of a declaration to structure the sorts is taken up in [Wa 82, GE 83] .

2. The basic idea

The conventional algebraic specification technique presents some cir= cumstantialities if the data type to be specified includes substruc= tures, so called subtypes or subsorts.

Example 2.1

Consider a conventional algebraic specification for the integers, which have the natural numbers as a subtype.

```
      spec nat included in int - conventional version
      srts nat , int
      opns zero : ---> nat ;
           succ : nat ---> nat ;
           0 : ---> int ;
           _+1 : int ---> int ;
           _-1 : int ---> int ;
           mk : nat ---> int
      vars n : nat ; i : int
      eqns (i+1)-1 = (i-1)+1 = i ;
           mk(zero) = 0 ;
           mk(succ(n)) = mk(n)+1
      ceps
```

The fact that the natural numbers are included in the integers is only implicit by the conversion function mk. There is no formal relation between the sorts nat and int. Another lack of the specification is the fact that a term denoting a natural number does not denote an integer, but every natural number is an integer number and therefore an adequate notation should be found. ***

The approach presented here allows to classify the set of sorts by a partial ordering, which expresses that one sort is a subsort of another sort. This concept has a deep influence on our notion of sig= nature : it is possible and sometimes necessary that one function has many domains and codomains or - for short - functions are overloaded :

- If a function is defined on certain sorts, the same function must be defined on all subsorts of the given ones.
- If a function has a certain value sort, then the same function must also be seen as a function having a supersort of the given one.

For example if nat < int is in the partial ordering and we have _-_ : int x int ---> int, then _-_ : nat x nat ---> int has to be in the signature too. And if 0 : ---> nat is a function, the the same will hold for 0 : ---> int. The exact definitions will be given in the following chapter.

Example 2.2

Let us now look at the example again and present our specification.

```
spec nat included in int - subsort version
srts nat , int with nat < int
opns 0 : ---> nat ;
     _+1 : nat ---> nat ;
     _+1 : int ---> int ;
     _-1 : int ---> int
vars i : int
eqns (i+1)-1 = (i-1)+1 = i
ceps
```

The ordering nat < int indicates that every term denoting a natural number also denotes an integer number. Therefore 0 is also a constant of sort int and _+1 : nat ---> nat can also be seen as a function from nat to int. But it is neccessary to declare that _+1 is a function from int to int, because not every function from nat to nat is also a function from int to int, for example the factorial function. The main point here is the fact that terms of the form $0(+1)^n$ can be recognised as natural numbers looking only at the signature.

It is also possible to define functions from subsorts into arbitrary sorts or from arbitrary sorts into subsorts. For example we can now specify the factorial function and the square

_! : nat ---> nat

$\_^2$: int ---> nat

by giving the equations

$0! = 0+1$

$(n+1)! = (n+1)*(n!)$

$i^2 = i*i$

using a variable n of sort nat and the multiplication _*_ : int x int ---> int . Please note that the equations are well typed. For example the left hand side of the last equation is of sort nat and therefore also of sort int and this matches the sort of the right side. ***

3. Signatures, algebras and morphisms

Our notions of signature, algebra and morphism must take into account that the same function name can be defined for different domains or codomains and that the same elements can occur in different carriers. But giving the same name to different functions implies that the func= tions behave in a similar way. Furthermore different occurences of identical elements in different carriers are not distinguished.

Definition 3.1

A signature is a triple $(S,\leq,\Sigma)$, where

(1) S is a set (of sorts) ,

(2) $\leq$ is a partial ordering of S and

(3) $\Sigma=\langle\Sigma_{w,s}\rangle_{w\in S^*,s\in S}$ is an $S^*\times S$-indexed family of sets of operation symbols such that

(4) $w'\leq w$ and $s\leq s'$ implies $\Sigma_{w,s} \subseteq \Sigma_{w',s'}$.

- By a partial ordering we mean a reflexsive, transitive and anti= symmetric relation. If $s\leq s'$, then we say that s is a subsort of s' and s' is a supersort of s. $s<s'$ means $s\leq s'$ and $s\neq s'$. If $w=s_1...s_n$ and $w'=s_1'...s_n'$, $w\leq w'$ means $s_i \leq s_i'$ for $i=1,...,n$.
- The sets $\Sigma_{w,s}$ are arbitrary, so the same operation symbol may occur in different sets even with a different number of arguments.
- Condition (4) means the following : If an operation symbol σ has arity $s_1...s_n$ and sort s, then σ will also be defined on all sub= sorts $s_1'...s_n'$ of the arity $s_1...s_n$ and σ will also be a function symbol having a supersort s' of sort s. For example if we have nat<int and _-_ : int x int ---> int, then _-_ : nat x nat ---> int will also be a part of the signature. On the other hand if 0 : ---> nat is in the signature, then the same will hold for 0 : ---> int.
- We will abbreviate $(S,\leq,\Sigma)$ by Σ and define $\tilde{\Sigma}=\{\sigma^{w,s}|w\in S^*,s\in S,\sigma\in\Sigma_{w,s}\}$.

Example 3.2

We give a signature describing some operations on integer numbers. Let S be the set {nat,int,bool} and nat<int be the partial ordering on S. The operation symbols are denoted in the usual way :

0 : ---> nat

0 : ---> int

_+1 : nat ---> nat

_+1 : nat ---> int

_+1 : int ---> int

_-1 : nat ---> int

_-1 : int ---> int

false , true : ---> bool

_≡_ : nat x nat ---> bool

_≡_ : nat x int ---> bool

_≡_ : int x nat ---> bool

_≡_ : int x int ---> bool

The given family of operations symbols satisfies condition (4) of our signature definition. ***

It is quite troublesome to repeat all operation symbols of the sig= nature with appropriate domains and codomains. A shorter notation for a signature would be useful and therefore we define what the com= pletion of an arbitrary family of operation symbols means.

Definition 3.3

Let $(S,\leq,\Sigma)$ be a triple consisting of a set S, a partial ordering $\leq$ on S and an arbitrary $S^{*}\times S$-indexed family of sets Σ .

$comp(\Sigma) = \langle\, comp(\Sigma)_{w,s} \,\rangle_{w\in S^{*},s\in S}$ with $comp(\Sigma)_{w,s} = \bigcup_{w\leq w',s'\leq s} \Sigma_{w',s'}$

is called the completion of Σ.

- For any arbitrary family Σ the completion $(S,\leq,comp(\Sigma))$ will be a signature. It will be convenient not to repeat the same function symbol in all sets. When we give an arbitrary family Σ and we speak of the signature Σ, we will allways mean the completion of Σ.

Example 3.4

Let S with $\leq$ be the same as in example 3.2 and let Σ be following family of operation symbols.

0 : ---> nat

_+1 : nat ---> nat

_+1 : int ---> int

_-1 : int ---> int

false , true : ---> bool

_≡_ : int x int ---> bool

The completion of the above family of operation symbols is identical to the signature given in example 3.2. It is also the least family such that its completion yields that signature. Note that _+1 : nat ---> nat reflects some important information about the successor operation +1 and that we do not have _-1 : nat ---> nat. ***

Definition 3.5

Let signature Σ be given. A Σ-algebra is a tuple (A,F), where

(1) $A=\langle A_s\rangle_{s\varepsilon S}$ is an S-indexed family of sets such that

(2) $s\leq s'$ implies $A_s \subseteq A_{s'}$ and

(3) $F=\langle\sigma_A^{w,s}\rangle_{\sigma^{w,s}\varepsilon\tilde\Sigma}$ is a $\tilde\Sigma$-indexed family of functions, for every $\sigma^{w,s}\varepsilon\tilde\Sigma$ there is a function $\sigma_A^{w,s}$: A_w ---> A_s such that

(4) $\sigma\varepsilon\Sigma_{w,s}\cap\Sigma_{w',s'}$ and $a\varepsilon A_w\cap A_{w'}$ implies $\sigma_A^{w,s}(a)=\sigma_A^{w',s'}(a)$.

- If $w = s_1...s_n$ is given , then A_w means the product $A_{s_1} \times ... \times A_{s_n}$.
- Clause (2) requires that if s is a subsort of s', then the corresponding carrier A_s will be included in $A_{s'}$. Thus for example the natural numbers will be included in the integer numbers.
- Condition (4) especially expresses : if $w=w'=\lambda$, then $\sigma_A^{w,s}=\sigma_A^{w',s'}$. It will also guarantee that we can speak of the function σ_A . Especially if $\sigma\varepsilon\Sigma_{w,s}$, $w'\leq w$ and $s\leq s'$, which of course implies $\sigma\varepsilon\Sigma_{w',s'}$, $A_{w'} \subseteq A_w$ and $A_s \subseteq A_{s'}$, then $\sigma_A^{w,s}|_{A_{w'}} = \sigma_A^{w',s'}$. This assures for example that the addition on integers is compatible with the addition on rational numbers.

  But even if the sorts are unrelated condition (4) must be valid. For example if the same constant symbol c occurs in $\Sigma_{\lambda,s}$ and $\Sigma_{\lambda,s'}$ and neither $s\leq s'$ nor $s'\leq s$ holds, then $c_A^{\lambda,s}=c_A^{\lambda,s'}$ must be true. We do not think it is natural in such a case that $c_A^{\lambda,s}$ and $c_A^{\lambda,s'}$ evaluate to different elements. If different evaluations are wanted, then there should be different names in the signature. Of course the same applies to functions. If f is in $\Sigma_{w,s}\cap\Sigma_{w',s'}$ and a is in $A_w\cap A_{w'}$, then $f_A^{w,s}(a)$ and $f_A^{w',s'}(a)$ have to be equal, because giving the same name to a function from A_w to A_s and to a function from $A_{w'}$ to $A_{s'}$, expresses that there are similarities between the functions. These similarities are the requirement that the functions behave in the same way when applied to the same arguments.
- We abbreviate (A,F) by A and define $\tilde A = \bigcup_{s\varepsilon S} A_s$.

Example 3.6

Recall the signature given in example 3.2. Let A_{nat}, A_{int} and A_{bool} be the set of natural numbers, integer numbers and truth values, re= spectively. Let 0, +1 and -1 be the obvious functions and let ≡ be the equality predicate on integers. Then the described entities form an algebra in the sense of definition 3.5. ***

Definition 3.7

Let signature Σ and Σ-algebras A and B be given. A Σ-algebra morphism $f : A \dashrightarrow B$ is an S-indexed family of mappings $f=\langle f_s \rangle_{s\varepsilon S}$, each $f_s : A_s \dashrightarrow B_s$ such that

(1) if $\sigma^{w,s} \varepsilon \tilde{\Sigma}$ with $w = s_1 \ldots s_n$ and $a_i \varepsilon A_{s_i}$ for $i = 1,\ldots,n$, then
$f_s(\sigma_A^{w,s}(a_1,\ldots,a_n))=\sigma_B^{w,s}(f_{s_1}(a_1),\ldots,f_{s_n}(a_n))$ and

(2) if $a \varepsilon A_s \cap A_{s'}$, then $f_s(a)=f_{s'}(a)$.

- Condition (1) is the usual requirement that morphisms respect the operational structure.
- Clause (2) reflects that we do not want to distinguish between equal elements in different carrier sets. It especially holds for the case $s \leq s'$, because then $A_s \subseteq A_{s'}$.
  If condition (2) would be dropped, then a situation like the one depicted in the figure below is possible. But a mapping like this does not reflect the structure of the algebra A in the algebra B, which is the usual requirement for a morphism from A to B.

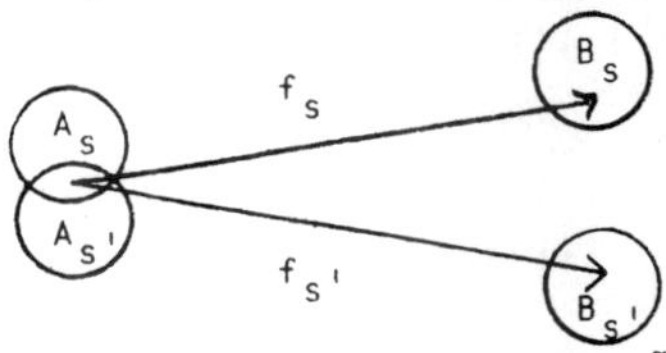

- A morphism $f : A \dashrightarrow B$ induces a mapping $\tilde{f} : \tilde{A} \dashrightarrow \tilde{B}$ that satis= fies $\tilde{f}(A_s) \subseteq B_s$ for $s \varepsilon S$.
- The category of all Σ-algebras with all morphisms between them is denoted by ALG_Σ.

Definition 3.8

Let signature Σ be given. The Σ-term algebra (T_Σ, F_Σ) is defined in the usual way.

$T_\Sigma = \langle T_s \rangle_{s\varepsilon S}$ is the least family of sets satisfying :

(1) $\Sigma_{\lambda,s} \subseteq T_s$ and

(2) $\sigma \varepsilon \Sigma_{w,s}$ with $w = s_1 \ldots s_n$ and $t_i \varepsilon T_{s_i}$ for $i = 1,\ldots,n$ implies
$\sigma(t_1,\ldots,t_n) \varepsilon T_s$.

$F_\Sigma = \langle \sigma_T^{w,s} \rangle_{\sigma^{w,s}\varepsilon\tilde{\Sigma}}$.

(3) $\sigma\varepsilon\Sigma_{\lambda,s}$ implies $\sigma_T^{\lambda,s} = \sigma$.

(4) $\sigma\varepsilon\Sigma_{w,s}$ with $w = s_1 \ldots s_n$ and $t_i\varepsilon T_{s_i}$ for $i = 1,\ldots,n$ implies
$\sigma_T^{w,s}(t_1,\ldots,t_n) = \sigma(t_1,\ldots,t_n)$.

- T_Σ is a Σ-algebra satisfying the conditions of our definition.
  (1) Let $s \leq s'$ be given. We have to show $T_s \subseteq T_{s'}$. Assume $t\varepsilon T_s$. If depth(t)=1, then $t=\sigma\varepsilon\Sigma_{\lambda,s}$. This implies $\sigma\varepsilon\Sigma_{\lambda,s'}$ and so $\sigma=t\varepsilon T_{s'}$. If depth(t)=n+1, then $t=\sigma(t_1,\ldots,t_n)$, $\sigma\varepsilon\Sigma_{w,s}$ with $w=s_1\ldots s_n$ and $t_i\varepsilon T_{s_i}$. This implies $\sigma\varepsilon\Sigma_{w,s'}$ and therefore $\sigma(t_1,\ldots,t_n)=t\varepsilon T_{s'}$.
  (2) Let $\sigma\varepsilon\Sigma_{w,s}\cap\Sigma_{w',s'}$ with $w=s_1\ldots s_n$ and $w'=s_1'\ldots s_n'$ and $t_i\varepsilon T_{s_i}\cap T_{s_i'}$ be given. We have to show : $\sigma_T^{w,s}(t_1,\ldots,t_n)=\sigma_T^{w',s'}(t_1,\ldots,t_n)$. But $\sigma_T^{w,s}(t_1,\ldots,t_n) = \sigma(t_1,\ldots,t_n) = \sigma_T^{w',s'}(t_1,\ldots,t_n)$ and if $w=w'=\lambda$, then $\sigma_T^{\lambda,s} = \sigma = \sigma_T^{\lambda,s'}$.
- We defined the term algebra in the standard way, but used in our examples a mix-fix notation for operation symbols. This does not present any difficulties as long as terms are put in parenthesis unequivocally.

Example 3.9

The term algebra of the signature of example 3.2 can be described by the following context-free productions :

<nat> ::= 0 | (<nat>)+1

<int> ::= 0 | (<int>)+1 | (<int>)-1

<bool> ::= false | true | (<int>)≡(<int>)

Of course we have L(<nat>) $\subseteq$ L(<int>). Therefore terms of the form $0(+1)^n$ are of sort nat and of sort int and cannot be parsed uniquely.

***

Theorem 3.10

Let signature Σ and Σ-algebra A be given. Then T_Σ is initial in ALG_Σ , i.e. there is a unique morphism $f : T_\Sigma \text{---}> A$.

Proof

We define $f = \langle f_s \rangle_{s\varepsilon S}$ in the usual way according to the structure of the terms.

$$f_s(t) = \begin{cases} \sigma_A^{\lambda,s} & \text{if } t=\sigma \text{ and } \sigma\varepsilon\Sigma_{\lambda,s} \\ \sigma_A^{w,s}(f_{s_1}(t_1),\ldots,f_{s_n}(t_n)) & \text{if } t=\sigma(t_1,\ldots,t_n)\text{ , }\sigma\varepsilon\Sigma_{w,s} \text{ with } w=s_1\ldots s_n \text{ and } t_i\varepsilon T_{s_i} \end{cases}$$

First we have to show that the definition is well-defined, because the choice of w is not unique. The following situation can occur :

$t = \sigma(t_1,\dots,t_n)$, $\sigma\varepsilon\Sigma_{w,s}\cap\Sigma_{w',s}$ with $w = s_1\dots s_n$, $w' = s_1'\dots s_n'$ and $t_i \ \varepsilon\ T_{s_i}\cap T_{s_i'}$. We have to prove that $\sigma_A^{w',s}(f_{s_1'}(t_1),\dots,f_{s_n'}(t_n)) = \sigma_A^{w,s}(f_{s_1}(t_1),\dots,f_{s_n}(t_n))$ is valid. But this is part of the proof for condition (2´) of our morphism definition :

Let $t\varepsilon T_s\cap T_{s'}$ be given. If depth(t)=1 , then t=σ and $\sigma\ \varepsilon\ \Sigma_{\lambda,s}\cap\Sigma_{\lambda,s'}$ and $f_s(t)=f_s(\sigma)=\sigma_A^{\lambda,s}=\sigma_A^{\lambda,s'}=f_{s'}(\sigma)=f_{s'}(t)$ is valid according to our defini= tion of algebra.

If depth(t)=n+1 , then $t=\sigma(t_1,\dots,t_n)$, $\sigma\varepsilon\Sigma_{w,s}\cap\Sigma_{w',s'}$ with $w=s_1\dots s_n$ and $w'=s_1'\dots s_n'$ and $t_i\epsilon T_{s_i}\cap T_{s_i'}$. According to the induction assumption $f_{s_i}(t_i)$ and $f_{s_i'}(t_i)$ are equal and therefore $f_{s_i}(t_i)=f_{s_i'}(t_i)\varepsilon A_{s_i}\cap A_{s_i'}$. Then the following equalities hold :

$$f_s(t) = f_s(\sigma(t_1,\dots,t_n)) = \sigma_A^{w,s}(f_{s_1}(t_1),\dots,f_{s_n}(t_n))$$
$$\overset{(*)}{=}\sigma_A^{w',s'}(f_{s_1'}(t\ ),\dots,f_{s_n'}(t\ )) = f_{s'}(\sigma(t_1,\dots,t_n)) = f_{s'}(t)\ .$$

(*) holds due to our definition of algebra. The proof that f respects the operations and its uniqueness property is analogous to the con= ventional case [ADJ 78]. q.e.d.

Example 3.11

The unique morphism f : T_Σ ---> A from the term algebra of example 3.9 into the algebra A of example 3.6 evaluates terms to the corresponding natural numbers, integer numbers and truth values, respectively. ***

4. Equations

Definition 4.1

Let signature Σ and Σ-algebra A be given. An S-indexed, pairwise dis= joint family of sets $V = \langle V_s \rangle_{s\varepsilon S}$ with each V_s disjoint from all $\Sigma_{w,s'}$ with $w\varepsilon S^*$ and $s'\varepsilon S$ denotes variables for Σ .

An assignment to (or interpretation of) the variables is an S-indexed family of mappings $I = \langle I_s \rangle_{s\varepsilon S}$, $I_s : V_s \text{ ---> } A_s$.

The extended signature (S,≤,Σ(V)) is the completion of $\langle\Sigma'_{w,s}\rangle_{w\varepsilon S^*,s\varepsilon S}$ with $\Sigma'_{w,s}$ = if w=λ then $\Sigma_{\lambda,s} \cup V_s$ else $\Sigma_{w,s}$ fi .

The result of applying the forgetful functor U : $ALG_{\Sigma(V)}$ ---> ALG_Σ to $T_{\Sigma(V)}$ is denoted by $T_\Sigma(V)$.

Lemma 4.2

Let signature Σ, variables V, Σ-algebra A and assignment I : V ---> A be given. Then there is a unique Σ-algebra morphism $I^\#$: $T_\Sigma(V)$ ---> A that extends I in the sense that $I(v)=I^\#(v)$ if vεV.

Proof

The Σ-algebra A can be made into a Σ(V)-algebra A_V by defining $v_A=I(v)$.

$T_{\Sigma(V)}$ is initial in $ALG_{\Sigma(V)}$ and therefore there is a unique morphism $f_V : T_{\Sigma(V)} \dashrightarrow A_V$. Then $U(f_V) : T_\Sigma(V) \dashrightarrow A$ is the unique morphism with $U : ALG_{\Sigma(V)} \dashrightarrow ALG_\Sigma$ the corresponding forgetful functor. q.e.d.

Definition 4.3

Let signature Σ, Σ-algebra A and an S-indexed family of relations $\equiv = \langle \equiv_s \rangle_{s\varepsilon S}$, $\equiv_s \subseteq A_s \times A_s$ be given. Let $\tilde{\equiv}$ denote the equivalence on $\tilde{A}$ generated by $\bigcup_{s\varepsilon S} \equiv_s$.

The family of relations $\equiv = \langle \equiv_s \rangle_{s\varepsilon S}$ is called an equivalence on A, iff $\tilde{\equiv}|_{A_s \times A_s} = \equiv_s$.

An equivalence $\equiv = \langle \equiv_s \rangle_{s\varepsilon S}$ is called a congruence on A, iff for all $\sigma\varepsilon\Sigma_{w,s}\cap\Sigma_{w',s'}$ with $w=s_1\ldots s_n$, $w'=s_1'\ldots s_n'$ and $a_i\varepsilon A_{s_i}$, $a_i'\varepsilon A_{s_i'}$ with $a_i\tilde{\equiv}a_i'$ for $i=1,\ldots,n$ $\sigma_A^{w,s}(a_1,\ldots,a_n)\tilde{\equiv}\sigma_A^{w',s'}(a_1',\ldots,a_n')$ is valid.

The factorisation $A/\equiv$ of an algebra by a congruence is defined in the following way :

$A/\equiv^- = \langle A/\equiv_s \rangle_{s\varepsilon S}$.

$A/\equiv_s = \{[a]|a\varepsilon A_s\}$ with $[a]=\{a'\varepsilon\tilde{A}|a\tilde{\equiv}a'\}$.

$F/\equiv = \langle \sigma_{A/\equiv}^{w,s} \rangle_{\sigma^{w,s}\varepsilon\tilde{\Sigma}}$.

$\sigma_{A/\equiv}^{w,s}([a_1],\ldots,[a_n]) = [\sigma_A^{w,s}(a_1',\ldots,a_n')]$ with

$w=s_1\ldots s_n$, $[a_i]\varepsilon A/\equiv_{s_i}$, $a_i'\varepsilon A_{s_i}$ and $[a_i]=[a_i']$.

- It is not sufficent to require each $\equiv_s$ to be an equivalence relation on $A_s \times A_s$. Consider the following example with sorts s and s' and operations

  a : ---> s   a : ---> s'

  b : ---> s   b : ---> s'

  Then it would be possible that a and b are equivalent under $\equiv_s$, but not under $\equiv_{s'}$: a $\equiv_s$ b and a $\not\equiv_{s'}$ b . But a case like this should be excluded.

- Also a weaker definition of congruence in the sense that "$a_i \equiv_{s_i} a_i'$ implies $\sigma_A^{w,s}(a_1,\ldots,a_n) \equiv_s \sigma_A^{w,s}(a_1',\ldots,a_n')$ with $w=s_1\ldots s_n$" does not work as well. Consider the following example with sorts s, s', s_1 and s_2 and operations

  a , b : ---> s

  a : ---> s_1

  b : ---> s_2

  c , d : ---> s'

  f : s_1 ---> s'

  f : s_2 ---> s'

and the algebra which is depicted below and where f(a)=c and f(b)=d is valid.

$A_s = \{ a , b \}$

$A_{s_1} = \{ a \}$ $A_{s_2} = \{ b \}$

$A_{s'} = \{ f(a)=c , d=f(b) \}$

Under the above weaker definition a congruence could then consist only of $a \equiv_s b$, but this would not imply $f(a)=c \equiv_{s'} d=f(b)$, which should be the case for a congruence.

- The factorisation $A/\equiv$ of an algebra by a congruence is a Σ-algebra satisfying our definition.
  (1) Let $s \leq s'$ be given. We have to show $A/\equiv_s \subseteq A/\equiv_{s'}$. If $[a] \varepsilon A/\equiv_s$, then there is an $a' \varepsilon A_s$ with $[a]=[a']$. But $a' \varepsilon A_s$ implies $a' \varepsilon A_{s'}$, because $s \leq s'$. Therefore $[a]=[a'] \varepsilon A/\equiv_{s'}$.
  (2) Let $\sigma \varepsilon \Sigma_{w,s} \cap \Sigma_{w',s'}$ be given. If $w=w'=\lambda$, then $\sigma^{\lambda,s}_{A/\equiv} = [\sigma^{\lambda,s}_A] = [\sigma^{\lambda,s'}_A] = \sigma^{\lambda,s'}_{A/\equiv}$.

  If $w=s_1 \ldots s_n$, $w'=s'_1 \ldots s'_n$ and $[b_i] \varepsilon A/\equiv_{s_i} \cap A/\equiv_{s'_i}$ for $i=1,\ldots,n$, then there are $a_i \varepsilon A_{s_i}$ and $a'_i \varepsilon A_{s'_i}$ with $[a_i] = [a'_i] = [b_i]$ for $i=1,\ldots,n$. Then the following equalities hold :

$$\sigma^{w,s}_{A/\equiv}([b_1],\ldots,[b_n]) = \sigma^{w,s}_{A/\equiv}([a_1],\ldots,[a_n]) =$$
$$[\sigma^{w,s}_A(a_1,\ldots,a_n)] \overset{(*)}{=} [\sigma^{w',s'}_A(a'_1,\ldots,a'_n)] =$$
$$\sigma^{w',s'}_{A/\equiv}([a'_1],\ldots,[a'_n]) = \sigma^{w',s'}_{A/\equiv}([b_1],\ldots,[b_n])$$

  (*) is valid due to our definition of congruence.

- If an arbitrary family of relations on an algebra is given, then there is allways a least congruence containing the family. It is called the congruence generated by this family of relations. This is the same as in the conventional case [ADJ 78].

<u>Lemma 4.4</u>

Let signature Σ and Σ-algebras A and B be given.

(1) A morphism f : A ---> B induces a congruence $\equiv$ on A.

(2) A congruence $\equiv$ on A induces an epimorphism f : A ---> A/$\equiv$.

<u>Proof</u>

(1) As usual we define $\equiv = \langle \equiv_s \rangle_{s \varepsilon S}$ by $a \equiv_s a'$ iff $f_s(a) =_s f(a')$. Assume $\equiv$ is not an equivalence on A. Then there is a sort s with $\equiv_s$ a proper subset of $\tilde{\equiv}|_{A_s \times A_s}$ and there are $a,a' \varepsilon A_s$ with $a \tilde{\equiv} a'$ and not $a \equiv_s a'$. But $\tilde{\equiv}$ is the equivalence generated by $\equiv$ and this implies $f_s(a)=f_s(a')$. Therefore $a \equiv_s a'$.

The congruence property is valid as well. Let $\sigma \in \Sigma_{w,s} \cap \Sigma_{w',s'}$ with $w = s_1 \ldots s_n$ and $w' = s_1' \ldots s_n'$ and $a_i \in A_{s_i}$, $a_i' \in A_{s_i'}$ with $f_{s_i}(a_i) = f_{s_i'}(a_i')$ for $i = 1, \ldots, n$ be given. Then the following equalities are valid :

$f_s(\sigma_A^{w,s}(a_1, \ldots, a_n) = \sigma_B^{w,s}(f_{s_1}(a_1), \ldots, f_{s_n}(a_n)) =$

$\sigma_B^{w,s}(f_{s_1'}(a_1'), \ldots, f_{s_n'}(a_n')) = \sigma_B^{w',s'}(f_{s_1'}(a_1'), \ldots, f_{s_n'}(a_n')) =$

$f_{s'}(\sigma_A^{w',s'}(a_1', \ldots, a_n'))$.

This implies $\sigma_A^{w,s}(a_1, \ldots, a_n) \tilde{\equiv} \sigma_A^{w',s'}(a_1', \ldots, a_n')$.

(2) We define $f = \langle f_s \rangle_{s \in S}$ by $f_s(a) = [a]$ as usual.

f respects the operational structure :

$f_s(\sigma_A^{w,s}(a_1, \ldots, a_n)) = [\sigma_A^{w,s}(a_1, \ldots, a_n)] = \sigma_{A/\equiv}^{w,s}([a_1], \ldots, [a_n]) =$

$\sigma_{A/\equiv}^{w,s}(f_{s_1}(a_1), \ldots, f_{s_n}(a_n))$

Condition (2) of our morphism definition is valid as well : $a \in A_s \cap A_{s'}$ implies $[a] \in A/\equiv_s \cap A/\equiv_{s'}$. Therefore $f_s(a) = [a] = f_{s'}(a)$ is true.

Furthermore f is surjective : Let $[a] \in A/\equiv_s$ be given. Then there is an $a' \in A_s$ with $[a] = [a']$ and so $f_s(a') = [a'] = [a]$. q.e.d.

<u>Definition 4.5</u>

Let signature Σ, variables V, $T_\Sigma(V)$ and Σ-algebra A be given. An <u>equation</u> is a tuple $l = r$ with $l, r \in T_\Sigma(V)_s$. An equation $l = r$ is <u>true</u> in A, iff for all assignments $I : V \longrightarrow A$ $I^\#(l) = I^\#(r)$.

Let E be a set of equations.

$E(T_\Sigma) = \{ \langle I^\#(l), I^\#(r) \rangle \mid l = r \in E \text{ and } I : V \longrightarrow T_\Sigma \text{ assignment} \}$

$\equiv_E$ denotes the congruence generated by $E(T_\Sigma)$.

<u>Example 4.6</u>

We give equations for the signature of example 3.2 using variables i and j of sort int and n of sort nat.

(i+1)-1 = i

(i-1)+1 = i

0≡0 = true

0≡n+1 = false

n+1≡0 = false

i+1≡j+1 = i≡j ***

<u>Theorem 4.7</u>

Let signature Σ, variables V and equations E be given and let $T_{\Sigma,E}$ denote the factorisation of T_Σ by $\equiv_E$. Then $T_{\Sigma,E}$ is initial in the category of all Σ-algebras satisfying E.

Proof

We know T_Σ is initial in the category of all Σ-algebras and therefore we have the following situation with unique morphisms f and g for a given Σ-algebra satisfying E.

f(t)=[t]

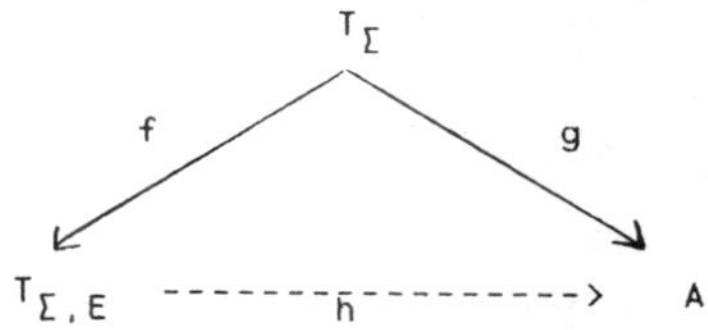

We define h([t]) = g(t). h is independant of representatives, it respects the operations and is unique. The proof is analogous to the conventional case [ADJ 78]. So we only have to prove condition (2) of our morphism definition is valid.

Let $[t] \varepsilon T/\equiv_s \cap T/\equiv_{s'}$ be given. Then $h_s([t]) = g_s(t) = g_{s'}(t) = h_{s'}([t])$ is true.

q.e.d.

Example 4.8

The quotient of the term algebra described in example 3.9 by the con= gruence $\equiv_E$ induced by the equations of example 4.6 is isomorphic to the algebra A of example 3.6 . Please note that the equality predicate on integers has been specified without hidden functions. This cannot be done by the conventional algebraic specification technique. ***

5. Error and exception handling

A quite useful application of our concepts is error and exception handling in abstract data types. One can introduce for each sort s a subsort s_{ok} representing only the ok values of the data type and classify the functions into those preserving ok values and those introducing errors when applied to ok elements.

Example 5.1

spec nat with error handling

srts nat, nat_{ok} with nat_{ok} < nat

opns 0 : ---> nat_{ok} ;

_+1 : nat_{ok} ---> nat_{ok} ;

_+1 : nat ---> nat ;

_-1 : nat ---> nat ;

error : ---> nat

vars n : nat_{ok}

<u>eqns</u> (n+1)-1 = n ;

0-1 = error ;

error+1 = error-1 = error

<u>ceps</u>

The specified data type consists of the natural numbers and exactly one error element. The main point here is that the variable n has the sort nat_{ok} and is actualized only by terms of the form $0(+1)^n$, which represent the ok values. 0 and +1 are functions preserving ok elements, -1 is an error introduction function and error of course an error con= stant. ***

The details of this approach can be found in [GDLE 82] , where a slightly different and easier notation is used. It is also shown there that this concept allows all forms of error handling : error intro= duction, error propagation and error recovery.

Acknowledgements

Thanks to Hans-Dieter Ehrich, Udo Lipeck, Axel Poigne and Klaus Drosten for fruitful discussions and constructive criticism.

References

ADJ 78 Goguen,J.A./Thatcher,J.W./Wagner,E.G. : An Initial Algebra Approach to the Specification, Correctness and Implementation of Abstract Data Types. Current Trends in Programming Metho- dology, Vol. IV (R.T.Yeh, ed.). Prentice Hall, Englewood Cliffs, 1978, pp. 80-149.

Bi 83 Bidoit,M.: Algebraic Specification of Exception Handling and Error Recovery in Abstract Data Types. 2nd Workshop on Theory and Applications of Abstract Data Types. Passau 1983.

Eh 79 Ehrich,H.-D.: On the Theory of Specification, Implementation and Parametrization of Abstract Data Types. Journal ACM, Vol.29, 1982, pp. 206 - 227.

EKMP 80 Ehrig,H./Kreowski,H.-J./Mahr,B./Padawitz,P.: Algebraic Imple= mentation of Abstract Data Types. Theoretical Computer Science, Vol. 20, 1982, pp. 209-263.

EKTWW 81 Ehrig,H./Kreowski,H.-J./Thatcher,J.W./Wagner,E.G./Wright,J.B.: Parameter Passing in Algebraic Specification Languages. Proc. Workshop on Program Specification, Aarhus 1981, LNCS 134, Berlin 1982, pp. 322-369.

GDLE 82 Gogolla,M./Drosten,K./Lipeck,U./Ehrich,H.D.: Algebraic and Operational Semantics of Exceptions and Errors. Proceedings 6th GI-Conference Theoretical Computer Science, Dortmund 1983, LNCS 145, pp. 141-151. Also : Forschungsbericht Nr. 140, 1982, Abteilung Informatik, Universitaet Dortmund.

GE 83 Gogolla,M./Ehrich,H.D.: Algebraic Specification with Subsorts Using Declarations. Bulletin of the EATCS, Vol. 21, October 1983.

Go 78 Goguen,J.A.: Order Sorted Algebras : Exception and Error sorts, Coercions and Overloaded Operators. Semantics and Theory of Computation Report No. 14, University of California, Los Angeles, Dec. 1978.

Gu 83 Guiho,G.: Multioperator Algebras. 2nd Workshop on Theory and Applications of Abstract Data Types. Passau 1983.

Gu 75 Guttag,J.V.: The Specification and Application to Programming of Abstract Data Types. Techn. Report CSRG-59, Univ. of Toronto, 1975.

Li 82 Lipeck,U.: Ein algebraischer Kalkuel fuer einen strukturier= ten Entwurf von Datenabstraktionen (Dissertation). For= schungsbericht Nr. 148, 1982, Abteilung Informatik, Universi= taet Dortmund.

LZ 74 Liskov,B./Zilles,S.: Programming with Abstract Data Types. SIGPLAN Notices Vol. 9, No. 4, April 1974, pp. 50-59.

SW 82 Sanella,D./Wirsing,M.: Implementation of Parametrized Speci= fications. Proc. 9th ICALP, LNCS 140, 1982, pp. 473-488.

Wa 82 Wadge,W.W.: Classified Algebras. University of Warwick, Theory of Computation, Report No. 46, October 1982.

WPPDB 80 Wirsing,M. / Pepper,P. / Partsch,H. / Dosch,W./ Broy,M. : On Hierachies of Abstract Data Types. Bericht TUM-I8007,Institut fuer Informatik, Technische Univ. Muenchen, Mai 1980.

NUMERATION MODELS OF λ-CALCULUS (EXTENDED ABSTRACT)

A. Kanda
Department of Computer Science
University of British Columbia
Vancouver, B.C. V6T 1W5
Canada

Abstract

Models of λ-calculus have been studied by Scott [7]. In these studies, finding solutions to the isomorphic equation $S \cong [S \to S]$ where $[S \to S]$ is a certain set of functions from S to S is the main issue. In this paper, we present an example of such solutions which fail to be a model of λ-calculus. This example indicates the necessity of careful consideration of the syntax of λ-calculus, especially for the study of constructive models of λ-calculus. Taking this into account, we axiomatically show when a numeration of Ersov [3] forms a model of λ-calculus. This serves as a general framework for countable models of λ-calculus. Various examples of such numerations are studied. An algebraic characterization of this class of numerations is also given.

§1. λ-Calculus

The λ-calculus developed by Church [2] is a formal system designed to study equivalence of functions composed from other functions in certain primitive ways. In this section, we briefly overview this calculus. As mentioned in the abstract, since the syntax of λ-calculus plays an important role in the construction of numeration models, we present the syntax in quite a detailed manner.

We start with assuming a countable set V of variables.

Definition 1.1 (λ-Terms)

1. If x is a variable in V, then x is a λ-term.
2. If M and N are λ-terms then so is (MN).
3. If x is a variable and M is a λ-term then so is (λx.M). □

Definition 1.2 (Occurrence)

We define a binary relation occurs over λ-terms as follows:

1. X occurs in X.
2. If X occurs in M or in N, then X occurs in (MN).
3. If X occurs in M, then for every variable y, X occurs in (λy.M). □

We write X ∢ Y for "X occurs in Y".

Definition 1.3 (Free and bound variables)

An occurrence of a variable x in M is bound if it is inside a part of M of the form $\lambda x.M$, otherwise it is free. We say x is free in Y if it has a free occurrence in Y. □

Definition 1.4 (Substitution)

For any terms M, N and any variable x, the result M[x:=N] of substituting N for each free occurrence of x in M (and changing bound variables to avoid clashes) is defined.

In λ-calculus, each λ-term is considered to be a representation for a function and the following three reduction rules are to establish equivalence of functions:

Reduction Rules

$(\alpha):(\lambda x.M) \rightarrow (\lambda y.M[x:=y])$ x is not bound in M and y∤M

$(\beta):((\lambda x.M)N) \rightarrow M[x:=N]$ $(\eta):(\lambda x.Mx) \rightarrow M$ x∤M □

§2. Reflexive Sets and Models of λ-Calculus

A reflexive set is a set which is a solution of the following isomorphic equation: $S \cong [S \rightarrow S]$ where $[S \rightarrow S]$ is a set of functions from S to S.

Given a reflexive set S with an isomorphism pair $(\Phi:S \rightarrow [S \rightarrow S],$ $\Psi:[S \rightarrow S] \rightarrow S)$, we build a model of λ-calculus as follows:

--An environment is a function $\rho:V \rightarrow S$. We denote the set of all environments by Env. Updating an environment is an operation
Upd : Env x V x S → Env such that:

$$\text{Upd}(\rho,x,s)(v) := \underline{\text{if}}\ x = v\ \underline{\text{then}}\ s\ \underline{\text{else}}\ \rho(v).$$

We write $\rho[x:=s]$ for $\text{Upd}(\rho,x,s)$.

--An interpretation is a function $\xi:T \times \text{Env} \rightarrow S$ defined by:

$$\xi(x,\rho) = \rho(x)$$
$$\xi((MN),\rho) = \Phi(\xi(M,\rho))(\xi(N,\rho))$$
$$\xi((\lambda x.M),\rho) = \Psi(\lambda s \in S.\xi(M,\rho[x:=s]))$$

It is important to notice that ξ is well-defined only when $\lambda s \in S.\xi(M,\rho[x:=s]) \in [S \rightarrow S]$. If this condition is satisfied we say S is a λ-Admissible reflexive set.

--Now we can establish the following theorem which states that every λ-admissible reflexive set forms a model of λ-calculus.

Theorem 2.1

(1) $\xi((\lambda x.M),\rho) = \xi((\lambda y.M[x:=y]),\rho)$ provided that x is not bound in M and $y \notin M$.

(2) $\xi(((\lambda x.M)N),\rho) = \xi(M[x:=N],\rho)$

(3) $\xi((\lambda x.Mx),\rho) = \xi(M,\rho)$ provided $x \notin M$. □

The term model of Church and lattice theoretic model of Scott are examples of λ-admissible reflexive sets. λ-admissibility is an important part of building models of λ-calculus which takes care of the interrelation between syntax and semantics. In fact, we can easily show examples of reflexive sets which are not models of λ-calculus.

Let [N→N] be the set of all total recursive functions from N to N. Then we have an isomorphism

$$N \cong [N \to N]$$

for we know that [N→N] is a countable set. It is well-known that this isomorphism can never be "effective". Due to this non-constructiveness,

$$\lambda n \in N.\xi(M,\rho[x:=N])$$

fails to be in [N→N]. Thus the reflexive set $N \cong [N \to N]$ does not form a model of λ-calculus.

This example indicates that finding reflexive sets is not difficult but what is not easy is finding reflexive sets which are λ-admissible. Also this indicates that careful treatment of the syntax of λ-calculus is important in building models of λ-calculus, especially when it comes to constructive models of λ-calculus. A detailed analysis of when a reflexive set is λ-admissible was done by Coppo et.al. [10].

It ought to be stressed that, in this section, we have established a general result that every λ-admissible reflexive set forms a model of λ-calculus. Thus building a model of λ-calculus now amounts to building a λ-admissible reflexive set.

In the rest of the paper, we develop a general framework for building models of λ-calculus with the effectiveness constraint.

§3. Gödelized λ-calculus

By Gödel numbering variables and λ-terms we can realize constructions of λ-calculus as recursive functions. It is easy to establish computable bijections $\upsilon: N \to V$ and $\tau: N \to T$ where T is the set of all λ-terms. The syntactic constructions of λ-calculus corresponds to the following system of recursive functions:

is-var(n) = <u>true</u> if $\tau(n)\varepsilon V$
<u>false</u> otherwise

is-apply(n) = <u>true</u> if $\tau(n) = (MN)$ for some $M,N\in T$
<u>false</u> otherwise

is-abst(n) = <u>true</u> if $\tau(n) = (\lambda x.M)$ for some $x\in V$ and $M\in T$
<u>false</u> otherwise

$\tau(\text{inc}(n)) = \nu(n)$

$\nu(\text{var}(n)) = \tau(n)$ if is-var(n)

is-apply(n) => τ(apply(rator(n),rand(n))) = $\tau(n)$

is-abst(n) => τ(abst(bound(n),body(n))) = $\tau(n)$

Conversion rules of λ-calculus are realizable in the following sense:

<u>Proposition 3.2</u>

There are recursive functions α,β,η s.t.

(1) $\alpha(n,m)$ = <u>true</u> if $\tau(n) \overset{\alpha}{=>} \tau(m)$
<u>false</u> otherwise

(2) $\beta(n,m)$ = <u>true</u> if $\tau(n) \overset{\beta}{=>} \tau(m)$
<u>false</u> otherwise

(3) $\eta(n,m)$ = <u>true</u> if $\tau(n) \overset{\eta}{=>} (m)$
<u>false</u> otherwise □

§4. Numerated Reflexive Sets

In §2, we generalized (abstracted) various mathematical structures which satisfy the equation $S\cong[S\to S]$ as reflexive sets and studied how reflexive sets form models of λ-calculus. Similar study for non-extensional λ-calculus was done by several authors (see Meyer [6] for example). In this section we make abstraction of constructive sets which satisfy $S\cong[S\to S]$ as numerated reflexive sets and in the next section, we study how a numerated reflexive set forms a model of λ-calculus.

<u>Definition 4.1</u> (<u>Numeration</u>) (Ersov [3])

A <u>numeration</u> γ is a pair (μ,S) where μ is a surjection from N to S. Let $\gamma_1 = (\mu_1,S_1)$ and $\gamma_2 = (\mu_2,S_2)$ be numerations. A morphism from γ_1 to γ_2 is a function $f:S_1\to S_2$ such that for some recursive function r_f, $f\cdot\mu_1 = \mu_2\cdot r_f$. Such an r_f is called a <u>realization</u> of f w.r.t. μ_1 and μ_2. If r_f is primitive recursive, we say the morphism f is <u>primitive</u>. □

<u>Proposition 4.2</u> (Ersov [3])

Numerations and morphisms among them form a category. □

If $\mu(n) = \mu(m)$ we write $n =_\mu m$. Obviously $=_\mu$ is an equivalence relation on N.

Definition 4.3

Let $\gamma_1 = (\mu_1, S_1)$ and $\gamma_2 = (\mu_2, S_2)$ be numerations. A numeration $\gamma = (\mu, \mathrm{Hom}(\gamma_1, \gamma_2))$ is admissible wrt γ_1 and γ_2 iff there are recursive functions υ, realize, and numerate s.t.

$\mu(n)(\mu_1(m)) = \mu_2(\upsilon(n,m))$

$r_{\mu(n)} = \phi_{\mathrm{realize}(n)}$

if ϕ_n is a realization of $f:\gamma_1 \to \gamma_2$ then $\mu(\mathrm{numerate}(n)) = f$.

$<\phi_i>$ is a Gödel numbering of partial recursive functions. If such a γ exists, we write $(\gamma_1 \to \gamma_2) = ((\mu_1 \to \mu_2), (S_1 \to S_2))$ to denote it. □

The following theorem states that there is only one admissible numeration of $\mathrm{Hom}(\gamma_1, \gamma_2)$.

Theorem 4.4

All admissible numerations of $\mathrm{Hom}(\gamma_1, \gamma_2)$ are recursively isomorphic. □

Definition 4.5

A numerated reflexive set (NRS) is a numeration $\gamma = (\mu, S)$ satisfying:

(1) An admissible numeration $(\gamma \to \gamma)$ exists

(2) $\gamma \cong (\gamma \to \gamma)$ in the category of numerations. □

Lemma 4.6 No non trivial NRS is finite. □

§5. Numeration Models of λ-Calculus

From an NRS, we build a model of λ-calculus as follows:

Definition 5.1

Let (ν, V) be the bijection discussed in §2 and let (μ, S) be an NRS. Let $(\Psi: S \to (S \to S), \Psi: (S \to S) \to S)$ be an isomorphism pair. An environment is a primitive morphism from (ν, V) to (μ, S). We write Env to denote the set of all environments. □

Since every λ-term has only finitely many occurrences of variables, it is sufficient to consider only primitive morphisms from (ν, V) to (μ, S).

The next theorem states that updating environments has a realization:

Theorem 5.2

(1) For each $\rho \in Env$, $x \in V$ and $s \in S$, $\rho[x:=s] \in Env$.

(2) There is a recursive function Update:$N^3 \to N$ s.t. if $r_\rho = \psi_i$ then

$$\psi_{Update(i,n,m)} = r_{\rho[\nu(n):=\mu(m)]},$$

where $<\psi_i>$ is a Gödel numbering of primitive recursive functions. □

We introduce a numeration (σ, Env) by:

$$\sigma_i = \rho \text{ s.t. } r_\rho = \psi_i.$$

As for the nonconstructive case, the interpretation function can be defined by:

$$\xi(\tau(n),\sigma_i) := \underline{\text{if}}\ \text{is-var}(n)\ \underline{\text{then}}\ \sigma_i(\tau(n))$$
$$\underline{\text{else}}\ \underline{\text{if}}\ \text{is-apply}(n)\ \underline{\text{then}}$$
$$\Phi(\xi(\tau(\text{rator}(n)),\sigma_i))(\xi(\tau(\text{rand}(n)),\sigma_i))$$
$$\underline{\text{else}}\ \underline{\text{if}}\ \text{is-abst}(n)\ \underline{\text{then}}$$
$$\Psi(\lambda s \in S.\xi(\tau(\text{body}(n)),\sigma_i[\tau(\text{bound}):=s]))$$

The well-definedness of ξ can be established as a part of the proof of the following theorem:

Theorem 5.3

The following recursive function realizes ξ:

$$e(n,i) := \underline{\text{if}}\ \text{is-var}(n)\ \underline{\text{then}}\ \psi_i(\text{var}(n))$$
$$\underline{\text{else}}\ \underline{\text{if}}\ \text{is-apply}(n)\ \underline{\text{then}}$$
$$\upsilon(r_\Phi \cdot e(\text{rator}(n),i),\ e(\text{rand}(n),i))$$
$$\underline{\text{else}}\ \underline{\text{if}}\ \text{is-abst}(n)\ \underline{\text{then}}$$
$$r_\Psi(\text{numerate}\cdot \text{ab}(n,i))$$

where ab is a recursive function satisfying:

$$\phi_{ab(n,i)}(m) = e(\text{body}(n),\ \text{Update}(i,\text{bound}(n),m)).$$

Proof

By induction on the structure of terms we will show:

$$\mu(e(n,i)) = \xi(\tau(n),\sigma_i).$$

For saving space, we prove only the is-abst(n)=true case of the induction step. The induction base and is-apply(n)=true case can be proved easily.

$$\mu(e(n,i)) = \mu(r_\Psi(\text{numerate}(\text{ab}(n,i))))$$
$$= \Psi((\mu \to \mu)(\text{numerate}\cdot \text{ab}(n,i)))$$

But $\lambda s \in S.\xi(\tau(\text{body}(n)),\sigma_i[\tau(\text{bound}(n)):=s])$ is realized by $\phi_{ab(n,i)} = \lambda m \in N.e(\text{body}(n),\ \text{Update}(i,\text{bound}(n),m))$ because we have:

$\mu(\phi_{ab(n,i)}(k))$
$= \mu(e(body(n), Update(i,bound(n),k)))$
$= \xi(\tau(body(n)),\sigma_i[bound(n):=\mu(k)])$ (Induction Hypothesis)
$= (\lambda s\in S.\xi(\tau(body(n)),\sigma_i[\tau(bound(n):=s]))(\mu(k))$.

Thus by the admissibility of $(\mu\to\mu)$ we have:

$(\mu\to\mu)(numerate\cdot ab(n,i)) =$
$\lambda s\in S.\xi(\tau(body(n)),\sigma_i[bound(n):=s])$. ----- (I)

Hence

$\mu(e(n,i)) = \Psi(\lambda s\in S.\xi(\tau(body(n)),\sigma_i[bound(n):=s]))$
$= \xi(\tau(n),\sigma_i)$. □

It is important to notice that (I) establishes:

$$\lambda s\in S.\xi(\tau(body(n)),\sigma_i \; bound(n):=s\;) \in (S\to S).$$

Therefore the interpretation function ξ is well-defined. This implies that the admissibility of a NRS coincides with the λ-admissibility of reflexive sets discussed in §2.

<u>Theorem 5.4</u>

(1) If $\alpha(m,n)$ = <u>true</u> then
$\xi(\tau(n),\sigma_i) = \xi(\tau(m),\sigma_i)$

(2) If $\beta(m,n)$ = <u>true</u> then
$\xi(\tau(n),\sigma_i) = \xi(\tau(m),\sigma_i)$

(3) If $\eta(m,n)$ = <u>true</u> then
$\xi(\tau(n),\sigma_i) = \xi(\tau(m),\sigma_i)$ □

In λ-calculus, we have a fixed-point combinator Y given by:

$$Y \equiv \lambda f.((\lambda x.f(xx))(\lambda x.f(xx))).$$

By β-reduction we have:

$$Y(f) \overset{\beta}{\to} (\lambda x.f(xx))(\lambda x.f(xx)) \overset{\beta}{\to} f(\lambda x.f(xx))(\lambda x.f(xx)).$$

Thus $\xi((Yf),\rho) = \xi((f(Yf)),\rho)$
$= \Phi((\xi(f,\rho))(\xi(Yf),\rho))$ for all $\rho\in Env$.

This indicates the following fixed-point theorem of a NRS.

<u>Theorem 5.5</u> (<u>The Fixed-point Theorem</u>)

If $\gamma = (\mu,S)$ is a numerated reflexive set then there is a recursive function fix s.t.

$$(\mu\to\mu)(n)(\mu(fix(n))) = \mu(fix(n)).$$ □

It can be shown that whenever a numeration $\mu\mapsto\mu:N\to\mathrm{Hom}(\gamma,\gamma)$ is admissible it satisfies the fixed-point theorem. Even though 5.5 is a special case of this general result, it is interesting because it is obtained through proof theory of λ-calculus.

Remark We have established that in order to show a numeration forms a model of λ-calculus, it is sufficient to show that the numeration is a NRS. It is important to notice that characterization of a NRS does not explicitly refer to the syntax of λ-calculus at all.

§6. Examples of Numerated Reflexive Sets

(Example) We show an order theoretic NRS. We form an effective reflexive set and directed indexing as an NRS. For details see Kanda [4], [5].

A domain is a partially ordered set $(X,<)$ such that

(1) For every subset $Z\subset X$, if Z has an upper bound then the least upper bound (lub) $\bigsqcup Z$ exists

(2) The set B_D of compact elements of X is countable

(3) For every element $x\in X$, $B_x = \{b\in B \mid b<x\}$ is directed and $x = \bigsqcup B_x$.

Let $\varepsilon:N\to B_D$ be a numeration. (X,ε) is an effectively given domain if there is a pair (b,ℓ) of recursive predicates satisfying:

$$b(x) \leftrightarrow \varepsilon(f_p(x)) \text{ has upper bound}$$

$$\ell(x,k) \leftrightarrow \varepsilon(k) = \bigsqcup \varepsilon(f_p(x))$$

where f_p is the standard enumeration of finite subsets of N. An element $x\in X$ is computable w.r.t. ε if for some recursively enumerable set W, $\varepsilon(W)$ is directed and $x = \bigsqcup \varepsilon(W)$. $\mathrm{Comp}(x,\varepsilon)$ denotes the set of all computable elements of (X,ε).

For every effectively given domain (X,ε) there is a recursive function $d_\varepsilon:N\to N$ s.t. for every $j\in N$, $\varepsilon(W_{d_\varepsilon(j)})$ is directed and if $\varepsilon(W_i)$ is directed then $\bigsqcup\varepsilon(W_i) = \bigsqcup\varepsilon(W_{d_\varepsilon(i)})$. This function gives us a numeration $\delta_\varepsilon:N\to\mathrm{Comp}(X,\varepsilon)$ defined by:

$$\delta_\varepsilon(i) = \bigsqcup\varepsilon(W_{d_\varepsilon(i)}).$$

Given effectively given domains (X,ε) and (X',ε'), let $[X\to X']$ be the set of all functions, called continuous functions, $f:X\to X'$ which preserve the lub of directed subsets, (i.e. if $D\subset X$ is directed then $f(D) = \{f(x) \mid x\in D\}$ is directed and $f(\bigsqcup D) = \bigsqcup f(D)$) with the following partial ordering: for $f,g\in[X\to X']$,

$$f<g \text{ iff } f(x)<g(x) \text{ for all } x\in X.$$

It is well-known that $[X \to X']$ is a domain where

$B_{[X\to X]}$ = the set of all possible finite joins of the step functions $[b,b']:X\to X'$ s.t. $b \in B_X$, $b' \in B_X{}'$ and $[b,b'](x) :=$ <u>if</u> $b<x$ then b' else $\bot$ where $\bot = \bigsqcup \phi$.

Let $(\varepsilon\to\varepsilon'):N\to B_{[X\to X']}$ be the following numeration:

$(\varepsilon\to\varepsilon')(n) :=$ <u>if</u> $\sigma(n)$ has a lub <u>then</u> $\bigsqcup \sigma(n)$ <u>else</u>

$\sigma(n) = \{[\varepsilon(i),\varepsilon'(j)] \mid (i,j) \in Pr(n)\}$

Pr: standard enumeration of finite subsets of NxN.

It is known that if (X,ε) and (X',ε') are effectively given domains then $([X\to X'],[\varepsilon\to\varepsilon'])$ is also an effectively given domain.

$f:X\to X'$ is <u>computable</u> w.r.t. $(\varepsilon,\varepsilon')$ iff $f\in Comp([X\to X'],[\varepsilon\to\varepsilon'])$.

<u>Proposition 6.3</u> (Weihranch & Schafer [8], Streicher [9])

Let (X,ε) and (X',ε') be effectively given domains. $f:X\to X'$ is computable w.r.t. $(\varepsilon,\varepsilon')$ iff $f|Comp(X',\varepsilon')$ is a morphism from $(\delta_\varepsilon, Comp(X,\varepsilon))$ to $(\delta_{\varepsilon'}, Comp(X',\varepsilon'))$. □

This theorem is a generalization of Myhill-Shefferdson theorem.

Now we are ready to build a constructive reflexive set. Let (X_0,ε_0) be any effectively given domain. Define effectively given domain (X_n,ε_n) recursively by:

$$X_{n+1} = [X_n \to X_n] \qquad \varepsilon_{n+1} = [\varepsilon_n \to \varepsilon_n]$$

Between (X_n,ε_n) and $(X_{n+1},\varepsilon_{n+1})$ there is an obvious projection pair $(f_n:X_n\to X_{n+1},\ f_n^R:X_{n+1}\to X_n)$ defined by:

$$f_0(x) = \lambda y.x, \qquad f_0^R(x) = x(\bot)$$

$$f_{n+1}(x) = f_n\cdot x\cdot f_n^R \qquad f_{n+1}^R(x) = f_n^R\cdot x\cdot f_n \quad .$$

It is obvious that both f_n and f_n^R are computable. It is not difficult to observe that for each $n\in N$, we can uniformly generate a pair (b_n,ℓ_n) of recursive predicates which makes ε_n effectively given, and n_1,n_2 s.t. $f_n = \delta_{[\varepsilon_n\to\varepsilon_{n+1}]}(n_1)$ $f_n^R = \delta_{[\varepsilon_{n+1}\to\varepsilon_n]}(n_2)$. This makes $((X_n,\varepsilon_n),(f_n,f_n^R))$ an effective sequence of embedding of effectively given domains as in [4,5].

The inverse limit $(X_\infty,\varepsilon_\infty)$ is defined by:

$$X_\infty = \{(x_0,x_1,x_2,\dots) \mid x_n\in X_n, x_n = f_n^R(x_{n+1})\}$$

$$(x_0,x_1,x_2,\dots) < (y_0,y_1,\dots) \text{ iff } x_i<y_i \text{ for all } i.$$

$$\varepsilon_\infty((n,m)) = f_{n\infty}(\varepsilon_n(m))$$

where $\quad (f_{n\infty}: X_n \to X_\infty,\ f^R_{n\infty}: X_\infty \to X_n)$ is a projection pair defined by:

$$f_{n\infty}(x) = (f^R_0 \cdot f^R_1 \cdots \cdot f^R_{n-1}(x), \cdots, f^R_{n-1}(x), x, f_1(x), f_2 \cdot f_1(x), \cdots)$$
$$f_{n\infty}((x_0, x_1, \ldots)) = x_n.$$

As shown in [4], $(X_\infty, \varepsilon_\infty)$ is an effectively given domain and there is a computable isomorphism due to Scott [7]:

$$X_\infty \underset{\Psi}{\overset{\Phi}{\rightleftarrows}} [X_\infty \to X_\infty]$$

$$\Phi(x) = \lambda y \varepsilon X_\infty \cdot \bigsqcup (x_{n+1}(y_n))$$
$$\Psi(g) = \langle g_{(0)}, g_{(1)}, \ldots \rangle$$

where $\quad x_k = f^R_{k\infty}(x) \quad$ and $\quad g_{(0)} = f^R_{0\infty}(g(|))$

$$g_{(n+1)} = f^R_{n\infty} \cdot g \cdot f_{n\infty}\ .$$

Think of the following numerations:

$$\gamma = (\delta_{\varepsilon_\infty}, \mathrm{Comp}(X_\infty, \varepsilon_\infty))$$
$$(\gamma \to \gamma) = (\delta_{[\varepsilon_\infty \to \varepsilon_\infty]}, \mathrm{Comp}([X_\infty \to X_\infty], [\varepsilon_\infty \to \varepsilon_\infty])).$$

<u>Theorem 6.4</u>

(1) The numeration $(\gamma \to \gamma)$ is admissible

(2) $\gamma \cong (\gamma \to \gamma)$ in the category of numerations.

Therefore γ is an NRS. □

§7. <u>An Algebraic Characterization of Numerated Reflexive Sets</u>

A countable applicative system is an algebra $(X, \cdot)$ where $\cdot$ is a binary operation over a countable set X. The set T(X) of <u>terms</u> (using countably many variables $x_0, x_1, \ldots$) over $(X, \cdot)$ is inductively defined as follows:

$$x_i \in T(X)$$
$$a \in X \to a \in T(X)$$
$$A, B \in T(X) \to (A \cdot B) \in T(X).$$

We assume that $\cdot$ associates to the left, also we will drop $\cdot$ if it does not cause much difficulty to read. Thus $A_1 A_2 \ldots A_n$ denotes $(\cdots(A_1 A_2)\cdots A_n)$. To denote that $A \in T(X)$ has variables $x_0, x_1, \ldots, x_n$, we write $A(x_0, x_1, \ldots, x_n)$. We can Gödel number terms. Let $\sigma: N \twoheadrightarrow T(X)$ be a Gödel numbering of terms.

Let $\gamma = (\mu: N \twoheadrightarrow X, X)$ be a numeration. We define $\gamma \times \gamma$ to be a numeration $(\mu \times \mu: N \twoheadrightarrow X \times X, X \times X)$ s.t.

$$\mu \times \mu(\langle n, m \rangle) = (\mu(n), \mu(m))$$

where <-,-> is a pairing function.

Definition 7.1

A realizably extensional combinatory algebra (RECA) is a 4-tuple $(X,\cdot,\gamma,\sigma)$ s.t.

(1) $(X,\cdot)$ is a countable applicative system

(2) $\gamma = (\mu:N\to X, X)$ is a numeration

(3) $\cdot : X\times X \to X$ is a morphism from $\gamma\times\gamma$ to γ, realized by a recursive function op.

(4) There is a recursive function λ s.t. if $\sigma(n) = A(x_1,\ldots,x_n)$ then $\mu(\lambda(n)) = f$ is a unique element of X satisfying:

$$fy_1 \ldots y_n = A(x_1{:=}y_1,\ldots,x_n{:=}y_n)$$

where $A(x_1{:=}y_1,\ldots,x_n{:=}y_n)$ is the result of substituting y_i for x_i in A $(1\leq i\leq n)$. □

Note that (4) is a realization of extensional combinatory completeness of Church [1]. Thus an RECA is a countable applicative system $(X,\cdot)$ where $\cdot$ is realizable and the extensional combinatory completeness is also realizable.

Definition 7.2

An RECA $(X,\cdot,\gamma,\sigma)$ is computationally complete iff there is a recursive function alg s.t. if ϕ_n realizes $f:X\to X$ then $\sigma(\mathrm{alg}(n))$ is a term with a free variable, say x and

$$f(z) = (\sigma(\mathrm{alg}(n)))(x{:=}z).$$ □

Lemma 7.3

If $(X,\cdot,\gamma,\sigma)$ is a computationally complete RECA then $\mathrm{Hom}(\gamma,\gamma) = \Phi(X)$ where Φ maps elements of X to functions $X\to X$ defined by: $\Phi(x)(x') = x\cdot x'$. □

Now let $(\gamma\to\gamma) = (\mu\to\mu, \mathrm{Hom}(\gamma,\gamma))$ be the following numeration: $(\mu\to\mu)(n) = \Phi(\mu(n))$.

Lemma 7.4

$(\gamma\to\gamma)$ is admissible. □

Theorem 7.5

If $(X,\cdot,\gamma,\sigma)$ is a computationally complete RECA, then γ is a NRS.

Proof It is sufficient to show $\gamma = (\gamma\to\gamma)$ in the category of numerations. Define Ψ:Hom$(\gamma,\gamma)\to X$ by:

$$\Psi(\Phi(x)) = x.$$

Then $\Phi(\Psi(\Phi(x))) = \Phi(x)$. Thus (Φ,Ψ) is an isomorphism. Both Φ and Ψ are realized by the identity function $N\to N$. Thus $\gamma\cong(\gamma\to\gamma)$ in the category of numerations. □

Before we prove the converse of 7.5, notice that we did not include constants in our language of λ-calculus. By trivial modification of 1.1 and definition of ξ, we can include constants. Under this modification, obviously 5.3, 5.4, 5.5 still hold.

Now let $\gamma = (\mu,X)$ be a NRS with an isomorphism pair (Φ,Ψ). Define an operation $\cdot:X\times X\to X$ by:

$$x\cdot y = \Phi(x)(y).$$

Theorem 7.6

If $\gamma = (\mu,X)$ is a NRS then $(X,\cdot,\gamma,\sigma)$ is a computationally complete RECA. □

Proof

(1) Since Φ and $\Phi(x)$ are morphisms, $\cdot$ is a morphism from $\gamma\times\gamma$ to γ.

(2) Let $\sigma(n) = A(x_1,\ldots,x_k)$. Then $\xi(\lambda x_1..\lambda x_k.A(x_1,\ldots x_k),\rho) = f$ is the unique element of X s.t. $fy_1..y_k = A(x_1:=y_1,..,x_k:=y_k)$. By 5.3 a recursive function λ s.t. $\mu(\lambda(n)) = f$ exists.

(3) Assume a recursive function ϕ_n realizes $f:X\to X$. Then for some recursive function g, $\Psi(f) = \mu(g(n))$. Let x be a variable and $\mu(g(n))\cdot x = \sigma(\text{alg}(n))$. Then alg is a recursive function and $f(z) = (\sigma(\text{alg}(n))(x:=z)$. □

Barendregt [1] showed that extensional combinatory systems serve as models of λ-calculus. 7.5 is a numeration version of his result. Meyer [6] characterized models of non-extensional λ-calculus as combinatory systems. It should be a routine modification of our development to obtain numeration version of Meyer's result.

§ 8. Concluding Remarks

Even though the term model of Church is a countable model, the numeration of the set of equivalence classes of terms via Gödel numbering of terms does not form a numeration model. This indicates the importance of order theoretic numeration model.

It should be stressed that in our construction of numeration models, environments and the interpretation function are just morphisms. Thus in the construction of order theoretic numeration models, we do not need to assume any order theoretic property of environments and the interpretation function. This suggests that in the denotational semantics of Scott [7], we do not need to consider collections of syntactic objects as order theoretic domains.

Acknowledgement

The author thanks the referees for very valuable comments. Especially lemma 4.6 is purely due to one of the referees.

REFERENCES

[1] Barendregt, H. The Type Free λ-calculus, Handbook of Math. Logic, J. Barwise, ed., North Holland, 1977.

[2] Church, A. The Calculi of Lambda-conversion. Princeton University Press, 1941.

[3] Ersov, Ju. L. Theorie der Numerierungen I. Zeitschrife fur Math. Logik, Bd 19, Heft 4, 1973.

[4] Kanda, A. Fully Effective Solutions of Recursive Domain Equations. Proc. of MFCS'79. Lecture Notes in Computer Science No. 74, 1979.

[5] Kanda, A. Constructive Category Theory I. Proc. of MFCS'81 Lecture Notes in Computer Science No. 118, 1981.

[6] Meyer, A. What Is a Model of λ-calculus? MIT/LCS/TM-201, 1981.

[7] Scott, D. Continuous Lattices, Lecture Notes in Mathematics No. 274, 1971.

[8] Weihrauch and Schafer, Admissible Representations of Effective CPO's. Proc. of MFCS'81, Lecture Notes in Computer Science, No. 118, 1981.

[9] Streicher, T. Scott Domains, Computability and the Definability Problem, Thesis, Johannes Kepler Universitat Lintz (1982).

[10] Coppo-Dezani-Honsell-Longo, "Extended type structures and filter lambda-models", Logic Coll. 82, (Lolli, Marlja, Longo, eds.), North-Holland (1982).

NEARLY TIGHT BOUNDS FOR THE LONGEST EDGE OF A TREE IN A VLSI LAYOUT

Michael Kaufmann
Fachbereich 10, Universität des Saarlandes
6600 Saarbrücken, West Germany

Abstract. In the last three years many results were published about graph layout in VLSI. One aspect of graph layout is the minimization of the longest edge; for this problem Bhatt and Leiserson (1981) recently demonstrated a new technique to shorten the longest edge, and they thus achieved an upper bound of $O(\sqrt{N}/\log N)$ for trees. Unfortunately, no good universal lower bounds exist.
This paper presents a general technique for proving lower bounds for trees. Furthermore new upper bounds are presented. The lower and upper bounds are almost tight asymptotically.

1. INTRODUCTION

For VLSI theory it is very interesting to consider how to lay out a graph in the plane. The reason is that a network in VLSI can be interpreted (with some simplifications) as a graph, with transistors corresponding to nodes and wires to the edges of the graph.

Thus we can solve many problems in VLSI by solving the related graph theoretic problems.
One important aspect here is the longest wire in a network layout. This wire can determine the performance of the circuit, if the time to propagate information through a wire grows with the length of the wire. The capacitive model by Mead and Conway (1980) supports this view. In systolic systems thus, the period of the system clock must be longer than the longest propagation delay.
For general graphs, there exist some results developed by Bhatt and Leiserson and by Leighton (1981,1982). But if we restrict ourselves to the class of trees, these results are rather weak; therefore this problem is mentioned as an open problem in all

of these papers.

We divide this paper into 4 sections. Section 2 reviews the standard model, as well as some definitions and lemmata. Then we present a nearly trivial lower bound for maximal edge length. In section 3, we develop the main result. We prove lower and upper bounds. We give a simple example which explains the technique of which we make use subsequently to obtain the lower bound. The upper bound is an application of the method of Bhatt/Leiserson. Thus we achieve nearly tight bounds for the considered classes of trees. Finally, section 4 summarizes the results for general trees.

2. BACKGROUND

The first model for graph layout was suggested by Thompson (1979). He considers the layout as an embedding in a two-dimensional grid. This grid consists of horizontal and vertical lines spaced apart at unit intervals.

A layout of a graph is an assignment of nodes to crossings of horizontal and vertical lines. The edges follow the lines, they may cross each other but not overlap for any distance, and they may not cross nodes which they are not connecting.

The area of the layout equals the product of the numbers of vertical and horizontal lines that contain a node or edge segment of the graph.

For this layout model, we restrict the graphs to those having nodes with degree at most four, and we only consider binary trees; extension to other classes of graphs is easy.

Most layout techniques base on the divide-and-conquer paradigm and use graph separators to recursively partition a given circuit. For trees, this technique yields a linear upper bound on the area.

Definition 1:

A class of graphs closed under the subgraph relation has an f(x)-separator theorem, if there are constants a,b with $0<a\le 1/2$ and $b>0$, such that by removing at most $b\cdot f(N)$ edges, every N-node graph of the class can be partitioned into disjoint subgraphs having $c\cdot N$ and $(1-c)\cdot N$ nodes, where $a\le c\le 1-a$.

<u>Definition 2:</u>

An $f(x)$-separator is said to be <u>perfect</u> if $c \cdot N = \lfloor N/2 \rfloor$ or $\lceil N/2 \rceil$.

The lemmata 1 and 2 below can be proved by familiar techniques.

<u>Lemma 1:</u>

Any tree has an $O(\log N)$-perfect separator.

A complete binary tree can be laid out as an H-tree (Figure 1) in linear area as shown by the recurrence equation for the side length s of the layout:

$$s(N) = 2s(N/4) + 1$$

If we extend the H-tree edges to channels with width $(N/2^i)^\alpha$ for level i, $1 \le i \le \log N$, $0<\alpha<1/2$, then the "1" in the recurrence equation is replaced by N^α (Figure 2).

<u>Lemma 2:</u>

The linear upper bound for the area still holds for an extended H-tree (used by Bhatt/Leiserson (1981)) with channel width $(N/2^i)^\alpha$ for all levels i, $1 \le i \le \log N$.

Figure 1: H-tree with 63 nodes

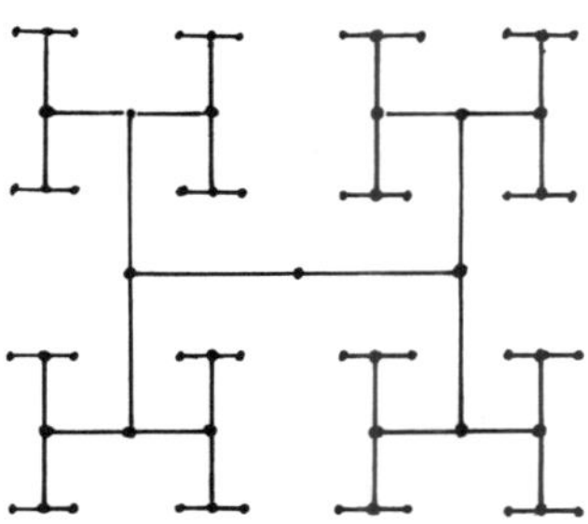

Figure 2: extended H-tree

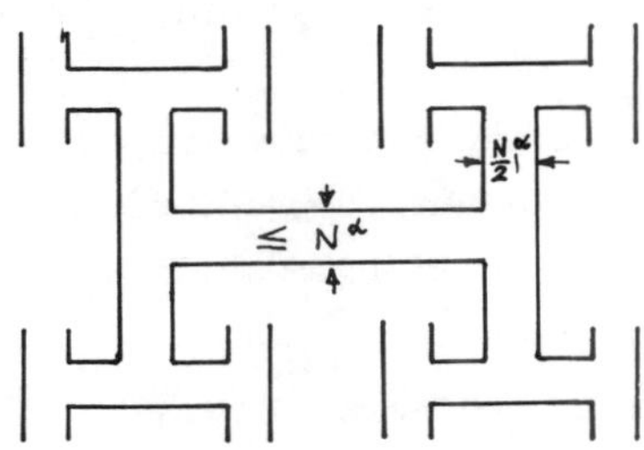

The following trivial lower bound shows that the upper bound of Bhatt and Leiserson is optimal for complete binary trees.

Lemma 3:

Let L be the maximal edge length for a layout of a tree, and let $v_1,\dots,v_N$ be its nodes. Let $MD = \sum_{i,j} d(v_i,v_j)/N^2$ be the average path length, where $d(v_i,v_j)$ is the number of nodes on the path from v_i to v_j. Then $L \geq \Omega(\sqrt{N}/MD)$.

Proof: Partition any layout into three stripes V_1,V_2,V_3, such that V_1 and V_3 each contain N/10 nodes.

Figure 3

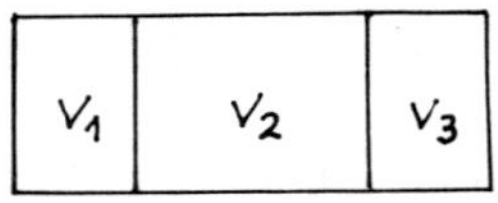

The paths between the nodes of V_1 and V_3 have at least length $\sqrt{N}$ (side length of linear layout area). Clearly, at least one path from a node in V_1 to a node in V_3 contains at most O(MD) nodes. Thus we can conclude that the longest edge must have a length of at least $\Omega(\sqrt{N}/MD)$.

The average number of nodes on a path between two nodes in a complete binary tree is O(log N). This implies a lower bound for the longest edge of a complete binary tree of size $\Omega(\sqrt{N}/\log N)$.
On the other hand, for the tree that consists of just one path we find a linear area layout with edge length 1.
Intuitively, we can conclude:
The denser the tree, the longer the longest edge.

To formalize the property "dense", we define a function $t: V \times N \to N$ called density, where t(v,k) is the number of nodes which can be reached from node v by a path passing through exactly k nodes.
We know: $\forall v,k: t(v,k) \leq 2^k$.
The above bounds are tight for exponential density. Let us thus assume that the density is bound by a polynomial:

$\forall v,k: t(v,k) \leq k^{i-1}$ for $i>1$, i constant.

3. NEW BOUNDS

3.1 Lower bounds

To explain the technique, we look at the following simple example.

Consider a complete binary tree of depth r, extended by paths of length m hanging down from the leaves.

It is clear that

$$N = 2^r m + 2^r - 1 \leq 2^{r+1} m$$

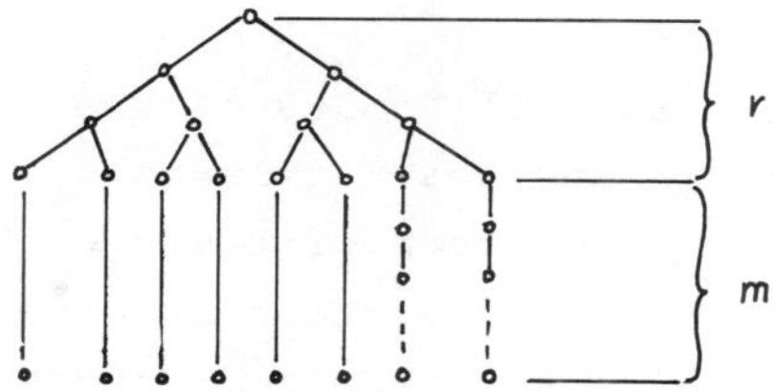

Figure 4

In any layout of the tree, let d be the radius of the smallest circle around the root which contains all nodes of the r upper levels.

$$\Rightarrow \quad L \geq d/r$$

$2^r - 2\pi d$ of the 2^r paths must lie completely inside the circle, since the circumference of the circle is only $2\pi d$.

Also we have:

$$\pi d^2 \geq (2^r - 2\pi d)m$$

$$\Rightarrow \quad d^2 \geq (2^r/\pi - 2d)m$$

We now consider 2 cases:

$$d \geq 2^{r-1}/2\pi \qquad \Rightarrow \quad L \geq 2^{r-1}/2\pi r$$

and

$$d < 2^{r-1}/2\pi \qquad \Rightarrow \quad d \geq 2^{r/2} m^{1/2}/\sqrt{2\pi} \geq \sqrt{N}/2\sqrt{\pi}$$

$$\Rightarrow \quad L \geq \sqrt{N}/2\sqrt{\pi} r$$

$$\Rightarrow \qquad L \geq \min\ (\sqrt{N}/2\sqrt{\pi} r,\ N/8\pi r m).$$

Choose m such that

$$\frac{\sqrt{N}}{2\sqrt{\pi} r} = \frac{N}{8\pi r m} \qquad \Rightarrow \quad m = \frac{\sqrt{N}}{4\sqrt{\pi}}; \qquad \Rightarrow \quad L \geq \Omega(\sqrt{N}/\log N). \quad \Box$$

In contrast, note that Lemma 3 yields only a lower bound of $\Omega(1)$, since MD $\simeq m/2 + r$.

Now we sketch the general method for lower bounds.
Suppose: $\exists v$: $c_4 k^{i-1} \le t(v,k) \le c_4' k^{i-1}$, $c_4, c_4' > 0$, $\forall k$: $1 \le k \le \ldots$
At the end of the proof, we will be able to bound k from above by $c_1 N^{1/2(i-1)}$, where $c_1 > 0$ is another constant.

Consider any layout of the tree with the assumptions made above, and draw a circle of radius $c_1\sqrt{N}$, $0<c_1<1$ around the node v.
Note that all nodes of the first $c_1\sqrt{N}/L$ levels lie inside the circle and that at least $c_4(c_1\sqrt{N}/L)^{i-1}$ subtrees hang down from the nodes of the $c_1\sqrt{N}/L$ -th level.
We assume that these subtrees have nearly equal size.
Let a be the number of these subtrees which lie completely inside the circle.
Note that

<u>at least</u> $\sum_{k=0}^{c_1\sqrt{N}/L} c_4 k^{i-1} \ge c_o(c_1\sqrt{N}/L)^i$ nodes and analogously

<u>at most</u> $c_6(c_1\sqrt{N}/L)^i$ nodes lie on the first $c_1\sqrt{N}/L$ levels

with constants c_o, c_6 which are valid for this class of trees.

Hence the area of the circle is bounded by

$$\pi c_1^2 N \ge a\left(\frac{N - c_6(c_1\sqrt{N}/L)^i}{c_4(c_1\sqrt{N}/L)^{i-1}}\right) + c_o(c_1\sqrt{N}/L)^i.$$

This provides us with an upper bound for a.
A lower bound for a follows from the fact that at least $c_4(c_1\sqrt{N}/L)^{i-1} - 2\pi c_1\sqrt{N}$ of the subtrees must lie completely inside the circle (since the circumference of the circle is bounded).
By replacing a in the inequality we get, after some technical transformations,

$$\underline{L \ge \Omega(\sqrt{N}/N^{1/2(i-1)}).}$$

Note that the assumption for the density only has to be valid for the first $O(N^{1/2(i-1)})$ levels depending on one node v only.

We can easily show that such trees exist by giving an algorithm which constructs a tree for any given i and N with density $\Theta(k^i)$ for all k.

3.2 Upper bounds

We only sketch the technique of embedding the tree, since it is nearly the same used by Bhatt/Leiserson (1981). We embed the tree in an H-tree widening the H-tree edges to channels. If the channel width meets the premise of Lemma 2, the area remains linear.
Using the technique of Leighton (1982) we know that $O(\log^2 N)$ edges are enough for a fully balanced decomposition of any tree. A decomposition is said to be fully balanced, if there is a perfect separation. In addition, the number of edges of G incident to precisely one node in a subgraph on level i differs by at most an additive constant from the number of edges of G incident to precisely one node in the corresponding subgraph on that level i for all $1 \le i \le \log N$.

Now, here is a sketch of the layout procedure:

Place the edges of the fully balanced decomposition at level 1 and the corresponding nodes parallel to each other with length L on the top channel and place the edges incident to the embedded nodes in such way that the distance between their nodes is L.

Figure 5: Embedding the tree in an H-tree

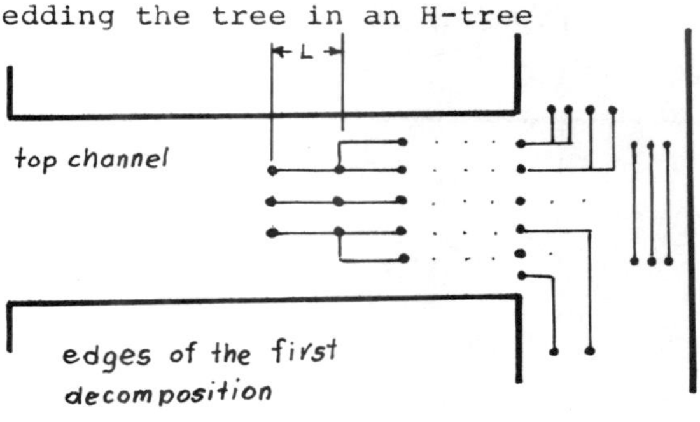

This step is repeated until some nodes are placed at the end of the top channel.
Then place the next edges using Leighton's decomposition technique such that about half of them goes to the right and half to the left of the second channel. In the middle of this channel place the edges of the second decomposition level,too.
Repeat this procedure until you reach the level where you can trivially lay out the remaining subtrees of size L^2 with maximal edge length L.

Note that the upper channel has length $O(\sqrt{N})$ as well as the path from the root of the H-tree to one leaf. Since we use the fully balanced decomposition, we know that the area remains linear, if the top channel is not too wide ($\leq N^{\alpha}$, $\alpha<1/2$) and we only need consider this channel.
We only need consider even the biggest subtree T on the top channel, since there are $O(\log^2 N)$ subtrees and
$\forall\alpha<1/2\ \exists\beta<1/2$: $N^{\alpha}\cdot\log^2 N \leq N^{\beta}$.
We suppose again that

$$\forall v,k:\ t(v,k) \leq k^{i-1} \text{ for a constant } i>1.$$

Let $depth_T$ be the depth of the subtree T that comes to lie inside the top channel of the H-tree.

Figure 6: Embedding of subtree T

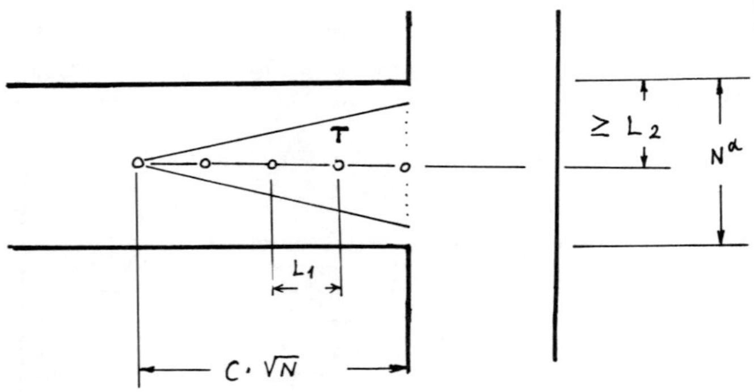

Then $depth_T = c\sqrt{N}/L_1$. Clearly, there are at most $(depth_T)^{i-1}$ nodes at the end of the top channel. We know that the length L_2 of the longest edge of T is not as long as the number of nodes at the channel end (Figure 6).
Thus

$$L_2 \le (c\sqrt{N}/L_1)^{i-1}.$$

Let $L = L_1 = L_2$ $\Rightarrow L \le c\sqrt{N}^{(i-1)/i} \le O(\sqrt{N}/N^{1/2i})$.

¤

Now we can formulate our main result:

> We can lay out any tree with density $t(v,k) = \Theta(k^{i-1})$ $\forall v,k$, $i>1$ constant, with a maximal edge length of
>
> $$\Omega(\sqrt{N}/N^{1/2(i-1)}) \le L \le O(\sqrt{N}/N^{1/2i}).$$

These bounds are nearly tight asymptotically.
This formulation of the results does not exploit our lower bound fully; for more details see the derivation of the bound.

<u>Remark:</u> Using the "L-shapes" of Paterson/Ruzzo/Snyder (1981) we achieve an upper bound of $O(\sqrt{N}/N^{1/2i + 1/i^2})$.
This technique, however, improves our upper bound only unessentially.

For different values for the density we obtain the following table:

density	lower bound	upper bound	
k^0	1	1	
k^1	1	$N^{1/4}$	
.	.	.	
.	.	.	
k^{10}	$N^{9/20}$	$N^{10/22}$	
.	.	.	
.	.	.	
$2^{\gamma k}$	$\gamma\sqrt{N}/\log N$	$\sqrt{N}/\log N$	$0<\gamma\le 1$ const.

4. CONCLUSION

We saw that the bounds obtained are nearly tight and that they (especially the lower bound) are applicable to other theorems and perhaps extendable for any density function.

For any tree, we derived the following lower bound:

$$\max_{ST} \left\{ \frac{\sqrt{N}_{ST}}{N_{ST}^{1/2(i-1)}} \;\middle|\; \begin{array}{l} N_{ST} \text{ is the number of nodes in subtree} \\ ST \text{ and } 1^{i-1} \text{ is the density on depth } 1 \end{array} \right\}$$

Furthermore, we proved the following upper bound:

$$\min_{\text{decomposition}} \; \max_{ST} \left\{ \frac{\sqrt{N}/2^{k/2}}{\left(\frac{N}{2^{k/2}}\right)^{1/2i}} \;\middle|\; \begin{array}{l} 1^{i-1} \text{ is the max. density of} \\ ST \text{ on depth } 1\text{; on level } k \text{ lie} \\ \text{its top edges} \end{array} \right\}$$

It is difficult to relate these bounds to each other since there are no theorems about different kinds of tree decompositions.

By our technique the lower bound for graphs with small separator can possibly be improved, too. If we consider a spanning tree of a density as high as possible, the layout of this tree might yield a better lower bound.

ACKNOWLEDGEMENT

I would like to thank Kurt Mehlhorn for stimulating my interest in graph layout and for various discussions, and Thomas Lengauer and Stefan Hertel for reading versions of this paper.

REFERENCES

Bhatt, S.N. & Leiserson, C.E. (1982). Minimizing the longest edge in a VLSI layout. M.I.T. VLSI Memo

Leighton, F.T. (1981). New lower bound techniques for VLSI. 22. Annual Symposium on Foundations of Computer Science IEEE

Leighton, F.T. (1982). A layout strategy for VLSI which is provably good. 14. Annual ACM Symposium on Theory of Computing

Mead, C.& Conway, L. (1980). Introduction to VLSI Systems. Addison-Wesley

Paterson, M.,Ruzzo, W. & Snyder, L. (1981). Bounds on minimax edge length for complete binary trees. 13. Annual ACM Symposium on Theory of Computing

Thompson, C.D. (1979). Area-time complexity for VLSI. 11. Annual ACM Symposium on Theory of Computing

UNIFORM TERMINATION OF TERM REWRITING SYSTEMS

Recursive Decomposition Ordering with Status

Pierre LESCANNE

Centre de Recherche en Informatique de Nancy
Campus Scientifique BP 239
54506 Vandoeuvre Cedex France

1. INTRODUCTION

The key of many algorithms that manipulate Term Rewriting Systems is proving their termination [12]. Unfortunately, as Lankford and Huet [3] showed, this problem like many other termination problems is undecidable. Thus the only hope is in providing very general methods that cover a large area in a specific domain. In this paper, we propose an algorithm well suited for proving termination of term rewriting systems that occur in Abstract Data Type Specifications and Functional Programming. The method that we propose here is based on orderings. In this paper, we provide a well-founded ordering ">" such that the system $\{l_i \dashrightarrow r_i\}$ terminates if $l_i > r_i$, for all rule. It is called the Recursive Decomposition Ordering with Status (RDOS in short). Because of this status, it improves the Recursive Decomposition Ordering introduced by Jouannaud, Lescanne and Reinig. Thus the RDOS can handle equations as frequent as associativity that the previous version of the Recursive Decomposition Ordering could not. It is also more powerful than an ordering it is often compared to, namely the Recursive Path Ordering. However it keeps its outstanding property of incrementality which makes the proofs of termination so easy in REVE. The Recursive Decomposition Ordering with Status is the only ordering actually implemented in the new term rewriting laboratory REVE 2 for proving termination. In Annex the reader will find a short survey on orderings in proving uniform termination of term rewriting systems.

2. THE RECURSIVE DECOMPOSITION ORDERING WITH STATUS

The Recursive Decomposition Ordering with Status we define here, written RDOS uses status on operators in its definition. We show it contains strictly the RPOS. In the following, let [] or 'box' be a specific given term. Box has no variable and is the least term for the RDOS. It can be seen either as the 'empty' term i.e., the term which has no symbol at all, or as a term which has only a specific constant symbol. Both possibilities will be allowed in REVE. The second could be useful when the set of rules REEE deals with has a unique constant, like the identity in groups or the empty stack in the specification of stacks. Notice that the precedence is a quasi-ordering, which means that equivalent symbols w.r.t. the precedence are allowed. We write 'f eq g' to denote that the operator f is equivalent to the operator g. In the following, we use 'occurrence' and 'path'. Occurrence is the classical concept used in terms (see [5])and the path to u (where u is an occurrence) is the set of occurrences that are prefix of u.

Definition 1: The *multiset elementary tripartite decomposition* of t at the occurrence u is the triple ed{u}(t) = <f, {t1,...,tn}, $d^u(c)$>. f is the *leader*, it is t(u) the symbol in t at the occurrence u, {t1,...,tn}, the *followers*, is a multiset of terms (no ordering on terms is required) where ti = t/ui, and $d^u(c)$ the *context* is the set of elementary decompositions to t(u <-- []) along the path u', u' is path to u except the occurrence u i.e. the set of the strict prefixes of u. t(u <-- []) is the term obtained by replacing the subterm t/u at the occurrence u by []. In particular if, u =/\ (the empty occurrence) c is [] and $d^u(c)$ is the empty set. []

Definition 2: The *lexicographical elementary decomposition* of t at u is the triple ed{u}(t) = <f, (t1,...,tn), $d^u(c)$>, where f and $d^u(c)$ are as above and (t1,..,tn) is the ordered sequence of t/u1,..t/un (left to right) or t/u1,...,t/un (right to left) according to the status of f. []

In order to know whether the RDOS has to consider a left-to-right lexicographical decomposition or a right-to-left lexicographical decomposition or a multiset decomposition, a status is assigned to each operator symbol.

Definition 3: *status* is a function from the set of operator symbols onto the set {m, l, r}. If status(f) = m, f is said to have a multiset status if status(f) = l or r, f is said to have a lexicographical status, 'left-to-right' with l and 'right-to-left' with r. []

Obviously two equivalent symbols w.r.t the precedence are supposed to have consistent status (i.e., both multiset or both lexicographical).

STATUS CONSISTENCY CONDITION:

f eq g ==> status(f) = status(g) = m

or status(f) E {l,r} and status E {l,r}.

In order to make the ordering stable for substitutions to variables we declare the following condition:

CONDITION ON VARIABLES IN THE PRECEDENCE: variables are comparable with no other variable and no function symbol in the precedence.

The RDO is a particular of the RDOS when all the status have a status m. We now define the comparison of two elementary decompositions.

Definition 4: *Comparing two elementary decompositions*. An elementary decomposition d = <f, S, dc> is less than an elementary decomposition d'= <g,T,dc'> if

f < g

or f eq g and T << S where << is the the extension of the RDOS to multisets (see [7]) if status(f) = status(g) = m and to sequences if status E {l,m} or f eq g and T = S and dc << dc' is the extension to sets of elementary decompositions of the ordering on elementary decompositions. []

We now introduce the concepts of path decompositions and decomposition that are the basis for the RDOS.

Definition 5 Path Decomposition: The path decomposition $d^P(t)$ along the path p in a term t is the set of the elementary decompositions of t for all the occurrences on p. []

Definition 6 Decomposition: The decomposition dec(t) of a term is the set of the path decompositions of t for all the paths in t. Indistinguishable path decompositions need not to be repeated, so that decompositions can be considered as a set. The decomposition of [] is the empty set. []

Definition 7 Ordering on Decompositions and Recursive Decomposition Ordering: The extension of the ordering on path decompositions and on decompositions are natural extensions of elementary decompositions to sets and sets of sets. We say that s $<_{RDOS}$ t if the decomposition of s is less than the decomposition of t. []

THEOREM 1: The RDOS is a partial quasi-ordering.

Proof: From Definition 7 the RDOS is trivially an ordering on decompositions. Because the mapping 'dec' from terms onto decompositions is many-to-one the decomposition ordering on terms is only a quasi-ordering. It is easy to check that two terms have the same decomposition if the are equal up to a permutation of the subterms below a symbol with status m.

Before giving Theorem 2 on connection between the RDOS and the RPOS let us first look at an example.

EXAMPLE 1 (Jouannaud): Consider

```
                  !                             not
                /   \                            |
       s = not    not          and      t =     &
            |      |                          /   \
            x      y                         x     y
```

Suppose the precedence is just ! < & and the status of !, & and 'not' are m (i.e., we consider only the RDO). dec(s) = {d^{11}(s), d^{21}(s)}.

d^{11}(s) is made of three elementary decompositions. Indeed

```
 11              not  not                      1     !
d   (s) = {<!, {|  ,   | }, {}>, <not, {x},d ( /     \ )>,
                x     y                        []    not
                                                      |
                                                      y
                                 !
                 <x, {}, /     \ > }
                           not   not
                            |     |
                           []     y
```

d^{21}(s) contains also three elementary decompositions and is defined in a symmetrical way, by changing the role of x and y.

dec(t) = {d^{11}(t), d^{12}(t)} where

```
 11                  &                        1 not
d   (t) = {<not, {/ \ }, {}>, <&, {x, y}, d ( | )>,
                x   y                        []

                   11  not
          <x, {}, d  (  |   )> }
                        &
                       / \
                      []  y
```

d^{12}(t) is also defined in a symmetrical way. Then we may conclude dc(s) < dec(t) because d^{11}(s) < d^{11}(t) and d^{21}(s) < d^{12}(t). Let us prove only d^{11}(s) < d^{11}(t). Indeed

```
            not not                        1 not
    a. <!, { | , | }, {}> < <&, {x, y}, d ( | )> because ! < &.
             x   y                         []
                  1    !                   &                           &
    b. <not, {x}, d ( / \)>  <  <not, {/ \}, {}> because x <RDOS      / \
                     [] not              x y                          x   y
                         |
                         y
```

from the subterm property of the RDOS (see Theorem 2).

```
                1     !                   1  not
   c. <x , {} , d ( /    \ )> < < x, {}, d (  |  )
                   not not                    &
                    |   |                    / \
                    []   y                  []  y

because d^1(...) = {<!,...>, <not,{[]},...>} is less than
 1  not                          &
d (  |  ) = {&, ...> , <not, { / \ },...>} by a similar reasoning.
    &                           []  y
   / \
  []  y
```

Thus $s <_{RDO} t$. However $s <_{RPO} t$ does not hold for the same precedence. Intuitively the RDO or the RDOS do not lose information about the other branches when traversing a branch. It is also possible to prove that the RDOS is more powerful than the RPOS. But before let us give the definition of what we call the Recursive Path Ordering with Status.

Definition 8 Recursive Path Ordering with Status: Given a status and a precedence, the Recursive Path Ordering is the ordering on terms that is the least fixed point of the following definition:

$$s = f(s1,\dots,sm) < g(t1,\dots,tn) = t$$

if

- (RPOS1-m) f eq g and status(f) = m and {s1,...,sm} << {t1,...,tm} (where << is the multiset ordering).

or - (RPOS1-l) f eq g and status(f) and status(g) are lexicographical and (s1,...,sm) << (t1,...,tm) (where << is the lexicographical ordering on sequences from left to right or right to left according to the status of f and g) and for each si, si < t.

or - (RPOS2) f < g and for each si, si < t

or - (RPOS3) there exists tj such that s < tj []

Notice first that the RPOS requires to check that the direct subterms si are bounded by the full term t when the root has a lexicographical status. A similar property is not necessary in the RDOS and, for this reason, the RDOS is more powerful with terms containing symbols with lexicographical status (see Example 2). Second the RPOS is intrinsically non deterministic because, with equivalent lexicographical roots, either (RPOS1-l) or (RPOS3) can be used.

THEOREM 2: If s $<_{RPOS}$ t then s $<_{RDOS}$ t.

Proof: To prove this theorem we must prove that the RDOS is also a fixed point of the definition of the RPOS. The proofs of each part of the definition are similar to those of [6] except for the proof of (RPOS1-1).

Let us prove it. If f eq g and status(f) and status(g) are lexicographical then at the root the decompositions are ed{/\}(t) = <f, (s1,...,sm), {}> and ed{/\}(t) = <g, (t1,...,tn), {}>. Obviously if (s1,...,sm) is lexicographically dominated by (t1,...tn) then ed{/\}(s) is dominated by ed{/\}(t). Use now the fact that each si is such that si < t to prove dec(s) < dec(t). Notice that the difference between ed{u}(si) and ed{iu}(s) is just in the context where the elementary decomposition ed{/\}(s) is (recursively) added. If now the proof of dec(si) < dec(t) uses ed{u}(si) < ed{v}(t), then ed{iu}(s) < ed{v}(t) because ed{/\}(s) added to the context is everywhere dominated by ed{/\}(t) as mentioned above. Thus dec(s) < dec(t) is proved by imitating the proofs of dec(si) < dec(t) meaning that each time we need to bound ed{iu}(s) by an ed{v}(t) we take the v used to prove dec{s}(si) < dec{v}(s) in the proof of dec(si) < dec(t).

Example 1 and Example 2 show that the inclusion of the RPOS into the RDOS is strict.

EXAMPLE 2: Suppose status(*) = 1 and there is no hypothesis on the precedence.

$$s = h(h(x) * x) >_{RDOS} x * h(x * x) = t$$

The proof is a little tedious and we refer to ANNEX where the reader will find a 'proof' proposed by REVE 2 in an implementation of the Knuth-Bendix procedure. As previously, we do not have s $>_{RPOS}$ t. Indeed h and * are incomparable and the RPOS tries to prove h(x) * x is less than x * h(x * x) and cannot succeed because it forgets the root symbol h on s that allows s to prevail on h(x * x) in the RDOS. However notice that s $>_{RPOS}$ t with both possible precedences h>* or h<*. This is not a surprise because Theorem 4.

Theorem 2 has an obvious corollary.

THEOREM 3: The RDOS is a simplification ordering.

Proof: An ordering is a simplification ordering if it contains the 'embedding' which is the least fixed point of the following definition:

s = f(s1,...,sm) < g(t1,...tn) = t
if
- f = g and for each i si < ti or si = ti.
or - there exists tj such that s < tj.

Obviously the RPOS is a fixed point of this definition, thus the RPOS contains the embedding and the RDOS does too.

The next theorem is the key for the incrementality property used extensively in REVE.

THEOREM 4: The RDOS is monotonic which means that when the precedence is increased the RDOS is also increased.

Proof: Suppose < is a precedence included in a precedence <'. If dec(s) < dec(t), obviously dec(s) <' dec(t). One has just to use the same comparisons between the same elementary decompositions in both cases.

3. IMPROVEMENTS ON RECURSIVE DECOMPOSITION WITH STATUS.

Some improvements similar to those proposed in [6] can be made to the RDOS to make it more efficient. However they have to be adapted to the presence of status.

1. In path decompositions, only elementary decompositions with maximal symbol as leader are kept and if two elementary decompositions have the same leader f with status m only the highest is kept. Formally let us define

$d^{p}_{+}(t)$ [$d^{p}(t)$ and

d' [$d^{p}(t)$ => there exists d [$d^{p}_{+}(t)$ such that
leader(d) > leader(d')
or leader(d) = leader(d') and status(leader(d)) = m
and occurrence(d) > occurrence(d')

and use only $d^{p}_{+}(t)$ as path decomposition.

2. In decompositions only maximal path decompositions are kept.

3. Instead of considering the following as multisets or sequences of terms, they can be seen as multisets or sequences of decompositions. Since decompositions of subterm have to be computed when the decomposition of full term is built, this improves further call of the RDOS.

4. Because elementary decompositions are considered on a path, let us say p, it is possible to discriminate among the followers of a leader with a status m and to split the followers by putting aside the path decomposition that corresponds to this path p (see [6]). This is implemented in REVE and

makes the RDOS an again more powerful ordering. For instance it is now possible to prove with this 'quadripartite' Recursive Decomposition Ordering,

EXAMPLE 3 [6]:

$$((x * x) * (x *)) * ((y * y) * (y * y)) >_{RDOS} (x * y) * (x * y)$$

See Annex.

4. SKETCH OF THE IMPLEMENTATION

The implementation of the RDOS was made in CLU [13] as the rest of REVE 1 [12] and REVE 2 [3] and is a very good exercise in this style of programming, because it provides interesting recursive data structures. More precisely we were lead to define three main clusters namely elem_dec, path_dec, and decomposition that refer to one another (see Figure 1).

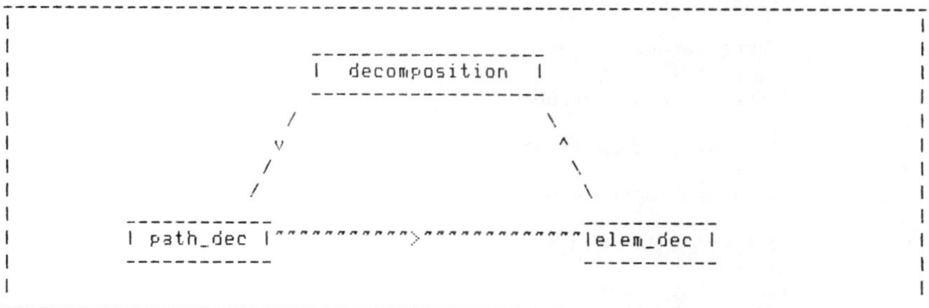

Figure 1: Simplified graph of cluster references

The representation of 'decomposition' refers to 'path_dec' via a cluster 'set'. The representation of 'path_dec' refers to 'elem_dec' and the representation of 'elem_dec' is a record which third field (context) refers to 'path_dec'. The second field (followers) allo refers to 'path_dec' if the improvement 4 is implemented and in any case to 'decomposition' via a cluster multiset or a cluster sequence.

The implementation of the comparison operations is easy, they return a value among 'eq', 'gt', 'lt' or 'undef' with obvious meanings. The implementation of the operations that build the decompositions is much more interesting. Indeed one constructs first the decompositions of the direct subterms for three purposes, for getting the elementary decomposition that corresponds to the root, for building the set of all the path decompositions belonging to the subterms, for preparing the root and the decompositions of its followers to be inserted into the already created elementary decompositions. In the next step the elementary decomposition at the root is inserted in the path decompositions already constructed Afterwards the root symbol and the decompositions of the direct subterms are added on the top of the context of the elementary decompositions already present.

5. CONCLUSION

Perhaps at first sight, the definition of the RDOS seems tricky, but the simple principles it is based upon,namely precedence and status, make it easy to understand. This is because the RDOS conforms to the natural idea one has on why 'a term prevails on another'.

Now we would like to say a word on how the incrementality works in REVE. Suppose we run a Knuth-Bendix algorithm. Then REVE generates equations that have to be oriented into rules and to be incorporated in a terminating set. If the RDOS and the precedence are able to orient such an equation, REVE does it, otherwise REVE returns a set of pairs of symbols that it suggests to incorporate into the current precedence. If the set contains only one pair or if REVE is 'greedy' (e.g. after setting a flag) then this pair (or these pairs) is (or are) added to the precedence. In other cases, the user is asked to choose the correct pair. If this step fails, REVE tries to set the status of one of the operators that occur in the equation. Presently, REVE does that by 'trial and error'. Annex 2 shows how the incrementality works in REVE 2.

In their paper Kamin and Levy proposed to include semantics in the RPO. It is possible to do the same with the RDO. Instead of comparing roots of subterms at certain occurrence as we do with decompositions we may perform more comparisons based on a semantics. That would involve changing the information contained in the first component of an elementary decomposition.

Acknowledgements: I am twice indebted to Jean-Pierre Jouannaud for the great part he took in defining the RDO and for stimulating discussions that lead me to the idea of lexicographical decompositions. I thank Randy Forgaard for allowing me to use his wonderful REVE 2 as an illustration in Annex. I am grateful towards ADI (contract 82/767) and Greco Programmation for their help.

6. REFERENCES

[1] BOOK R., 'Confluent and others types of Thue systems,' J. of Ass. Comp. Mach. 29 (1982) , 223-229.

[2] DERSHOWITZ N., 'Ordering for Term Rewriting systems' Theoretical Computer Science 17 (1982), 279-301.

[3] FORGAARD R., 'A Program for Generatingand Analizing Term Rewriting Systems' Master's Thesis, MIT Lab. for Computer Science, Cambridge Massachusetts USA (1984) (To appear).

[4] HUET G., LANKFORD D., 'On the Uniform halting Problem for Term Rewriting Systems' Rapport 283, IRIA, Mars 1978, INRIA Rocquencourt, France.

[5] HUET G., 'Confluent Reductions: Abstract Properties and Applications to Term Rewriting Systems,' J of Ass. Comp. Mach. 27, (1980) 797-821.

[6] JOUANNAUD J-P., LESCANNE P., REINIG F., 'Recursive Decomposition Ordering' Conf. on Formal Description of Programming Concepts II, North Holland, (D. Bjorner Ed.) (1982), pp 331-346.

[7] JOUANNAUD J-P., LESCANNE P., 'On Multiset Orderings' Inf. Proc. trs, 10 (1982), pp 57-63

[8] KAMIN S., LEVY J-J., 'Attempts for Generalizing the Recusive Path Ordering' Unpublished manuscript, Feb. 1980.

[9] KNUTH D.E., BENDIX P.B., 'Simple Word problems in Universal Algebras,' in Computational Problems in Abstract Algebra, Ed. Leech J., Pergamon Press (1969), 263-297.

[10] LANKFORD D., 'On Proving Term Rewriting Systems are Noetherian' MTP-3 Math Dept Louisiana Tech U (May 1979).

[11] LESCANNE P. 'Some properties of the Decomposition Ordering, a Simplification Ordering to prove termination of rewriting systems', RAIRO Informatique Theorique / Theoritecal Informatics, 16 (1982), pp 331-347.

[12] LESCANNE P., 'Computer Experiments with the REVE Term Rewriting System Generator' 10th ACM Conf. on Priciples of Programming Languages, Austin Texas, 24-26 January, 99-108.

[13] LISKOV B., ATKINSON R., BLOOM T., MOSS E., SCHAFFERT J.G., SCHEIFFLER R., SNYDER A., 'CLU Reference Manual' Lecture Notes in Computer Science vol. 114 (1981).

[14] NIVAT M., 'Congruences Parfaites et Quasi-Parfaites', Seminaires Dubreuil, 25eme annee, (1971).

[15] PLAISTED D., A Recursively Defined Ordering for Proving Termination of Term Rewriting Systems', Dept. of Computer Science Report 78-943, Univ. of Illinois at Urbana Champaign Sept. 1978.

ANNEX: Experiments with the RDO in REVE 2

```
-------------
| EXAMPLE 1 |
-------------

REVE 2.1

Welcome to REVE, a Rewrite Rule Laboratory.
Copyright 1983 Pierre Lescanne, John Guttag, and Randy Forgaard
Type `?', followed by a carriage return, for help.

-> read

The equations in the file you specify will replace the rules and equations that
are currently in the system.
The default suffix for equation files is `.eqn'.  To see a list of available
example files, type `?'.

Specify a file to be read: ex_1

Equations:

1.   not((x & y)) == (not(x) | not(y))


Rewrite Rules:


-> kb

Starting Knuth-Bendix...

The following equation currently cannot be ordered:

not((x & y)) == (not(x) | not(y))

The following precedence suggestions may allow the equation to be ordered:

    1.  & > not
    2.  & > |
    3.  not > |

If you accept all of the above suggestions, the equation can be ordered
as it stands.  Do you accept all of them (y/n)? n

Please type a sequence of numbers indicating your choices, or SKIP this
equation, REVERSE it, INTERRUPT Knuth-Bendix, UNDO,
or repeat the CHOICES (#///r/i/u/c): 2

Equation has been ordered:
    not((x & y)) == (not(x) | not(y))

Rule added to rewriting system:
    not((x & y)) -> (not(x) | not(y))
```

```
Equations:


Rewrite Rules:

1.    not((x & y)) -> (not(x) | not(y))

Your system is complete!




-------------
| EXAMPLE 2 |
-------------


REVE 2.1

....

Equations:

1.    h((h(x) * x)) == (x * h((x * x)))


Rewrite Rules:


-> status

For which operator would like to set the status? *
Would you like LEFT-to-right status, or RIGHT-to-left status (l/r)? l

-> kb

Starting Knuth-Bendix...

Equation has been ordered:
    h((h(x) * x)) == (x * h((x * x)))

Rule added to rewriting system:
    h((h(x) * x)) -> (x * h((x * x)))

Interrupt...
```

```
-------------
| EXAMPLE 3 |
-------------


REVE 2.1


Equations:

1.   (((x * x) * (x * x)) * ((y * y) * (y * y))) == ((x * y) * (x * y))


Rewrite Rules:


-> kb

Starting Knuth-Bendix...

Equation has been ordered:
    (((x * x) * (x * x)) * ((y * y) * (y * y))) == ((x * y) * (x * y))

Rule added to rewriting system:
    (((x * x) * (x * x)) * ((y * y) * (y * y))) -> ((x * y) * (x * y))

Interrupt...
```

ALTERNATING FINITE AUTOMATA ON ω-WORDS

Satoru Miyano
Department of Mathematics, Kyushu University 33, Fukuoka 812, Japan

Takeshi Hayashi
College of General Education, Kyushu University 01, Ropponmatsu, Fukuoka 810, Japan

Abstract. The classes of ω-languages defined by alternating finite automata are investigated and characterized under four types of acceptance conditions. It is shown that for each acceptance condition alternating finite automata on ω-words accept only ω-regular laguages and for one type of acceptance condition alternation increases the power in comparison with nondeterminism but for other three cases it does not.

1. Introduction

We characterize the classes of ω-languages defined by alternating finite automata on ω-words for four basic acceptance definitions including ones in Büchi(1960) and Landweber(1969). An ω-word is an infinite sequence of symbols of finite kinds and ω-language is a set of ω-words. Various types of automata which process ω-words have been considered and their accepting ω-language classes have been investigated (Büchi 1960; Choueka 1974; Cohen & Gold 1977 a,b, 1978 a,b). In particular, the classes of ω-languages accepted by nondeterministic and deterministic finite automata on ω-words have been extensively studied and the characterizations of these classes have been obtained in terms of regular sets (Büchi 1960; Eilenberg 1974; Hartmanis 1967; Hossley 1972; Kobayashi et al. 1983; Landweber 1969; McNaughton 1966; Nivat 1981; Rabin 1969; Staiger & Wagner 1974; Wagner 1977,1979).

Alternation has been introduced as an extended notion of

nondeterminism in Chandra et al. (1981). When finite automata are viewed as a method of describing sets of ω-words, alternation has a benefit that it makes the descriptions easy and simple. It is known that alternating finite automata on finite length words accept only regular sets whether they have one-way input head or two-way input head (Chandra et al. 1981; Ladner et al. 1978). On the other hand, for ω-words, nondeterministic finite automata define a larger class of ω-languages than deterministic ones for some acceptance definition. Our interest here is how alternation affects the accepting power of ω-languages for finite automata on ω-words. We compare the classes of ω-languages accepted by alternating finite automata on ω-words with nondeterministic ones. We show that for one of the four types of acceptance definitions alternation increases it accpeting power but for other three cases it does not. Our results are summarized in Table I of Section 3 in comparison with nondeterministic and deterministic classes. The table shows that any ω-language accepted by alternating finite automaton is ω-regular language (McNaughton 1966) for each cases. More interesting point is that the nondeterministic and deterministic classes differ for the acceptance definition introduced by Büchi (1960) and the nondeterministic and alternating classes differ for its dual acceptance definition.

2. Preliminaries

Let Σ be a finite alphabet. We denote by Σ^ω the set of all infinite sequences over Σ. Elements in Σ^ω are called *ω-words* and a subset L of Σ^ω is called an *ω-language*.

Definition 2.1. An *alternating finite automaton* (abbreviated *afa*) is a sextuple $M=(Q,f,\Sigma,\Delta,q_0,\mathfrak{F})$, where

(1) Q is a finite set of states and f is a mapping f: $Q \rightarrow \{and, or\}$. If $f(q)=and$ (resp. or), q is called a *universal state* (resp. *existential state*).

(2) Σ is a finite alphabet.

(3) Δ is a subset of $Q\times\Sigma\times Q$ such that the set $\Delta(q,a)=\{p \mid (q,a,p)$ is in $\Delta\}$ is not empty for any q in Q and any a in Σ. Elements in Δ are called *transitions*.

(4) q_0 is a state in Q called the *initial state*.

(5) $\mathfrak{F}$ is a family of subsets of Q. For F in $\mathfrak{F}$, F is called a *final set* and elements in F are called *final states*. If $\mathfrak{F}$ consists of a single final set, then we say that M is *simple*.

Definition 2.2. A *nondeterministic finite automaton* (abbreviated *nfa*) is an *afa* whose states are all existential states and we omit the function f from notation. A *deterministic finite automaton* (abbreviated *dfa*) is an *nfa* with the property that $|\Delta(q,a)|=1$ for each q in Q and each a in Σ.

Definition 2.3. Let $x=x_1x_2x_3\ldots$ be in Σ^ω, where x_n is in Σ for $n\geqq 1$. A *computation tree* $T(M,x)$ *of* M *on* x is an infinite labelled tree satisfying the following conditions:

(1) $T(M,x)$ has no leaf.

(2) The nodes are labelled with the elements in Q. In particular, the root of $T(M,x)$ is labelled with q_0.

(3) For each $n\geqq 1$, the edges between level n and level $n+1$ are labelled with x_n.

(4) If node v in level n is labelled with a universal state q, then v has a child labelled with p for each p in $\Delta(q,x_n)$.

(5) If node v in level n is labelled with an existential state

q, then v has exactly one child labelled with p for some p in $\Delta(q, x_n)$.

Definition 2.4. An infinite path α in $T(M,x)$ beginning at the root is called a *run in* $T(M,x)$. For a run α, we define

(1) $\mathrm{I}(\alpha)=\{q \mid$ state q occurs in α infinitely many times$\}$,

(2) $\mathrm{O}(\alpha)=\{q \mid$ state q occurs in $\alpha\}$.

Definition 2.5. For an *afa* $M=(Q,f,\Sigma,\Delta,q_0,\mathfrak{F})$ and x in Σ^ω, we say that M accepts x in the sense of C_i $(i=1,\ldots,4)$ if there exists a computation tree $T(M,x)$ such that for each run α in $T(M,x)$, there exists F in $\mathfrak{F}$ satisfying the condition C_i, where

(C_1) $\mathrm{I}(\alpha)\cap F\neq\phi$.

(C_2) $\mathrm{I}(\alpha)\subseteq F$.

(C_3) $\mathrm{O}(\alpha)\cap F\neq\phi$.

(C_4) $\mathrm{O}(\alpha)\subseteq F$.

We call $T(M,x)$ an *accepting computation tree* of M on x in the sense of C_i, respectively. For $i=1,\ldots,4$, we denote by $L_i(M)$ the set of ω-words accepted by M in the sense of C_i and we say that M *recognizes* an ω-language L in the sense of C_i if $L=L_i(M)$.

Definition 2.6. For $i=1,\ldots,4$, we define

(1) $\mathfrak{A}_i=\{L_i(M) \mid M$ is an *afa*$\}$,

(2) $\mathfrak{A}_i^s=\{L_i(M) \mid M$ is a simple *afa*$\}$,

(3) $\mathfrak{N}_i=\{L_i(M) \mid M$ is an *nfa*$\}$,

(4) $\mathfrak{N}_i^s=\{L_i(M) \mid M$ is a simple *nfa*$\}$,

(5) $\mathfrak{D}_i=\{L_i(M) \mid M$ is a *dfa*$\}$,

(6) $\mathfrak{D}_i^s=\{L_i(M) \mid M$ is a simple *dfa*$\}$.

3. Overview of the classes concerned

The classes $\mathfrak{D}_i$ and $\mathfrak{N}_i$ $(i=1,\ldots,4)$ have been characterized in terms of general topology and the representations of the ω-languages in these classes have been obtained by applying several operations to regular languages. In the following sections we will determine the classes for alternating finite automata on ω-words by establishing the relationship between $\mathfrak{A}_i$ and $\mathfrak{N}_i$ for $i=1,\ldots,4$. We will be concerned with the classes denoted by R, G^R, F^R, G^R_δ and F^R_σ, which are defined as follows:

(1) R: An ω-language in R is of the form $\cup_{i=1}^{n} U_i \cdot V_i^\omega$ for some regular languages U_i and V_i, where we define $U^\omega = \{ y_1 y_2 \ldots y_n \ldots \mid y_j$ is a nonempty word in U for $j \geq 1\}$ for $U \subseteq \Sigma^*$. R is called the class of ω-regular languages (McNaughton 1966).

(2) G^R: An ω-language in G^R is of the form $U \cdot \Sigma^\omega$, where U is a regular languages and Σ is a finite alphabet.

(3) F^R: For a set $U \subseteq \Sigma^*$, $A(U)$ denotes the set $\{w \mid w \in \Sigma^*$ and w is an initial segment of some word in $U\}$. An ω-language in F^R is described as $C(U) = \{x \mid x \in \Sigma^\omega$ and each initial segment of x is in $A(U)\}$ for some regular language U.

(4) F^R_σ: An ω-language in F^R_σ is of the form $\cup_{i=1}^{n} U_i \cdot C(V_i)$ for some regular languages U_i and V_i.

(5) G^R_δ: An ω-language L in G^R_δ is written as $L = \{x \mid x \in \Sigma^\omega, A(x) \cap W$ is infinite $\}$ for some regular language $W \subseteq \Sigma^*$, where $A(x) \subseteq \Sigma^*$ denotes the set of the initial segments of x.

We summarize in Table I our new results together with the former results on deterministic and nondeterministic finite automata on ω-words. For $\mathfrak{D}_i$ and $\mathfrak{N}_i$, we refer the reader to the table in Wagner (1979, p. 129).

TABLE I

	C_1	C_2	C_3	C_4
$\mathfrak{D}_i$	G_δ^R	F_σ^R	G^R	F^R
$\mathfrak{N}_i$	R	F_σ^R	G^R	F^R
$\mathfrak{A}_i$	R	R	G^R	F^R

As shown in Table I, C_1 type acceptance separates the nondeterministic and deterministic classes and C_2 type acceptance separates the alternating and nondeterministic classes. On the other hand, no changes occur under C_3 and C_4 type acceptances.

4. Simple alternating finite automata

It is known that a single final set is sufficient for nondeterministic and deterministic cases under all acceptance conditions C_i, *i.e.*, $\mathfrak{D}_i=\mathfrak{D}_i^S$ and $\mathfrak{N}_i=\mathfrak{N}_i^S$ for $i=1,\ldots,4$ (Staiger & Wagner 1974). The purpose of this section is to show that the same fact also holds for alternating finite automata on ω-words.

Theorem 4.1. $\mathfrak{A}_i=\mathfrak{A}_i^S$ *for* $i=1,\ldots,4$.

Proof. Let $M=(Q,f,\Sigma,\Delta,q_0,\mathfrak{F})$, For each $i=1,\ldots,4$, we construct a simple *afa* which recognizes the same ω-language as M in the sense of C_i.

Case (i) C_1: Consider a simple *afa* $M^S=(Q,f,\Sigma,\Delta,q_0,\{F^S\})$, where $F^s = \{q \mid q \in F,\ F \in \mathfrak{F}\}$. Then M and M^s recognize the same ω-language in the sense of C_1 .

Case (ii) C_2: We define a simple afa $M^s = (Q^s, f^s, \Sigma, \Delta^s, q_0^s, \{F^s\})$ in the same way as Staiger & Wagner (1974, Lemma 4).

(1) $Q^s = \{(q, \mathfrak{F}') \mid q \in Q,\ \mathfrak{F}' \subseteq \mathfrak{F},\ q$ is in F for each F in $\mathfrak{F}'\}$.

(2) $f^s(q, \mathfrak{F}') = f(q)$ for $(q, \mathfrak{F}')$ in Q^s .

(3) $q_0^s = (q_0, \emptyset)$.

(4) For each transition (q, a, p) in Δ, Δ^s contains $((q, \mathfrak{F}'), a, (p, \{F \mid F \in \mathfrak{F}',\ p \in F\}))$ for all $\emptyset \neq \mathfrak{F}' \subseteq \mathfrak{F}$ and $((q, \emptyset), a, (p, \{F \mid F \in \mathfrak{F},$ and $p \in F\}))$.

(5) $F^s = \{(q, \mathfrak{F}') \mid (q, \mathfrak{F}') \in Q^s$ and $\mathfrak{F}' \neq \emptyset\}$.

Let x be in Σ^ω. Then it should be noticed that there is a one-to-one correspondence between the computation trees of M on x and the computation trees of M^s on x. Namely, for a computation tree $T(M, x)$ of M on x, we associate it with a computation tree $T(M^s, x)$ of M^s on x that begins with the root $(q_0, \emptyset)$ and is created by expanding it according to the transitions corresponding those in $T(M, x)$. Conversely, for $T(M^s, x)$, we associate it with $T(M, x)$ by replacing label $(q, \mathfrak{F}')$ by q for each node. Let $T(M, x)$ and $T(M^s, x)$ be the computation trees of M on x and M^s on x corresponding to each other. For a run α in $T(M, x)$, we denote by α^s the corresponding run in $T(M^s, x)$ and vice versa. We will show that the following two statements are equivalent:

(6) For each run α in $T(M, x)$, there exists F in $\mathfrak{F}$ such that $\mathrm{I}(\alpha) \subseteq F$.

(7) For each run α^s in $T(M^s, x)$, $\mathrm{I}(\alpha^s) \subseteq F^s$.

Let α and α^s be

$$\alpha : q_0 \xrightarrow{x_1} q_1 \xrightarrow{x_2} \cdots \xrightarrow{x_n} q_n \xrightarrow{x_{n+1}} \cdots$$

$$\alpha^s : (q_0, \mathfrak{F}_0) \xrightarrow{x_1} (q_1, \mathfrak{F}_1) \xrightarrow{x_2} \cdots \xrightarrow{x_n} (q_n, \mathfrak{F}_n) \xrightarrow{x_{n+1}} \cdots$$

Then note that there exists an integer k_0 such that for any $k \geqq k_0$, $\mathrm{I}(\alpha)=\{q_n \mid n \geqq k\}$. Similarly, there exists an integer $k_1 \geqq k_0$ such that $\mathrm{I}(\alpha^s)=\{(q_n, \mathfrak{F}_n) \mid n \geqq k\}$ for all $k \geqq k_1$. Assume that (6) holds. If $\mathfrak{F}_m=\phi$ for some $m \geqq k_1$, then $\mathfrak{F}_n=\phi$ for infinitely many $n \geqq k_1$. Since $\mathfrak{F}_m=\phi$ and $\mathrm{I}(\alpha)=\{q_n \mid n \geqq m\} \subseteq F$, we can see by the definition of Δ^s that $\mathfrak{F}_{m+1}$ contains F. Therefore again by the definition of Δ^s, $\mathfrak{F}_n$ contains F for all $n>m$. Hence $\mathfrak{F}_n \neq \phi$ for all $n>m$. This is a contradiction. Therefore $\mathfrak{F}_n \neq \phi$ for all $n \geqq k_1$. Hence $\mathrm{I}(\alpha^s) \subseteq F^s$. Conversely assume that $\mathrm{I}(\alpha^s) \subseteq F^s$. Then by the definition of Δ^s, $\mathfrak{F}_{n+1} \subseteq \mathfrak{F}_n$ and $\mathfrak{F}_n \neq \phi$ for all $n \geqq k_1$. Since $\mathfrak{F}_n$ is finite, there exists F such that F is in $\mathfrak{F}_n$ for all $n \geqq k_1$. Hence q_n is in F for all $n \geqq k_1$. Therefore $\mathrm{I}(\alpha) \subseteq F$. Hence M and M^s define the same set of ω-words.

Case (iii) C_3: The same as case (i).

Case (iv) C_4: We define a simple *afa* $M^s=(Q^s, f^s, \Sigma, \Delta^s, q_0^s, \{F^s\})$ as follows:

(1) $Q^s=\{(q, \mathfrak{F}') \mid q \in Q,\ \mathfrak{F}' \subseteq \mathfrak{F},\ q \text{ is in } F \text{ for all } F \text{ in } \mathfrak{F}'\}$.

(2) $f^s(q, \mathfrak{F}')=f(q)$ for $(q, \mathfrak{F}')$ in Q^s.

(3) $q_0^s=(q_0, \mathfrak{F}_0)$, where $\mathfrak{F}_0=\{F \mid q_0 \in F,\ F \in \mathfrak{F}\}$.

(4) For each transition (q, a, p) in Δ, Δ^s contains $((q, \mathfrak{F}'), a, (p, \{F \mid F \in \mathfrak{F}',\ p \in F\}))$ for all $\mathfrak{F}' \subseteq \mathfrak{F}$.

(5) $F^s=\{(q, \mathfrak{F}') \mid (q, \mathfrak{F}') \in Q^s \text{ with } \mathfrak{F}' \neq \phi\}$.

In the same way as case (ii), there is a one-to-one correspondence between the computation trees of M on x and the computation trees of M^s on x. We use the same notations as case (ii). We will show the equivalence of the following two statements:

(6) For each run α in $T(M, x)$, there exists F in $\mathfrak{F}$ such that $\mathrm{O}(\alpha) \subseteq F$.

(7) For each run α^s in $T(M^s,x)$, $O(\alpha^s)\subseteq F^s$.

Let α and α^s denote the same paths as in case (ii). Assume that $O(\alpha)-\{q_n \mid n\geq 0\}\subseteq F$ for some F in $\mathfrak{F}$. By definition, $F\in\mathfrak{F}_0$ and therefore $F\in\mathfrak{F}_n$ for all $n\geq 0$. Hence $O(\alpha^s)\subseteq F^s$. Conversely assume that $O(\alpha^s)\subseteq F^s$. Since $\mathfrak{F}_{n+1}\subseteq\mathfrak{F}_n$ and $\mathfrak{F}_n\neq\phi$ for all $n\geq 0$, there exists F such that $F\in\mathfrak{F}_n$ for all $n\geq 0$. By the definition of Δ^s, $q_n\in F$ for all $n\geq 0$. Hence $O(\alpha)\subseteq F$. □

5. Comparison with the nondeterministic classes

Theorem 5.1. $\mathfrak{A}_1=\mathfrak{N}_1$.

Proof. The containment $\mathfrak{N}_1\subseteq\mathfrak{A}_1$ is obvious. Let L be an ω-language in $\mathfrak{A}_1$ and let $M=(Q,f,\Sigma,\Delta,q_0,\{F\})$ be a simple *afa* which recognizes L in the sense of C_1. To show the containment $\mathfrak{A}_1\subseteq\mathfrak{N}_1$, we construct an *nfa* M' which recognizes L in the sense of C_1. Before describing M', we need several preliminary notations and observations. Let x be in Σ^ω and let T be a computation tree of M on x. For a node u of T, we denote by $T(u)$ the subtree of T with root u. For $n\geq 1$, $V(n,T)$ denotes the set of the nodes in level n. Given $n\geq m\geq 1$, we divide $V(n,T)$ as follows:

(1) $V_0(n,m,T)=\{u \mid u$ is in $V(n,T)$ and the path between u and the node in level m does not hold any element in $F\}$.

(2) $V_1(n,m,T)=V(n,T)-V_0(n,m,T)$.

$V_0(n,m,T)=\phi$ means that all the paths between level n and level m hold some elements in F. For $n\geq m\geq 1$, we define an equivalence relation $R(n,m,T)$ on $V(n,T)$ by $uR(n,m,T)v$ if (3) and (4) hold.

(3) Both u and v are in $V_0(n,m,T)$ or both u and v are in $V_1(n,m,T)$.

(4) u and v hold the same label.

Assume that M accepts x in the sense of C_1. Then we show that there exist an accepting computation tree T and a sequence $0=r_0<r_1<\ldots<r_n<\ldots$ of integers satisfying (5) and (6).

(5) $r_{n+1}=\min\{m \mid m>r_n \text{ and } V_0(m, r_n+1, T)=\phi\}$ for $n\geqq 0$.

(6) For each n, m with $r_n<m\leqq r_{n+1}$, if $uR(m, r_n+1, T)v$, then the transitions taken at u are the same as those at v.

In order to show that such T and $\{r_n\}_{n=0}^{\infty}$ exist, we define a sequence $\{T_n\}_{n=0}^{\infty}$ of accepting computation trees of M on x. We define T_n and r_n inductively. Let $r_0=0$ and T_0 be an arbitrary accepting computation tree of M on x. Assume that T_n and r_m are defined but T_{n+1} and r_{m+1} are not. Moreover assume that $n\geqq r_m$ and $V_0(l, r_m+1, T_n)\subseteqq V_0(l, r_m+1, T_{r_m})$ for $l>r_m$. Let $C[u_1], \ldots, C[u_k]\subseteqq V(n+1, T_n)$ be the equivalence classes of $R(n+1, r_m+1, T_n)$, where u_j $(j=1, \ldots, k)$ are their representative nodes in level $n+1$. Then in T_n, for each j $(j=1, \ldots, k)$ we replace the subtree $T_n(u)$ at u by $T_n(u_j)$ for all u in $C[u_j]$. Let T_{n+1} be the tree obtained by the above replacement. Then notice that T_{n+1} is an accepting computation tree of M on x. If $V_0(n+1, r_m+1, T_n)=\phi$, then we define $r_{m+1}=n+1$ else r_{m+1} is not yet defined. Since T_{r_m} is an accepting computation tree, there exists an integer $l>r_m$ such that $V_0(l, r_m+1, T_{r_m})=\phi$. By (3) and (4), we see that $V_0(l, r_m+1, T_{n+1})\subseteqq V_0(l, r_m+1, T_n)$ for all $l>r_m$. Therefore $V_0(l, r_m+1, T_{n+1})\subseteqq V_0(l, r_m+1, T_{r_m})$. Since $V_0(l, r_m+1, T_{r_m})=\phi$, r_{m+1} will be eventually defined. Then note that r_{m+1} is defined to be $\min\{l \mid l>r_m \text{ and } V_0(l, r_m+1, T_l)=\phi\}$. Hence $\{r_n\}_{n=0}^{\infty}$ and $\{T_n\}_{n=0}^{\infty}$ are defined. Then there exists a computation tree T such that T coincides with T_n up to level n for all $n\geqq 0$. Then by the choice of $\{r_n\}_{n=0}^{\infty}$, $V_0(r_{n+1}, r_n+1, T)=\phi$ for all $n\geqq 0$. Hence T is an accepting computation tree of M on x. Obviously, T and $\{r_n\}_{n=0}^{\infty}$ satisfy (5) and (6).

We now describe the moves of M'. Let $x=x_1x_2x_3\ldots$ be in Σ^{ω}. If

M accepts x in the sense of C_1, then by the above observation there exist an accepting computation tree T and a sequence $\{r_n\}_{n=0}^{\infty}$ satisfying (5) and (6). M' has two variables Q_0 and Q_1 that take subsets of Q as values. M' on x simulates T level by level. In simulating the level n ($r_m<n\leqq r_{m+1}$) of T, M' keeps the labels of the nodes in $V_i(n,r_m+1,T)$ in Q_i for $i=0,1$. By (3)-(6), M' need not keep all the nodes in level n. Initially, if q_0 is in F, then $Q_0=\phi$ and $Q_1=\{q_0\}$ else $Q_0=\{q_0\}$ and $Q_1=\phi$. Assume that in level n, $Q_0=Q_0^{(n)}$ and $Q_1=Q_1^{(n)}$. In level $n+1$, variables Q_0 and Q_1 are changed in the following way:

(1) $Q_0^{(n)}\neq\phi$: For each universal state q in $Q_0^{(n)}$ and for each state p in $\Delta(q,x_n)$, if p is in F then p is put into Q_1 else into Q_0. For each existential state q in $Q_0^{(n)}$, M' nondeterministically chooses a state p in $\Delta(q,x_n)$ and puts p into Q_1 if p is in F else into Q_0. For each universal state q in $Q_1^{(n)}$ all states in $\Delta(q,x_n)$ are put into Q_1 and for each existential state q in $Q_1^{(n)}$, exactly one state is nondeterministically chosen from $\Delta(q,x_n)$ and is put into Q_1.

(2) $Q_0^{(n)}=\phi$: In this case we say that M' is in the reset mode. For each universal state q in $Q_1^{(n)}$ and for each state p in $\Delta(q,x_n)$, if p is in F then p is put into Q_1 else into Q_0. For each existential state q in $Q_1^{(n)}$, a state p in $\Delta(q,x_n)$ is nondeterministically chosen and M' puts p into Q_1 if p is in F else into Q_0.

Then it should be noticed that M' on x can pass the reset mode infinitely often. Conversely, if M' on x can pass the reset mode infinitely often, then it is easily observed that there is an accepting computation tree of M on x in the sense of C_1. By this observation, we define the set F' of final states of M' by the set of states in the reset mode. Then L is recognized by M' in the sense of C_1. □

Theorem 5.2. $\mathfrak{A}_3=\mathfrak{N}_3$.

Proof. For a simple *afa* M, let M' be the same simple *nfa* as the one constructed in Theorem 5.1. Then we can show in a similar way that M' recognizes the same ω-language as M in the sense of C_3 . □

Theorem 5.3. $\mathfrak{A}_4=\mathfrak{N}_4$.

Proof. Let $M=(Q,f,\Sigma,\Delta,q_0,\{F\})$ be a simple *afa*. A simple *nfa* M' that recognizes the same ω-language as M in the sense of C_4 moves as follows: M' has a variable S which takes a subset of Q as a value. Assume that an input $x=x_1x_2x_3\ldots$ is given. Initially M' puts $S=\{q_0\}$. Assume that at step n, $S=S_n$. S is updated as follows: For each universal state q in S_n, all states in $\Delta(q,x_n)$ are put into S and for each existential state q in S_n, exactly one state in $\Delta(q,x_n)$ is chosen and is put into S. The set F' of final states of M' is $\{Q' \mid \phi\neq Q'\subseteq F\}$. Then it is easily observed that M accepts x in the sense of C_4 if and only if M' accepts x in the sense of C_4 . □

Lemma 5.4 (Büchi 1960). *$\mathfrak{N}_1$ is closed under complement.*

Theorem 5.5. $\mathfrak{A}_1=\mathfrak{A}_2$.

Proof. We show that for $L\subseteq\Sigma^\omega$, L is in $\mathfrak{A}_1$ if and only if $\overline{L}=\Sigma^\omega-L$ is in $\mathfrak{A}_2$. We first prove that $L\in\mathfrak{A}_1$ implies $\overline{L}\in\mathfrak{A}_2$. Assume that L is in $\mathfrak{A}_1$ and let $M=(Q,f,\Sigma,\Delta,q_0,\{F\})$ be a simple *afa* that recognizes L in the sense of C_1 . We show that $\overline{L}$ is in $\mathfrak{A}_2$. By definition, the following two statements are equivalent:

(1) x is in $\overline{L}$.

(2) For any computation tree $T(M,x)$, there exists a run α in $T(M,x)$ such that $\mathrm{I}(\alpha)\subseteq \bar{F}$, where $\bar{F}=Q-F$.

Then consider a simple afa $\bar{M}=(Q,\bar{f},\Sigma,\Delta,q_0,\{\bar{F}\})$, where $\bar{f}(q)=and$ if $f(q)=or$, $\bar{f}(q)=or$ if $f(q)=and$. Then notice that the following statement is equivalent to (2):

(3) There exists a computation tree $T(\bar{M},x)$ of $\bar{M}$ on x such that for any run α in $T(\bar{M},x)$, $\mathrm{I}(\alpha)\subseteq\bar{F}$.

Hence $\bar{L}$ is in $\mathcal{A}_2$. The converse implication can be proved in the same way. By Theorem 5.1 and Lemma 5.4, $\mathcal{A}_1$ is closed under complement. Therefore by the above equivalence we see that $\mathcal{A}_1=\mathcal{A}_2$. □

By the theorems of this section and the results already known for $\mathcal{N}_i$ $(i=1,\ldots,4)$, the proof of Table I is completed.

Concluding remarks

In the definition of alternating finite automata, we have assumed that $\Delta(q,a)\neq\phi$ for each q in Q and each a in Σ. In the literatures (Hossley 1972; Wagner 1979), the case allowing $\Delta(q,a)=\phi$ has been also discussed. We call an afa which allows the case $\Delta(q,a)=\phi$ a partial afa. Partial nfa and dfa can be similarly defined. Let $\mathcal{PD}_i$, $\mathcal{PN}_i$, $\mathcal{PA}_i$ $(i=1,\ldots,4)$ be the classes of ω-languages recognized by partial dfa's, partial nfa's, partial afa's in the sense of C_i, respectively. It is not hard to show that the partial and nonpartial classes are equal under C_1, C_2 and C_4 type acceptances for deterministic, nondeterministic and alternating cases. For C_3 type acceptance, $\mathcal{PD}_3$ and $\mathcal{PN}_3$ have been already determined (Wagner 1979). To determine $\mathcal{PA}_3$, first note that the classes of ω-languages recognized by simple partial afa's in the sense of C_3 is equal to $\mathcal{PA}_3$. Then we can prove $\mathcal{PA}_3=\mathcal{PN}_3$ by taking care of the undefined transitions in the construction of the *nfa* in the proof of Theorem 5.1. Table II summarizes the classes for partial finite automata on ω-words.

TABLE II

	C_1	C_2	C_3	C_4
$\mathcal{PD}_i$	G^R_δ	F^R_σ	$G^R\Delta F^R$	F^R
$\mathcal{PN}_i$	R	F^R_σ	F^R_σ	F^R
$\mathcal{PA}_i$	R	R	F^R_σ	F^R

$G^R\Delta F^R=\{L_1\cap L_2 \mid L_1\in G^R, L_2\in F^R\}$.

We have not examined the acceptances defined by the conditions

(C_5) $\mathrm{I}(\alpha)\in\mathfrak{F}$,

(C_6) $\mathrm{O}(\alpha)\in\mathfrak{F}$.

In Wagner(1979), the ω-languages defined by deterministic finite automata under C_5 and C_6 type acceptances were thoroughly studied.

References

Büchi, J.R.(1960). On an decision method in restricted second order arithmetic, *International Congress on Logic Methodology and Philosophy of Science*, Stanford, Calif.

Chandra, A.K., Kozen, D.C. & Stockmeyer, L.J.(1981). Alternation. *J. Assoc. Comput. Mach.* 28, 114-133.

Choueka, Y.(1974). Theories of automata on ω-tapes: A simplified approach. *J. Comput. System Sci.* 8, 117-142.

Cohen,R.S. & Gold, A.Y.(1977). Theory of ω-languages I: Characterizations of ω-context-free languages. *J. Comput. System Sci.* 15, 169-184.

Cohen, R.S. & Gold, A.Y.(1977). Theory of ω-languages II: A study of various models of ω-type generation and recognition. *J. Comput. System Sci.* 15, 185-208.

Cohen, R.S. & Gold, A.Y.(1978). ω-computations on deterministic pushdown machines. *J. Comput. System Sci.* 16, 275-300.

Cohen, R.S & Gold, A.Y.(1978). ω-computations on Turing machines. *Theoret. Comput. Sci.* 6, 1-23.

Eilenberg, S.(1974). *Automata, Lanugages, and Machines*, Vol. A. New York: Academic Press.

Hartmanis, J. & Stearns, R.E.(1967). Set of numbers defined by finite automata. *Amer. Math. Monthly* 74, 539-542.

Hossley, R.(1972). Finite tree automata and ω-automata. TR MAC TR-102, MIT. Cambridge, Mass.

Kobayashi, K., Takahashi, M & Yamasaki, H.(1983). Characterization of ω-regular languages by first-order formulas. TIT Research Report C-48. (to appear in *J. Comput. System Sci.*)

Ladner, R.E., Lipton,R.J. & Stockmeyer,L.J.(1978). Alternating pushdown automata. *Proc. 19th IEEE Symposium on Foundations of Computer Science*, 92-106.

Landweber, L.H.(1969). Decision problems for ω-automata. *Math. Systems Theory* 4, 376-384.

McNaughton, R.(1966). Testing and generating infinite sequences by a finite automaton. *Inform. Contr.* 9, 521-530.

Nivat, M.(1981). Behaviours of processes and synchronized systems of processes. Lecture note at Marktoberdopf NATO Summer School.

Rabin, M.O.(1969). Decidability of second-order theories and automata on infinite trees. *Trans. Amer. Math. Soc.* 141, 1-35.

Staiger,L. & Wagner, K.(1974). Automatentheoretische und automatenfreie Charakterisierungen topologischer Klassen regularer Folgenmengen. *EIK* 10, 379-392.

Wagner, K.(1977). Eine topologischer Charakterisierung einiger Klassen regularer Folgenmengen. *EIK* 13, 473-487.

Wagner, K.(1979). On ω-regular sets. *Inform. Contr.* 43, 123-177.

PROOF BY INDUCTION IN EQUATIONAL THEORIES WITH RELATIONS BETWEEN CONSTRUCTORS

E. Paul
Centre National d'Etudes des Telecommunications
38/40, Rue du General Leclerc
92131 Issy les Moulineaux, France

Abstract. This paper proposes a generalization of the inductive proof method of Huet and Hullot [3] to the case where there are relations between constructors. These relations can be simplifiers, or commutativity/associativity, or any combination of these two types, provided the following conditions are met:
1-One can build from these relations a complete term rewriting system (in the ordinary sense, or in the sense defined by Peterson and Stickel [9] if there are commutative/associative constructors).
2-These relations have a property which we have called "inductive completeness".
The results of this paper are similar to those of Remy [10]. The main differences are:
-the introduction of the notion of inductive completeness, which removes a failure case in the inductive completion algorithm.
-the introduction of a method of automatic simplification of equations, which avoids, in some cases, a loop forever of the completion algorithm.

1 INTRODUCTION-DEFINITION OF INDUCTIVE COMPLETENESS

When there are no relations between constructors, the generation of such a relation by the Knuth and Bendix completion algorithm, applied to the initial set of equations + the theorem to be proved, entails the disproof of this theorem.

Conversely, if there are relations between constructors, the algorithm may generate a new relation which is in fact an inductive consequence of the initial set of relations, and we cannot conclude anything.

To solve this problem, we will require that the relations between constructors have a property which we have called "inductive completeness". Intuitively, this property means that all inductive consequences of these relations have been obtained.

More formally, let F be a set of operators, every operator being given with its arity. Let T be the set of terms constructed from operators in F and variables in a given denumerable set V. Let E be a set of equations, i.e a set of equalities M=N, with M and N in T. The pair (F,E) is called an (equational) specification.

To simplify the notations, we assume we have only one sort; all the results of this paper carry over to many-sorted equational theories without difficulty.

We define two relations over T, =E (equational equality) and =IE (inductive equality) in the following way:

M =E N iff M=N is valid in all the models of (F,E). It is well known that this is equivalent to whether M=N can be derived from E, using only instantiation and replacement of equals by equals (Birkhoff's theorem). M =IE N iff M=N is valid in the initial algebra defined by (F,E). It is equivalent to say that, for every ground substitution s, Ms =E Ns

We obviously have: M =E N => M =IE N

The specification (F,E) is <u>inductively complete</u> iff the inverse property is true, i.e: M = IE N => M =E N.

This concept has been already used by Tarski [13] and Henkin [2], with a different name: an inductively complete equational specification is called a "base" for the initial algebra defined by this specification.

We give in annex some examples of inductively complete equational specifications. It seems that this property is not very difficult to obtain for the usual specifications, if we restrict to the inductive completeness of the sub-system of relations between constructors. This is sufficient for using the Knuth and Bendix completion algorithm as an inductive theorem prover.

However, in some cases (see annex), we can prove the inductive completeness of an equational specification including relations between defined operators. This result is interesting, since it shows that it is useless to look for inductive theorems other than the ones already obtained (note that we only deal with <u>equational theorems</u>. Non equational theorems, such as Fermat's conjecture, are not relevant to this method).

But we can not always obtain, from a given equational specification, a finite equational specification equivalent (i.e defining the same initial algebra) and inductively complete. We give in annex an example in which there is no finite inductively complete specification equivalent to the initial specification. In other words, whatever theorems we have already proved, we are sure that there are other theorems which are valid in the initial algebra, and which are not pure equational consequences of the already proved theorems.

Of course, such a specification (which we call an "inductive closure" of the initial specification) always exist if we accept infinite (denumerable) specifications: the set of all theorems valid in the initial algebra is an inductive closure.

The organization of the paper is as follows:

-In section 2, we give a criterion for proving or disproving theorems in the initial algebra.

-In section 3, to be able to use this criterion in practice, we orient the equations to form a rewriting system. We describe the modifications of the Knuth and Bendix completion algorithm for using it as an inductive theorem prover.

-In section 4, we examine the problem of completeness.

-In section 5, we propose an extension to the notion of constructor which allows to speed up the disproofs of theorems.

-In section 6, we propose an improvement of the inductive completion algorithm. This improvement is based on a procedure of automatic

simplification of equations.
-In annex, we give some examples of inductively complete equational specifications, and we give an example of a specification with no finite inductive closure.

2 PROOF OR DISPROOF OF THEOREMS IN THE INITIAL ALGEBRA OF AN EQUATIONAL THEORY

2.1 Notations

Let (F,E) be a specification as defined above. F is partitioned: F = C u D. We call the operators in C the constructors, and the operators in D the defined operators.

T is the set of terms constructed from operators in F and variables in a given denumerable set V.
Tc is the set of terms constructed from C and V.
G is the set of ground terms (i.e containing no variables) constructed from F.
Gc is the set of ground terms constructed from C.
M,N,P,Q,M1,N1,P1,Q1 are any terms.
m,n,p,q,m1,n1,p1,q1 are any ground terms.
X,Y,Z,X1,Y1,Z1 are variables.
s is a substitution. If M is a term, s(M) is denoted Ms.
I = G/=E is the initial algebra defined by the specification (F,E).

The set of equations E is partitioned : E = Ec u Ed, and for each equation M=N of Ec, we assume that M and N are in Tc. The set Ec is called "relations between constructors".

2.2 Principle of induction

To be able to prove (or disprove) theorems in the initial algebra I defined by (F,E), we assume that this specification meets the three following properties:

-The sub-specification (C,Ec) is inductively complete.
-The specification (F,E) is <u>complete</u> w.r.t. (C,Ec), i.e:
For every m in G, there is n in Gc such that m =E n.
-The specification (F,E) is <u>consistent</u> w.r.t. (C,Ec), i.e:
For every m,n in Gc, m =E n => m =Ec n.

From the completeness and consistency of (F,E) w.r.t.(C,Ec), it is easy to prove that the initial algebra I defined by (F,E) is the same as the initial algebra defined by (C,Ec): I = G/=E = Gc/=Ec.

2.3 Criterion for proving or disproving theorems

Let E1 be a set of equations that we want to prove in the initial algebra I. Let F1 be the set of new operators introduced by E1 (F1 may be empty).

Proving E1 is the same as proving that the initial algebra defined by the specification (FuF1,EuE1) is identical with the initial algebra defined by (F,E). Therefore, it is the same as proving that (FuF1,EuE1) is complete and consistent w.r.t. (F,E).

We suppose that we have proved the completeness of

(FuF1,EuE1) w.r.t. (F,E). This problem will be examined in section 4. Note that the completeness is obvious if F1 is empty.

Proving E1 is then the same as proving the consistency of (FuF1,EuE1) w.r.t.(F,E), i.e the following property:

For every m,n in G, m =EuE1 n => m =E n (1)

It is easy to prove, from the completeness and consistency of (F,E) w.r.t. (C,Ec), that (1) is equivalent to:

For every m,n in Gc, m =EuE1 n => m =Ec n (2)

The following theorem, which is the base of this paper, states that (2) can be extended to terms containing variables:

<u>Theorem A</u>:
(2) is equivalent to:
For every M,N in Tc, M =EuE1 N => M =Ec N (3)

Proof: (3) => (2) is obvious. Conversely, let us assume that (2) is true, and let M and N be in Tc such that M =EuE1 N.

Let s be a ground substitution such that, for every variable X occuring in M or N, Xs is in Gc.
Ms and Ns are in Gc, and Ms =EuE1 Ns. Therefore, by (2): Ms =Ec Ns

This equality holds for every ground substitution s. Therefore, from the definition of inductive equality: M =IEc N and from the inductive completeness of (C,Ec): M =Ec N. Therefore (3) is true.

3 <u>KNUTH AND BENDIX ALGORITHM AS AN INDUCTIVE THEOREM PROVER</u>

We assume familiarity with term rewriting systems and the Knuth and Bendix completion algorithm, as presented for instance in Huet [4]. If P and Q are two terms and R a term rewriting system, P =R Q denotes that P and Q have the same R-normal form.

From now on, we suppose that we can build from the equational system Ec a complete term rewriting system Rc (complete on terms, or on equivalence classes of terms if there are associative/ commutative constructors, as defined by Peterson and Stickel).

We can also declare some defined operators as associative/ commutative.

We assume given a well-founded partial ordering on terms >>, compatible with the term structure and stable by substitution, with which we prove the termination of the successive sets of rewrite rules.

To prove the set of equations E1, we run the Knuth and Bendix completion algorithm, initializing the set of rewrite rules to Rc and the set of equations to Ed u E1 (if there are AC operators, we run the Peterson and Stickel completion algorithm).

The only modification occurs in the step in which a pair of terms, coming from either a simplified critical pair or a reduced rewrite rule, is considered for orientation before being added as a new rewrite rule. This step should be modified as follows, assuming that (M,N) is the current candidate rewrite rule, with M # N:

- If M and N are in Tc, stop "disproof".
- If M is in Tc, and N is not in Tc:
    - If N >> M ,introduce new rule N -> M.
    - Otherwise stop "failure".
- If N is in Tc, and M is not in Tc:
    - If M >> N ,introduce new rule M -> N.
    - Otherwise stop "failure".

-If M is not in Tc, and N is not in Tc:
- -If M >> N ,introduce new rule M -> N.
- -If N >> M ,introduce new rule N -> M.
- -Otherwise stop "failure".

The rewriting system Rc, present at initialization, is kept without any modification all along the running of the algorithm. For if l->r is a rewrite rule in Rc, l and r are in Tc. Since it is forbidden to add rules whose left-hand sides are in Tc, l and r are irreducible all along the running of the algorithm.

Theorem B:
-If the algorithm stops with success, or if it runs for ever, (FuFl,EuEl) is consistent w.r.t.(F,E).
-If the algorithm stops with disproof, (FuFl,EuEl) is inconsistent w.r.t (F,E).

Proof: If the algorithm stops with success or runs for ever, let R be the final rewriting system constructed by the algorithm (R may be finite or infinite). We have R = Rc u Rl, and left-hand sides of rules in Rl are not in Tc. Let P and Q be two terms in Tc such that P =EuEl Q. From the confluence of R, we have: P =R Q. But P and Q, elements of Tc, are not reducible by rules of Rl. Therefore, P =Rc Q and P =Ec Q. From theorem A, (FuFl,EuEl) is consistent w.r.t.(F,E).

If the algorithm stops with disproof, we have found two terms M and N in Tc such that M =EuEl N and M #R N, R being the current rewriting system constructed by the completion algorithm. As Rc $\subseteq$ R, we have M #Rc N and M #Ec N. From theorem A, (FuFl,EuEl) is inconsistent w.r.t.(F,E).

Remark 1: If the set of equations Ed has been compiled before by the Knuth and Bendix algorithm, producing the complete rewriting system Rc u Rd, we can initialize the set of rewrite rules to Rc u Rd and the set of equations to El. In the same manner, once El has been proved, producing the complete rewriting system Rc u Rl, we can try to prove a new set of equations E2, initializing the set of rewrite rules to Rc u Rl and the set of equations to E2. Thus, we can build an iterative proof system as in [3]. The rewriting systems successively obtained are all in the form R = Rc u Rl where Rc is the initial rewriting system linking the constructors.

Remark 2: if we do not suppose that the system Ec is inductively complete, we can also run this algorithm with the following difference: if M and N are in Tc and M or N is not ground, we stop with failure, since the new relation between constructors may be (or not) an inductive consequence of the initial set of relations.

4 PROBLEMS OF COMPLETENESS

So far, we have assumed that, if the set of equations El we are trying to prove introduces new operators Fl, the specification (FuFl,EuEl) is complete w.r.t.(F,E),i.e. w.r.t. (C,Ec), because (F,E) is complete w.r.t.(C,Ec) by the principle of induction.

Actually, this property of completeness can be checked by examining the final rewriting system R produced by the completion algorithm. For this purpose, we need the two following lemmas:

Lemma 1: (FuF1,EuE1) is complete w.r.t.(C,Ec) iff the R-normal form of any ground term belongs to Gc.
Proof: obvious.

Lemma 2: (FuF1,EuE1) is complete w.r.t.(C,Ec) iff any defined operator f, with arity n, has the following property:
For all m1,...,mn in Gc in normal form, f(m1,...,mn) is R-reducible (i)
Proof: from lemma 1, by induction on the structure of ground terms.

Note that it is sufficient to check property (i) with terms mi in normal form. For if mi is not in normal form, the term f(m1,...,mn) is obviously reducible.

In practice, it is sufficient to check property (i) for the operators in F1, i.e. the newly introduced operators. For if f is a (non-constructor) operator in F, as (F,E) is complete w.r.t.(C,Ec) by the principle of induction, any term f(m1,...,mn) with mi in Gc is E-equal to a term in Gc. Therefore, such a term is reducible by confluence of R.

A well known sufficient condition to ensure the property (i) is the following:
-for any f in F1 with arity n, there is in R a set {Ri} of rules whose left-hand sides are in the form f(Si1,...,Sin).
-the set of n-tuples Si = {Si1,...,Sin} is complete for the constructors (see [3],[10] for a precise definition of that concept).

If there are no relations between constructors, the rules Ri can be regarded, in a natural way, as an inductive definition of operator f by cases on arguments constructed over the constructors. But if there are relations between constructors, this sufficient condition may be too restrictive in practice, since it does not take into account the fact that we have to check property (i) only when the terms mi are in normal form.

For example, let us take natural numbers, with constructors 0,1,+ and relations between constructors:
X+0 = X , X+Y = Y+X , X+(Y+Z) = (X+Y)+Z
(it is easy to verify that this specification is inductively complete)

Let us add to this specification the following equations defining the operator S(SUM_OF_INTEGERS): S(0) = 0 , S(X+1) = S(X)+X+1.

When we apply the Peterson and Stickel completion algorithm to these equations, we obtain the following rewriting system, confluent w.r.t.associativity/commutativity of +:

X+0 -> X
S(0) -> 0
S(1) -> 1
S(X+1) -> S(X)+X+1

A complete set of arguments constructed over the constructors is: {0,1,X+Y} , X and Y being two variables.

To prove the completeness of the definition of S by using the sufficient condition described above, it would be necessary that the terms S(0), S(1), S(X+Y) are left-hand sides of rules, and that is not the case for S(X+Y). More generally, it is easy to see that it is impossible to give a definition of S over any complete set of arguments constructed over the constructors 0,1,+.

Nevertheless, we can check that the definition of S is complete by a direct verification of property (i): any term m of Gc in normal form is obviously in one of the forms: 0, 1, 1+...+1, and it is easy to verify that any term in the form S(m) is R-reducible.

This example shows that the nice criterion of completeness, based on the definition of functions over complete sets of arguments, cannot always be applied when there are relations between constructors; if not, it is necessary to directly check property (i).

5 EXTENSION OF THE NOTION OF CONSTRUCTOR

If we look again at the results of sections 2 and 3, we can see that these results are always valid if we introduce in the set C, in addition to constructors, other non-constructor operators, provided that the equational system Ec linking together all these operators (constructors or not) would still be inductively complete. For example, in the algebraic examples given in annex, we can introduce the operator x (multiplication) in C.

The advantage of such an extension of the family of constructors is to speed up the disproofs of theorems. For example, in an arithmetical proof , if the completion algorithm generates the equation XxY = X+Y (X and Y being two variables) we can at once conclude that there is inconsistency, although x is not a constructor.

But there is a drawback: this method may increase the failure cases of the completion algorithm, because it increases the set Tc (terms built from constructors) and therefore increases the constraints when orienting a rewrite rule (no left-hand sides in Tc).

Note that the usual concept of constructors is still useful for the problem of completeness of new operators.

6 SIMPLIFICATION OF EQUATIONS

If there are no relations between constructors, the Huet and Hullot algorithm [3] is in fact more powerful than the algorithm described in section 3, because it comprises a procedure of simplification of equations which avoids, in some cases, an infinite loop of the algorithm. Furthermore, the disproof criterion is more efficient than the one used here. In this section, we generalize these methods when there are relations between constructors.

6.1 No relations between constructors

If there are no relations between constructors, when an equation M=N is generated by the Knuth and Bendix completion algorithm with M=C(M1,...,Mp) and N=C1(N1,...,Nq), C1 and C being two constructors, the Huet-Hullot algorithm proceeds in the following way (see [3] for a justification):

-If C=C1 (hence p=q), the equation M=N is replaced by the p equations Mi=Ni.
-If C#C1 , the algorithm stops with "disproof".

We can consider that these deductions are based on implicit non equational relations between constructors, namely (Xi,Yi are variables):

-For any constructor C:
C(X1,...,Xp)=C(Y1,...,Yp) => Xi=Yi for i=1,2,...,p (1)

-For any constructors C,C1 with C#C1:
C(X1,...,Xp)=C1(Y1,...,Yq) => TRUE=FALSE (2)

These relations are used by the completion algorithm as INFERENCE RULES. These inference rules can:
-either deduce from an equation other more simple equations, which allow to delete the initial equation (relations (1)).
-or disprove an equation (relations (2)).

The way these inference rules interact with the equations generated by the completion algorithm is exactly an application of the <u>resolution principle</u>, introduced by Robinson for automatic theorem proving in first order predicate calculus (see [12] for details about resolution).

The equation Mi=Ni is a resolvent between the unit clause C(M1,...,Mp)=C(N1,...,Np) and clause (1), and the equation TRUE=FALSE (which we assimilate to the empty clause) is a resolvent between the unit clause C(M1,...,Mp)=C1(N1,...,Nq) and clause (2).

6.2 Relations between constructors

To generalize these methods when there are relations between constructors, we assume that there exist between these constructors, besides the equational relations Ec, non-equational relations in the following form:

P1=Q1 => P=Q
with P1 and Q1 belonging to Tc and:
-either P and Q belonging to Tc(generalization of relations of type (1))
-or P=TRUE and Q=FALSE (generalization of relations of type (2))

These non-equational relations are given to the completion algorithm at the beginning. We suppose that these relations have been proved as valid in the initial algebra defined by the equations Ec. (note that, as these relations are not equational, their proofs are not relevant to the method described in this paper). We denote NE the set of non equational relations.

These relations are considered as lemmas, that we use for simplifying or disproving the new equations produced by the completion algorithm. For that, we extend the computation of critical pairs between rewrite rules to the computation of critical pairs between a rewrite rule and a relation in NE.

<u>Definition</u>

Let R1: M -> N be a rewrite rule
Let R2: P1=Q1 => P=Q be a relation in NE

A "critical pair" between R1 and R2 is defined as a resolvent(if it exists) of R1 and R2 considered as clauses. Such a resolvent exists iff both literals (M=N) and (P1=Q1) are unifiable; if s is the most general unifier of these literals, the resolvent is the equation Ps=Qs.

If there are commutative/associative operators, we use commutative/associative unification, as we do for the computation of ordinary critical pairs. In this case, we may obtain several resolvents. To take into account the commutativity of equality, we also have to compute resolvents between R1 and the "reverse" of R2, i.e the rule Q1=P1 => P=Q (another equivalent method consists in building the commutativity of = in the unification algorithm, as we do for commutative/associative operators)

We can now describe the modifications of the Knuth and Bendix completion algorithm, when it is used as an inductive theorem prover, to take into account non-equational relations:

-When computing critical pairs: compute also critical pairs between the rewrite rules and the rules of NE.
-When considering an equation for orientation:
 -stop "disproof" if this equation is TRUE=FALSE.
 -otherwise, proceed as described in section 3.

Note that this algorithm may stop with disproof either by detection of a new relation between constructors or by detection of the equation TRUE=FALSE.

This algorithm may generate new equations which are not equational consequences of the initial set of equations, unlike the ordinary Knuth and Bendix algorithm. Consequently, these new equations are not valid in all models of the initial set. But they are valid in the initial algebra (and that is in fact the only model which interests us when we are doing inductive proofs), for all non-equational inference rules are valid in this algebra by hypothesis.

The correction of the algorithm comes from the following facts:
-All generated equations are sound consequences of the initial set of equations in the initial algebra. Therefore, if the algorithm stops with disproof, the initial set of equations is inconsistent.
-If the algorithm stops with success or loops forever, the final (finite or infinite) rewriting system R constructed by the completion algorithm is equivalent to or stronger than the initial set of equations EuE1 (i.e $=_{EuE1} \subseteq =_R$). It is easy to verify that the proof of consistency performed in theorem B is always correct if we suppose only $=_{EuE1} \subseteq =_R$.

Let us take an example, to see how the use of non-equational inference rules can improve the working of the completion algorithm:
The natural numbers can be defined by two different theories:
-Theory 1: constructors 0 and SUCC without relations.
-Theory 2: constructors 0,1,+ and relations:
X+0 = X, X+Y = Y+X , X+(Y+Z) = (X+Y)+Z
In theory 1, we have between the constuctors the following (implicit) non equational relations:
SUCC X = SUCC Y => X = Y
SUCC X = 0 => TRUE = FALSE
These relations are easily transposed in theory 2:
X+1 = Y+1 => X = Y
X+1 = 0 => TRUE = FALSE

In theory 1, using the Huet-Hullot algorithm, the generation by the completion algorithm of the equation SUCC M = SUCC N entails its replacement by the equation M = N. The generation of the equation SUCC M = 0 entails the disproof.

In theory 2, the generation by the completion algorithm of the rewrite rule M+1 -> N+1 entails the generation of the equation M = N by superposition with the relation X+1 = Y+1 => X = Y. When it is transformed into a rewrite rule, this equation entails the deletion of the rule M+1 -> N+1. In a similar way, the generation of the rewrite rule M+1 -> 0 entails the disproof.

Note that, unlike Huet-Hullot, we do not eliminate at once the rule M+1 _-> N+1. Thus we are sure that, at each step of the algorithm, the new system is equivalent to or stronger than the old one.

6.3 Possible extensions

At first, it is important to note that the non-equational relations are not implicit as in Huet-Hullot [3], but provided by the user. That gives us a means for increasing significantly the "intelligence" of the completion algorithm. For example, the relation X+1 = Y+1 => X = Y can be generalized as:

X+Z = Y+Z => X = Y (cancellation law)

This relation will result in automatic elimination of terms that are common to both members of an equation.

In the same way, the relation X+1 = 0 => TRUE = FALSE can be generalized as X+Z = 0 => X = 0 (the relation X+Z = 0 => Z = 0 is unnecessary if we have declared the operator + as commutative).

We can further extend the use of this method, by allowing in NE non-constructors operators. For example, let us consider integers with operators 0,1,+,-,x as defined in annex. We can introduce in NE the following relations:

XxX = 0 => X = 0

(XxX)+(YxY) = 0 => X = 0

Another way for extending this method consists in allowing the introduction in NE of inference rules in the form:

(P1=Q1)↑(P2=Q2)↑...↑(Pn=Qn) => (P=Q) (↑ is the boolean conjunction)

with either P and Q are two terms, or P=TRUE and Q=FALSE.

Such non-equational rules correspond exactly to HORN clauses, i.e clauses with at most one positive literal. The non-equational rules that were studied so far correspond to n=1. With such rules, we can generalize the definition of critical pairs in the following way:

Let R be the non-equational rule: (P1=Q1)↑(P2=Q2)↑...↑(Pn=Qn) => (P=Q).
Let F be a family of n rewrite rules: {l1->r1,l2->r2,...,ln->rn} which are not necessarily all distinct.

If it is possible to unify simultaneously each (li=ri) with each (Pi=Qi), let s be the most general simultaneous unifier. The "critical pair" between R and F is the equation Ps=Qs. This computation corresponds exactly to the operation called, in the vocabulary of resolution, "hyperresolution".

On the other hand, we cannot generalize the method to non-HORN clauses, because such clauses will generate, by hyperresolution with the rewrite rules, disjunctions of equations which require a cases analysis. For example, we cannot use the following relation:

XxY = 0 => X=0 v Y=0 (v is the boolean disjunction)

ANNEX
SOME EXAMPLES OF INDUCTIVELY COMPLETE EQUATIONAL SPECIFICATIONS

For S1, S2, S3, the specifications are given directly under the form of rewriting systems confluent w.r.t. the associativity/ commutativity of + and x. Note that we do not use in examples S1 and S2 the usual constructors SUCC or SUCC and PRED. If necessary, they can be introduced via the definitions SUCC X -> 1+X, PRED X -> -1+X.

The inductive completeness of the specifications S1 and S2 has been remarked by Tarski [13], Henkin [2], Degano and Sirovich [1].

S1: NATURAL NUMBERS

Constructors: 0,1,+
Defined operator: x
Specification:

```
X+0 -> X
Xx1 -> X
Xx0 -> 0
Xx(Y+Z) -> (XxY)+(XxZ)
```

S2: INTEGERS

Constructors: 0,1,+,-
Defined operators: x
Specification:

```
X+0 -> X
-X+X -> 0
-0 -> 0
-(-X) -> X
-(X+Y) -> (-X)+(-Y)
Xx1 -> X
Xx0 -> 0
Xx(Y+Z) -> (XxY)+(XxZ)
Xx(-Y) -> -(XxY)
```

For these two systems, it is easy to check that the operator x is completely defined w.r.t.constructors, by using the method described in section 4.

The normal forms of terms are isomorphic to the polynomials. Therefore, the inductive completeness of these systems is a consequence of the following proposition: if a polynomial P is zero for all (positive) integer values of its variables, it is identically zero. That is a well known algebra theorem, which is proved by induction over the number of variables of P. If P is a one-variable polynomial, we use the fact that an one-variable polynomial over a field cannot have more roots than its degree.

It is easy to prove that the subsystem of relations between constructors is also inductively complete, for S1 and S2.

We can complete the specification S1 with the following definition of exponential:

```
Xexp(Y+Z) = (XexpY)x(XexpZ)        Xexp0 = 1
(XxY)expZ = (XexpZ)x(YexpZ)        Xexp1 = X
Xexp(YxZ) = (XexpY)expZ            1expX = 1
```

Tarski has conjectured that this system is inductively complete. Although some partial results have been obtained (see [2], [11]), the general problem remains unsolved.

S3: INTEGERS MODULO p

Let p be a prime number. "Integers modulo p", denoted by Z/p, can be defined as the initial algebra generated by the following system:

Constructors: 0,1,+
Defined operators: x
Specification:
(R1) X+0 -> X
(R2) pX -> 0
(R3) Xx1 -> X
(R4) Xx0 -> 0
(R5) Xx(Y+Z) -> (XxY)+(XxZ)
(pX denotes X+X+...+X p times)

It is easy to prove that the system of relations between constructors is inductively complete and that the operator x is completely defined w.r.t.constructors.

But the whole system is not inductively complete. Indeed, according to the arithmetic theorem known as "Fermat's little theorem", any integer raised to the pth power is equal to itself in Z/p. This theorem can be expressed by the following relation:

$X^p = X$ (X^p denotes XxXx...xX p times)

This relation is <u>not</u> an equational consequence of the initial set of equations.

At first, we will prove this theorem by using the method described in this paper. Then, we will prove that the initial system, completed with this theorem, is inductively complete.

Proof of Fermat's little theorem:

To prove this theorem, we add the rewrite rule R6: X^p -> X to the rewriting system, and we check that all critical pairs are confluent. We must also take into account the "extensions rules" as defined by Peterson and Stickel. In fact, we only have to consider extensions of rules R2 and R6, for the extensions of other rules are instances of existing rules. These extensions are:
(RE2) Y+pX -> Y
(RE6) YxX^p -> YxX

The following diagram gives the proof of confluence in the only non obvious case, namely the superposition of rules R5 and R6:

$(Y+Z)^p$

(Application of rule 6) → $Y+Z$

(Repeated applications of rule 5: binomial formula) → $Y^p + Z^p + \sum_{i=1}^{p-1} \frac{p!}{i!(p-i)!} Y^i Z^{p-i}$

Since p is a prime number, $\frac{p!}{i!(p-i)!}$ is divisible by p for any i such that $0<i<p$.

By using rules R2 and R6, we can reduce to Y+Z the right-hand branch, which proves the confluence.

Inductive completeness of the final system:

The running of the proof is the same as for the proof of inductive completeness of systems S1 and S2. The only difference appears when we have to prove that a one-variable polynomial, which is zero for all values of the variable, is identically zero. The proof is as follows: let P be such a polynomial, and let d be the degree of P. By using rewrite rule R6, we can assume that $d<p$. If $d>0$, P cannot have more than d roots, which is a contradiction because it has p roots (all elements of Z/p). Therefore $d=0$ and P is identically zero.

Remark: If $p=2$, the confluent rewriting system that we have obtained is isomorphic to the system discovered by Hsiang for propositional calculus, with the following meaning of operators:
0 : FALSE 1 : TRUE x : AND + : EXCLUSIVE OR

Therefore, the proof of inductive completeness of this system can be regarded as a new proof of the completeness of propositional calculus.

S4: SETS

Let IT1,IT2,...,ITi,... be a denumerable set of constants which we call "items". Let us define the finite sets of items as the initial algebra generated by the following equational system:

Constructors: emptyset
insert

Equations (s being a variable of sort SET, it1,it2 being variables of sort ITEM):
insert(insert(s,it1),it2) = insert(insert(s,it2),it1)
insert(insert(s,it1),it1) = insert(s,it1)

By using these equations, any term can be transformed into a expression of the form:
insert(insert(...(insert(s,it1)...itn) ITi1)... ITim)
with:
s being either the constant emptyset, or a variable of sort SET.
it1,...,itn being distinct variables of sort ITEM.
ITi1,...,ITim being distinct constants of sort ITEM.

Using this normal form, it is easy to prove, by instantiating variables with distinct constants, that this specification is inductively complete.

Note that we use in this proof the fact that there are infinitely many constants of sort ITEM. So we can choose instances of variables iti all distinct and different from all constants which are already present in the expression. If there are only finitely many constants of sort ITEM, this specification is not inductively complete. For instance, if we have only two items IT1 and IT2, the following equation, which is not an equational consequence of the initial set, is true for each set s:

insert(insert(s,IT1),IT2) = insert(insert(emptyset,IT1)IT2)

S5: AN EQUATIONAL SPECIFICATION WITH AN INFINITE INDUCTIVE CLOSURE

We consider the specification S1 of natural numbers. We add to this specification a new operator P defined by the following equations: P(0,0)=0, P(0,X+1)=1, P(X+1,0)=1, P(X+1,Y+1)=P(X,Y). Let E be this equational specification. E can be compiled into the following rewriting system, confluent w.r.t.the associativity/ commutativity of + and x:

```
X+0 -> X                  P(0,1) -> 1              P(X+1,1) -> P(X,0)
Xx1 -> X                  P(1,0) -> 1              P(1,X+1) -> P(0,X)
Xx0 -> 0                  P(0,X+1) -> 1            P(1,1)   -> 0
Xx(Y+Z) -> (XxY)+(XxZ)    P(X+1,0) -> 1
P(0,0) -> 0               P(X+1,Y+1) -> P(X,Y)
```

Considering this rewriting system, it is easy to check that the new operator P is completely defined w.r.t constructors 0,1,+.

P can be interpreted as an equality symbol. For if m and n are two natural numbers, we have P(m,n)=0 if m=n, and P(m,n)=1 if m#n. This interpretation allows to transform non-equational theorems (without existential quantifiers) into equational theorems; once they have been transformed, we can apply the method described in this paper for proving or disproving them. For example, the non equational theorem X+Y = X+Z <=> Y = Z is transformed into P(X+Y,X+Z) = P(Y,Z), which is easily proved by our method.

It is well known that certain arithmetical problems are undecidable; we use this fact for proving that any inductive closure of E is not finite, nor even recursively enumerable. More precisely, we will use the indecidability of Hilbert's tenth problem, proved by Matiyasevich (1970). This problem is as follows: given two polynomials M and N, and {X1,X2,...,Xn} being the set of variables occuring in M or N:

There exist X1,X2,...,Xn natural numbers such that M = N.

This problem is not decidable, but it is semi-decidable: a simple semi-decision algorithm consists in enumerating all possible values of the n-tuple {X1,X2,...,Xn} and, for each value, in verifying if M = N.

We prove that, if the inductive closure of E was recursively enumerable, the negation of Hilbert's tenth problem would be semi-decidable. A problem which is semi-decidable, and whose negation is semi-decidable, is decidable: thus we obtain a contradiction.

The negation of Hilbert's tenth problem is the following theorem:

For all X1,X2,...,Xn natural numbers, M # N

This theorem can be transformed into an equational one:
For all X1,X2,...,Xn natural numbers, P(M,N) = 1

That is: P(M,N) =IE 1 (let us recall that =IE denotes the inductive equality, or equality over the initial algebra).

Let us call C an equational system which is an inductive closure of E. From the definition of inductive closure, =IE = =C. If C were recursively enumerable, =C would be semi-decidable; therefore, negation of Hilbert's tenth problem would be semi-decidable.

REFERENCES

[1] DEGANO P. and SIROVICH F., On solving the equivalence problem for a sub-class of primitive recursive functions, Nota Scientifica S-79-18, June 1979.

[2] HENKIN L., The logic of equality , annual meeting of the MAA, San Francisco, January 1974.

[3] HUET G. and HULLOT J.M., Proofs by induction in equational theories with constructors , Proc.21st Symposium on Foundations of Computer Science (1980).

[4] HUET G., A complete proof of correctness of the Knuth-Bendix completion algorithm , Rapport de recherche INRIA No 25, July 1980.

[5] HUET G., Confluent reductions: abstract properties and applications to term rewriting systems, JACM, Vol.27, No 4, October 1980, pp 797-821.

[6] HUET G., OPPEN D.C., Equations and rewrite rules: a survey , Technical Report CSL-11,SRI International, Jan.1980.

[7] HULLOT J.M., A catalogue of canonical term rewriting system, Technical report CSL-113, SRI International, April 1980.

[8] KNUTH D. and BENDIX P., Simple word problems in universal algebra Computational problems in abstract algebra, Ed. Leech J., Pergamon Press, 1970, 263-297.

[9] PETERSON G.E and STICKEL M.E, Complete Sets of Reductions for some equational theories, JACM, Vol.28, No2, April 1981, pp233,264.

[10] REMY J.L., Etude des systemes de reecriture conditionnels et application aux types abstraits algebriques, These docteur es sciences, Centre de recherche en informatique de Nancy, July 1982.

[11] RICHARDSON D., Solution of the identity problem for integral exponential functions, Zeitschr.f.math.Logik und Grundlagen d.Math. Bd.15, S.333-340 (1969)

[12] ROBINSON J.A., A machine-oriented logic based on the resolution principle , JACM,Vol.12, No 1, January 1965, pp23-41.

[13] TARSKI A., Equational logic and equational theories of algebras, Contributions to mathematical logic (K.Schutte.Ed), North-Holland, Amsterdam, 1968.

PROOFS IN THE FINAL ALGEBRA

L. Puel
LITP Université Paris 7
2 Place Jussieu 75005 Paris France

Abstract. We show how to prove (and disprove) theorems in the final algebra of an equational variety by modifying both the Knuth-Bendix completion algorithm and its extension proposed by Huet-Hullot.

Résumé. Nous montrons comment faire des preuves (et des réfutations) dans l'algèbre terminale d'une variété équationnelle en modifiant l'algorithme de complétion de Knuth-Bendix, ainsi que l'extension de cet algorithme faite par Huet-Hullot.

0 INTRODUCTION

An abstract data type is an isomorphism class of Σ-algebras. The abstract data type usually chosen for an equational data type $T = (S,\Sigma,E)$ is the class of initial algebras of the (Σ,E)-algebras. Initial algebra distinguishes two terms the equality of which cannot be deduced from the axioms of E. Nevertheless we often have to consider terms which satisfy certain properties as equivalent even if they are not equal in the initial algebra. In particular these properties can be characterized by functions with a codomain in a reference type $T_0 = (S_0,\Sigma_0,E_0)$ included in T and it is the final semantics which distinguish the terms. Example: the type integer being already defined, we can be interested by the congruence modulo 2. The reference type is then the boolean one with constants T, F and operator $\neg$. The integer modulo 2 type includes boolean type and integers with operators 0, succ and one more operator f which associates to a boolean an integer. T = (Int U Bool; T,F,$\neg$,0,succ,f; E). E is the set of equations: $\neg F=V$; $\neg V=F$; $f(0) = V$; $f(succ\ x) = \neg f(x)$.

The final algebra contains exactly two elements: the class of 0 and the one of succ(0). Remember the initial algebra owns an infinite number of terms which are $succ^n(0)$, $n \geq 0$. One of the advantages of initial algebra is the possibility to make proofs using the Knuth-Bendix completion algorithm as G.Huet and J.M.Hullot have done [5]. In this work our goal is to obtain a similar method in the final point of view. Schematically, we start by showing that if the type T satisfies hypotheses of sufficient completeness and consistency (Guttag & Horning [2]) and if the abstract data type associated to T_0 is initial algebra, then a non trivial final algebra for T exists. We characterize then final equivalence between two terms M and N of $T_\Sigma(X)$ by $M \approx N$ if and only if for every ground substitution σ and for every context C $\sigma(C(M)) \equiv_E \sigma(C(N))$. Then we show that with a simple modification of the Knuth-Bendix completion algorithm - forbidding the creation of rules the members of which are elements of $T_{\Sigma_0}(X)$ and whose associated equation is not valid in the initial algebra $I(\Sigma_0, E_0)$- we may prove t=t'in the final algebra by showing that E U {t=t'} is consistent.

After a section devoted to recall properties and notations we introduce in section 2 algebraic framework for the final approach of an abstract data type. In section 3 we describe completion algorithms and set out the corresponding theorems of correctness. Lastly, in section 4 we use this method to make proofs in initial algebra with equations between constructors.

1 BASIC DEFINITIONS AND RESULTS

We will use the mathematical theory of abstract data types created by the ADJ group [1]. And here we recall some notations. A specification of a data type T is a triple (S, Σ, E) where S is the set of sorts, Σ is the signature and E is a set of equations. We denote by T_Σ the algebra of ground terms over Σ and if X is a denumerable set of variables, we note $T_\Sigma(X)$ the set of terms with variables over Σ and X. When we have to specify the sort s we note $T_{\Sigma,s}$. $\equiv_E$ is the congruence closure of E. A Σ-algebra that is a model of E is a (Σ,E)-algebra. We denote by $I(\Sigma,E)$ the initial algebra of the variety $M(E)$ (the class of all models of E). A Σ-algebra A is minimal if the homomorphism $T_\Sigma \to A$ is surjective. Let A be an algebra of signature Σ and let Σ_0 be a signature included in Σ, we mean by $\langle A \rangle_{\Sigma_0}$ the Σ_0-subalgebra of A generated by the constants and operators of A named in Σ_0. Let t be a term of type s in $S-S_0$ a context C of t is a term belonging to $T_{\Sigma,s_0}(X)$, with exactly one occurrence of one variable of sort s. Moreover we will use without describing it the Knuth- Bendix completion algorithm settled out by G.Huet [4].

2 ABSTRACT DATA TYPE. FINAL ALGEBRA

Let $T = (S,\Sigma,E)$ be a specification of a data type including a primitive type specified by $T_0 = (S_0,\Sigma_0,E_0)$. We make the following semantic choice: two terms t and t' belonging to $T_\Sigma(X)$ are equivalent if and only if they have the same "behaviour towards primitive type". In this section we set up the algebraic framework fitting this choice and we make hypotheses needed to show the existence of a non trivial final model (the type T being equational an unit Σ-algebra is a final model of E).

2.1 Existence of a non trivial final model

We suppose that the specification $T=(S,\Sigma,E)$ satisfies the following properties :

a)the abstract data type associated to T_0 is the initial algebra of $M(E_0)$.

1)the primitive type is not modified by the axioms of E (consistency)

$$(1)\ \forall\ t_0, t'_0 \in T_{\Sigma_0,S_0},\ t_0 \equiv_E t'_0 \Rightarrow t_0 \equiv_{E_0} t'_0$$

2)each term of primitive type is equivalent to a primitive term. (sufficient completeness)

$$(2)\ \forall\ t \in T_{\Sigma_0,s_0}\ \exists\, t_0 \in T_{\Sigma_0,s_0} \qquad t \equiv_E t_0$$

We denote by $\mathbf{M}(E)$ the set of minimal (Σ,E)-algebra whose restriction to E_0 is the initial (Σ_0,E_0)-algebra and by $T(\Sigma,E)$ the final algebra of $\mathbf{M}(E)$.

Proposition 2.1.1

Let $T=(S,\Sigma,E)$ including $T_0=(S_0,\Sigma_0,E_0)$ be a specification satisfying properties (a),(1),(2), then there exists a non trivial final algebra in $\mathbf{M}(E)$.

Proof

Let A_0 be initial algebra of the (Σ_0,E_0)-algebras, and A an algebra of $\mathbf{M}(E)$, A models $T'=(S,\Sigma,E')$ with E' defined by $E'= E \cup \{ t\neq t' \mid A_0 \models t\neq t'\}$. As A_0 is an initial algebra we can take $E' \cup \{ t=t' \mid A_0 \models t=t'\}$ instead of E'. The final algebra of $\mathbf{M}(E)$ is then the final algebra of the models of T'(if such an algebra exists). The existence of a final model for T' is shown by the next theorem (M.Wirsing, M. Broy [7]) given in the special case where the axioms are of the form t=t' or t≠t'.

Theorem 2.1.2

Let $T=(S,\Sigma,E)$ a data type with $E = E_1 \cup E_2$ where the axioms of E_1 are equations and those of E_2 of the form t≠t', if T has a finitely generated model and if for each t≠t' of E_2 the equation t=y (for new y) is maximal then T has a final finitely generated model.

A Σ-algebra A is finitely generated if the homomorphism $h: T_\Sigma(X) \rightarrow A$ is surjective and an equation t = y is maximal if for any ground substitution σ either $\sigma(t)=\sigma(y)$ is valid in any model of T or $\sigma(t)\neq\sigma(y)$.
This theorem proves that T' including inequalities has a non trivial final model. We have then shown the existence of a final algebra of $\mathbf{M}(E)$.

2.2 Final model's characterization

Let H be a subset of M(E), we define in T_Σ the relation $\approx$ (relative to H) by : $M \approx N$ if and only if there exist a finite sequence $A_1,\ldots,A_n$ in H and a sequence $M_0,\ldots,M_n$ in T_Σ such that $M_0=M$, $M_n=N$ and for every i $(1\leq i\leq n)$ $A_i \models M_{i-1}=M_i$. $\approx$ is an equivalence in T_Σ and we denote by $T_{\Sigma/\approx}$ the quotient set. We can state then the following properties :

Proposition 2.2.1

$T_{\Sigma/\approx}$ is a (Σ, E)-algebra and if H has a non trivial final algebra this algebra is isomorphic to $T_{\Sigma/\approx}$.

In the previous section we have shown the existence of non trivial final algebra of $\mathbf{M}(E)$. Taking $\mathbf{M}(E)$ as H we have then:

Proposition 2.2.2

Let $T=(S,\Sigma,E)$ including $T_0=(S_0,\Sigma_0,E_0)$ be a specification satisfying (1) and (2), $T_{\Sigma/\approx}$ is a non trivial final algebra of $\mathbf{M}(E)$.

2.3 Final equivalence in $T_{\Sigma/\approx}$.

Definition 2.3.1

$M \approx_E N$ if and only if there exist a finite sequence $M_0,\ldots,M_n$ in $T_\Sigma(X)$ and a finite sequence of algebras $B_1,\ldots,B_n$ in $\mathbf{M}(E)$ with $B_i \models M_i = M_{i-1}$ for every i ($1 \leq i \leq n$).

Definition 2.3.2

Let m and n be ground terms, $m \approx_E^g n$ if and only if there exist a finite sequence $m_0=m,\ldots,m_n=n$ in T_Σ and a finite sequence $A_1,\ldots, A_n$ of (Σ, E)-algebras restriction to T_0 of which is the initial algebra with $A_i \models m_{i-1}= m_i$ for every i ($1 \leq i \leq n$).

If m and n are ground terms, $m \approx_E n$ if and only if $m \approx_E^g n$ since every algebra includes a minimal one.

Proposition 2.3.3

$M \approx_E N$ if and only if for every ground substitution σ $\sigma(M) \approx_E^g \sigma(N)$.

proof

If $M \approx_E N$ there are a finite sequence $M_0,\ldots,M_n$ in

$T_\Sigma(X)$ with $M_0 = M$ and $M_n = N$ and a finite sequence $B_1,\ldots,B_n$ of algebras in $\mathbf{M}(E)$ satisfying for every i $(1 \leq i \leq n)$ and for every assignment v_i from X to B_i $h_{B_i,v_i}(M_{i-1}) = h_{B_i,v_i}(M_i)$. Let σ be a ground substitution, v_1 is the assignment from X to B_1 such that the following diagram is commutative. We denote by h_{B_1,v_1} the unique homomorphism from $T_\Sigma(X)$ to B_1 extending v_1.

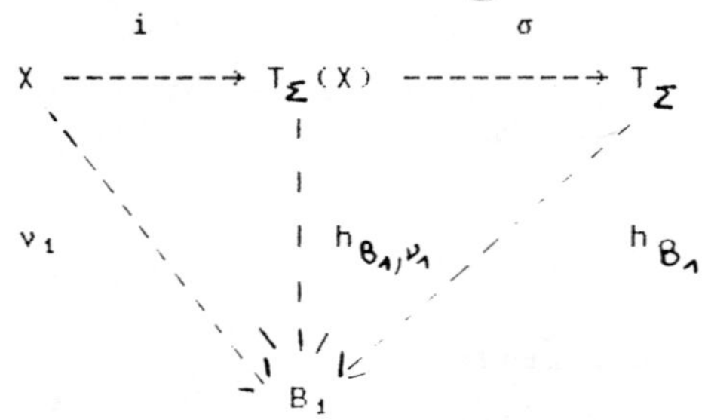

Then for every i $(1 \leq i \leq n)$ $\sigma(M_{i-1}) = \sigma(M_i)$ holds in B_i and therefore $\sigma(M) \approx_E^g \sigma(N)$. If for any ground substitution σ, $\sigma(M) \approx_E^g \sigma(N)$ then $\sigma(M) \approx_E \sigma(N)$ and $T_{\Sigma/\approx}$ valids $\sigma(M)=\sigma(N)$: we note that $\approx_E$ restricted to ground terms is the relation defined in the previous section with $\mathbf{M}(E)$ as H. Let v be an assignment from X to $T_{\Sigma/\approx}$, for every variable x there is t_x in T_Σ with $v(x) = h_{T_{\Sigma/\approx}}(t_x)$. Let σ be the substitution defined for every x by $\sigma(x) = t_x$, we have the following equalities:

$$h_{T_{\Sigma/\approx},v}(M) = h_{T_{\Sigma/\approx}}(\sigma(M)) = h_{T_{\Sigma/\approx}}(\sigma(N)) = h_{T_{\Sigma/\approx},v}(N)$$

In conclusion, $T_{\Sigma/\approx}$ valids M=N and $M \approx_E N$.

$\approx_E^g$ is the greatest non trivial congruence including every ground instance $\sigma(G) = \sigma(D)$ of the equations of E the restriction to primitive terms of which is $\equiv_E$. Thus the final algebra of $\mathbf{M}(E)$ is $T_{\Sigma/\approx_E^g}$.

<u>Definition 2.3.4</u>

Let $T = (S,\Sigma,E)$ including $T_0 = (S_0,\Sigma_0,E_0)$ be a specification and A be an algebra in $\mathbf{M}(E)$, we define a relation $\approx_A$ in A by $t_1 \approx_A t_2$ if and only if for every s_0 in S_0, for every context C of t_1 and t_2 in $T_{\Sigma,s_0}(X)$ and for every assignment v from X to A, $h_{A,v}(C(t_1)) = h_{A,v}(C(t_2))$.

Proposition 2.3.5

$A/\approx_A$ is a final algebra of $\mathbf{M}(E)$.

From the previous proposition we can deduce that if T is a specification satisfying (1) and (2) and if t and t' are terms in T_Σ we have the following equivalences :

$t \approx^g_E t' \iff [t] \approx_{T_{\Sigma/\approx}} [t']$	[t] denotes the class of t in $T_{\Sigma/\approx}$.
$\iff [C(t)] = [C(t')]$	for every context C of t and t'.
$\iff C(t) \equiv_E C(t')$	C(t) and C(t') are of primitive sort .

Thus we have characterized final equivalence between M and N in $T_\Sigma(X)$ by $M \approx_E N$ if and only if for every ground substitution σ and for every context C in $T_{\Sigma,s_0}(X)$, $\sigma(C(M)) \equiv_E \sigma(C(N))$.

We can see that the notion of final algebra fits the notion of terms' observability in primitive type (terms are observed through contexts) and the notion of observable equality (two terms are equal if for every context of primitive type we get the same result using one or the other term).

3 PROOFS IN THE FINAL ALGEBRA

Let $T = (S,\Sigma,E)$ and $T_0 = (S_0,\Sigma_0,E_0)$ be specifications which verify the following assumptions:

a) $S_0 \subset S$, $\Sigma_0 \subset \Sigma$, $E_0 \subset E$.

b) Sufficient completeness of T.

(1) $\forall s_0 \in S_0 \quad \forall t \in T_{\Sigma,s_0} \quad \exists t_0 \in T_{\Sigma_0,s_0} \quad t \equiv_E t_0$

c) Consistency of T.

(2) $\forall s_0 \in S_0 \quad \forall t_0,t'_0 \in T_{\Sigma_0,s_0} \quad t_0 \equiv_E t'_0 \implies t_0 \equiv_{E_0} t'_0$

We present a method to prove theorems in the final algebra of the (Σ,E)-algebras whose restriction to Σ_0 is the initial algebra of the (Σ_0,E_0)-algebras. Our process is similar to the one given by G.Huet and J.M.Hullot [5] to make proofs in the initial algebra of an equational variety.

First we show that on the assumption that the specification T is sufficiently complete, proving the validity of a theorem $t = t'$ in the final algebra $T(\Sigma, E)$ and proving the consistency of $E \cup \{t = t'\}$ are equivalent problems. Then we give a Knuth-Bendix completion algorithm modified to protect the initial algebra of T_0 which, when it stops with success, prove the consistency of $E \cup \{t = t'\}$.

Theorem 3.1

Let E be a set of equations satisfying (1) . Let E' be a set of equations in $T_\Sigma(X)$ such that E' contains E, the following properties are equivalent:

(i) E' satisfies (2).

(ii) E satisfies (2) and every equation of E'-E holds in $T(\Sigma, E)$.

Proof

(i) ==> (ii) E satisfies (2) : obvious . If there is an equation $t = t'$ in E'-E which does not hold in $T(\Sigma, E)$, there is a context C and a ground substitution σ such that $\sigma(C(t)) \not\equiv_E \sigma(C(t'))$ with $\sigma(C(t)) \equiv_{E'} \sigma(C(t'))$ by hypothesis. Therefore E satisfying (1), there are t_0 and t'_0 in T_{Σ_0, s_0} such that $\sigma(C(t)) \equiv_E t_0$ and $\sigma(C(t')) \equiv_E t'_0$. Then $t_0 \equiv_{E'} t'_0$ and E' fulfilling (2) $t_0 \equiv_{E_0} t'_0$. This property refutes the assumption and every equation in E'- E holds in $T(\Sigma, E)$.

(ii) ==> (i) Let t_0 and t'_0 be elements of T_{Σ_0, s_0} such that $t_0 \equiv_{E'} t'_0$, there is a finite sequence $t_1, \ldots, t_n$ in T_{Σ_0, s_0} with $t_{i-1} \equiv_{E'} t_i$, $t_0 \equiv_{E'} t_1$ and $t'_0 \equiv_{E'} t_n$. For every t_i in the sequence there are an equation G=D in E' and a ground substitution σ such that $t_{i+1} = t_i\,[u \leftarrow \sigma(D)]$ or $t_i = t_{i+1}[u \leftarrow \sigma(D)]$. Then for every i, $t_{i+1} = \sigma(C(D))$ (C context) and $t_i = \sigma(C(G))$ (or the opposite); G = D being valid in $T(\Sigma, E)$ $t_i \equiv_E t_{i+1}$ and then $t_0 \equiv_E t'_0$. E satisfying (2), $t_0 \equiv_{E_0} t'_0$.

The Knuth-Bendix completion algorithm that we shall use to prove consistency is modified to prevent a rule the associated equation of which would not hold in the initial algebra $I(\Sigma_0, E_0)$. First we give an algorithm without specifying the process of the proof in $I(\Sigma_0, E_0)$ and then an algorithm fitting the case where Σ_0 contains constructors, defined operators and with no equation between constructors.

Completion algorithm 3.2

We state the following assumptions:

$T(S, \Sigma, E)$ fulfills properties (a), (1), (2) and there is a confluent and noetherian rewriting system, R_0, such that $\equiv_{R_0} = \equiv_{E_0}$. $>$ is a reduction ordering.

The completion algorithm is the one described by G.Huet [4]. The only modified steps are initialization and decision to add a new rule.

Step 1 Initialization $\mathbb{E}_0 = E' - E_0$, $\mathbb{R}_0 = R_0$, $i=0$, $p=0$.

Step 2 If $\mathbb{E} \neq \emptyset$ then go to 4 .

Step 3 Compute critical pairs If all rules in $\mathbb{R}_i$ are marked, stop with success. Otherwise, select an unmarked rule in $\mathbb{R}_i$, say with label k. Let $\mathbb{E}_{i+1}$ be the set of all critical pairs computed between rule k and any rule of $\mathbb{R}_i$ of label not greater than k. Let $\mathbb{R}_{i+1}$ be the same as $\mathbb{R}_i$ except that rule k is now marked. Increment i by 1 and go to 2.

Step 4 Reduce equation Select equation $M=N$ in $\mathbb{E}$. Let $M\downarrow$ (resp. $N\downarrow$) be an $\mathbb{R}_i$-normal form of M (resp. N) obtained by applying rules of $\mathbb{R}_i$ in any order, until none applies.

Step 5 If $M\downarrow = N\downarrow$, then let $\mathbb{E}_{i+1} = \mathbb{E}_i - \{ M=N \}$, $\mathbb{R}_{i+1} = \mathbb{R}_i$, increment i by 1 and go to 2 .

Step 6 Decision to add a rule

if $M\downarrow \in T_{\Sigma_0, S_0}(X)$ then

if $N\downarrow \in T_{\Sigma_0, S_0}(X)$

Let us prove $M\downarrow = N\downarrow$ in the initial algebra $I(\Sigma_0, E_0)$.

If the algorithm used to do this proof stops with failure (resp. false) then failure (resp. false) else add the rules created during the proof of $M\downarrow = N\downarrow$.

else if $N\downarrow > M\downarrow$ then let $\lambda = N\downarrow$, $\rho = M\downarrow$

else failure .

else if $N\downarrow \in T_{\Sigma_0,s_0}(X)$ do symmetrically as above .

else if $M\downarrow > N\downarrow$ then let $\lambda = M\downarrow$, $\rho = N\downarrow$

else if $N\downarrow > M\downarrow$ then $\lambda = N\downarrow$, $\rho = M\downarrow$

else stop with failure .

Step 7 Add a new rule Let K be the set of labels k of rules of $\mathbf{R}_i$ whose left-hand side λ_k is reducible by $\lambda \to \rho$, say to to λ'_k . Let $\mathbf{E}_{i+1} = \mathbf{E}_i - \{M=N\} \cup \{\lambda'_k = \rho_k \mid k:\lambda_k \to \rho_k \in \mathbf{R}_i$ with $k \in K\}$. Increment p by 1. Let $\mathbf{R}_{i+1} = \{j:\lambda_j \to \rho'_j \mid j:\lambda_j \to \rho_j \in \mathbf{R}_i$ with $j \notin K\} \cup \{p: \lambda \to \rho\}$, where ρ'_j is a normal form of ρ_j, using rules from $\mathbf{R}_i \cup \{\lambda \to \rho\}$. The rules coming from $\mathbf{R}_i$ are marked or unmarked as they were in $\mathbf{R}_i$, the new rule $\lambda \to \rho$ is unmarked. Increment i by 1 and go to 2 .

Remark 3.3

For every rule $G \to D$ with G in $T_{\Sigma_0,S_0}(X)$ and for every ground substitution σ, $\sigma(G) \equiv_{E_0} \sigma(D)$.

Theorem 3.4

(i) If the algorithm stops with success, every equation in E'-E holds in the final algebra $T(\Sigma, E)$.

(ii) The resulting term rewriting system satisfies (1) and (2).

(iii) If the algorithm stops with disproof, some equation of E'-E does not hold in $T(\Sigma . E)$.

(iv) If some equation in E'- E does not hold in $T(\Sigma, E)$,the algorithm stops with either disproof or failure (if the algorithm used to make proofs in the initial algebra $I(\Sigma_0, E_0)$ has the same property).

Proof

(i) If the algorithm stops with success the

resulting term rewriting system is confluent and noetherian and $\equiv_{E'} \subset \equiv_{R}$. E' satisfies (2) because every rule $G \rightarrow D$ with left-hand side G in $T_{\Sigma_0, S_0}(X)$ belongs to R_0 or fulfills $\sigma(G) \equiv_{E_0} \sigma(D)$.

(ii) Obvious.

(iii) The algorithm stops with disproof if at step i we obtain two terms t_0 and t'_0, elements of $T_{\Sigma_0, S_0}(X)$, such that there is a ground substitution σ with $\sigma(t_0) \not\equiv_{E_0} \sigma(t'_0)$ and $t_0 \equiv_{E_i \cup R_i} t'_0$. Therefore E' does not satisfy (2).

(iv) Let t_0 and t'_0 be elements of T_{Σ_0, S_0} such that $t_0 \equiv_{E'} t'_0$ and $t_0 \not\equiv_{E_0} t'_0$. If the algorithm generates an infinite set of rewrite rules R_∞, this set is confluent and there is an element t of T_{Σ_0, S_0} such that $t_0 \overset{*}{\underset{R_\infty}{\rightarrow}} t \overset{*}{\underset{R_\infty}{\leftarrow}} t'_0$. This fact refutes $t_0 \not\equiv_{E_0} t'_0$.

<u>Example 3.5</u>

T_0 = (Bool ; T , F , ⌉ ; E_0)

T = (Bool , Int ; T , F , ⌉ ,0, succ , + ,•f ; E)

| ⌉T = F | E_0
| ⌉F = T |
| f(succ(x)) = ⌉f(x) E
| f(0) = V
| x+0 = x
| x+succ(y) = succ(x+y)
| succ(x) + y = succ(x+y)

We direct equations from left to right and we get terms rewriting rules. Let us show that x+succ(x) = 0 is false in the final algebra. The algorithm generates new rules : x+succ(x) → 0; succ(x+x) → 0; ⌉f(x+x) →T and then the critical pair (T,F). We can also show that x+x = 0 is true ; the generated rules are x+x → 0 and succ(succ(0)) → 0 and the algorithm stops with success .

We can now study the special case where Σ_0 contains constructors and defined operators with no equation between constructors. We use the completion algorithm version given by G. Huet and J.M.Hullot [5] . We denote by

$\mathbf{C}_0$ the set of constructors , $\mathbf{D}_0$ the set of defined operators and $\Sigma_0 = \mathbf{D}_0 \cup \mathbf{C}_0$. In this section we state the following assumptions :

$T_0 = (S_0, \Sigma_0, E_0)$ satisfies the "principle of definition":

(1') $\forall\, t_0 \in T_{\Sigma_0,s_0} \quad \exists t'_0 \in T_{\mathbf{C}_0,s_0} \quad t_0 \equiv_{E_0} t'_0$.

(2') $\forall\, t_0 , t'_0 \in T_{C_0,s_0}$, $t_0 \equiv_{E_0} t'_0 \implies t_0 = t'_0$.

$T = (S, \Sigma , E)$ satisfies (a),(1)and (2).

<u>Lemma 3.6</u>

On the assumptions above , if $M = C(M_1,..,M_n)$, $N = C(N_1,..,N_n)$ with C in $\mathbf{C}_0$ and $M \equiv_E N$ then for every i $(1 \leq i \leq n)$ $M_i = N_i$ holds in $T(\Sigma , E)$.

If $M \equiv_E N$ then for every ground substitution σ , $C(..,\sigma(M_i),..) \equiv_E C(..,\sigma(N_i),..)$ and for every i $(1 \leq i \leq n)$ there are t_i and t'_i in T_{Σ_0,s_0} such that $t_i \equiv \sigma(M_i)$, $t'_i \equiv \sigma(N_i)$. We have then $C(..,t_i,..) \equiv_E C(..,t'_i ,..)$ and by (2) $C(..,t_i,..) \equiv_{E_0} C(..,t'_i,..)$ and by (2') $t_i = t'_i$. From this we deduce $\sigma(M_i) \equiv_E \sigma(N_i)$ and $M_i = N_i$ holds in $T(\Sigma ,E)$.

<u>Remark 3.7</u>

Let E containing M=N with $M = C(M_1,..,M_n)$, $N = C(N_1,..N_n)$ and C in $\mathbf{C}_0$. If $E' = E - \{M=N\} \cup \{M_i = N_i \mid 1 \leq i \leq n\}$ then $T(\Sigma ,E) = T(\Sigma ,E')$ and $T = (S,\Sigma ,E')$ satisfies (a),(1), (2),(1'),(2').

<u>Lemma 3.8</u>

Let $T = (S,\Sigma ,E)$ satisfying (a), (1), (1'), (2'), $M=C(..,M_i ,..)$, $N=D(..,N_j ,..)$ with C and D two distinct constructors and $M \equiv_E N$ then T does not satisfy (2') .

<u>proof</u>

Let σ be any ground substitution and $M \equiv_E N$, then for every i $(1 \leq i \leq n)$, for every j $(1 \leq j \leq p)$ there are t_i and t'_j in T_{Σ_0,s_0} such that $\sigma(M_i) \equiv_E t_i$ and $\sigma(N_j) \equiv_E t'_j$. If T satisfies (2) then $C(..,t_i ,..) \equiv_{E_0} D(..,t'_j ,..)$. This fact contradicts (2').

Lemma 3.9

Let $T = (S,\Sigma,E)$ satisfying (a),(1),(1'),(2'). Let $M = C(..,M_i,..)$ with C a constructor. Let N be a variable and $M \equiv_E N$. Then T does not satisfy (2).

Completion algorithm 3.10

The previous properties show us that we can use to prove theorems in the final algebra $T = (S,\Sigma,E)$ the induction algorithm of G.Huet and J.M.Hullot [5] in which the step of decision to add a rule is modified as follows:

If $M = C(..,M_i,..)$ with C in $\mathbf{C}_0$,then:

If $N = C(..,N_i,..)$ then replace the pair (M,N) by the n pairs (M_i,N_i).

If $N = D(..,N_j,..)$ with D in $\mathbf{C}_0$ and $C \neq D$ or $N = x$ with x a variable then stop with "disproof".

Otherwise:

If $N > M$,introduce new rule $N \rightarrow M$.

Otherwise stop with "failure".

Otherwise:

If $N = C(..,N_i,..)$ with C in $\mathbf{C}_0$ do symmetrically as above.

Otherwise:

If $M > N$, introduce new rule $M \rightarrow N$.

If $N > M$, introduce new rule $N \rightarrow M$.

Otherwise stop with "failure".

The theorem 3.4 holds for this algorithm.

4 PROOFS IN THE INITIAL AGEBRA WITH EQUATIONS BETWEEN CONSTRUCTORS

Let $T = (S,\Sigma,E)$ be the specification of a data type. Let the signature Σ includes constructors $\mathbf{C}$ and defined operators $\mathbf{D}$. Let E_0, included in E, be the set of equations between constructors. We denote by $T_{\mathbf{C}}$ the set of ground terms over $\mathbf{C}$. The initial algebra of the equational variety $M(E)$ is isomorphic to $T_{\mathbf{C}}/\equiv_{E_0}$.We assume that T satisfies the following properties:

(1') $\forall\ t \in T_{\Sigma}$ $\exists\ t_0 \in T_C$ $t \equiv_E t_0$

(2') $\forall\ t_0, t_0' \in T_C$, $t_0 \equiv_E t_0' \Longrightarrow t_0 \equiv_{E_0} t_0'$ Then we can prove the next theorem .

Theorem 4.1

Let E be a set of equations satisfying (1') and let E' be a set of equations in $T_{\Sigma}(X)$ including E , the following properties are equivalent :

i) E' satisfies (2')

ii) E satisfies (2') and every equation in E'- E holds in $I(\Sigma, E)$

The properties (1') and (2') and this theorem are the analogue of the "principle of definition" and the correspondent theorem of G.Huet and J.M.Hullot [5] . Then we use to prove theorems in the initial algebra the Knuth-Bendix completion algorithm [G.Huet 4] in which we modify the decision to add a rule in the following way : if the normal forms M↓ and N↓ are ground terms over constructors then stop with disproof else if they belong to T (X) then we replace (M↓,N↓) by the set of pairs obtained taking the derivatives of M↓ and N↓ with respect to a variable (we replace x by $C_i(..,x,..)$ in which C_i is a constructor) else we consider the equation for orientation and generation of a new rule.

Theorem 3.4 (i) (ii) holds for this algorithm. We apply this method to an example given by E.Paul [6] to illustrate another method of proof .

Integer modulo p (p primary)

constructors 0,1,+ ; defined operator * ;

equations E_0 | x+0 = x

| x+..+x = 0 (with p-1 +)

| x+y = y+x

| x+(y+z) = (x+y)+z

equations used to define *

1*x=x; 0*x=0; x*(y+z)=x*y+x*z; x*y=y*x; x*(y*z)=(x*y)*z;

We use the associative commutative completion algorithm. In order to show $x^p = x$ we add the rule $x^p \to x$ and the only non trivial critical pair is $(y+z, \sum_{i=0}^{p} C_p^i z^i y^{p-i})$. But p is primary and then for every i $(1 \leq i \leq p-1)$ C_p^i is a multiple of p. There is no rule to add and the resulting system is complete; $x^p = x$ holds in the initial algebra .

5 CONCLUSION

We have designed an algorithm which can be used to prove theorems in the final algebra of an equational variety. This algorithm, when it stops with success, generates a term rewriting system R such that $\equiv_E \subset \equiv_R$. We know this property is not necessary and it is sufficient to have a system R such that $\approx_E = \approx_R$. Therefore in case of inability to orientate to an equation t=t', we adapt the algorithm by replacing the equation by the set of equations C(t) = C(t') with C context of t and t'. When the specification $T=(S,\Sigma,E)$ contains constructors, destructors and tests, the number of distinct equations generated when we add contexts is finite.

REFERENCES

[1] ADJ J.A. Goguen , J.W. Thatcher , E.G.Wagner
An initial algebra approach to the specification, correctness and implementation of abstract data types . R.T. Yeh (Ed.) Current trends in Programming Methodology .Vol.3 Data Structuring N.J. Prentice Hall 1978

[2] Guttag J.V. , Horning J.J.
The algebraic specification of abstract data types. Acta Informatica 10 1978

[3] Guttag J.V , Horowitz R. , Musser D.R.
The design of data types specifications . Current Trends in Programming Methodology Vol IV R.Yeh (Ed) Prentice Hall (1978)

[4] Huet G.
A complete proof of correctness of the Knuth - Bendix completion algorithm J.C.S.S. 23 1 11-21 1981

[5] Huet G. , Hullot J.M.
Proofs by induction in equational theories with constructors Rapport Inria 1980

[6] Paul E.
Preuves par induction dans les théories équationnelles en présence de constructeurs . (à paraitre)

[7] Wirsing M. Broy M.
Abstract data types as lattices of finitely generated models. 9th. M.F.C.S. L.N.C.S. 88 Springer Verlag . Berlin pp 673-685 (1980)

O N   G R A P H   R E W R I T I N G S

J.-C. Raoult
LRI, bat 490, Faculté d'Orsay, F-91405 ORSAY CEDEX

Abstract. The purpose of the present paper is twofold: Firstly, to show that it is possible to rewrite graphs in a way equivalent to, and in fact slightly more powerful than that of Ehrig et alii (1973). Our method consists in using a single push-out of partial morphisms and is described in section 3. Section 1 is devoted to the elementary definitions concerning graphs and related terms. Section 2 contains the set-theoretic prerequisites for the sequel and may be skipped by people already knowing what push-outs and pull-backs are about.
Secondly, we indicate in section 4 why this method is not really fit for rewriting graphs that represent collapsed terms (i.e. sharing common subterms) and we introduce push-outs of total functions, which are not morphisms everywhere on their domain. This method is connected to the classical rewriting of the corresponding terms. The adequacy of these new rewriting rules is then tested to prove a local confluence criterion à la Knuth-Bendix (1970) in section 5. All missing proofs can be found in Raoult (1984).

1. INTRODUCTION

There are so many different definitions of graphs that we feel it useful to explicitly choose one for the rest of the paper.

Definition 1. A graph is a set G of vertices together with a mapping succ:G->G* . For each vertex s, succ(s) is the list of all successors of s. Its i-th successor is denoted by $succ_i(s)$. Furthermore, each vertex v has a label lab(v).

Hence the graphs that we are considering are directed and ordered: A vertex has a first successor, a second successor, etc. The following figure shows two different graphs. (see figure 1 next page).

The corresponding morphisms are defined without any originality, except perhaps for the role of the variables.

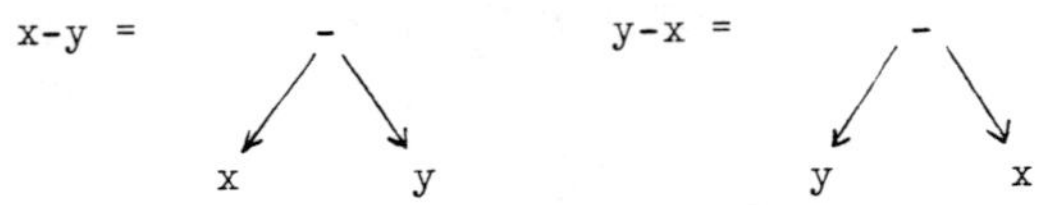

Figure 1

Definition 2. A mapping f:G->H is a morphism at s $\in$ G when
(i) lab(f(s)) = lab(s),
(ii) if succ(s) = $s_1 \ldots s_n$, then succ(f(s)) = $f(s_1) \ldots f(s_n)$.

A mapping is a morphism when it is a morphism at all vertices. A mapping is an occurrence when it is a morphism at all vertices except perhaps at the leaves having label in X.

Therefore, a morphism is a fortiori an occurrence. Figure 2 shows two occurrences; the last one is a morphism.

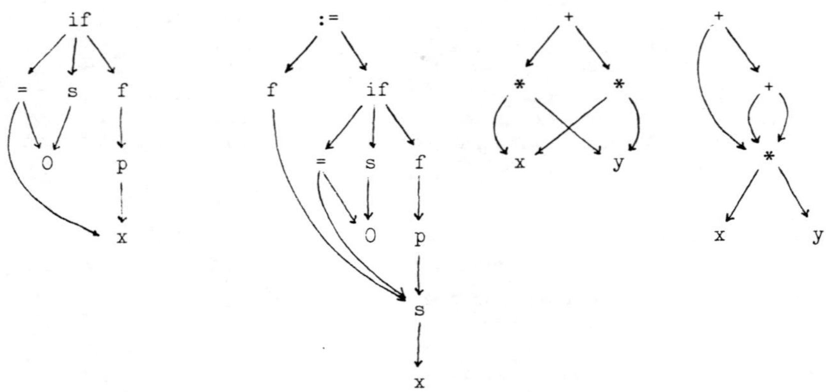

Figure 2

It is clear that the identity is a morphism (and an occurrence), and that the composition of two morphisms (or two occurrences) is again a morphism (or an occurrence).

With each graph G, acyclic and having a unique root, is associated a term in T(F,X), defined by induction on G.
(i) If G = {s} , then exp(G) = lab(s).

(ii) Otherwise, let s be the root of G, f its label and $s_1,\ldots,s_n$ its successors. Then

$$\exp(G) = ft_1\ldots t_n \text{ where } t_i = \exp(s_i).$$

Conversely, given a term t, there exist several graphs G such that exp(G)=t. At one extreme is the tree "tree(t)" which is the least contracted representation. At the other extreme is the graph defined by the following method.

Definition 3. For a term t, let gra(t) be the set of all subterms of t; define the mapping succ at a vertex s of gra(t) by

$$\text{succ}(s) = s_1\ldots s_n \text{ if } s=fs_1\ldots s_n.$$

The graph gra(t) has a property that we shall demand of all graphs henceforth.

Assumption. Two different vertices may not be labelled by the same variable.

2. COMMUTATIVE SQUARES OF MAPPINGS

Before rewriting graphs, we shall first rewrite sets. More precisely, we work in the category (Psets) the objects of which are sets and the arrows of which are partial functions. A partial function f:A --> B is a mapping f:dom(f) -> B where $\text{dom}(f)=f^{-1}(B)$ is a subset of A called the domain of f. Two partial functions are equal when they have same domain and coincide on this domain. The composition of f:A --> B and g:B --> C has domain

$$\text{dom}(gf) = f^{-1}(g^{-1}(C)) = f^{-1}(\text{dom}(g)),$$

and on this domain is the composition of the mappings. The identity mapping satisfies clearly its usual equations and the composition is associative; we have just defined the category (Psets).

Recall that the push-out of two arrows f:A --> B & g:A --> C is the smallest commutative square built on f and g: There exist two arrows h:B --> D

& k:C --> D satisfying hf=kg and such that for any two arrows u:B --> X & v:C --> X satisfying also uf=vg, there exists a unique arrow w:D --> X with u=wh & v=wk.

Proposition 3. Push-outs exist in (Psets).

To define the push-out D, we let A' be the greatest subset of dom(f) $\cap$ dom(g) closed under the equivalence relation R generated by

$$f(a) = f(a') \text{ or } g(a) = g(a')$$

The set D is defined as the union (B-f(A))+(C-g(A))+Q where q:A'->Q is the quotient of A' under R.

<u>Remark</u>: D is the push-out in (Sets) of the following diagram

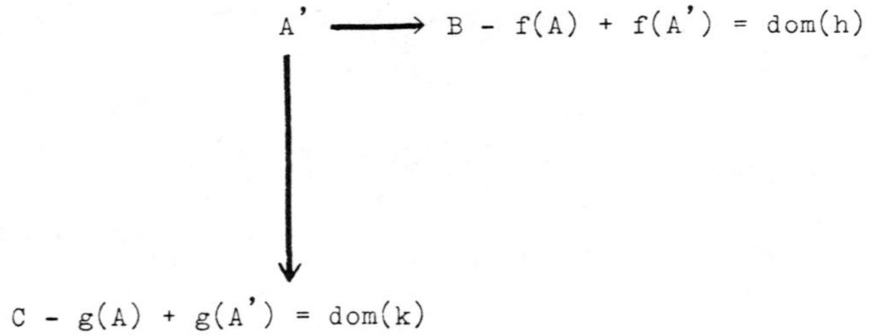

Figure 3

3. REWRITING GRAPHS WITH PARTIAL MORPHISMS

Suppose that our graphs have no variable; or equivalently, consider the category of partial morphisms, i.e. partial functions f:A --> B that are morphisms on their domain. According to definition 2 section I, it means that if $s \in$ dom(f) and succ(s)=$s_1 \ldots s_n$, then

$$(\forall i)\ s_i \in \text{dom}(f)\ \&\ \text{succ}(f(s))=f(s_1)\ldots f(s_n).$$

The domain of f must therefore be a full subgraph of A.

Proposition 5. Let f:A --> B, g:A -> C, h:B -> D, k:C --> D be a push-out of partial functions, and suppose that f and g are morphisms on their domain. Then there exists an unique graph structure on D

such that h and k are morphisms on their domain if and only if
(i) no vertex in B-f(A) has a successor in f(A)-f(A'), and
(ii) no vertex in C-g(A) has a successor in g(A)-g(A').

The exclusion of variables is unrealistic insofar as the graphs represent terms, but it is suited to representing graphs by edges E and vertices V as in Ehrig et alii(1973). The set of vertices of the representing graph is E+V, and the function successor is defined by

succ(s) = ε (empty chain) if s belongs to V,
succ(e) = st if e ∈ E with source s and target t.

The morphisms as defined in section I correspond exactly to the morphisms defined in the usual way by two functions, on the edges and on the vertices, such that the following two squares commute.

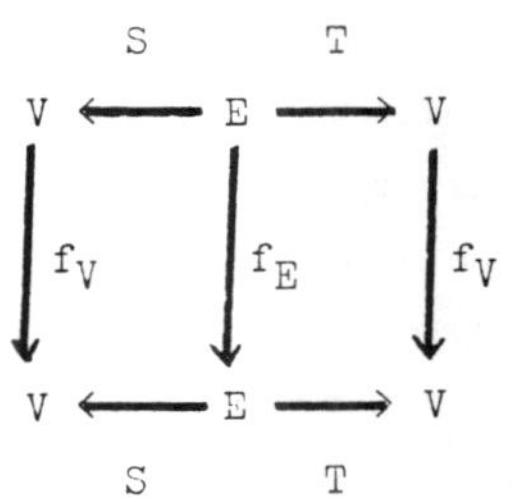

Figure 4

Further, labelled graphs correspond exactly to their coloured graphs, so that automatically, our morphisms correspond to the morphisms of coloured graphs.

Having this representation in mind, the conditions of proposition 5 recall the "gluing condition" of Ehrig et alii (1973). In fact, proposition 5 is more general than the existence of the graph deduced from their "fast productions".

Corollary. With the same notations as in proposition 5, assume that
(i) g is a total morphism,
(ii) no vertex in C-g(A) has a successor in g(A-dom(f));
(iii) dom(f) contains $ker(g) = \{c \in C;\ (\exists_{c' \neq c})\ g(c')=g(c)\}$,

then the following two squares are push-outs in the category of graphs with total graph morphisms.

$$\begin{array}{ccccc} A & \longleftarrow & \mathrm{dom}(f) & \xrightarrow{f} & B \\ \downarrow g & & \downarrow & & \downarrow h \\ C & \longleftarrow & \mathrm{dom}(h) & \xrightarrow{k} & D \end{array}$$

Condition (i) by itself cannot ensure that h is also total; this is one reason of introducing condition (iii).

The two squares above are nothing else than the construction of the graph D obtained from C by applying the "fast production" A<-dom(f)->B.

4. ANOTHER APPROACH TO GRAPH REWRITING

The necessary and sufficient condition of proposition 5 is useful as long as the graphs are represented by vertices and edges. But it is not satisfied, in general, by the graphs of the form gra(t) in which t is a term in T(F,X). For instance, how can one apply the following production? (see figure 5 next page). In fact, we do not want to loose any vertex because we do not know in advance whether a vertex will be a successor of a vertex outside the pattern g(A). The interface graph need be the whole of C. Here is another way around the problem: remark that the desired rewriting consists in

1) making a copy of B and C,

2) redirecting all edges, in the copy of C, pointing on the root r of A, onto the root of B;

3) redirecting all edges of B pointing to variable leaves s in f(A) onto $f^{-1}(s)$;

4) The resulting graph is generated by the root of the copy of C.

Operation number 4 consists in running a garbage collector, and we shall not bother to do it except for the root of B: we are sure that no edge is left pointing to this root because of action 2. If these operations are performed on the example above, they yield the graph on the right of figure 5.

It is possible to get the same result with the help of proposition 5, provided that we slightly modify the graph rewriting rule asso-

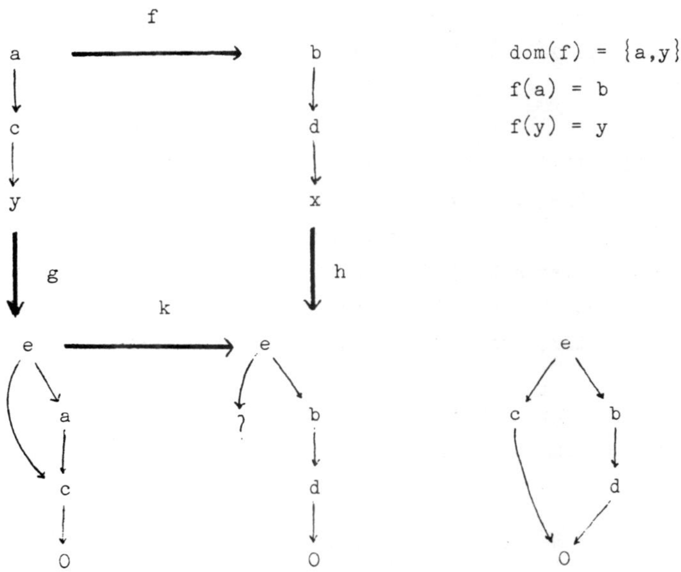

The function f is not a morphism on its domain and there are two edges having source e and target in g(A)-g(A') so that none of the conditions of proposition 5 is satisfied. The graph on the right is the desired result.

Figure 5

ciated with the rule g->d over the terms. We need here introduce functions that are not morphisms over their domain.

Notation. Given a function f:C -> D between two graphs, the set of vertices at which f is a morphism is denoted by mor(f) and the set of all other vertices is denoted by rew(f).

The intuitive idea is that the points of mor(f) are preserved in D whereas the points of rew(f) are "rewritten", so that the category of graphs together with total (set-theoretic) functions as arrows may be called the category of graph-rewritings.

Theorem 1. Let A, B, C be three graphs, and f:A->B and g:A->C two total functions. Let h:B->D and k:C->D be the push-out of f and g in the category (Sets). Suppose further

$$\ker(g) \subseteq mor(f) \ \& \ \ker(f) \subseteq mor(g) .$$

Then there exists a unique structure of graph upon D such that rew(h)=f(rew(g)) and rew(k)=g(rew(f)) if and only if

$$mor(f) \cup mor(g) = A$$

Furthermore, let u:B->X and v:C->X be two functions such that uf=vg, and w:D->X be the unique function such that u=wh and v=wk; then

$$mor(w) \supseteq h(mor(h) \cap mor(u)) \cup k(mor(k) \cap mor(v))$$

The graph structure on D is defined by h on h(mor(h)) and k on k(mor(k)). The following example shows why g should be one-to-one outside mor(f).

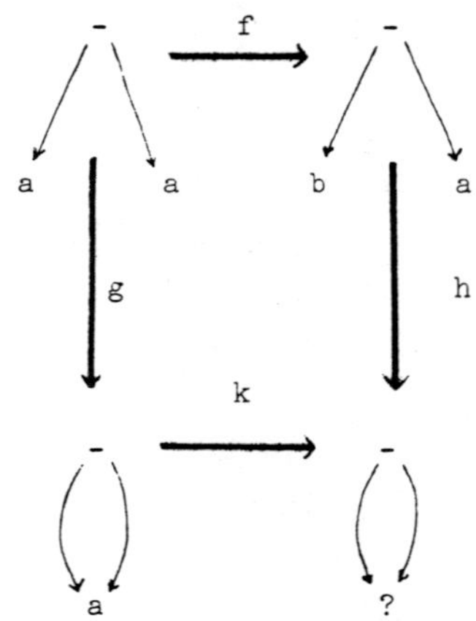

Figure 6

Here the function g identifies two points, one of which belongs to rew(f). Which label should have the leaf of D? Theorem 1 can be seen as a confluence property in the case when f and g rewrite disjoint sets of vertices. Indeed, we have

$$mor(f) \cup mor(g)=A \iff rew(f) \cap rew(g)=\emptyset.$$

It turns out that the situation of theorem 1 is precisely that which is got after applying operations 1, 2 and 3 to A itself then to C, when A, B and C represent collapsed terms, as in the following figure.

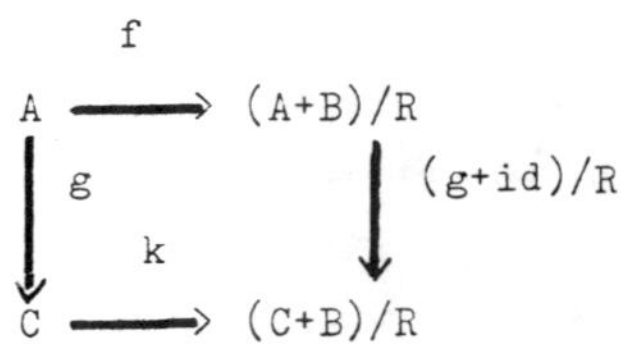

Figure 7

Proposition 6. Consider figure 12, in which A, B and C are dags having a unique root, g is an occurrence, and f, k are the insertions in the disjoint union, followed by the projection onto the quotient. This square is a push-out in the sense of theorem 1. Furthermore, exp(C) ->* exp(C+B)/R under the rewriting rule exp(A)->exp(B).

This proposition justifies the following definition.

Definition 4. A graph rewriting rule is a total function f:A->B which is a morphism at the leaves labelled with variables and which does not identify any vertex with a variable leaf. A rule f is applicable at the occurrence g when mor(f)containsker(g). Applying rule f at the occurrence g consists in constructing the push-out D as in theorem 1.

The first condition ensures ker(f)$\subseteq$mor(g) because our graphs have at most one leaf labelled with a given variable.

5. A CRITERION FOR CONFLUENCE

In this section is described a criterion for testing the local confluence of a finite system of graph rewriting rules which is analogous to the criterion proposed in Knuth & Bendix (1970).

To define the succession of two rewritings, we use the following well known result.

Proposition 7. A composition of two push-outs in (Sets) is a pushout.

This result will be used in the following settings:
(i) A->B is a rewriting rule, A->C is an occurrence of the pattern A in C, C->E is another occurrence. If we apply the rule in C, we get D. If we apply the rule C->D in E, we get F. The proposition above tells us that if we can apply A->B in E, then we get F.
(ii) f:A->A' and f':A'->A" are two rewritings and g:A->B is an occurrence. Then the squares I and II in the following figure are built successively, and the proposition above implies that the succession I.II is the application of rule f'f at the occurrence g.

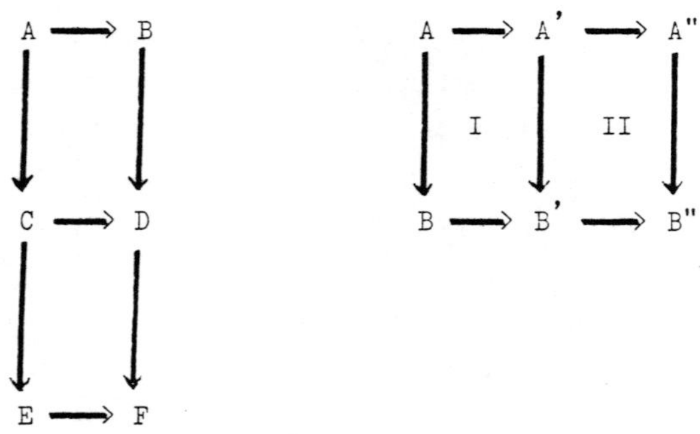

Figure 8

Give now a graph G and two rewritings of this graph under the rules f:A->B and f':A'->B'. Let I be the pull-back of f and f', and let S denote the push-out of I->A and I->A', which exist thanks to the following proposition.

Proposition 10. In the category of graphs with occurrences, push-out and pull-backs exist.

Then S can be rewritten under the rule f at the occurrence A->S, giving T, and also under the rule f' at the occurrence A'->S, giving T'. We get in this way the following diagram, in which all arrows which are not rewritings are occurrences. (see figure 9 next page).

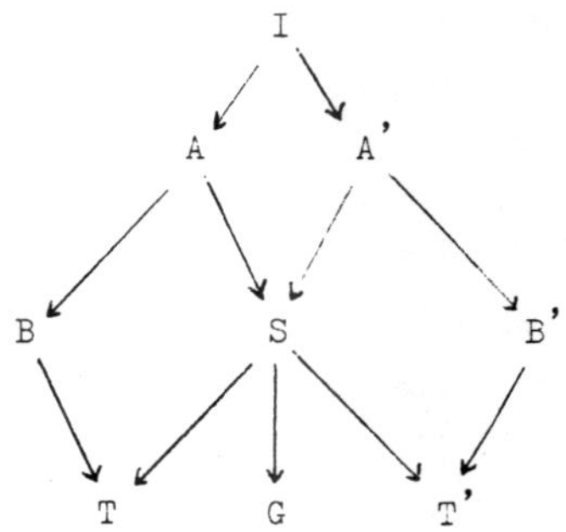

Figure 9

Definition 5. A pair of morphisms T<-S->T' as in figure 17, is called a critical pair.

For instance, suppose the following three rules, where the numbers at the vertices indicate the images of f.

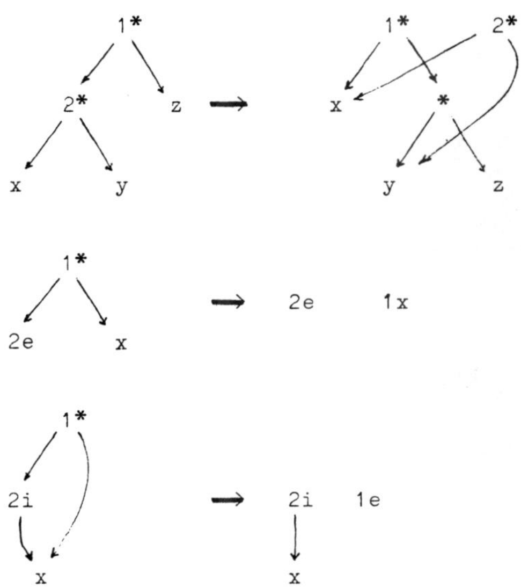

Figure 10

There exists a critical pair, between the first and the last axiom, which is described by the figure next page.

If the rewriting relation is to be locally confluent, there must exist two chains of rewritings T->*V and T'->*V. The following theorem shows that this condition is also sufficient.

Theorem 2. A system of rewriting rules is locally confluent if and only if for all critical pairs T<-S->T' there exist two chains of rewritings T->*V and T'->*V.

Proof: Very simple. The remark following the proposition above shows that, given a chain of arbitrary rewritings starting at S, it can be pushed out into a chain of rewritings starting at G. The situation is depicted by the following diagram, where the small diamond may be seen under the big one.

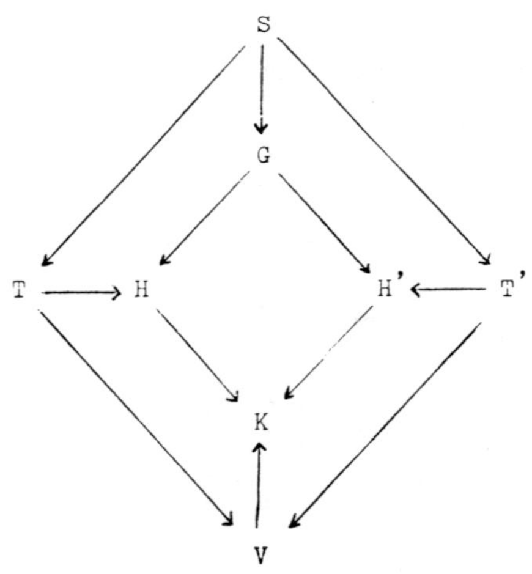

Figure 11

The graph K is the push-out of G and V under S, QED.

6. CONCLUSION

We have shown that a precise definition of graph rewritings coincides with the intuition: replace in a text graph an occurrence of an old pattern by an occurrence of a new pattern. This is accomplished, as is suggested by this informal definition in a unique commutative square: a push-out in a suitable category. Choosing the category of partial morphisms yields a definition essentially equivalent to that of Ehrig & alii (1973). A more restrictive definition is given section 4, which is more related to first-order term rewritings. In fact, it can be checked that when terms are represented as graphs, then proposition 6 ensures that the rewritten graph represents the rewritten term. No miracle occurs, though. If a variable occurs more than once in the left-hand side of a rewriting rule, then this variable is shared in the representing graph A, as demanded section I. In order to apply the rule at a given occurrence, one must check that the image of this variable is unique in the text graph C. In general, it is not unique, so that is is necessary to check for the equality of two subgraphs. Offhand, it seems that little is won over the classical term representation where the same verification must be carried on the relevant subterms. Nevertheless, not only can this verification be performed in linear time, as in Cocke & Schwartz (1970) but it also takes care of many further equalities. Consider for instance the following caricature.

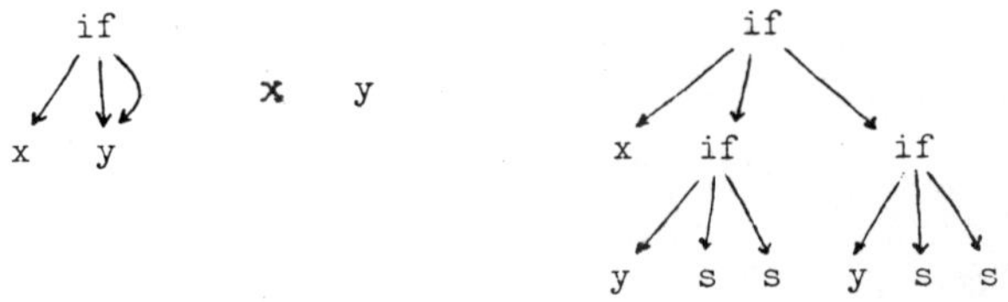

Figure 12

We want to apply the rewriting rule on the left at the root of the term represented on the right. The subsequent check transforms the graph into the following. (see figure 13 next page). The rewriting rule can now be applied at the root, then at the root of the result without further ado. The graph structure has remembered more sharing than we were looking for at first. This remark, together with theorems 1 and 2 are a strong hint that matters are as simple with graphs as with terms. In fact, they may be simpler: compare the proof of the local Church-Rosser property, in section 5, with a classical proof.

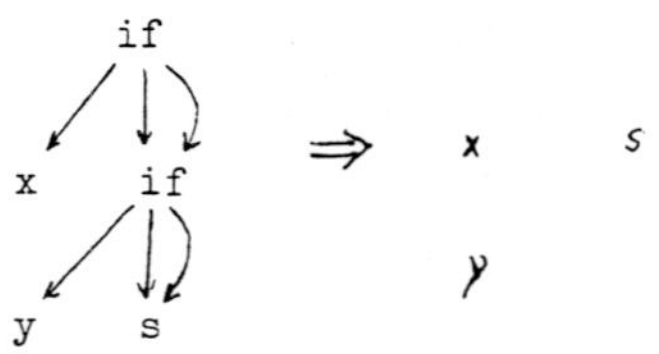

Figure 13

REFERENCES

Barendregt H.P. (1981): The lambda calculus, its syntax and semantics. Studies in logic and the foundations of mathematics, vol. 103, North-Holland.

Cocke J. & Schwartz J.T. (1970): Programming languages and their compilers, preliminary notes, Second revised version. In Courant Institute of Mathematical Science, New-York.

Ehrig H., Pfender M. & Schneider H.J. (1973): Graph grammars: an algebraic approach. In Proc. 14th ann. IEEE Symposium on Switching and Automata Theory, Iowa City, pp. 167-180.

Huet G. (1980): Confluent reductions, abstract properties and application to term rewriting systems, in JACM, vol. 27, num. 4, pp. 797-821.

Knuth D.E. & Bendix P. (1970): Simple word problems in universal algebras. In Computational Problems in Abstract Algebras, J. Leech ed., Pergamon Press, Braunschweig.

Lévy J.-J. (1978): Réductions correctes et optimales dans le lambda-calcul. Thèse d'état, Paris VII.

Montangero C., Pacini G. & Turini F. (1974): Graph representation and computation rules for typeless recursive program schemes. In 2nd Colloq. Automata, Languages and Programming, Saarbruecken (1974), Springer Verlag, LNCS 14.

Raoult J.-C. (1984): On graph rewriting. Internal report, LRI, Bat. 490, Faculté d'Orsay, F-91405 ORSAY CEDEX. Also, to appear in TCS.

BOUNDARY NLC GRAMMARS

G. Rozenberg
Institute of Applied Mathematics and Computer Science,
University of Leiden, Leiden, The Netherlands.

E. Welzl
Institute of Applied Mathematics and Computer Science,
University of Leiden, Leiden, The Netherlands.
on a year's absence from
Institutes for Information Processing, IIG, Technical University of Graz and Austrian Computer Society, Graz, Austria.

INTRODUCTION

Graph grammars are used to define collections of graphs, applying similar methods as they are used in string grammars for formal string languages. On the one hand this is motivated by investigations in structural pattern recognition, database theory, and compiler construction. On the other hand graph theory is full of graph grammar-like concepts, using generative (iterative) tools to describe graph languages with certain properties, as, e.g., Tutte's characterization of 3-connected graphs (Tutte, 1961).

In recent years the systematic and mathematical investigation of so-called _node-label controlled graph grammars_ (NLC grammars) has been initiated (Janssens & Rozenberg, 1980). In an NLC grammar the embedding of a new graph D replacing a node v is constructed only on the basis of the node labels involved, that is, the labels of the nodes of the embedded graph D and the labels of the neighbors of the replaced node v. Let the set of nodes which can be rewritten in a graph H be the boundary of this graph H. In a _boundary NLC_ (BNLC) _grammar_ the boundary of every graph generated from the axiom consists of pairwise nonadjacent nodes. Besides this the rewriting is defined as for NLC grammars.

Here we present the outcome of initial investigations of the basic properties of BNLC grammars and their generated graph languages (BNLC languages). Thus we give normal forms and closure properties of this new class of graph languages. Emphasis is on graph theoretic properties, e.g., the set of connected (or nonplanar) graphs in a BNLC language forms a BNLC language. Then we give some insight into the combinatorial structure of BNLC languages, e.g., we give an upper asymptotic bound for the number of graphs with up to n nodes (for positive integers n) in a BNLC language.

The presentation is informal and does not include proofs. It is aimed at an overview which reveals the essential properties of BNLC languages and which indicates directions for further research. For a more detailed presentation (with proofs) we refer to Rozenberg & Welzl (1983a, 1983b).

DEFINITIONS AND EXAMPLES

GRAPHS: An undirected, node-labelled graph is a system $H=(V_H,E_H,\Sigma_H,\varphi_H)$, where V_H is a finite nonempty set (of nodes), E_H is a set of subsets of cardinality two of V_H (the set of edges), Σ_H is a finite set of labels and φ_H is a function from V_H into Σ_H (the labelling function). For a node v in V_H its neighboorhood in H is defined by $neigh_H(v)=\{w\in V_H \mid \{v,w\}\in E_H\}$, its (label-)context in H is defined by $cont_H(v)=\{\varphi_H(w) \mid w\in neigh_H(v)\}$. H is called a graph over Σ if $\Sigma_H\subseteq\Sigma$. The underlying unlabelled graph H' of H is the pair $H'=(V_H,E_H)$.

The following graph-theoretic notions are used in the usual way, see, e.g., Harary (1969): graph isomorphism, subgraph of a graph, discrete graph, complete graph, connected graph, planar graph, k-colorable graph (for a positive integer k), graph homeomorphic to a given graph, clique of a graph, chromatic number etc.

NLC GRAMMARS: A node-label-controlled (NLC) grammar is a system $G=(\Sigma,\Delta,P,conn,Z)$, where

- Σ is a finite nonempty set of labels,
- Δ is a finite nonempty subset of Σ (set of terminals),
- P is a finite set of pairs (a,D), where a is a label in Σ and D is a (nonempty!) graph over Σ (set of productions),
- conn is a function from Σ into set of subsets of Σ (connection function). (We use here a connection function instead of the usual connection relation $C\subseteq\Sigma\times\Sigma$. The direct correspondence is given by $C=\{(a,b) \mid b\in conn(a)\}$.)
- Z is a graph over Σ (the axiom).

The set $\Sigma_N=\Sigma-\Delta$ is the set of nonterminals of G. A node in a graph is called nonterminal node if its label is in Σ_N. If $H,\overline{D},\overline{H}$ are graphs over Σ with $V_H\cap V_{\overline{D}}=\emptyset$, and v is a node in H, then we say H directly c-derives $\overline{H}$ (in G), replacing v by $\overline{D}$, denoted by

$$H \Rightarrow_{(v,\bar{D})} \bar{H},$$

if there is a production (a,D) in P, such that D is isomorphic to $\bar{D}$, $a = \varphi_H(v)$, and

(a) $V_{\bar{H}} = (V_H - \{v\}) \cup V_{\bar{D}}$,

(b) $E_{\bar{H}} = (E_H - \{\{v,w\} \mid w \in neigh_H(v)\}) \cup E_{\bar{D}}$
$\cup \{\{u,w\} \mid u \in neigh_H(v), w \in V_{\bar{D}}, \text{and } \varphi_H(u) \in conn(\varphi_{\bar{D}}(w))\}$,

and

(c) $\varphi_{\bar{H}}(w) = \varphi_H(w)$ for $w \in V_H - \{v\}$,
$= \varphi_D(w)$ for $w \in V_{\bar{D}}$.

Intuitively, we replace the node v in H by the graph $\bar{D}$ and connect a node w in $\bar{D}$ to a (former) neighbor u of v if and only if $\varphi_H(u) \in conn(\varphi_{\bar{D}}(w))$. $H \Rightarrow_{(v,\bar{D})} \bar{H}$ is called a <u>concrete derivation step</u>. A graph H <u>directly derives</u> a graph H', in symbols $H \Rightarrow H'$, if there is a concrete derivation step $H \Rightarrow_{(v,\bar{D})} \bar{H}$, and H' is isomorphic to $\bar{H}$. $\overset{*}{\Rightarrow}$ is the reflexive transitive closure of $\Rightarrow$. We say H <u>derives</u> H', if $H \overset{*}{\Rightarrow} H'$. $H \Rightarrow H'$ is called a <u>derivation step</u>. A sequence of successive (concrete) derivation steps is a <u>(concrete) derivation</u>. The <u>exhaustive language</u> generated by G is defined as $S(G) = \{H \mid Z \overset{*}{\Rightarrow} H\}$, and the <u>language generated</u> by G is $L(G) = \{H \in S(G) \mid H \text{ is a graph over } \Delta\}$.

<u>Example 1</u>: Let $G = (\Sigma,\Delta,P,conn,Z)$ be an NLC grammar with
$\Sigma = \{0,1,2,\tilde{1},\tilde{2}\}$,
$\Delta = \{0\}$,
$conn(0) = conn(1) = conn(2) = \Sigma$,
$conn(\tilde{1}) = \{0,1,\tilde{1}\}, conn(\tilde{2}) = \{0,2,\tilde{2}\}$,
$Z = \bullet^0$
and P consists of the productions:

(1) $(0,\bullet^1)$, (4) $(\tilde{1},\bullet^0)$,
(2) $(1,\bullet^2)$, (5) $(\tilde{2},\bullet^0)$, and
(3) $(2,\bullet^0)$, (6) $(0,\bullet^{\tilde{1}}\!-\!\!-\!\!-\bullet^{\tilde{2}})$.

Fig. 1 shows two derivations in G. Note that we are applying in both cases the same productions to the same two nodes of the initial graph - we only change the order - but we obtain two different graphs.

The language L(G) generated by G is the set of all connected graphs over {0}. (Every application of a production (6) in G is the inverse of an edge contraction, see Harary, 1969.)

Fig. 1

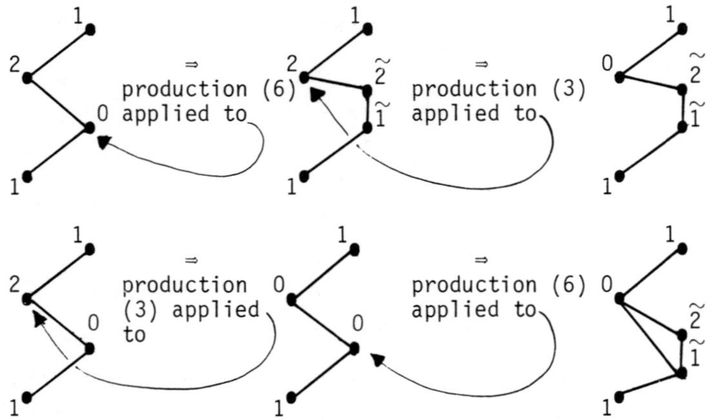

A graph language L is an <u>NLC language</u>, if there is an NLC grammar such that L=L(G). Example 1 shows that the set of all connected graphs with a single label is an NLC language, and the reader may easily find an NLC grammar generating all graphs with a single label. For more detailed definitions and results for NLC grammars we refer to Janssens & Rozenberg (1980a,1980b, 1981) or Janssens (1983)

<u>BNLC GRAMMARS</u>: Let $G = (\Sigma,\Delta,P,conn,Z)$ be an NLC grammar, where for every production (a,D) in P, a is a nonterminal. (It is known that every NLC language can be generated by such an NLC grammar). G is called <u>boundary NLC</u> (BNLC) <u>grammar</u>, if for every production (a,D) in P, the set of nonterminal nodes in D (= <u>boundary of</u> D) is discrete (i.e., the nonterminal nodes in D are pairwise not adjacent) and the boundary of the axiom Z is discrete. For a BNLC grammar G, L(G) and S(G) are defined as for NLC grammars. A graph language L is a <u>BNLC language</u>, if there is a BNLC grammar G such that L=L(G).

<u>Example 2</u>: Let $G = (\Sigma,\Delta,P,conn,Z)$ be a BNLC grammar with

$\Sigma = \{A,B,a,b,c\}$,

$\Delta = \{a,b,c\}$,

conn(A) = conn(B) = $\emptyset$,

conn(a) = conn(b) = conn(c) = Σ,

Z = $\bullet^{A}$,

and P consists of the productions

(1) (A, 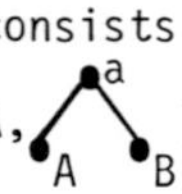

), (2) (A, 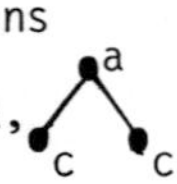

),

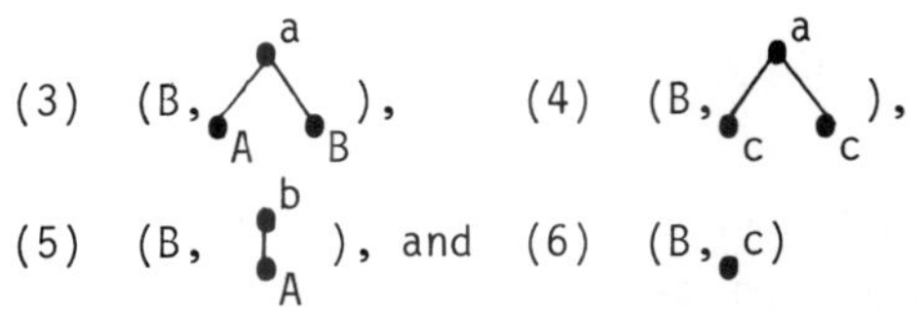

Fig. 2 depicts a derivation of a graph in L(G). L(G) consists of a class of rooted trees, whicn are used for certain dynamic datastructures (respectively the balanced instances of these trees). Roughly speaking, a tree in L(G) is of order 2, the root is the only a-labelled node with two neighbors, the leaves are labelled by c, and whenever an internal node has only one son, then this node is labelled by b, its brother has two sons, and its son has two sons.

Fig. 2

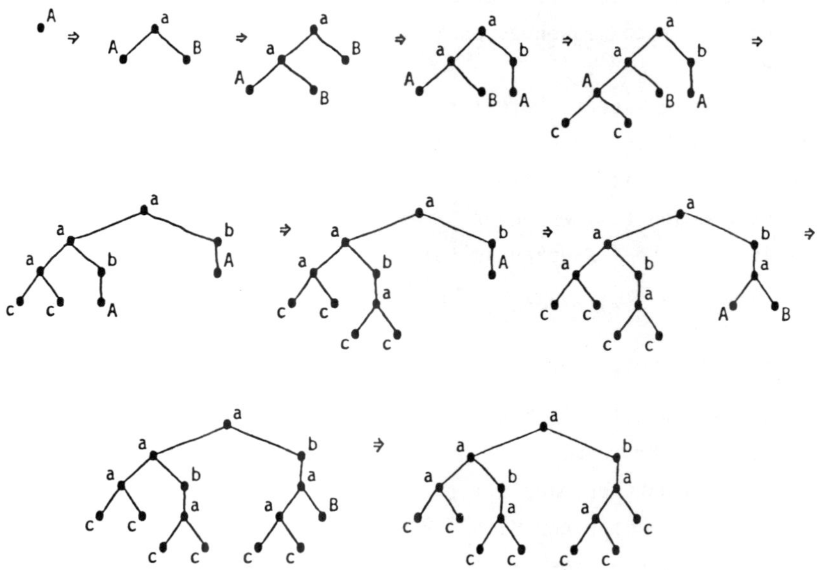

Consider now the BNLC grammar G' = $(\Sigma,\Delta,P,conn',Z)$ which is identical to G exept for the connection function conn': conn'(A) = conn'(B) = {b}, and conn'(a) = conn'(b) = conn'(c) = Σ. Then the generated graph language L(G') consists of all graphs which can be obtained from the trees in L(G) by inserting edges between every b-labelled node and the nodes in its subtree. Fig. 3 shows the derivation of the graph corresponding to the one in Fig. 2.

Note that for a BNLC grammar G every graph in S(G) has a discrete boundary. This implies that there is no interaction between nonterminal nodes in derivations. Thus, if we have two nodes in a graph H to which we apply two productions, then the order of applying these productions does not influence the resulting graph. This is in contrast to our observation for NLC grammars in Fig. 1 .

Fig. 3

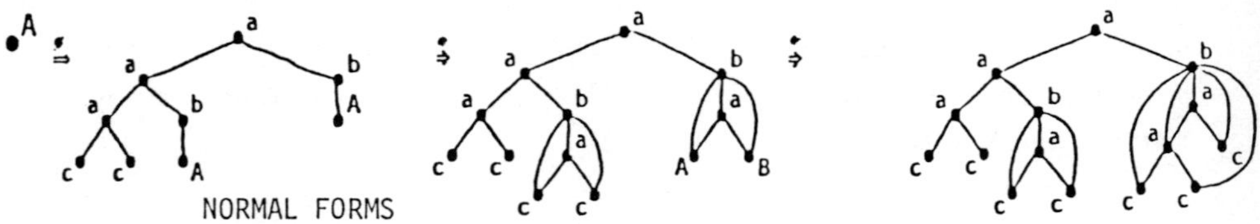

NORMAL FORMS

We present here some normal form results for BNLC grammars which considerably ease some proofs for BNLC grammars and which have some interesting direct consequences as it will be seen, e.g., in the section on enumeration.

One essential feature of BNLC grammars not true for general NLC grammars is that in a derivation the neighborhood of a nonterminal node never changes (until it is rewritten). Hence the context of a nonterminal node v (i) never changes and (ii) whenever $H \Rightarrow_{(v,\bar{D})} \bar{H}$, then the context of a node $w \in V_{\bar{D}}$ in $\bar{H}$ can be expressed as follows:

$$\mathrm{cont}_{\bar{H}}(w) = \mathrm{cont}_{\bar{D}}(w) \cup (\mathrm{cont}_{H}(v) \cap \mathrm{conn}(\varphi_{\bar{D}}(w))).$$

(Note that (ii) holds for all NLC grammars.)

This fact is exploited in many proofs for BNLC grammars, as, e.g., in the following normal form result.

A BNLC grammar $G = (\Sigma,\Delta,P,\mathrm{conn},Z)$ is called <u>context-consistent</u>, if there exists a mapping $\eta\colon \Sigma_N \to 2^{\Delta}$, with the following property. Whenever a nonterminal node v appears in a graph H in S(G), then $\mathrm{cont}_H(v) = \eta(\varphi_H(v))$. This means that whenever two nonterminal nodes with the same label appear in not necessarily distinct graphs H_1 and H_2 from S(G), then they have the same context. It can be proved that, in general, the following result does not hold for NLC languages.

<u>Theorem</u> 1: For every BNLC language L there is a context-consistent BNLC grammar with L = L(G).

By definition every NLC grammar is monotone in the sense that a node is always replaced by a graph with at least one node. However, edges can be erased in a derivation step. For BNLC grammars we can find a normal form which is also monotone with respect to edges.

Let $G = (\Sigma,\Delta,P,\text{conn},Z)$ be an NLC grammar. A concrete derivation step $H \Rightarrow_{(v,\bar{D})} \bar{H}$ is <u>connection-preserving</u>, if

$$\text{neigh}_H(v) \subseteq \bigcup_{w \in V_{\bar{D}}} \text{neigh}_{\bar{H}}(w).$$

G is called <u>connection-preserving</u>, if every concrete derivation step applied to a graph in S(G) is connection-preserving.

<u>Theorem</u> 2: For every BNLC language L there is a connection-preserving BNLC grammar with L = L(G).

The last normal form concerns the size of the right-hand side of productions in an NLC grammar. Let $G = (\Sigma,\Delta,P,\text{conn},Z)$ be an NLC grammar. A production (a,D) in P is a <u>chain-rule</u>, if $|V_D| = 1$ and the node in D is labelled by a nonterminal. In the following theorem we summarize all normal forms we have obtained for BNLC grammars so far (in order to express that they can be simultaneously achieved).

<u>Theorem</u> 3: For every BNLC language L there is a context-consistent, connection-preserving BNLC grammar G without chain-rules such that L = L(G).

CLOSURE PROPERTIES

For the family of NLC languages it has been shown that in general the set of connected graphs in an NLC language is no NLC language. It is even not decidable whether an NLC language contains a connected graph or not. The same results hold for graph properties like discreteness, planarity, and k-colorability (for a positive integer k).

For a BNLC language a number of these subsets specified by a graph property appear to be again BNLC languages. We summarize some of these properties.

<u>Theorem</u> 4: Let L be a BNLC language, k be a positive integer and H be an unlabelled graph. Then the sets of graphs in L which

(i) are connected,

(ii) are disconnected,

(iii) are k-colorable,

(iv) are discrete,

(v) have a subgraph homeomorphic to H,

(vi) are nonplanar

are BNLC languages.

LARGEST COMPLETE SUBGRAPH VERSUS CHROMATIC NUMBER

Let us briefly recall a result due to Erdös (1961). (We need and present here a weaker version of the original result.)

Proposition: For every pair of integers n,m, $2 \leq n \leq m$, there is a graph H (i) which has no complete subgraph on more than n nodes and (ii) whose chromatic number is not less than m.

This means, e.g., that the set of all triangle-free graphs (i.e., no subgraph on three nodes is complete) contains for every integer m, $m \geq 2$, a graph with chromatic number greater than m. Such an "independence" of largest complete subgraph and chromatic number does not hold in BNLC languages. (For a graph H, ch(H) denotes the chromatic number of H, and mc(H) denotes the maximal number of nodes of a complete subgraph of H.)

Theorem 5: Let L be a BNLC language. Then there is a positive integer function f_L, such that for every graph H in L we have $ch(H) \leq f_L(mc(H))$.

This theorem gives us first insight about what BNLC grammars can*not* do:

Corollary 6: The set of all graphs is not the underlying unlabelled graph language of a BNLC language.

Corollary 7: The set of all triangle-free graphs is not the underlying unlabelled graph language of a BNLC language.

Corollary 8: The family of underlying unlabelled graph languages of BNLC languages is a proper subset of the family of underlying unlabelled graph languages of NLC languages.

DECIDABILITY

Most of the positive decidability results we have for BNLC languages follow immediately from the (constructive) closure properties for BNLC languages and from the fact that for NLC grammars (and so for BNLC grammars) the emptiness of their generated languages is decidable. Let us summarize some of these results. (Problems (ii), (iii), and (iv) are known to be undecidable for NLC languages.)

Theorem 9: For a BNLC grammar G it is decidable whether all graphs in L(G) (i) are connected, (ii) are disconnected, (iii) are planar, (iv) are not k-colorable (for a given positive integer k).

A graph language L is of bounded chromatic number, if there is a positive integer n, such that, for every graph H in L, $ch(H) \leq n$ holds. Analogously, L is of bounded clique number, if there is a positive integer m such that, for every graph H in L, $mc(H) \leq m$ holds. Theorem 5 in the former section implies

Lemma 10: A BNLC language L is of bounded chromatic number if and only if it is of bounded clique number.

It is not difficult to show that the set of complete subgraphs of graphs in a BNLC language is a BNLC language. Since the finiteness problem is decidable for NLC (and so for BNLC) grammars, we have

Theorem 11: Let G be a BNLC grammar. Then it is decidable whether or not (i) L(G) is of bounded clique number (ii) L(G) is of bounded chromatic number.

It is still open whether the maximal chromatic number of a BNLC language can be computed (whenever it exists) from a generating BNLC grammar. Another interesting open problem is: Is it decidable whether or not a BNLC grammar generates a planar graph?
The classical decision problems from formal language theory, like the emptiness of intersection problem or the equivalence problem are undecidable for BNLC grammars. However, the cofiniteness problem is decidable for BNLC grammars, since - as we will see in one of the following sections - no BNLC language is cofinite.

RELATIVE INDEX

Let $G = (\Sigma,\Delta,P,conn,Z)$ be a BNLC grammar. Consider a graph H in S(G) - L(G) and a nonterminal node v in H. Whenever a node from H is rewritten in G, all of its neighbors are labelled by elements of Δ. Hence, if a node w is derived (possibly in a number of steps) from v, then, for each $a \in \Delta$, either w is adjacent to all a-labelled neighbors of v or to none of them. In other words: Every node derived from v can "distinguish" nodes in $neigh_H(v)$ by their labels only and these (that is nodes and labels) do not change during the derivation any more. We will exploit this observation to get another combinatorial property of BNLC languages.
By this we will be able to show also for some graph languages of bounded

chromatic number, that they are not BNLC languages. (This was not possible using Theorem 5 only.)

Let $H = (V_H, E_H)$ be an unlabelled graph, $X \subseteq V_H$, and $Y = V_H - X$. Two nodes v_1 and v_2 in Y are called X-<u>equivalent</u>, in symbols $v_1 \sim_X v_2$, if they have the same neighborhood in X, formally

$$\mathrm{neigh}_H(v_1) \cap X = \mathrm{neigh}_H(v_2) \cap X.$$

The <u>index</u> <u>of</u> H <u>relative</u> <u>to</u> X, $\mathrm{index}_X(H)$ for short, is the number of different equivalence classes w.r.t. $\sim_X$ on Y.

<u>Lemma</u> 12: Let H be a graph, $X \subseteq V_H$, $Y = V_H - X$. Then

$$\log_2(\mathrm{index}_Y(H)) \leq \mathrm{index}_X(H) \leq 2^{\mathrm{index}_Y(H)} .$$

(Let us briefly go back to the example from the beginning of this section. For a label $a \in \Delta$, every a-labelled neighbor of v in H has the same neighborhood in the set X of nodes which are derived from v. Consequently, two a-labelled neighbors of v are X-equivalent in a derived graph $\bar{H}$. That is, $\mathrm{index}_X(\bar{H}) \leq |\Delta| + 1$, and, for $Y = V_{\bar{H}} - X$, $\mathrm{index}_Y(\bar{H}) \leq 2^{|\Delta| + 1}$.)

<u>Theorem</u> 13: For every BNLC language L there is a positive constant c, $c \geq 2$, for which the following holds: For every graph H in L there is a subset X of V_H such that (i) $|V_H|/c \leq |X| \leq |V_H|/2$, and (ii) $\mathrm{index}_X(H) \leq c$.

Let us consider, e.g., the set of <u>square grid graphs</u>. For a positive integer k, the unlabelled graph $H_k^\square = (V_{H_k^\square}, E_{H_k^\square})$ is defined by

$V_{H_k^\square} = \{(i,j) \mid i,j \text{ integers with } 0 \leq i, j \leq k\}$ and

$E_{H_k^\square} = \{\{(i,j),(i',j')\} \mid |i-i'| + |j-j'| = 1\}$. Fig. 4 depicts $H_1^\square, H_2^\square$, and $H_3^\square$.

Fig. 4.

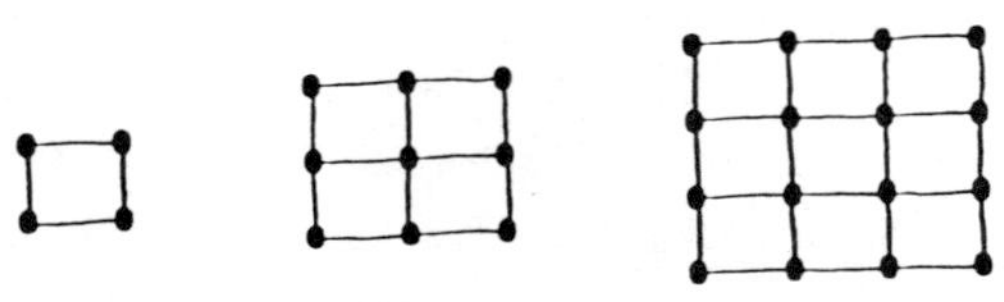

It is easily seen that all these graphs are bipartite and planar. Concerning the distinction number we state the following:

Lemma 14: Let k be a positive integer. Then for every subset X of $V_{H_k^\square}$ with $|X| \geq k$ we have $\mathrm{index}_X(H_k^\square) \geq \sqrt{k}/4$.

This lemma shows not only that the set $\mathcal{H}^\square = \{H_k^\square | k = 1,2,\ldots\}$ is not the underlying unlabelled graph language of a BNLC language, but also that it is so even for every superset of $\mathcal{H}^\square$.

Corollary 15: The set of planar graphs is not the underlying unlabelled graph language of a BNLC language.

Corollary 16: The set of bipartite graphs is not the underlying unlabelled graph language of a BNLC language.

(STRONGLY) BNLC PROHIBITIVE GRAPH LANGUAGES

The results in Theorems 5 and 13 and their implications lead us to the following definitions. An unlabelled graph language L is BNLC prohibitive, if no superset L´of L is the underlying unlabelled graph language of a BNLC language. An infinite unlabelled graph language L is strongly BNLC prohibitive, if the intersection with every underlying unlabelled graph language L´of a BNLC language is finite. Clearly every strongly BNLC prohibitive graph language is BNLC prohibitive. We have seen already a number of BNLC prohibitive graph languages, e.g., the set of planar graphs, the set of 2-colorable graphs (and so the set of k-colorable graphs, for $k \geq 2$) and the set of triangle-free graphs. From the previous results we get the following examples of strongly BNLC prohibitive graph languages:

Theorem 17: (i) $\mathcal{H}^\square$ is a strongly BNLC prohibitive graph language. (ii) Let $\mathcal{H}^{\not\triangle}$ be an infinite set of triangle-free graphs, such that for each positive integer m almost al graphs in $\mathcal{H}^{\not\triangle}$ have a chromatic number exceeding m. Then $\mathcal{H}^{\not\triangle}$ is strongly BNLC prohibitive.

ENUMERATION

We have seen already that the set of all graphs (over a fixed but arbitrary alphabet) is not a BNLC language. Here we will strengthen this result. Let L be a graph language. Then we define an integer function numb_L by $\mathrm{numb}_L(n) = |\{H \in L \,|\, |V_H| \leq n\}|$. It is well known that for an alphabet Δ, the set L of all graphs satisfies $\mathrm{numb}_L(n) \in \Omega(C^{n^2})$, where C is a positive integer. Let now $G = (\Sigma,\Delta,P,conn,Z)$ be a BNLC grammar without chain-rules. If we consider a concrete derivation of a graph H in L(G):

$$Z = H_0 \Rightarrow_{(v_0,D_1)} H_1 \Rightarrow_{(v_1,D_2)} H_2 \cdots \Rightarrow_{(v_{m-1},D_m)} H_m = H,$$

then the graph H is uniquely defined by the sequence of replacements in this derivation:

$$(*) \qquad (v_0,D_1),(v_1,D_2), \ldots (v_{m-1},D_m).$$

That is, we can encode the graph H by the sequence (*). Every pair (v_i,D_{i+1}), $0 \le i \le m-1$, can be encoded in less than $c \cdot \log_2 n$ bits, (where c is a constant number depending on G, and n is the number of nodes in H). Hence the whole sequence (*) (and thus the graph H) can be encoded by $\bar{c} \cdot n \cdot \log_2 n$ bits. (Since G is chain-rule free, we have $m \le 2n$). This shows that $numb_{L(G)}(n) \le 2^{\bar{c}n\log_2 n}$, that is $numb_{L(G)}(n) \in \mathcal{O}(C^{n\log_2 n})$, with $C = 2^{\bar{c}}$. One can even prove the following result.

Theorem 18: Let L be a BNLC language. Then $numb_L(n) \in \mathcal{O}(C^n)$, for some constant C depending on L.

MEMBERSHIP COMPLEXITY

It is known that the membership problem for NLC grammars is PSPACE-complete. (See Garey & Johnson (1979) for basic notions in complexity theory.) There is even a fixed NLC language, for which the membership problem is PSPACE-complete. This stems essentially from the fact that - in some sense - every context-sensitive string language can be generated by an NLC grammar.

Since every BNLC language L is generated by a BNLC grammar G without chain-rules, for every graph H in L there is a derivation in G which has length linear in the number of nodes in H. This easily implies:

Theorem 19: Let L be a BNLC language. Then the membership problem for L is in NP.

The problem whether the membership problem for BNLC languages is NP-hard is still open. (Note that if the membership problem is not NP-hard for BNLC languages, then the 3-colorability problem for graphs in a BNLC language is not NP-hard: see Theorem 4 (iii).)

CONCLUSION

We have presented a number of results on BNLC grammars and languages. The major outcome of these basic investigations is:

(i) The class of BNLC languages has a number of nice properties, as closure w.r.t. graph properties and decidability results which do not hold for the class of NLC languages.

(ii) BNLC grammars have a rather restricted generative power compared to NLC grammars. An outstanding example is that the set of all graphs is no BNLC language.

Although (ii) appears as a disadvantage at first sight, especially the fact that BNLC grammars cannot generate the set of all graphs(and the implications of Theorems 5, 13 and 19) opens a number of possibilities for complexity results. As we have mentioned, e.g., an upper bound for the complexity of membership in BNLC languages is also an upper bound for the complexity of testing 3-colorability of graphs in a BNLC language. Of course, we have no results so far which actually prove results in this direction, rather we would like to stress these aspects for further research on BNLC languages.

Finally, we mention an implication of our research for NLC languages. It is an easy observation that every underlying unlabelled NLC language has an infinite subset which is the underlying unlabelled graph language of a BNLC language. This implies that a strongly BNLC prohibitive graph language is never an underlying unlabelled graph language of an NLC language. Hence many "BNLC results" are applicable to the general NLC case (e.g., $H^{\square}$ is not an underlying unlabelled graph language of an NLC language).

ACKNOWLEDGEMENT: The second author's research has been supported by the Austrian "Fonds zur Förderung der wissenschaftlichen Forschung".

REFERENCES

Erdös, P. (1961), Graph theory and probability II, Canad. J. Math. 13, 346-356.

Garey, M.R. & Johnson, D.S. (1979), "Computers and Intractability - A Guide to the Theory of NP-completeness", Freeman, San Francisco.

Harary, F. (1969), "Graph Theory", Addison-Wesley, Reading Mass.

Janssens, D. (1983), "Node Label Controlled Graph Grammars", Ph.D. Thesis University of Antwerp, Belgium.

Janssens, D. & Rozenberg, G. (1980a), On the structure of node-label controlled graph languages, Inform. Sci. 20, 191-216.

Janssens, D. & Rozenberg, G. (1980b), Restrictions, extensions and variations of NLC grammars, Inform. Sci. 20, 217-244.

Janssens, D. & Rozenberg, G. (1981), Decision problems for node-label controlled graph grammars, J. Comp. Syst. Sci. 22, 144-177.

Rozenberg, G. & Welzl, E. (1983a), Boundary NLC grammars: Variations and graph theoretic closure properties, Manuscript.

Rozenberg, G. & Welzl, E. (1983b), Combinatorial properties of boundary NLC languages,Manuscript.

Tutte, W.T. (1961), A theory of 3-connected graphs, Indag. Math. 23, 441-455.

AVERAGE EFFICIENCY OF PATTERN-MATCHING ON LISP-EXPRESSIONS (Extended Abstract)

Michèle SORIA

Laboratoire de Recherche en Informatique, Bat 490, Université Paris Sud, 91405 ORSAY CEDEX, FRANCE.

Jean-Marc STEYAERT

Laboratoire de Mathématiques Appliquées, Ecole Polytechnique, 91128 PALAISEAU CEDEX, FRANCE.

Abstract: *We study the average time complexity of a generalized Pattern Matching algorithm commonly used in A.I. programs. Using methods based on combinatorial analysis and asymptotic analysis, we show that the search of a pattern in Lisp expressions is linear on the average in the size of the input, contrasting with a polynomial worst case .*

1. INTRODUCTION

The search of occurrences of a pattern in expressions is a very common problem in Computer Science that arises in many situations : compiling (abstract syntax trees) , program transformations in view of optimization (semantic trees) , theorem proving (expression trees) ,algebraic manipulations (algebraic expressions) , string searching in text editors (words) ...

Since pattern-matching on strings has been thoroughly investigated ([KMP77], [BM77],[GO77]), we focus our attention on pattern-matching on tree structures ; in this area much work has been done on efficient algorithms for locating patterns or more generally families of patterns in trees, with or without preprocessing :[HO82] and [OVL79] give various methods with accurate estimates for their worst case behaviours . The average performance of these algorithms is generally left aside although [SF82] give a detailed analysis of a simple algorithm on trees representing algebraic expressions . In [DZ81] various combinatorial formulae are given for occurrences of patterns or sets of patterns in general trees : these results extend those previously known, but their applicability to pattern-matching is not studied .

In this paper we start from a simple recursive algorithm given in [Wi77] which searches for occurrences of patterns with "don't care" symbols in Lisp-expressions; this algorithm is widely used in man-machine dialogue softwares that require the search of sequences of keywords [We67]. Furthermore this algorithm, whose worst case behaviour can be readily evaluated, does not reduce to the one studied in [SF82]; the possible occurrence of "don't care" symbols makes it harder to analyse in its average behaviour . Following Knuth's paradigm [Kn68,Kn73] we perform a flow analysis of the algorithm, using methods developped in [SF82] ; we will make an intensive use of generating series for enumeration problems, and of complex analysis for asymptotic estimates .

The main result is that Winston's algorithm keeps linear on the average in the size of the inputs, whereas it can become exponential in the number of "don't care" symbols in especially bad configurations, for a large class of patterns ; as the reader will see, this last condition is quite natural and eliminates only cases considered as pathological by any reasonable programmer .

The plan of the paper is as follows :

Paragraph 2 is devoted to the presentation of the algorithm on the most widely used data structure for Lisp expressions.

Paragraph 3 gives enumeration results for trees and occurrences of patterns, with an emphasis on asymptotic estimates.

Paragraph 4 contains the analysis of the average performance of the algorithm based on the estimate of the number of node comparisons.

Paragraph 5 contains a discussion of the practical implications of this result.

2. LISP-EXPRESSIONS , PATTERNS AND THE ALGORITHM

The Lisp-expressions in which we want to search patterns will be called texts ; we will take into consideration the most commonly used representation of Lisp-expressions and therefore identify texts with binary trees whose internal nodes are labelled by "cons" operators, whereas the leaves contain atoms ; the rightmost leaf of any branch is labelled by "nil" which factually represents the end of a list . Figure 1 displays an example of a text together with its canonical representation (in the list notation, the dot represents the infix "cons" operator).

T = (A.(B.(E.G.F).(X.(Y.Z).(A.B)).C).(X.C.U).A.D)

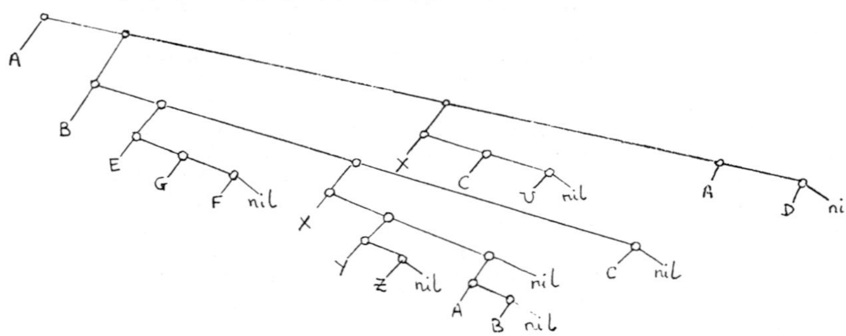

-Figure 1-
A list and its tree representation

With the conventions of these notations,it is easy to see that the number of symbols necessary to write a Lisp-expression is precisely the number of nodes of its tree representation ; we will call it the size of the expression and denote it by $|T|$ where T is the expression or equivalently the tree that represents it .

A pattern is a Lisp-expression with two special atoms : star (*) and sharp (#), which can be repeated any number of times (including none).
An example is given in Figure 2 .

The number of stars,sharps and other nodes in a pattern will be denoted by e,d and i respectively ; the total number of nodes is therefore e+d+i , and the number of "cons" (or internal nodes) is (e+d+i-1)/2 .

P = (A.(*.(X.(Y.Z).#).#).*.#.*)

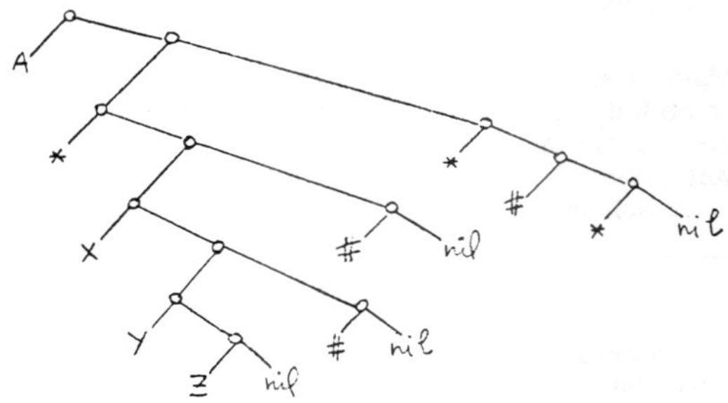

-Figure 2-
A pattern with e=2,d=3 and i=20

Sharps and stars in patterns play the role of don't care symbols, that can be substituted by expressions or strings of expressions in the following way :

a "#" can be substituted by any expression (atom or list) ,

a "*" can be substituted by any sequence (possibly empty) of expressions.

On the examples of Figures 1 and 2 , T can be recovered from P by substituting :

B.(E.G.F) to the first *

(A.B) to the first #

C to the second #

(X.C.U).A to the second *

D to the third #

empty list to the third *

or , with the same first three instances by substituting :

empty list to the second *

(X.C.U) to the third #

A.D to the third *

etc...

It is important to notice that # is a pattern whereas * is not ; however (*) is a pattern .

A pattern P is said to occur at the root of a text T if T can be recovered from P by appropriate subtitutions ; as we can see on the above example , this operation can be done in several ways which will be counted separately (on this example P occurs 3 times at the root of T).

The general problem of matching a pattern in a text is to determine all occurrences of the pattern, either at the root of the text or at the root of any full subexpression (list or atom) of the text : by "full subexpression" we mean a parenthesed sublist of the text . On our example of Fig.1, (X.C.U) is a full subexpression of T whereas C.U is not . Full subexpressions happen to be left subtrees of some "cons" node in the tree representation .
(Note that this is not a restriction , since searching occurrences of a pattern $P=(L_1.L_2.....L_k)$ in a non full subexpression is equivalent to searching occurrences of $(*.L_1.L_2.....L_k)$ in our sense) .

The pattern matching problem is easily solved by the two recursive procedures of Figure 3 : procedure **match** detects all root occurrences of a pattern in a text , while procedure **occur** repeats this operation on all full subexpressions of the text. Procedure **match** proceeds by a parallel preorder traversal of a pattern and a text according to the scheme :

-atoms are tested for equality ,

-#'s match any tree ,

-*'s are treated as follows : whenever a subpattern of the form (*.P) is detected, procedure **match** is called recursively between P and all subtrees of the text T rooted on its right branch .

```
Function match ( P:pattern , T:text ) : Boolean ;
 Begin
  Case P.info = # : match := True ;
       P.info = T.info = nil : match := True ;
       P.info = T.info in ATOM : match := True ;
       P.info = cons And T.info = nil :
               If P.left.info = * And P.right.info = nil Then match := True ;
       P.info = T.info = cons :
               Case P.left.info = * : match := match (P.right , T) ;
                          match := match Or match (P , T.right) ;
                    P.left.info = cons Or ATOM :
                          If match (P.left , T.left) Then
                               match := match (P.right , T.right) ;
               End ;
      otherwise : match := False ;
  End ;
 End .

Procedure occur ( P:pattern , T:text ) ;
 Begin
  B := match (P , T) ;
  If T<>nil Then Begin occur (P , T.left) ;
                 While T.right<>nil Do Begin
                                 T := T.right ; occur (P , T.left)
                               End
            End ;
 End.
```

-Figure 3-

3. COMBINATORIAL CONSIDERATIONS

In order to analyse the average behaviour of pattern-matching we need information on the number of texts of a given size and on the number of occurrences of a pattern in texts of a given size . These evaluations are performed according to a general scheme [FS82] which is twofold :

first we establish an equation on generating functions by considering the inductive definition of the objects we count

secondly we study the dominating singularities of the series thus obtained and derive the asymptotic behaviour of its coefficients using the Darboux method [He74].

Let **A** be the finite set of atoms on which Lisp-expressions are built , and let **L** be the class of all these expressions ; the class **L** is defined as the least fixed point of equation

$$\mathbf{L} = \mathbf{A} + (\,\mathbf{L}\,) + (\,\mathbf{L}.\mathbf{L}\,) + (\,\mathbf{L}\,.\,\mathbf{L}\,.\,\mathbf{L}\,) + \cdots \qquad (1)$$

which simply describes ,in the list notation, the trees associated to Lisp-expressions.

Let α = card (**A**) ; we then have :

PROPOSITION 1 : The number l_n of Lisp-expressions of odd size n satisfies asymptotically as $n \to \infty$:

$$l_n = \sqrt{\frac{2}{\pi}}\alpha^{\frac{1}{4}} \rho^{-n} n^{-\frac{3}{2}} (1+O(\frac{1}{n}))$$

Proof : From equation (1) we derive that the series $L(z) = \sum l_n z^n$ satisfies :

$$L(z) = \alpha z + \sum_{n=1}^{\infty} L(z)^n z^{n+1}$$

Hence

$$L(z) = \alpha z + \frac{z^2 L(z)}{1-zL(z)}$$

and solving this equation we get :

$$L(z) = \frac{1+(\alpha+1)z^2-\sqrt{(1-z^2(1+\sqrt{\alpha})^2)(1-z^2(1-\sqrt{\alpha})^2)}}{2z} \qquad (2)$$

The series L(z) has therefore $\rho = \dfrac{1}{1+\sqrt{\alpha}}$ as radius of convergence and two dominant singularities in $z = +\rho$ and $z = -\rho$. Using the Darboux method, we thus conclude [SF82] that :

$$l_n = \sqrt{\frac{2}{\pi}}\alpha^{\frac{1}{4}} \rho^{-n} n^{-\frac{3}{2}} (1+O(\frac{1}{n})) \quad \text{if n is odd}$$

$$0 \quad \text{if n is even.}$$

Occurences of a pattern P in a text T can be defined inductively as those occuring at the root of T and those occuring at the roots of all left subtrees of T ; let $\mathbf{O}_P$ and $\mathbf{H}_P$ denote respectively the sets of texts weighted by occurrences of P and root occurrences of P , and let $\mathbf{K} = \mathbf{L} - \mathbf{A} + \{\text{nil}\}$, we have :

$$\mathbf{O}_P = \mathbf{H}_P + \mathbf{O}_P.\mathbf{K} + \mathbf{L}.\mathbf{O}_P.\mathbf{K} + \mathbf{L}.\mathbf{L}.\mathbf{O}_P.\mathbf{K} + \cdots \qquad (3)$$

*PROPOSITION 2 : The average number of occurrences of a pattern P (with e *'s , d #'s and i other nodes) in a text T of size n satisfies :*

$$\overline{o_n^P} = \frac{1}{2}\rho^{i-2e}\tau^{d-1} n \, (1+O(\frac{1}{n})).$$

Proof : Let h_n^P be the number of root occurrences of P in all texts of size n ; then

$$H_P(z) = \sum_{n\geq 0} h_n^P z^n$$

satisfies

$$H_P(z) = z^{i-e}.L^d(z).\frac{1}{(1-zL(z))^e} \qquad (4)$$

From equation (3) we derive that the series

$$O_P(z) = \sum_{n\geq 0} o_n^P z^n$$

satisfies

$$O_P(z) = H_P(z) + \frac{z\,O_P(z).K(z)}{1-zL(z)}$$

where K(z) = L(z) - (α-1)z .
Hence

$$O_P(z) = H_P(z)\,.\,\frac{1}{1-\dfrac{z^2}{(1-zL(z))^2}} \qquad (5)$$

The analytic study of $O_P(z)$ shows that its dominant singularities are located in z=+ρ and z=-ρ . Its local behaviour in these points is easily evaluated from (2) and (5) . Using again the Darboux method we derive ,for odd n :

$$o_n^P = \frac{1}{\sqrt{2\pi}}\alpha^{\frac{1}{4}}\,\rho^{i-2e}\,\tau^{d-1}\,\rho^{-n}\,n^{-\frac{1}{2}}\,(1+O(\frac{1}{n})) ,$$

from which the proposition follows .

4. ANALYSIS OF THE ALGORITHM.

In this section we prove that the average running time of the pattern-matching algorithm is linear in the size of the text which contrasts with a polynomial worst case . The core of the argument is the evaluation of the average number of node comparaisons performed during the search of occurrences ; although the number of machine instructions varies according to the nature of the test performed, this gives a good approximation of the actual running time . A more detailed study is possible which is too intricate to be exposed in a few pages ; our evaluation illustrates the method and allows us to determine the major contribution to the actual cost .

Let P be a pattern with d #'s , e *'s and i other nodes . We rank the nodes different from * of its tree representation in preorder from 1 to d+i .

DEFINITIONS : For $1\leq k \leq d+i$, the *k-segment of P*, denoted $[P]_k$, is the tree obtained from P by pruning all nodes of rank $\geq k$, and by replacing pruned subtrees by a # .

For any pattern P , we define **P** to be *the family of all patterns obtained by replacing all *'s in the list-representation of P by an arbitrary number of #'s (possibly 0)* .

Elements of **P** will be called *instances* of P ; they contain no *'s , and it is clear that P occurs at the root of a text if and only if one of its instances does .

The notion of family of instances is easily generalised to k-segments of a pattern : it will be denoted by $\mathbf{P}_k$.

Examples of k-segments and of instances are given in Figure 4 with their tree representation .

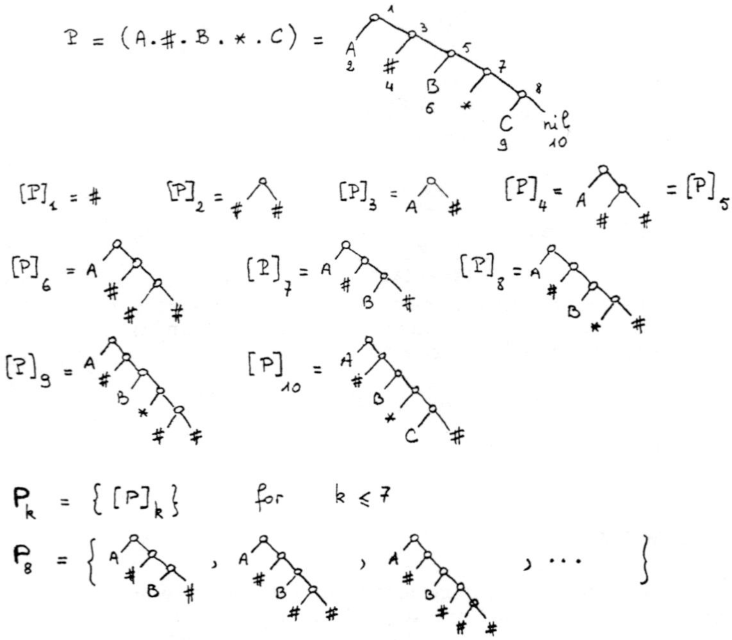

-Figure 4-

With these definitions , the number of comparaisons and tests performed during the execution of procedure match can be expressed in the following way :

THEOREM 1 : Let P be a pattern of characteristic (d,e,i) , and U be a text ; the cost of procedure match (P, U) is

$$\tau match(P,U) = \sum_{k=1}^{d+i} \sum_{M \in \mathbf{P}_k} H(M,U) \quad ,$$

where

$H(M,U)$ = 1 if *M occurs at the root of U,*

0 *otherwise.*

Let us first notice that since any instance M contains no *'s , either it occurs once at the root of U or does not occur at all .
The proof is long and tedious and is done by induction on the structure of the pattern . Basically this result is related to the recursive search performed for each * in the pattern .

Let now $\tau occur$ be the cost (in terms of comparaisons) of detecting all occurrences of P in T ; from the definition of procedure **occur** it is clear that $\tau occur$ is the sum of the costs of running procedure **match** (P,U) on all left subtrees U of T (denoted U<T) :

$$\tau occur = \sum_{U<T} \tau match(P,U) \ .$$

Hence by theorem 1

$$\tau occur = \sum_{U<T} \sum_{k=1}^{d+i} \sum_{M \in \mathbf{P}_k} H(M,U) \quad ,$$

and exchanging the order of summations :

$$\tau occur = \sum_{k=1}^{d+i} \sum_{M \in \mathbf{P}_k} \sum_{U<T} H(M,U) \quad .$$

We thus have from the definition of occurrences and instances :

$$\tau occur = \sum_{k=1}^{d+i} O^{[P]_k}(T) \qquad (6)$$

where $O^{[P]_k}(T) = \sum_{M \in \mathbf{P}_k} O^M(T)$, and $O^M(T)$ denotes the total number of occurrences of M in T .

We now have to sum equation (6) over all texts of a given size n .

DEFINITION : For any k-segment $[P]_k$ of a pattern P , let $\delta(k)$ be the *number of* #'s , $\varepsilon(k)$ be the *number of* *'s , and $\sigma(k)$ be the *number of other nodes* (internal nodes and atoms) .

Using proposition 2 we obtain from equation (6) :

THEOREM 2 : The average cost of searching a pattern P in a text T of size n is linear in n :

$$\overline{\tau occur}(P,n) = \omega_P \ . \ n \ \ (1 + O(\frac{1}{n}))$$

where ω_P is a constant depending only on P .
With the above notations,

$$\omega_P = \frac{1}{2} \sum_{k=1}^{i+d} \rho^{\sigma(k)-2\varepsilon(k)} \ \tau^{\delta(k)-1} \quad .$$

5. DISCUSSION

Let us start with an example and define the family of patterns

$$P_e = (\ *.A\ *.A\ *\ldots\ *.A\ *\ )$$

where P_e contains e *'s , hence 3e-1 other nodes, and no # . Let

$$T_n = (\ A.A.A\ldots.A\ )$$

be a text with n A's , and size 2n+1 .
The number of occurrences of P_e in T_n (certainly smaller than the cost of

occur(P_e, T_n)) is obviously

$$\binom{n}{e-1} \approx \frac{n^{e-1}}{(e-1)!} \quad \text{as } n \to \infty .$$

On the other hand ,

$$\omega_{P_e} = \frac{1}{2}[\ 1 + \rho^{-1} + (\tau + \rho + 1)\ \frac{1-\rho^{e-1}}{1-\rho}]$$
$$< \frac{1}{2}(\ 1 + \rho^{-1} + \tau)\ \frac{1}{1-\rho} \quad \text{since } \rho<1.$$

We can see on this example that the algorithm,and even *any* algorithm detecting all occurrences of pattern P_e, has a polynomial worst case behaviour -in $O(n^e)$, where e is the number of stars in the pattern-, whereas it has an average searching time which is linear in the size of the text, the coefficient of linearity being bounded independently of the size of the pattern .

Let us now examine the pattern

$$S_e = (\ *.*.*\ldots *)$$

formed with e *'s . For this pattern

$$\omega_{S_e} = \frac{\rho^{-e-1}-1}{\rho^{-1}-1}$$

which tends to infinity as e → ∞ .

Similarly the pattern

$$U_e = (\ *.\#.*.\#\ldots *.\#.*)$$

with e *'s is such that ω_{U_e} also diverges :

$$\omega_{U_e} = 1 + \rho^{-1} + (2 + \rho^{-1})\ \frac{\tau^e - \tau}{\tau - 1}$$

These patterns are rather pathological ; and it is clear that from a searching point of view, pattern S_e is equivalent to pattern (*) , and similarly pattern U_e is equivalent to pattern (#.#.#....#.*) -with $e-1$ #'s-.

If we reject patterns with such distributions of stars, and only consider those patterns such that their list notation contains at least one atom between every two consecutive stars , then it is possible to find an absolute constant ω_∞ which is greater than ω_P for any such pattern .

For this large class of patterns we thus conclude that the average behaviour of the algorithm is always linear in the size of the text, with no influence from the pattern .

BIBLIOGRAPHY

[BM77]Boyer,R.S.,& Moore,J.S. A Fast String Searching Algorithm. *Commun. ACM* vol.20,no.10, 1977 .

[DZ81]Dershowitz,N.,& Zaks,S. Applied Tree Enumeration. *Proceedings of CAAP 81*, Springer-Verlag 1981 .

[GO77]Guibas,L.J.,& Odlyzko,A. A New Proof of the Linearity of the Boyer & Moore String Searching Algorithm. *Proceedings of 18th IEEE conference on FOCS*, Providence, 1977 .

[He74]Henrici,P. " Applied and Computational Complex Analysis". J.Wiley New-York, 1974 .

[HO82]Hoffmann,C.M.,& O'Donnel,M.J. Pattern Matching in Trees. *Journal of the ACM* vol.29,no.1, 1982 .

[Kn68]Knuth,D. " The Art of Computer Programming, Vol 1 : Fundamental Algorithms". Addison-Wesley, Reading, Mass., 1968.

[Kn73]Knuth,D. "The Art of Computer Programming, Vol 3 : Searching and Sorting". Addison-Wesley, Reading, Mass., 1973 .

[OVL79]Overmars,M.H.,& Van Leeuwen,J. Rapid Subtree Identification Revisited. Tech.Rep. CS-79-3, Univ. of Utrecht, Utrecht, Netherlands, 1979 .

[SF82]Steyaert,J.M.,& Flajolet,P. Patterns and Pattern Matching in Trees : an Analysis . *Rapport no 77, Centre de Math. appli., Ecole Polytechnique 1982* . To appear in *Information & Control* .

[We67]Weizenbaum,J. Contextual Understanding by Computers. *Commun. of the ACM* vol.10,no.8, 1967 .

[Wi77]Winston,P. "Artificial Intelligence". Addison Wesley, 1977 .

A THEORY OF REPRESENTABLE CPO'S

Konrad R. Theobald
-FernUniversität-Gesamthochschule-
Fachbereich Mathematik & Informatik
Postfach 94o - D-58oo Hagen

Abstract. This paper presents a uniform approach to a general theory of complete partial orders (cpo's). It is available for most of the effectivizations of cpo's. Moreover it can be used to show that nearly all these subclasses coincide - up to computable isomorphic cpo's.

We confine ourselves to bounded-complete, ω-continuous cpo's, called npo's - the underlying class of most the effectivizations. The notions in this paper are attached to a type 2-recursion theory and the theory of representations (i.e. ERSOV's [4] theory of numberings for type 2-recursion theory).

1 *Introduction*

During the last ten years the study of complete partial orders (cpo's) has become of general interest in computer science. Mainly the results of these studies can be used in programming language semantics. In this kind of an abstract mathematical semantic the meaning of a program can be regarded as a computable function from and to a cpo-domain. SCOTT [18] suggested the importance of a profound knowledge of continuity and computability in those structures. This knowledge is of use in the field of recursive analysis, too (see SCOTT [17]).

Up to the present day several authors have introduced a lot of different effectivized classes of cpo's:

- continuous lattices (SCOTT [18]);
- continuous lattices having additional properties (TANG [2o]);
- message sets (REYNOLDS [13]);
- effective cpo's having additional properties (EGLI/CONSTABLE [3]; MARKOWSKY/ROSEN [11];
- effectively given domains (SMYTH [19]);
- admissible coherent cpo's (SCIORE/TANG [15], [16]);

- a universal domain (PLOTKIN [12]);
- recursive cpo's (WEIHRAUCH/DEIL [21]);
- zulässige cpo's (KREITZ [9]).

Most of these effectivizations are subclasses of the so-called *natural partial orders (npo's)* - i.e. bounded-complete, ω-continuous cpo's. We confine ourselves to that class. With the exception of class inclusion all efforts to compare the effectivizations mentioned above have failed (see SMYTH [19]; KANDA/PARK [8]). Yet it was possible to formulate demands on such a class (TANG [2o]):

- each structure of the class should have an effective base,
- the class should be effectively closed under some operations like product-cpo, continuous function-space-cpo, retract-cpo, etc.,
- the class should include a structure giving an effective theory for the real numbers.

In this context *effective* means something like computable. We also look at a constructive version of these demands (exchange effective by constructive). Here *constructive* means something like continuous. In this paper we shall give these terms this meaning.

Thus in order to unify the presented effectivizations a general approach to effectiveness in cpo's has to be developped. The first formulations of such a theory has been done by KANDA [5]; [6]; [7] and WEIHRAUCH/SCHÄFER [23] independently. Unfortunately they look at a fixed base numbering of a cpo and characterize all representations of the cpo-domain - admissible only for this base numbering. However it is well-known that there are cpo's having two really different (i.e. not recursively equivalent) base numberings, that determine the same effective theory: E.g. look at a cpo on intervals of real numbers and take an effective numbering of intervals with rational ends resp. of intervals with ends in $\{\frac{\ell-m}{2^n} | \ell,m,n \in \mathbb{N}\}$. Then the numberings are not equivalent but each system of effective nested intervals with rational ends can be transformed to an equivalent system of the other set of intervals. Hence the computability does not differ for these base numberings.

This paper overcomes these difficulties by looking at *represented cpo's* (pairs of cpo and representation of the cpo-domain). A *representation* is a surjective function from $\mathbb{F}$ (the set of total functions from $\mathbb{N}$ to $\mathbb{N}$) to the represented set. A continuity and recursion theory on $\mathbb{F}$ can be found in DETTKI/SCHUSTER [1]. Looking at a representation this theory can be applied to any represented set (see KREITZ/WEIHRAUCH [1o] and DEIL [2]). We shall introduce three different classes of represented cpo's: $\mathfrak{K}$ resp. $\mathfrak{Z}$ - the class of constructivly resp. admissibly represented npo's, i.e. the representation is continuous- resp. computable-equivalent to those given by $\sqsubseteq$-directed and $\prec$-directed sets of base elements with respect to (w.r.t) the base numbering - and $\mathfrak{E}$ - a subclass of $\mathfrak{Z}$ that satisfies the effective version of the Tang-demands. Then comparisons of the effectivizations to $\mathfrak{E}$ can be done. Indeed this subclass $\mathfrak{E}$ is the closure of most the effectivizations with computable isomorphic cpo's. This interrelation between those effectivizations is a confirmation of the profundity of the presented general theory.

2 *Recursion Theory, Numbered and Represented Sets*

In order to define a recursion theory for any set up to the cardinality of the sequence space of the natural numbers, we firstly define a recursion theory on two special sets.

- $\mathbb{N}$, the set of natural numbers (for the countable case),
- $\mathbb{F} := \{f: \mathbb{N} \dashrightarrow \mathbb{N} \mid f \text{ is a total function}\}$ ($\longrightarrow$ will indicate a total function in this paper).

A recursion theory for $\mathbb{N}$ can be found in ROGERS [14] or WEIHRAUCH ET AL. [22]. We denote *the set of computable functions from* $\mathbb{N}$ *to* $\mathbb{N}$ (e.g. Turing-computable) by P and $P \cap \mathbb{F}$, *the set of the total computable functions from* $\mathbb{N}$ *to* $\mathbb{N}$ by R.

For $\mathbb{F}$ we select a subset of *the set of operators* ($\{F \mid F:\mathbb{F} \dashrightarrow \mathbb{F}\}$) by introducing continuous operators. We take as topological base $\mathcal{B} := \{\{f\in \mathbb{F} \mid (\forall i\in\mathbb{N}, 0\leq i\leq n)\ g(i)=f(i)\} \mid g\in\mathbb{F} \wedge n\in\mathbb{N}\}$. Define $\mathcal{O}$ as the set of all unions of subsets of $\mathcal{B}$. $(\mathbb{F},\mathcal{O})$ is called the *Baire topology* of $\mathbb{F}$. Then we choose $\mathfrak{C} := \{F : \mathbb{F} \dashrightarrow \mathbb{F} \mid (\forall o\in \mathcal{O})(\exists o'\in\mathcal{O})\ o'=f^{-1}o \cap \mathrm{Def}(F)\}$. We call $\mathfrak{C}$ *the set of the continuous operators* and $\mathfrak{T}$ *the set of the total continuous operators*. We define computability on $\mathfrak{C}$ by *$\mathbb{F}$-Turing machines*. These machines have an oneway-read-only-inputtape, an oneway-write-only-outputtape and a twoway-worktape.

Physical model of a $\mathbb{F}$-Turing machine started on the code of a function $f \in \mathbb{F}$ on the inputtape.

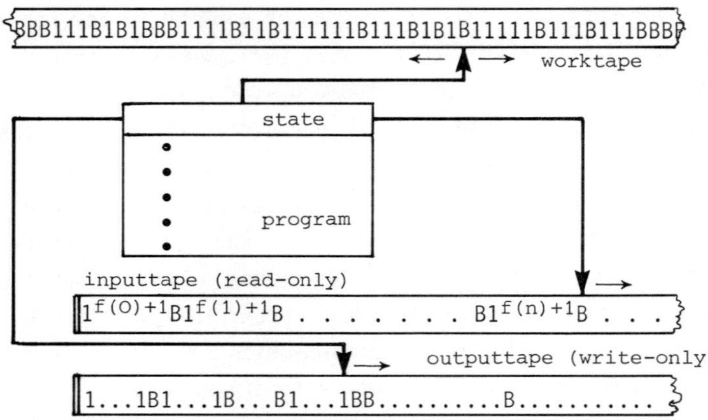

Then we call an operator F of $\mathfrak{C}$ *computable*, iff there exists a $\mathbb{F}$-Turing-Machine, that - started on the *code of a function* f of $\mathbb{F}$ ($1^{f(o)+1}B\ 1^{f(1)+1}B \ldots B\ 1^{f(n)+1}B \ldots$) - either computes the code of the function F(f) if F(f) exists or diverges or computes no code of a function if F(f) does not exist. *The set of all computable operators* is denoted by $\mathfrak{P}$ and $\mathfrak{P} \cap \mathfrak{T}$ the set of all total computable operators by $\mathfrak{R}$. A theory of continuity and computability of these sets (i.e. standard representation, universal operator of $\mathfrak{C}$, smn-theorem, recursion theorem, etc) can be found in DETTKI/SCHUSTER [1].

Let M be a set. If there exists a surjective function $\nu : \mathbb{N} \dashrightarrow M$, we call ν *a numbering of* M and the pair (M,ν) *a numbered set*. If there exists a surjective function $\delta : \mathbb{F} \dashrightarrow M$, we call δ *a representation of* M and the pair (M,δ) *a represented set*. Using numberings and representations we can derive a recursion theory for numbered and represented sets from those for $\mathbb{N}$ and $\mathbb{F}$.

2.1 *Definition*

(1) Let (M_1,ν_1), (M_2,ν_2) be two numbered sets and $f:M_1 \dashrightarrow M_2$ a function. f is called *(ν_1,ν_2)-computable*, iff there exists

a $g \in P$, such that (s.t.) $g\ \mathrm{dom}\ (\nu_1) \subseteq \mathrm{dom}\ (\nu_2)$ and $(\forall\ n \in \mathrm{dom}\ (\nu_1))\ f\nu_1(n) = \nu_2 g(n)$ holds.

(2) Let (M_1,δ_1), (M_2,δ_2) be two represented sets and $f:M_1 \dashrightarrow M_2$ a function. f is called (δ_1,δ_2)-continuous [(δ_1,δ_2)-computable], iff there exist a $F \in \mathfrak{C}[\mathfrak{P}]$, s.t. $F\ \mathrm{dom}\ (\delta_1) \subseteq \mathrm{dom}\ (\delta_2)$ and $(\forall\ h \in \mathrm{dom}\ (\delta_1))\ f\delta_1(h) = \delta_2 F(h)$ holds.

We illustrate the meaning of the definition for representations. A function $f:M_1 \dashrightarrow M_2$ is (δ_1,δ_2)-continuous [(δ_1,δ_2)-computable], iff there exists a continuous (computable) operator F, s.t. the following diagram commutes on dom (δ_1).

$$\begin{array}{ccc} \mathbb{F} & \overset{F}{\dashrightarrow} & \mathbb{F} \\ \delta_1 \downarrow & & \downarrow \delta_2 \\ M_1 & \overset{f}{\dashrightarrow} & M_2 \end{array}$$

For a represented set (M,δ) we call $\Delta_\delta := \delta R$ - the image of the total computable functions w.r.t δ - *the set of computable elements* of (M,δ). We define a standard numbering $\nu_\delta : \mathbb{N} \dashrightarrow \Delta_\delta$ of Δ_δ by $\nu_\delta := \delta\varphi$ where φ is a suitable fixed numbering of P (s. ROGERS [14]).

In order to compare represented sets we introduce two equivalence relations, called isarithmorphism relations (ισον-(mathematically) equal, ἀριθμος -number; μορφη-configuration).

2.2 *Definition*

Let (M_1,δ_1), (M_2,δ_2) be represented sets.

(1) (M_1,δ_1) is called *isarithmorphic* to (M_2,δ_2) (shortly: $(M_1,\delta_1) \boxed{\equiv} (M_2,\delta_2)$), iff there exists a bijective (δ_1,δ_2)-continuous function $f:M_1 \longrightarrow M_2$, s.t. f^{-1} is (δ_2,δ_1)-continuous.

(2) (M_1,δ_1) is called *computable isarithmorphic* to (M_2,δ_2) (shortly: $(M_1,\delta_1) \equiv (M_2,\delta_2)$), iff there exists a bijective (δ_1,δ_2)-computable function $f:M_1 \longrightarrow M_2$, s.t. f^{-1} is (δ_2,δ_1)-computable.

We call the functions mentioned in definition 2.2 *(computable) isarithmorphisms*. They have the following properties.

2.3 THEOREM

Let (M_i,δ_i), (M_i',δ_i') be represented sets (i=1,2).

(1) Let $(M_i,\delta_i) \boxminus (M_i',\delta_i')$ by g_i. Define I for any $h \in \mathbb{F}$ by $I(h) := g_2 h g_1^{-1}$. Then we have for any $h \in \mathbb{F}$:
h is (δ_1,δ_2)-continuous $\Leftrightarrow$ I(h) is (δ_1',δ_2')-continuous.

(2) Let $(M_i,\delta_i) \equiv (M_i',\delta_i')$ by g_i. Define I as above. Let $h \in \mathbb{F}$.
Then (a), (b), (c) hold:
(a) h is (δ_1,δ_2)-computable $\Leftrightarrow$ I(h) it (δ_1',δ_2')-computable,
(b) $g_1\ \Delta_{\delta_1} = \Delta_{\delta_2}$,
(c) the restriction of g_1 on Δ_{δ_1} is $(\nu_{\delta_1},\nu_{\delta_1})$-computable (by a <u>total</u> computable function).

Hence the isarithmorphisms harmonize to the concepts of continuity and computability. Altogether we have introduced a general theory of continuity and computability of numbered and represented sets. All necessary definitions are quite canonical. Moreover - for represented sets - we have formulated the intuitive idea of "effective" translatability of objects by the computable isarithmorphism relation. We shall apply this theory to cpo's.

3 *Represented Natural Partial Orders*

Below we summarize the most important definitions of cpo-theory. Let (D,ρ) be a relation. A subset $M \subseteq D$ is *ρ-bounded*, if there exists a $x \in D$, s.t. $(\forall\, m \in M)\ m\,\rho\, x$ holds. If for any two elements $m,m' \in M$ a $\overline{m} \in M$ exists, s.t. $m\,\rho\,\overline{m}$ and $m'\rho\,\overline{m}$ hold, then M is called *ρ-directed*. If any ρ-directed (ρ-bounded) subset M of D has a least upper bound (denoted by $\bigsqcup$), we call (D,ρ) *complete (bounded-complete)*.

Let $(D,\sqsubseteq)$ be a partial order (reflexive, antisymmetric and transitive) with least element $\perp$. Then we call $(D,\sqsubseteq,\perp)$ *complete partial order (cpo)*, iff $(D,\sqsubseteq)$ is complete. For a cpo $(D,\sqsubseteq,\perp)$ we define $(D,\prec)$ by

$$x \prec y :\Longleftrightarrow (\forall M \subseteq D,\ M\ \sqsubseteq\text{-directed})\ [y \sqsubseteq \bigsqcup M \Rightarrow (\exists m \in M)\ x \sqsubseteq m]$$

and call this relation the *Scott-relation*. A subset $B \subseteq D$ is called a *base of* $(D,\sqsubseteq,\bot)$, if for any $x \in D$ the set $B_x^{\prec} := \{b \in B \mid b \prec x\}$ is $\sqsubseteq$-directed and $x = \bigsqcup B_x^{\prec}$ holds. A bounded-complete cpo having a countable base is called *natural partial order (npo)*. Let now $(D,\sqsubseteq,\bot)$, $(D',\sqsubseteq',\bot')$ be two cpo's. A function $f : D \longrightarrow D'$ is called $((D,\sqsubseteq,\bot), (D',\sqsubseteq',\bot'))$-*continuous*, if for any $M \subseteq D$, M $\sqsubseteq$-directed the set fM is $\sqsubseteq'$-directed and $f(\bigsqcup M) = \bigsqcup fM$ holds. More detailed definitions and their interrelations can be found in WEIHRAUCH/DEIL [21].

In a general way we lay down properties of representations for npo's. As well as in the constructive, in the effective case we demand the existence of an base with a numbering, s.t. any represented element x can be transformed to a $\prec$-directed, x approximating set of base elements and any $\sqsubseteq$-directed set of base elements to an index representing the least upper bound of this set w.r.t. the given representation and the existing numbering of the base. We formulate that idea below:

3.1 *Definition*

Let $\bar{D} = (D,\sqsubseteq,\bot)$ be a npo and δ a total representation of D. Define for any base B and total numbering β of B representations $\gamma_\beta, \gamma_\beta^{\prec}$ of D by $\gamma_\beta(f) :=$ [if $\beta f \mathbb{N}$ $\sqsubseteq$-directed then $\bigsqcup \beta f \mathbb{N}$ else divergent] and $\gamma_\beta^{\prec}(f) :=$ [if $\beta f \mathbb{N}$ $\prec$-directed then $\bigsqcup \beta f \mathbb{N}$ else divergent].

(1) $(\bar{D},\delta)$ is called *constructively represented npo*, iff there exists a base B and a total numbering β of B, s.t. id_D is $(\delta,\gamma_\beta^{\prec})$-continuous and id_D is (γ_β,δ)-continuous by a total function. The class of all such represented npo's is denoted by $\mathbb{K}$.

(2) $(\bar{D},\delta)$ is called *admissibly represented npo*, iff there exists a base B and a total numbering β of B, s.t. id_D is $(\delta,\gamma_\beta^{\prec})$-computable and id_D is (γ_β,δ)-computable by a total function. The class of all such represented npo's is denoted by $\mathbb{Z}$.

For $(\bar{D},\delta)$ of $\mathbb{K}$ resp. $\mathbb{Z}$ we call an existing base numbering β that has the properties of definition 3.1 *constructive* resp. *admissible*.

We illustrate the definition above by the following diagram. The total continuous operators A and S exist by definition 3.1.

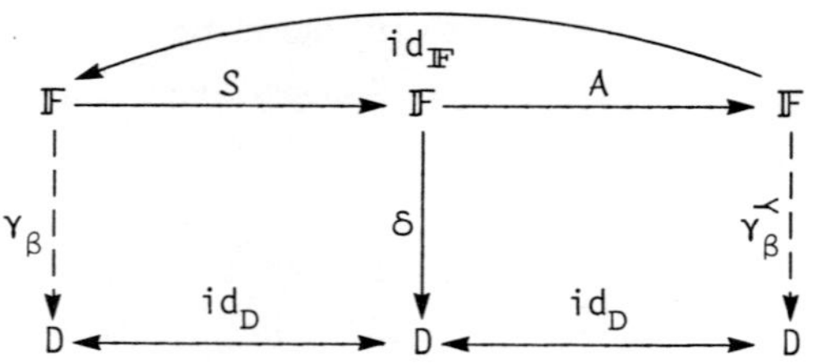

The properties of A and S in $\mathfrak{T}$ resp. $\mathfrak{R}$ can be axiomized as follows:

$(A)\quad (\forall f \in \mathbb{F})\,[\beta A(f)\,\mathbb{N}\ \prec\text{-directed} \wedge \delta(f) = \bigsqcup \beta A(f)\,\mathbb{N}],$

$(S)\quad (\forall f \in \mathbf{F})\,[\beta f\,\mathbb{N}\ \sqsubseteq\text{-directed} \Rightarrow \delta S(f) = \bigsqcup \beta f\,\mathbb{N}].$

We can prove any npo to have a constructive representation.

3.2 THEOREM

Let $\overline{D} = (D,\sqsubseteq,\perp)$ be a npo with a base B. Let β be any base numbering of B. Then there exists a representation δ_β of D, s.t. $(\overline{D},\delta_\beta)$ is in $\mathbb{K}$.

Using this theorem and proof ideas of SCOTT [17], [18] and SMYTH [19] in the appropriate modification we get the following result.

3.3 THEOREM

The class $\mathbb{K}$ satisfies the constructive versions of the Tang-demands.

Thus the class $\mathbb{K}$ has reasonable properties. Now we shall have a look at continuity definitions usable for the class $\mathbb{K}$. There are two different types of continuity of functions for $\mathbb{K}$: cpo-continuity and continuity w.r.t. representations. We can prove them not to differ.

3.4 THEOREM

Let $((D,\sqsubseteq,\perp),\delta)$, $((D',\sqsubseteq',\perp'),\delta')$ be in $\mathbb{K}$. Let $f : D \longrightarrow D'$ be a function. Then we have:

f is $((D,\sqsubseteq,\perp),(D',\sqsubseteq',\perp'))$-continuous $\Longleftrightarrow$ f is (δ,δ')-continuous.

As a conclusion of this theorem we get that the isarithmorphism relation does not differ from the isomorphism relation for cpo's (in order to simplify the following formulations we shall use the relations ⊑ and ≡ synonymously for members of $\mathbb{K}$, too).

We can characterize the concepts of computability - given in part 2 for represented sets - for the class $\mathbb{Z}$ by standard concepts of cpo-theory.

3.5 THEOREM

Let $((D,\sqsubseteq,\perp),\delta)$ be in $\mathbb{Z}$ and β an admissible base numbering. Then the following equation holds:

$$\Delta_\delta = \{x \in D \mid (\exists A \subseteq \mathbb{N}, A \text{ recursively enumerable}) [\beta A \text{ is } \sqsubseteq\text{-directed} \wedge x = \bigsqcup \beta A]\}.$$

But the characterization in the right side is exactly the ordinary computability concept of elements in cpo-theory, given e.g. in KANDA [7]. A similar result holds for the computability concept of functions.

3.6 THEOREM

Let $((D,\sqsubseteq,\perp),\delta)$, $((D',\sqsubseteq',\perp'),\delta')$ be in $\mathbb{Z}$ and β, β' two corresponding admissible base numberings. Let $f: D \longrightarrow D'$ be a function. Then (1) and (2) are equivalent:

(1) f is (δ,δ')-computable,

(2) there exists a recursively enumerable set $M \subseteq \mathbb{N}$, s.t. for any $A \subseteq \mathbb{N}$ with βA is $\sqsubseteq$-directed (a) and (b) hold:
 (a) $X := \{\beta'(j) \mid (\exists i \in A) \langle j,i \rangle \in M\}$ is $\sqsubseteq'$-directed,
 (b) $\bigsqcup X = f(\bigsqcup \beta A)$, for X defined as in (a).

($\langle\ ,\ \rangle$ is an appropriate effective bijective function from $\mathbb{N}^2$ to $\mathbb{N}$, see e.g. the pairing function of ROGERS [14]).

Since part (2) of theorem 3.6 is the characterization of a computable function in SMYTH [19] we have no difference between ordinary cpo-computability and computability given by the representations.

Thus the presented theory harmonizes with well-known standard notions of cpo-theory. But now we get this theory by a natural restriction of the constructively represented npo's to those that fulfills the properties of definition 3.1(1) in an effective way. Above those properties we have not demanded any effectivity, e.g. effectivity of the bounded-completeness.

We want to note some secondary effects of the theorems of this section. The ordinary cpo-concepts depend on the choice of the base and the base numbering. Here (see theorem 3.4, 3.5, and 3.6) we have the possibility to change the bases and base numberings for a fixed represented npo within the scope of the constructivity resp. the admissibility of base numberings (the definitions in part 2 are independent of a special base numbering). Indeed within this theory we can conclude that the theory of continuity and computability for the two numberings in the example of the introduction does not differ because both are admissible base numberings to an appropriate representation of the intervals.

To resume the main results of this section we note that we have introduced a reasonable general theory of continuity and computability based on a reasonable class of cpo's.

4 *Effective Represented Natural Partial Orders*

In the last section we have only specified a class ($\mathfrak{K}$) fulfilling the constructive version of the Tang-demands. Now we shall look at a suitable class fulfilling the effective version of the Tang-demands. The class $\mathfrak{Z}$ - the possibly biggest subclass of $\mathfrak{K}$ with a reasonable theory of computability - seems not to fulfill the Tang-demands. Almost all approaches to develop an effectivization of cpo's that is closed w.r.t. constructions of the cpo of the continuous functions demand some effectiveness of the bounded-completeness. For that reason we reduce the class $\mathfrak{Z}$ to those members having such a property and denote the resulting class by $\mathfrak{E}$. We choose a modified form of SMYTH's [19] effectively given domains in order to characterize this class $\mathfrak{E}$. First of all we shall demand the existence of a least element, then we generalize his CR-structures (see the definition of the approximation relation below) and finally we call only those cpo's effective represented npo which are computable isarithmorphic to the completion of one of the modified CR-structures. Whereas the generalization is necessary to prove the equivalence to other effectivizations, the restriction to the computable isarithmorphic cpo's is necessary, since only isarithmorphic, i.e. the same as isomorphic cpo's (see theorem 3.4) do not have the same theory of computability (see KANDA/PARK [8]).

We formulate these ideas in the following definitions which are rather incomprehensible for those people not familiar with these notions. Let E be a countable set and $(E,<)$ be a transitive relation. We call a set $A \subseteq E$ <-closed, if $(\forall e \in E)\,[(\exists a \in A)\; e < a \Longrightarrow e \in A]$. Then define D_E by $D_E := \{A \subseteq E \mid A \text{ is } <\text{-directed} \wedge A \text{ is } <\text{-closed}\}$ and $E_e^<$ by $E_e^< := \{a \in E \mid a < e\}$ for any $e \in E$. If for any $e \in E$ $E_e^<$ is <-directed (i.e. $E_e^<$ is in D_E) and there exists a least element $e_o \in E$ w.r.t. to <, then $(D_E, \subseteq, E_{e_o}^<)$ - called *the completion of* $(E,<,e_o)$ - is an npo, iff for any finite <-bounded set $A \subseteq E$ the set $\{E_a^< \mid a \in A\}$ has a least upper bound - called $\overline{\sqcup}A$ - in D_E w.r.t. $\subseteq$. If all these properties hold for a transitive relation $(E,<)$ and a element $e_o \in E$, we call $(E,<,e_o)$ a *complete basis structure*. For these structures we can define constructivity and effectiveness.

4.1 *Definition*

A tuple $\hat{E} = (E,<,\eta,c,k)$ is called *a constructively complete base structure*, iff $(E,<,\eta(k))$ is a complete basis structure, η is a total numbering of E, $k \in \mathbb{N}$ and $c \in \mathbb{F}$ a function having the following property:

$$\{j \in \mathbb{N} \mid \eta D_j \text{ is } <\text{-bounded}\} \subseteq c^{-1}\{0\} \subseteq \{j \in \mathbb{N} \mid \overline{\sqcup}\eta D_j \text{ exists}\}$$

(Here D is a total bijective numbering of $\{N \subseteq \mathbb{N} \mid N \text{ is finite}\}$ see ROGERS [14]).

Then the set $AR(\hat{E}) := \{\langle i,j\rangle \mid c(j) = 0 \wedge \eta(i) \in \overline{\sqcup}\eta D_j\}$ is called *the approximation relation of* $\hat{E}$. If $c \in R$ holds and $AR(\hat{E})$ is a recursively enumerable set, then $\hat{E}$ is called *an effectively complete basis structure*.

For the above defined structures we can define a standard representation σ_E of D_E. Let f be in $\mathbb{F}$. Define $A_f(n) := \{f(0),\dots,f(n)\}$ and $N(f) := \{n \in \mathbb{N} \mid (\forall i \in \mathbb{N})\,[D_i \subseteq A_f(n) \Longrightarrow c(i) = 0]\}$. Then we can choose $\sigma_E(f) := \bigcup_{n \in N(f)} \overline{\sqcup}\eta A_f(n) \cup E_{\eta(k)}^<$. Having defined σ_E in this way, we get the following result:

4.2 THEOREM

For any constructively complete base structure $\hat{E} = (E,<,\eta,c,k)$ the pair $\overline{\overline{E}} := ((D_E,\subseteq,E^<_{\eta(k)}),\sigma_E)$ is in $\mathbb{K}$ and for any member $\mathbf{k}$ of $\mathbb{K}$ there exists such a structure $\hat{E}$, s.t. $\mathbf{k} \equiv \overline{\overline{E}}$ holds. Furthermore, if $\hat{E}$ is effectively complete, then $\overline{\overline{E}}$ is in $\mathbb{Z}$.

Since we suppose that there exists members in $\mathbb{Z}$ being not computable isarithmorphic to a completion of an effectively complete base structure, we define the class of such members in $\mathbb{Z}$ and denote it by $\mathbb{E}$.

4.3 *Definition*

Define $\mathbb{E} := \{\mathbf{k} \in \mathbb{K} \mid (\exists (E,<,\eta,c,k)$ effectively complete basis structure$)\ ((D_E,\subseteq,E^<_{\eta(k)}),\sigma_E) \equiv \mathbf{k}\}$. Then $\mathbb{E}$ is called *the class of the effective represented npo's*.

Now for this class $\mathbb{E}$ we are able to prove the following theorem.

4.4 THEOREM

The class $\mathbb{E}$ fulfills the effective version of the Tang-demands.

Hence we have found a subclass of $\mathbb{Z}$ that has the same properties as $\mathbb{K}$ - but now in an effective version. Since we can use the theory of continuity and computability on $\mathbb{Z}$ for this class $\mathbb{E}$, this subclass turns out to be an intuitively good effective class of cpo's. The final section will confirm this conjecture.

5 *Comparisons with other Effectivizations*

Briefly we shall describe three known effectivizations of npo's.

Let $(D,\sqsubseteq,\bot)$ be a npo with a countable base B. $(D,\sqsubseteq,\bot)$ is called *an algebraic npo w.r.t.* B, if $B = \{x \in D \mid x \prec x\}$. Now we call $(D,\sqsubseteq,\bot,\beta)$ *a recursive cpo*, iff β is a base numbering of $(D,\sqsubseteq,\bot)$, $(D,\sqsubseteq,\bot)$ is an algebraic npo w.r.t. $\beta\,\mathbb{N}$, $\{\langle i,j\rangle \mid \beta(i)\sqsubseteq\beta(j)\}$ and $M := \{k \in \mathbb{N} \mid \beta D_k$ is $\sqsubseteq$-bounded$\}$ are recursive, and there exists a $q \in R$, s.t. $\beta q(k) = \bigsqcup \beta D_k$ holds for any $k \in M$ (see WEIHRAUCH/DEIL [21]).

A $((D,\sqsubseteq,\perp),(D,\sqsubseteq,\perp))$-continuous function $f\colon D \longrightarrow D$ - having the property $f^2=f$ is called a *retraction*. A retraction of a recursive cpo $(D,\sqsubseteq,\perp,\beta)$ is called *computable*, if $\{\langle i,j\rangle \mid \beta(i) \prec f\beta(j)\}$ is recursively enumerable. Let f be a retraction. Then $\overline{D}:=(fD,\sqsubseteq|_{fD},f(\perp))$ is a npo, called *retract* of $(D,\sqsubseteq,\perp)$ w.r.t. f. For any retract $\overline{D}$ of a recursive cpo w.r.t. a computable retraction we can construct a standard representation $\delta_{\overline{D}}$ of fD, s.t. $(\overline{D},\delta_{\overline{D}})$ is in $\mathfrak{Z}$. At last we define $\mathfrak{Z}_R := \{\mathfrak{k}\in\mathfrak{K} \mid (\exists\,\overline{D}$ retract of a recursive cpo w.r.t. a computable retraction) $\mathfrak{k}\equiv(\overline{D},\delta_{\overline{D}})\}$.

For any not empty set M with a total numbering μ and a truth function C of the power set of M we call $\overline{M}:=(M,C,\mu)$ *an effective message set*, iff $C(\emptyset)$ is true, $[C(X) \Leftrightarrow (\forall S\subseteq X, S \text{ finite})C(S)]$ holds for any subset X of M, and $\{i \in \mathbb{N} \mid C(\mu D_i)\}$ is a recursive set (see: REYNOLDS [13], SMYTH [19]). Then $\overline{D_M}:=(\{X\subseteq M \mid C(X)\},\subseteq,\emptyset)$ is a npo with base $\{S\subseteq M \mid C(S)\wedge S$ finite$\}$. A retraction f of $\overline{D_M}$ is called effective, if $\{\langle i,j\rangle \mid C(\mu D_j)\wedge \mu(i)\in f(\mu D_j)\}$ is *recursively enumerable*. We can prove a retract $\overline{\overline{M}}$ of an effective message set w.r.t. an effective retraction - completed with an appropriate standard representation $\delta_{\overline{\overline{M}}}$ of $\{X\subseteq M \mid C(X)\}$ - to be in $\mathfrak{Z}$. Then we define $\mathfrak{Z}_M:=\{\mathfrak{k}\in\mathfrak{K} \mid (\exists\overline{\overline{M}}$ retract of an effective message set w.r.t. an effective retraction) $\mathfrak{k}\equiv(\overline{\overline{M}},\delta_{\overline{\overline{M}}})\}$.

As the last effectivization mentioned in this paper we define the "zulässige cpo" (zcpo) of KREITZ [9]. A tuple $\widetilde{D}=(D,\sqsubseteq,\perp,e,U,r)$ is called *zcpo*, iff $(D,\sqsubseteq,\perp)$ is a npo with base $e\mathbb{N}$ $(e\colon\mathbb{N}\longrightarrow D)$, $U\colon\mathbb{N}\longrightarrow\{X \mid X\subseteq D\}$ is a function, s.t. for any $x\in D$ $E(x):=\{e(i) \mid x\in U(i)\}$ is $\sqsubseteq$-directed and $\bigsqcup E(x)=x$ holds, and $r\in R$ a function, s.t. $\{k\in\mathbb{N} \mid \bigcap_{i\in D_k} U(i)\neq\emptyset\},\{k\in\mathbb{N} \mid (\exists j\in\mathbb{N})\, D_k=\{j\}\} \subseteq r^{-1}\{0\} \subseteq \{k\in\mathbb{N} \mid \bigsqcup e\,D_k \text{ ex.}\}$ holds (we denote $(D,\sqsubseteq,\perp)$ by $S_{\widetilde{D}}$). Then we can define for any zcpo $\widetilde{D}$ a standard-representation $\delta_{\widetilde{D}}$, s.t. $(S_{\widetilde{D}},\delta_{\widetilde{D}})$ is in $\mathfrak{Z}$. In the same way as above we define $\mathfrak{Z}_K:=\{\mathfrak{k}\in\mathfrak{K} \mid (\exists\,\widetilde{D}$ zcpo$)$ $(S_{\widetilde{D}},\delta_{\widetilde{D}})\equiv\mathfrak{k}\}$.

Now the theory presented in the sections 2 and 3 allows us to prove the following theorem.

5.1 THEOREM

$$\mathfrak{Z} = \mathfrak{Z}_R = \mathfrak{Z}_M = \mathfrak{Z}_K .$$

Thus our conjecture at the end of part 4 has been confirmed by the equivalence of most the effectivizations mentioned in part 1. In order to verify this statement we have to remark, that REYNOLDS [13] message sets are generalizations of the continuous lattices and that the class $\mathfrak{E}_K$ is a generalization of SCIORE/TANG'S [15], [16] admissible coherent cpo's.

We conclude our investigation of classes of bounded-complete cpo's and its effectivizations by setting up the following thesis:

5.2 THESIS

The class $\mathfrak{E}$ is exactly the class of those natural partial orders that are intuitively effective.

Beside the accordance with so many other effectivizations of natural partial orders this thesis has been confirmed by the validity of the effective versions of the Tang demands.

Reference List

H.J. Dettki/H. Schuster - "Rekursionstheorie auf $\mathbb{F}$" - Informatik Berichte Nr. 34 (5/1983) - FernUniversität - Gesamthochschule - in Hagen - 1983 [1]

T. Deil - "Darstellungen und Berechenbarkeit reeller Zahlen" - Dissertation am Fachbereich Mathematik & Informatik - FernUniversität - Gesamthochschule - Hagen - 1983 [2]

H. Egli/R. Constable - "Computability Concepts for Programming Languages Semantics" - Theoretical Computer Science; Vol. 2 - 1976; 133 - 145 [3]

Ju.L. Eršov - "Theorie der Numerierungen I" - Zeitschrift für mathem. Logik & Grundlagen der Mathematik; Band 19, Heft 4 - 1973; 289 - 388 [4]

A. Kanda - "Data Types as Effective Objects" - Theory of Computation Report, No. 22 - Warwick University - 1977 [5]

A. Kanda - "Effective Solutions of Recursive Domain Equations" - Ph. D. thesis - Warwick University - 198o [6]

A. Kanda - "Göbel Numbering of Domain Theoretic Computable Functions - A Generalization of Rogers Indexing Theory - Department of Computer Studies, Report No. 138 - University of Leeds - 198o [7]

A. Kanda/D. Park - "When are two Effectively Given Domains Identical?" - Theor. Comp. Sci., 4th GI-confer. Aachen, LNCS67 - Springer - 1979; 17o - 181 [8]

Chr. Kreitz - "Zulässige cpo's: Ein Entwurf für ein allgemeines Berechenbarkeitskonzept" - Schriften zur Informatik & angewandten Mathematik Nr. 76 - RWTH Aachen - 1982 [9]

Chr. Kreitz/K. Weihrauch - "Towards a Theory of Representations" - Informatik Berichte - Nr. 4o (7/1983)- FernUniversität - Gesamthochschule - in Hagen - 1983 [1o]

G. Markowsky/B. Rosen - "Bases for Chain-Complete Posets" - IBM Journal of Research & Development; Vol. 2o - 1976; 138 - 147 [11]

G. Plotkin - "$\mathbb{T}^{\omega}$ as a Universal Domain" - Journal of Computer & System Science; Vol. 17 - 1978; 2o9 - 236 [12]

J. Reynolds - "On the Interpretation of Scott's Domain" - Symposia Mathematica N$\underline{\text{o}}$ 15 - 1975 ; 123 - 135 [13]

H. Rogers - "Theory of Recursive Functions and Effective Computability" - McGraw-Hill New York - 1967 [14]

E. Sciore/A. Tang - "Admissible Coherent cpo's" - Automata, Languages & Programming Proceedings 1978, LNCS62 - Springer Berlin - 1978; 44o - 456 [15]

E. Sciore/A. Tang - "Effective Domains" - Princeton University, New Jersey - 1978 [16]

D. Scott - "Outline of a Mathematical Theory of Computation" - Proceedings of the 4th Annual Princeton-Conference on Information Science & Systems, New Jersey - 197o; 169 - 176 [17]

D. Scott - "Data Types as Lattices" - SIAM Journal on Computing; Vol. 5 - 1976; 522 - 587 [18]

M.B. Smyth - Effectively Given Domains" - Theoretical Computer Science; Vol. 5 - 1977; 257 - 274 [19]

A. Tang - "Recursion Theory and Descriptive Set Theory in Effectively Given T_o-Spaces" - Ph. D. thesis - University of Princeton, New Jersey - 1974 [2o]

K. Weihrauch/T. Deil - "Berechenbarkeit auf cpo's" - Schriften zur Informatik & angewandten Mathematik Nr. 63 - RWTH Aachen - 198o [21]

K. Weihrauch et al. - "Theorie der Berechenbarkeit " - Kurs Nr. 168o/1; FernUniversität - Gesamthochschule - in Hagen - 1982 [22]

K. Weihrauch/G. Schäfer - "Admissible Representations of Effective cpo's"- Theoretical Computer Science; Vol. 26 - 1983; 131 - 147 [23]

YIELDS OF INFINITE TREES

Erick TIMMERMAN

- Laboratoire d'Informatique Fondamentale de Lille (L.A. 369 associé au C.N.R.S.)
- I.U.T. "A" de Lille-I, Département Informatique, B.P. 179, 59653 - Villeneuve d'Ascq Cédex (France)

Abstract. We introduce yield of infinite trees. Trees are provided with usual syntactic order, words with a new order that canonically makes concatenation continuous. "Yield" operation is continuous. Our main result consists in the decidability of yield's equality for infinite regular trees.

Résumé. Nous introduisons le feuillage d'arbres infinis. Les arbres munis de l'ordre syntaxique habituel, les mots d'un nouvel ordre rendant canoniquement la concaténation continue. L'opération "Feuillage" est continue. Notre principal résultat est la décidabilité de l'égalité des feuillages pour les arbres infinis réguliers.

INTRODUCTION

Infinite words, as usually defined, are not suitable for extending relations between finite trees and words to infinite ones. The basic reason lies in the non-compatibility of the order relation on words ("left factor") with the concatenation, and with syntactic order on trees.

By definition we impose good properties on yield operation :
- order relation on words has to make concatenation continuous in the corresponding CPO.
- yield operation (its domain is the CPO of trees with syntactic order) having to be then continuous.

The researched yield's notion is obtained by constructing the free object that fits these specifications.

Infinite words, here considered, are more general than those introduced by Nivat, and bi-infinite words defined by Nivat & Perrin (1981). They are close to generalized infinite words or arrangements (or strings) studied by Courcelle (1978) and Heilbrunner (1980). Arrangements enable to define the frontier of an infinite tree and the link with algebraic systems is done through the frontier of derivation trees. This side is used for solving quasi-rational (Courcelle, 1978) and algebraic (Heilbrunner, 1980) systems of equations. Unfortunately, frontier operation is not continuous and the decidability of frontier's equality of regular trees is an open problem.

Our notion of infinite words (we will call them infinite terms) seems to be poorer than arrangements : it does not take into account the way a sequence of words tends toward infinity.

Considering infinite regular trees, we prove the decidability of yield equality. The principle is to deduce a rational language from a regular tree, this language being a directed subset whose lub is the yield of the tree. This can be done in two different ways :

- constructing an automaton from a system that represents a regular tree,
- using Heilbrunner's results and tranforming his regular expressions (that represent arrangements) into rational ones that represent languages we are looking for. This is going to be presented in this way (although it is less general since it just holds for locally finite regular trees).

1 YIELD OPERATION

Context and notations

Let Σ be a ranked alphabet, Ω be the undefined symbol of arity 0 such that $\Omega \notin \Sigma$. We consider $T^{\infty}_{\Omega}(\Sigma) = T^{\infty}(\Sigma \cup \{\Omega\})$ the set of finite and infinite trees over $\Sigma \cup \{\Omega\}$ (that is the usual magma of infinite trees, Nivat 1973). $T^{\infty}_{\Omega}(\Sigma)$ provided with the syntactic order relation is an ω-algebraic complete partial ordered set (CPO); its finitary basis is $T_{\Omega}(\Sigma)$ the set of finite trees over $\Sigma \cup \{\Omega\}$. We will classically note : $T^{\infty}(\Sigma)$ the set of maximal trees and $T^{Loc}(\Sigma)$ the set of locally finite trees (see Courcelle 1983, for more precise definitions).

For each tree t in $T^{\infty}_{\Omega}(\Sigma)$, dom(t) denotes its tree-domain and fr(t) the subset of dom(t) of terminal nodes, i.e. :

$$fr(t) = \{u \in dom(t) / t(u) \in \Sigma_o \cup \{\Omega\}\}$$

where Σ_o is the set of constant symbols (arity 0) in Σ ; t being considered as a partial mapping : $N_+^* \to \Sigma \cup \{\Omega\}$ with the usual properties.

The yield operation is only defined for finite trees (i.e. for all t in $T_\Omega(\Sigma)$) by $fg : T_\Omega(\Sigma) \to (\Sigma_o \cup \{\Omega\})$

- if $dom(t)$ is empty, $fg(t) = \varepsilon$ (the empty word)
- if $dom(t) = \{\varepsilon\}$, $fg(t) = t(\varepsilon)$
- if $t = f(t_1,\ldots,t_p)$, $f \in \Sigma_p$ (arity p)

$$fg(t) = fg(t_1) . \ldots . fg(t_p)$$

In other words, if $u_1,\ldots,u_k$ is the increasing sequence, (w.r.t. lexicographic order) of the words in $fr(t)$ then :

$$fg(t) = t(u_1) . \ldots . t(u_k).$$

It is quite clear we cannot satisfactorily extend this operation to : $T_\Omega^\infty(\Sigma) \to (\Sigma_o \cup \{\Omega\})^\infty$ (the set of finite and infinite words over $\Sigma_o \cup \{\Omega\}$).

Specifications

We now define, in a general way, the conditions of a generalized yield operation.

Let M be a set such that Ω belongs to it.

Conditions on M :

1) M provided with an order relation $(<)$ is a CPO and its least element is Ω .

2) M provided with a concatenation operation $(\circ)$ is a monoïd.

3) The order relation is compatible with the concatenation, i.e. : $x < y$ & $z < t$ implies $x \circ z < y \circ t$.

4) The concatenation is continuous, i.e. whenever D and D' are directed subsets of M , $Lub(D) \circ Lub(D') = Lub(D \circ D')$, where $D \circ D'$ is the directed subset (by 3)) : $\{x \circ y \mid x \in D \;\&\; y \in D'\}$

Definition : For such a set M , we call "yield" a mapping $\phi : T_\Omega^\infty(\Sigma) \to M$ such that :

- ϕ is strict, increasing and continuous,

and - for all $t \in T_\Omega^\infty(\Sigma)$, if $t = f(t_1,\ldots,t_p)$, $f \in \Sigma_p$, then $\phi(t) = \phi(t_1) \circ \ldots \circ \phi(t_p)$.

Immediate property : For each finite tree t , if $u_1,\dots,u_k$ is the increasing sequence (w.r.t. lexicographic order) of the words of $fr(t)$ then $\phi(t)=\phi(t(u_1))\circ\dots\circ\phi(t(u_k))$ where $t(u_i)$ represents the tree whose domain is $\{\varepsilon\}$ and whose symbol is $t(u_i) \in \Sigma_o \cup \{\Omega\}$.

Consequence : ϕ is completely defined by its values on Σ_o , whenever it exists.

Construction

From now on, everything is canonical from a categorical point of view; we just make explicit constructions.

Let X be an alphabet such that $\Omega \notin X$. On can first note that there is no order relation on $(X \cup \{\Omega\})^*$ such that Ω is the least element and compatible with concatenation.

Let $\leq_\Omega$ denote the relation on $(X \cup \{\Omega\})^*$ defined by : for all $x,y \in (X \cup \{\Omega\})^*$:

$$x \leq_\Omega y \text{ iff : } \begin{cases} - \; x \in X^* \text{ and } x = y \\ - \text{ or } x = x_o\,\Omega\, x_1\, \Omega \dots \Omega\, x_n \;,\; x_i \in X^* \\ \quad\;\; y = x_o\, y_1\, x_1\, y_2 \dots y_n\, x_n \;,\; y_j \in (X \cup \{\Omega\})^* \\ \quad\;\; n \in N^+ \end{cases}$$

It is easy to check that $\leq_\Omega$ is the least preorder on $(X \cup \{\Omega\})^*$ compatible with the concatenation , such that Ω is less than each word (even the empty word).

Let $\simeq$ denote the congruence on $(X \cup \{\Omega\})^*$ generated by $\Omega\Omega \simeq \Omega$; then we have : for all $v,w \in (X \cup \{\Omega\})^*$ $v \simeq w$ iff $v \leq_\Omega w$ and $w \leq_\Omega v$. Thus $(X \cup \{\Omega\})^*/\simeq$ is a partially ordered set and Ω its least element. An ω-algebraic CPO is obtained by completion (by equivalence of directed subsets) Let us denote $W^\infty(X)$ this CPO, $W(X)$ its finitary basis (i.e. $(X \cup \{\Omega\})^*/\simeq$) and $W^\omega(X)$ the set of non-finitary words or "infinite terms" $(W^\omega(X) = W^\infty(X)\backslash W(X))$.

By continuity the concatenation is extended and confers to $W^\infty(X)$ a structure of monoïd : every condition of definition of a yield mapping is then satisfied.

Let us consider $T^\infty_\Omega(\Sigma)$ and $W^\infty(X)$ with $\Sigma_o = X$.

Let $\phi : T^{\infty}_{\Omega}(\Sigma) \rightarrow W^{\infty}(X)$ be the mapping, in accordance with the specifications, defined by :

- $\phi(\Omega) = \Omega$ (ϕ is strict)
- $\phi(x) = x$ for all x in Σ_o .

One can explicitly define ϕ , first as an application from $T_{\Omega}(\Sigma)$ into $W(X)$, then by continuous extension.

Let us remark ϕ is onto and for each finite tree t we have $fg(t) \simeq \phi(t)$. Considering locally finite trees we have : $\phi(T^{Loc}(\Sigma)) = \{\phi(t) \ / \ t \in T^{Loc}(\Sigma)\}$ is strictly included in $W^{\infty}(X)$; we will note $W^{Loc}(X)$ this set.

Theorem.-

$\phi : T^{\infty}_{\Omega}(\Sigma) \rightarrow W^{\infty}(X)$ is the initial yield (the only one within an isomorphism). i.e. : For any yield $\phi_m : T^{\infty}_{\Omega}(\Sigma) \rightarrow M$, there is one and only one continuous morphism of monoid h such that $\phi_m(t) = h(\phi(t)$ for all tree t .

The proof rests on the construction of the morphism h , and on the lemma : $\phi(t) = \phi(t')$ implies $\phi_m(t) = \phi_m(t')$.

2 YIELD AND FRONTIER

The notion of frontiers of infinite trees, introduced by Courcelle (1978) is based on the definition of arrangements or generalized infinite words. We just recall the main definitions and properties and then compare yield and frontier, infinite terms and arrangements.

Arrangements

Let X be an alphabet. An arrangement over X is a triple $u = \langle D,\pi,h \rangle$ consisting of a set D , a total order π or D , and a mapping $h : D \rightarrow X$. u is said countable whenever D is.

$A_{\omega}(X)$ denotes the set of countable arrangements. The words of X^{*} are identified with the finite arrangements $\langle [n],\leq,h \rangle$ where $[n] = \{1,2,\ldots,n\}$ and $\leq$ the natural order on integers. The arrangements

$<N_+,\leq,h>$ correspond to the infinite words of X^ω .

An equivalence relation on arrangements is defined as follows : if $u = <D,\pi,h>$ and $u' = <D',\pi',h'>$, u and v are said equivalent ($u \equiv v$) iff there exists a bijective order preserving mapping $f : D \to D'$ such that $h = h' \circ f$. The concatenation of arrangements is also defined (see Courcelle (1978) and Heilbrunner (1980)).

<u>Frontiers of infinite trees</u> (Courcelle (1978)).

We consider $T^\infty(\Sigma)$ the set of trees over Σ (i.e. the set of maximal trees in $T^\infty_\Omega(\Sigma)$).

For each tree $t : dom(t) \to \Sigma$, the "frontier" of t is the countable arrangement $\psi(t) = <fr(t),\leq_\ell,t>$, where $\leq_\ell$ is the lexicographic order. Let us recall :

<u>Properties</u> : - if $t = f(t_1,\ldots,t_p)$, $f \in \Sigma_p$ then : $\psi(t) = \psi(t_1)\ldots\psi(t_p)$
- for each finite tree $t : \psi(t) \equiv fg(t)$

<u>Theorem</u> (Courcelle)

$$A_\omega(\Sigma_o) = \{\psi(t)/t \in T^\infty(\Sigma)\}$$
$$= \{\varepsilon\} \cup \{\psi(t)/t \in T^{Loc}(\Sigma)\}$$

<u>Yield and frontier</u>

Let us recall that ψ is not "continuous" in $T^\infty_\Omega(\Sigma)$, i.e. : if $(t_i)_{i\in N}$ and $(t'_i)_{i\in N}$ are increasing sequences of trees in $T_\Omega(\Sigma)$ such that $\psi(t_i) \equiv \psi(t'_i)$ for all i in N , this does not imply $\psi(lub\{t_i/i \in N\}) \equiv \psi(lub\{t'_i/i \in N\})$.

<u>Consequence</u> : For all $t,t' \in T^{Loc}(\Sigma)$
$\phi(t) = \phi(t')$ does not imply $\psi(t) \equiv \psi(t')$.

Conversely we have the following

<u>Property</u> : For all $t,t' \in T^{Loc}(\Sigma)$

$$\psi(t) \equiv \psi(t') \quad \text{implies} \quad \phi(t) = \phi(t')$$

Note that this property does not generally hold in $T^{\infty}(\Sigma)$. The proof is based, besides definitions of the yield, frontier, équivalence of arrangements, and properties of ω-algebraic CPO's, on manipulations of tree-domains.

<u>Consequence</u> : There exists an onto mapping s , $s : A_{\omega}(X) \to W^{Loc}(X)$, that can be defined by : for each u in $A_{\omega}(X)$, let t be a locally finite tree such that $\psi(t) \equiv u$; then $s(u) = \phi(t)$. A direct definition of s can be done :

- u represents a word w in X whenever u is finite and then $s(u) = w$,
- let $u = \langle D,\pi,f\rangle$ be an infinite arrangement in $A_{\omega}(X)$ and ν be a bijective enumeration of D ($\nu : N_+ \to D$) .

For all $n \in N_+$ let $i_1,\ldots,i_n$ the increasing sequence of the elements in $[n]$ ordered by : i is less than j iff $\nu(i)\ \pi\ \nu(j)$ in D , and v_n be the word in $W(X)$ defined as follows :

$$v_n = \alpha_o . f(\nu(i_1))\ \alpha_1 \ldots \alpha_{n-1} . f(\nu(i_n))\ \alpha_n$$

where α_i belongs to $\{\Omega,\varepsilon\}$ for all $i \in [0,n]$ and :

- $\alpha_o = \varepsilon$ iff $\nu(i_1)$ is the least element in D
- $\alpha_n = \varepsilon$ iff $\nu(i_n)$ is the greatest element in D
- for all $i \in [1,n-1]$, $\alpha_j = \varepsilon$ iff $\nu(i_j)$ is the successor of $\nu(i_{j-1})$ and $\nu(i_{j+1})$ is the successor of $\nu(i_j)$ according to the total order π on D .

The set : $\{v_n / n \in N\}$ defined in this way, is an increasing sequence of $W(X)$ whose lub is in $W^{Loc}(X)$ and $s(u) = \mathrm{Lub}\{v_n / n \in N\}$. We have the following properties :

- for all u,w in $A_{\omega}(X)$: $u \equiv w$ implies $s(u) = s(w)$
  $s(u.w) = s(u).s(w)$
- for all t in $T^{Loc}(\Sigma)$: $\phi(t) = s(\psi(t))$; note that it is not necessarily true if t is not locally finite.

Regular expressions.

In order to solve quasi-rational and algebraic systems, Courcelle (1978) and Heilbrunner (1980) define "regular expressions" (r.e.) that represent countable arrangements, using the operations of concatenation, exponentiation (to ω and $-\omega$) and "shuffle".

With any regular expression E , in Heilbrunner's sense, one can associate the rational expression $g(E)$ that defines a rational language of $(X \cup \{\Omega\})^*$, g being recursively defined as follows :

- $g(\varepsilon) = \varepsilon$
- $g(\alpha) = \alpha$ for each letter α in X
- $g(E\cdot E') = g(E) . g(E')$ whenever E and E' are r.e.'s
- $g(E^{\omega}) = (g(E))^*\Omega$
- $g(E^{-\omega}) = \Omega(g(E))^*$
- if $E_1,\dots,E_n$ are r.e.'s and $E = \{E_1,\dots,E_n\}$ (E^{η} denotes the shuffle of the set E) then $g(E^{\eta}) = (\Omega(g(E_1) + \dots + g(E_n)))^*\Omega$

Proposition.-

Let E be a regular expression that denotes an arrangement u in $A_{\omega}(X)$. Then $s(u) = \mathrm{Lub}(g(E)/\simeq)$.

Sketch of the proof : $u \equiv w$, $w \in X^*$ whenever u is finite and then $g(E) = w = s(u)$.

If u is infinite, E contains at least one of the symbols : ω , $-\omega$, η.

a) Let us suppose $E = E_1.E_2$ with E_1 and E_2 satisfying the proposition. Then $u = u_1 u_2$ and $s(u) = s(u_1) s(u_2)$ (by property of s)
$= \mathrm{lub}(g(E_1)/\simeq).\mathrm{lub}(g(E_2)/\simeq) = \mathrm{lub}(g(E_1).g(E_2)/\simeq)$
(by the property of the CPO $W^{\infty}(X)$).
Thus $s(u) = \mathrm{lub}(g(E_1.E_2)/\simeq) = \mathrm{lub}(g(E)/\simeq)$

b) Let α be a letter in X , and $E = \alpha^{\omega}$
E is the solution (given by Courcelle or Heilbrunner) of the equation $x = \alpha x$. Let t be the infinite derivation tree of this system. It is easy to see that :

$\phi(t) = \mathrm{lub}(\alpha^{*}\Omega) = \mathrm{lub}(g(E)/\simeq)$. Furthermore $\psi(t) \equiv u$, thus $s(u) = \mathrm{lub}(g(E)/\simeq)$ since $\phi(t) = s(\psi(t))$. In the same way, if $E = \alpha^{-\omega}$ the result is obtained as before by using the equation $x = x\alpha$.

c) Let $\alpha_1,\ldots,\alpha_n$ be letters in X , $\alpha = \{\alpha_1,\ldots,\alpha_n\}$ and $E = \alpha^{\eta}$. E is the solution (given by Heilbrunner's algorithm) of the equation $x = x\,\alpha_1\,x\,\ldots\,x\,\alpha_n\,x$. As before, t is the maximal derivation tree of this system, $u \equiv \psi(t)$ and $\phi(t) = s(\psi(t))$ (t is locally finite). By considering finite approximations of t and $\phi(t)$, one can prove that $\phi(t) = \mathrm{lub}((\Omega(\alpha_1 + \ldots + \alpha_n))^{*}\Omega/\simeq)$ and thus we get :

$$\phi(t) = s(u) = \mathrm{lub}(g(E)/\simeq) .$$

d) It remains to be proved that $s(w) = \mathrm{lub}(g(\Theta(E))/\simeq)$, where w is the arrangement denoted by $\Theta(E)$, whenever an arrangement u is denoted by the expression E and satisfies $s(u) : \mathrm{lub}(g(E)/\simeq)$, and Θ is a substitution of the expression E_{α} for the letter α such that : $s(u_{\alpha}) = \mathrm{lub}(g(E_{\alpha})/\simeq)$. We only need to remark that $g(\Theta(E))$ is equal to $\tau(g(E))$ with τ the substitution of the expression $g(E_{\alpha})$ for the letter α .

3 YIELDS OF INFINITE REGULAR TREES

A tree is regular iff it has a finite number of distinct subtrees, iff it is a component of the unique solution of a regular system of equations (see Courcelle, 1983).

Let $V = \{x_1,\ldots,x_n\}$ be a set of syntactic variables; a regular system (of equations) is a system of the form : $S = \langle x_1 = u_1,\ldots,x_n = u_n\rangle$ with the u_i's in $T(\Sigma \cup V)$; S can also be viewed as a deterministic regular tree-grammar (one production rule for each syntactic variable).

Let $\bar{S}$ be the derived system, associated with S and defined by : $\bar{S} = \langle x_1 = \phi(u_1),\ldots,x_n = \phi(u_n)\rangle$; $\bar{S}$ is an algebraic system or, as previously recalled, a deterministic context-free grammar.

Let $h : (\Sigma_o \cup V)^{*} \rightarrow (\Sigma_o \cup \{\Omega\})^{*}$ be the morphism defined by :

- $h(x_i) = \Omega$ for each x_i in V
- $h(\alpha) = \alpha$ for each letter α in Σ_o .

It can be noted that $h(u) \leq_\Omega h(v)$ whenever $u \xrightarrow[\bar{S}]{*} v$; so the set $\{h(w)/x_i \xrightarrow[\bar{S}]{*} w\}/\simeq$ is a directed subset of $W(\Sigma_o)^S$ and, by definition, its lub is the infinite term generated by $\bar{S}$ from x_i ; it is equal to the yield of the maximal derivation-tree obtained from x_i .

Property.- Let t_i be, for each x_i in V, the regular tree generated by S from x_i then its yield $\phi(t_i)$ is the infinite term generated by $\bar{S}$ from x_i .

Let $Id(L)$ be, for any language L of $(\Sigma_o \cup \{\Omega\})^*$, the set $Id(L) = \{w \in (\Sigma_o \cup \{\Omega\})^*/\exists\ v \in L \ \&\ w \leq_\Omega v\}$.

Let $\rho : (\Sigma_o \cup \{\Omega\})^* \to (\Sigma_o \cup \{\Omega\})^*$ be the mapping that gives the unique normal form for any word, according to the congruence $\Omega\Omega \simeq \Omega$, i.e. : $\rho(w)$ is the shortest word u such that $u \simeq w$ (ρ suppresses useless Ω). One can easily prove :

Lemma.- For any rational language R of $(\Sigma_o \cup \{\Omega\})^*$ one can construct the rational language $\rho(Id(R))$.

We can now give a fundamental property that enables us to solve the problem of decision.

Property.- For any algebraic system $G = \langle x_1 = w_1,\ldots,x_n = w_n\rangle$ $n \in N_+$, $w_i \in (\Sigma_o \cup V)^*$, for each x_i in V , one can construct a rational language $R_i \subseteq (\Sigma_o \cup \{\Omega\})^*$ such that $R_i/\simeq$ is a directed subset whose lub is the infinite term generated by G from x_i .

The complete proof consists in the construction of an automaton associated with G (see Timmerman [10]).

A partial proof can be done : using Heilbrunner's algorithm to solve the system G , we obtain a regular expression E_i that represents an arrangement u_i equivalent ($\equiv$) to the frontier of the maximal derivation tree (t_i) obtained with G from x_i . By the mapping g (previously defined) we get a rational expression $g(E_i)$ defining a rational language R_i of $(\Sigma_o \cup \{\Omega\})^*$, and we have :

$$s(u_i) = s(\psi(t_i)) = \text{lub}(g(E_i)/\simeq) .$$

Furthermore $\phi(t_i)$ is equal to the infinite term generated by G from x_i and $\phi(t_i) = s(\psi(t_i))$ whenever t_i is locally finite.

Theorem.- Yield's equality for regular trees is decidable.

Proof.- Let t,t' be regular trees given by the regular systems S and S' . Let $\bar{S}$ and $\bar{S}'$ be the derived systems (defined as above). By the previous property we can construct the rational languages R and R' and we have : $\phi(t) = \phi(t')$ iff $R/\simeq$ and $R'/\simeq$ are equivalent directed subsets, iff $\rho(\text{Id}(R)) = \rho(\text{Id}(R'))$: this equality is decidable since they are rational languages, by the lemma.

Examples.-

1) Let t and t' be the regular trees defined by the systems S and S' :

$$S = \langle x = f(a,x) \rangle$$
$$S' = \langle y = h(a,y,y) \rangle$$

Then we get the derived systems :

$$\bar{S} = \langle x = ax \rangle$$
$$\bar{S}' = \langle y = ayy \rangle$$

Using Heilbrunner's algorithm to solve them we obtain the regular expressions : $x = a^\omega$ and $y = a^\omega(a^\omega)^\eta$ that respectively represent $\psi(t)$ and $\psi(t')$. $(\psi(t) \neq \psi(t'))$. Then :

$$g(x) = a^*\Omega \quad \text{and} \quad \phi(t) = \text{lub}(a^*\Omega/\simeq)$$

and

$$g(y) = a^*\Omega(\Omega(a^*\Omega))^*\Omega \simeq (a^*\Omega)^* \quad \text{and} \quad \phi(t') = \text{lub}((a^*\Omega)^*/\simeq)$$

One can see that $(a^*\Omega/\simeq)$ and $((a^*\Omega)^*/\simeq)$ are equivalent directed subsets, thus $\phi(t) = \phi(t')$.

2) Let now t and t' be defined by :

$$S = \langle x = f(a,x,x,b) \rangle$$
$$S' = \langle x_o = h(x_1,x_2,x_3),\ x_1 = k(a,x_1),\ x_2 = h(x_3,x_1,x_2),\ x_3 = k(x_3,b) \rangle$$

Then $\bar{S} = \langle x = axxb \rangle$

$\bar{S}' = \langle x_o = x_1 x_2 x_3 \ , \ x_1 = ax_1 \ , \ x_2 = x_3 x_1 x_2 \ , \ x_3 = x_3\ b) \rangle$

$\bar{S}'$ is quasi rational (in Courcelle's sense) and is solved by the expression $x_o = a^{\omega}(b^{-\omega}a^{\omega})^{\omega}\ b^{-\omega}$ that represents $\psi(t')$.

$\bar{S}$ is not quasi-rational and, by Heilbrunner's algorithm, is solved by $x = a^{\omega}(b^{-\omega}a^{\omega})^{\eta}\ b^{-\omega}$ that represents $\psi(t)$.

Let us note that $\psi(t) \not\equiv \psi(t')$. With g we obtain :

$$g(x_o) = a^{*}\Omega(\Omega b^{*}a^{*}\Omega)^{*}\Omega\Omega b^{*} \simeq a^{*}\Omega(b^{*}a^{*}\Omega)^{*}b^{*}$$

and $$g(x) = a^{*}\Omega((\Omega(\Omega b^{*}a^{*}\Omega))^{*}\Omega)\Omega b^{*} \simeq a^{*}\Omega(b^{*}a^{*}\Omega)^{*}b^{*}$$

thus $$\phi(t) = \phi(t') = \text{lub}((a^{*}\Omega b^{*})^{*}/\simeq)$$

3) Let t be defined by $S = \langle x = f(x,a,b,x) \rangle$.
$\bar{S} = \langle x = xabx \rangle$ that is solved by $x = (ab)^{\eta}$; $g(x) = (\Omega ab)^{*}\Omega$ and $\phi(t) = \text{lub}((\Omega ab)^{*}\Omega/\simeq)$.

Let t' be defined by $S' = \langle x = f(x,a,y,b,x)\ ,\ y = k(y,y) \rangle$.
Then $\bar{S}' = \langle x = xaybx\ ,\ y = yy \rangle$ and $x = (ayb)^{\eta}$, $y = \varepsilon$ and thus $x = (ab)^{\eta}$

We have $\psi(t) \equiv \psi(t')$. The tree t' is not locally finite and $\phi(t')$ is different from $\phi(t)$ since $\phi(t') = \text{lub}((\Omega a\Omega b)^{*}\Omega/\simeq)$ and the subsets $(\Omega ab)^{*}\Omega/\simeq$ and $(\Omega a\Omega b)^{*}\Omega/\simeq$ are not equivalent directed subsets of $W(\Sigma_o)$

ACKNOWLEDGMENTS

I thank Max DAUCHET for giving me the idea of this work and Bruno COURCELLE for his comments and suggestions about first version of the communication.

REFERENCES

[1] COMYN, G. (Mars 1982). Objets Infinis Calculables, Thèse d'Etat

[2] COURCELLE, B. (1978). Frontiers of Infinite Trees, In RAIRO, Informatique Theorique, Col. 12, pp. 319-337

[3] COURCELLE, B. (1983). Fundamental Properties of Infinite Trees. In Theoretical Computer Science, 25, pp. 95-169

[4] HEILBRUNNER, S. (1980). An Algorithm for the Solution of Fixed Point Equations for Infinite Words, In RAIRO, Informatique Theorique, Vol. 14, pp. 131-141

[5] LEGUY, B. (1980) Réductions, Transformations et Classification des Grammaires Algébriques d'Arbres. Thèse de 3ème Cycle

[6] NIVAT, M. (1973). Langages Algébriques sur le Magma Libre et Sémantique des Schémas de Programmes. In Automata, Langages and Programming, 1st Colloquium, North-Holland, pp. 293-307

[7] NIVAT, M. (1978). Sur les Ensembles de Mots Infinis Engendrés par une Grammaire Algébrique, In RAIRO, Informatique Théorique, Vol. 12, pp. 259-278

[8] NIVAT, M. (1979). Infinite Words, Infinite Trees, Infinite Computations. In Mathematical Centre Tracts, vol.109, pp.1-52.

[9] NIVAT, M.,PERRIN, D. (1981). Ensembles Reconnaissables de Mots Bi Infinis, Rapport L.I.T.P., 52

[10] TIMMERMAN, E. (To appear) Feuillages d'Arbres Infinis, Thèse de 3ème Cycle.

OPTIMAL DECISION TREES AND ONE-TIME-ONLY BRANCHING PROGRAMS FOR SYMMETRIC BOOLEAN FUNCTIONS

I. Wegener

FB-20 Informatik, Johann Wolfgang Goethe-Universität,
6000 Frankfurt a.M., Fed. Rep. of Germany

Abstract. Combinational complexity and depth are the most important complexity measures for Boolean functions. It turned out to be very hard to prove good lower bounds on the combinational complexity or the depth of explicitly defined Boolean functions. Therefore one has restricted oneself to models where non trivial lower bounds are easier to prove. Here we consider decision trees, branching programs and one-time-only branching programs where each variable may be tested on each path of computation only once. We present efficient algorithms for the construction of optimal decision trees and optimal one-time-only branching programs for symmetric Boolean functions. Furthermore we prove the following trade-off results. We show an exponential lower bound on the decision tree complexity of some Boolean function having linear formula size and linear one-time-only branching program complexity. Furthermore we show a quadratic lower bound on the one-time-only branching program complexity of some Boolean function having linear combinational complexity. Finally we present some new results on the complexity of decision trees and one-time-only branching programs for the clique function.

1. INTRODUCTION

One of the fundamental problems of complexity theory is to estimate the relative efficiency of different models of computation. In this paper we treat the complexity of Boolean functions. The most important model for the computation of Boolean functions is the Boolean network or circuit model. The proper complexity measures are the Boolean network complexity (combinational complexity) and the depth of Boolean functions. By a result of Spira (1971) the formula size of Boolean functions is closely connected to the depth of these functions.

Until now one knows that nearly all functions have only non polynomial networks and only networks of linear depth but one is not able to prove nontrivial lower bounds for explicitly defined Boolean functions. Therefore one is interested in the complexity of Boolean functions in other models, for example monotone networks. Here we consider decision trees and branching programs for the computation of Boolean functions.

In Chapter 2 we summarize all necessary definitions and show that branching programs/decision trees are Boolean networks/formulae for a complete basis consisting of only one function with the strange restriction that one input has to be a variable. This result opens a lot of new problems: we may consider other bases of this type. Furthermore we see that it is easier to prove lower bounds for branching programs and decision trees than for Boolean networks and formulae.

The depth of decision trees has been considered by many authors. In Chapter 3 we cite some of the known results. We show how the result of Spira (1971) may be applied in order to obtain networks of small depth from good decision trees. On the other hand we show that a result similar to that of Spira does not hold for decision trees.

In Chapter 4 we present an efficient algorithm for the construction of optimal decision trees for symmetric Boolean functions. The size of its running time equals the size of the constructed decision tree. By this algorithm we can deduce a trade-off result. We show that for some explicitly defined Boolean function each decision tree has exponential size while there exist Boolean formulae and one-time-only branching programs of linear size.

In Chapter 5 we treat restricted models of branching programs. Borodin et al.(1983) handle branching programs of width 2 only. They also mention that Masek (1976) has already used one-time-only branching programs. These programs fulfil the restriction that each variable may be tested on each path of computation only once. We are able to present also for this model an efficient algorithm for the construction of optimal programs for symmetric Boolean functions. By this result we construct explicitly functions whose Boolean network complexity is linear but whose complexity for these restricted branching programs is quadratic.

Summarizing we obtain two classes of results. We get efficient algorithms for the construction of some optimal computation schemes. In the whole field of complexity theory there are only few results of this type. Furthermore we obtain some interesting trade-off results.

In Chapter 6 we state some new results on the complexity of decision trees and one-time-only branching programs for clique functions.

2. BASIC DEFINITIONS AND RESULTS

At first we repeat the definitions of the models of computation and of the complexity measures we like to compare.

Definition1: Let Ω be a finite set of Boolean functions. A Boolean formula (over Ω) is a labelled tree where the leaves are labelled by Boolean variables or constants and the inner nodes -also called gates- are labelled by some $\omega \in \Omega$. The edges of the tree are directed from the leaves to the root. If a gate G is labelled by ω where $\omega:\{0,1\}^r \rightarrow \{0,1\}$ it has exactly r predecessors $G_1,\ldots,G_r$ which are completely ordered. The function computed at G, called res(G), is defined by induction by $res(G)=\omega(res(G_1),\ldots,res(G_r))$. The result of a leaf is equal to its label.

Definition 2: A Boolean network (over Ω) is a labelled acyclic graph where the labelling and the mode of computation are defined in the same way as for Boolean formulae.

Definition 3: i) The Boolean network complexity of f over Ω is the minimum number of gates in a Boolean network computing f: $C_\Omega(f)$.
ii) The depth of f over Ω is the minimum depth of a network computing f: $D_\Omega(f)$. Here the depth of a network is the length of its longest path.
iii) The formula size of f over Ω is the minimum number of gates in a Boolean formula computing f: $L_\Omega(f)$.

A basis Ω is called complete if all Boolean functions may be computed by a Boolean network over Ω. Since the network complexity and the depth may only vary by a constant factor if we switch from one complete basis to another (see Savage (1976)) we often suppress the index Ω if we handle the set of all binary functions.

Definition 4: A decision tree is a binary labelled tree where the leaves are labelled by Boolean constants and the inner nodes by Boolean variables. The edges are directed from the root to the leaves. A decision tree computes a Boolean function in the following way. One starts at the root which may be labelled by x_i. If the input vector $a \in \{0,1\}^n$ has the property $a_i=0$ we go to the left successor otherwise to the right successor. If we reach a leaf labelled b: $f(a)=b$.

Definition 5: A branching program is an acyclic labelled graph with one source and arbitrarily many sinks. Each node has outdegree 0 or 2. The labelling and the mode of computation are the same as for decision trees.

Definition 6: $C^*(f)$, $D^*(f)$ and $L^*(f)$ are the branching program complexity, branching program depth and decision tree complexity respectively, defined in an obvious way.

Definition 7: One-time-only branching programs or *-branching programs are those branching programs where on each path at most one node is labelled x_i. The proper complexity measure is denoted by C^{**}.

By our notation we suggest some connections between the complexity measures defined above. In fact we get easily the following basic result. By sel we denote the selection function: $sel(x,y,z)=y$ if $x=0$ and $sel(x,y,z)=z$ if $x=1$.

Theorem 1: $C(f) \leq 3\ C_{\{sel\}}(f) \leq 3\ C^*(f) \leq 3\ C^{**}(f)$

$$D(f) \leq 2\ D_{\{sel\}}(f) \leq 2\ D^*(f)$$

$$L_{\{sel\}}(f) \leq L^*(f)$$

Proof: The inequalities on $C(f)$ and $D(f)$ are obvious since $sel(x,y,z)=\bar{x}y \vee xz$ which implies $C(sel)=3$ and $D(sel)=2$. Given a decision tree for f we may construct a Boolean formula for f over {sel} with the same underlying tree. The same procedure works for branching programs and Boolean networks. At first we reverse the direction of the edges. A node G with predecessors G_1 and G_2 and with label x_i gets a new predecessor G_0 labelled x_i. G is labelled by sel and the order of the predecessors is G_0, G_1, G_2. We may easily prove by induction on the number of gates of the decision tree resp. formula that this formula computes again f.

Q.E.D.

Remark: We note an interesting difference between Boolean networks and formulae on one hand and branching programs and decision trees on the other hand. The information flow is reversed. Thus some ideas for the construction of efficient algorithms for f may work better for one model while others may work better for the other. By Theorem 1 we see that it will perhaps be easier (in any case not harder) to prove lower bounds on the complexity of Boolean functions using branching programs or decision trees.

Here we may ask whether we may construct from a Boolean network or formula for f over {sel} a branching program or decision tree of nearly the same size. In Chapter 4 resp. Chapter 5 we disprove the claim for decision trees resp. one-time-only branching programs.

We now define the function sel* which works like sel but which is restricted to inputs where the first input is a Boolean variable. Given a Boolean network or formula over {sel*} we may follow the proof of Theorem 1 in the other direction and obtain a branching program or decision tree of the same size for the same function. Thus we have proved

<u>Corollary 1:</u> $C^*(f)=C_{\{sel^*\}}(f)$, $D^*(f)=D_{\{sel^*\}}(f)$, $L^*(f)=L_{\{sel^*\}}(f)$.

{sel*} is even a complete basis, since $f=sel^*(x_1, f_{|x_1=0}, f_{|x_1=1})$. Thus C*, D* and L* are also Boolean network and formula complexity measures for the strange but complete basis {sel*}. This result should motivate the investigation of other bases of this type. The input of the functions of the basis is partially restricted to special functions but the basis is even under these restrictions complete. Of course the result that network complexity and depth of Boolean functions do change only by a constant factor by switching from one complete basis to another does not include complete bases of restricted functions.

3. ON THE DEPTH OF DECISION TREES

Obviously all Boolean functions may be computed by decision trees of depth n. On the other hand one was successful in proving that explicitly defined Boolean functions are exhaustive, that means they have indeed depth n (see Bollobàs (1978)).

Rivest & Vuillemin (1976) proved the Aanderaa-Rosenberg conjecture that the depth of decision trees for Boolean functions deciding any non trivial monotone graph property on n-vertex graphs is quadratic. They also proved that Boolean functions where $|\{x|f(x)=1 \text{ and } x_1+\ldots+x_n \text{ even}\}| \neq |\{x|f(x)=1 \text{ and } x_1+\ldots+x_n \text{ odd}\}|$ are exhaustive and that therefore the fraction of nonexhaustive Boolean functions is $O(2^{-n/2})$. Thus we cannot hope to construct Boolean networks or formulae with small depth by constructing decision trees with small depth. Indeed it is easy to show that there exist functions f where $D(f)=\lceil \log n \rceil$ and $D^*(f)=n$.

<u>Proposition 1:</u> There exist Boolean functions f on n variables where $D(f)=\lceil \log n \rceil$ and $D^*(f)=n$, for example $f=x_1 \vee \ldots \vee x_n$.

For $f=x_1 \vee \ldots \vee x_n$ obviously $D(f)=\lceil \log n \rceil$. Therefore Proposition 1 follows from the following lemma.

Lemma 1: If f is nonconstant and symmetric $D^*(f)=n$. Each decision tree for f contains a path on which all variables are tested.

Proof: We describe symmetric functions f by their value vectors $v(f)=(v_0,\dots,v_n)$ where $v_i=1$ iff $f(x_1,\dots,x_n)=1$ for all $(x_1,\dots,x_n)$ where $x_1+\dots+x_n=i$. The lemma is obviously correct for n=1. For n>1 we consider an optimal decision tree for f. The root is labelled (because of the symmetry of f) w.l.o.g. by x_n. Either $f_{|x_n=0}$ with value vector $(v_0,\dots,v_{n-1})$ or $f_{|x_n=1}$ with value vector $(v_1,\dots,v_n)$ is nonconstant. Following the proper edge we reach a decision tree for a nonconstant and symmetric Boolean function of n-1 variables having by induction hypothesis depth n-1 and including a path where all n-1 variables are tested.

Q.E.D.

Proposition 1 and Lemma 1 do not mean that we cannot obtain good results on the depth of Boolean functions by results on decision trees.

Proposition 2: $D(f) \leq c \log (L^*(f)+1)$ where $c=4/(\log 3-1)\approx 6.84$.

Proof: This result is only an application of a result of Spira (1971). As we have seen in Chapter 2 decision trees are also Boolean formulae over the restricted basis {sel*} and especially over the basis {sel}. Thus by the result of Spira: $D_{\{sel\}}(f)\leq c' \log(L^*(f)+1)$ where $c'=(D_{\{sel\}}(sel)+1)/(\log 3-1)=2/(\log 3-1)$. Obviously $D(f)\leq 2\, D_{\{sel\}}(f)$, thus $c=2\,c'$ is appropriate.

Q.E.D.

Since obviously $L^*(f)=n$ for $f=x_1 \vee\dots\vee x_n$ we may obtain a logarithmic upper bound on D(f) by Proposition 2. Certainly one obtains $D(f)=\lceil \log n\rceil$ in an obvious way. A natural question is whether the theorem of Spira may be generalized to decision trees. This would yield an inequality $D^*(f)\leq c^* \log (L^*(f)+1)$ for some constant c^*. This is impossible since we have proved for $f=x_1 \vee\dots\vee x_n$ that $D^*(f)=L^*(f)=n$.

4. AN EFFICIENT ALGORITHM FOR THE CONSTRUCTION OF OPTIMAL DECISION TREES FOR SYMMETRIC FUNCTIONS

The main purpose of this chapter is indicated in the title. A further purpose is to prove a trade-off result. The most important part of this theorem, the lower bound on the decision tree complexity of p_n, is an easy special case of the proposed efficient algorithm.

Theorem 2: For the parity function $p_n(x_1,\dots,x_n)=x_1 \oplus \dots \oplus x_n$ it holds that
(i) $L(p_n)=n-1$, (ii) $C^*(p_n)=2n-1$, (iii) $L^*(p_n)=2^n-1$.

Proof: The property $L(p_n)=n-1$ is obvious. For all functions f on n variables it holds that $L^*(f) \leq 2^n-1$ since we may label the root by x_n and may construct two subtrees for $f_{|x_n=0}$ and $f_{|x_n=1}$.

We like to notice that by the general upper bound on $L^*(f)$ we prove here the largest possible gap between formula size and decision tree complexity.

To prove the second assertion we construct a combined branching program for p_n and $\bar{p}_n$. The program has two sources, one for p_n and one for $\bar{p}_n$, both labelled x_n. The 0-successor of p_n and the 1-successor of $\bar{p}_n$ are combined as a source for p_{n-1} while the 1-successor of p_n and the 0-successor of $\bar{p}_n$ are combined as a source for $\bar{p}_{n-1}$. Thus by an easy induction $C^{**}(p_n,\bar{p}_n) \leq 2n$. We may drop the source for $\bar{p}_n$ in order to obtain a branching program for p_n only. Therefore $C^*(p_n) \leq C^{**}(p_n) \leq 2n-1$.

For the lower bound we prove at first $C^*(p_n,\bar{p}_n) \geq 2n$. The assertion holds clearly for n=1. For $n > 1$ we may assume w.l.o.g. that the source for the computation of $\bar{p}_n$ lies not on a path starting from the source for p_n. In general in branching programs for more than one function some sources need not to be sources of the graph. A similar property holds for Boolean networks for several outputs where outputs for some functions need not to be sinks of the graph. Because of the symmetry of p_n we may assume w.l.o.g. that the source for p_n is labelled by x_n. The two direct successors are sources for p_{n-1} and $\bar{p}_{n-1}$.

These two nodes form the sources of a branching program for p_{n-1} and $\bar{p}_{n-1}$ which does not contain the necessarily different sources for p_n and $\bar{p}_n$. Thus $C^*(p_n,\bar{p}_n) \geq 2+C^*(p_{n-1},\bar{p}_{n-1})$ yielding $C^*(p_n,\bar{p}_n) \geq 2n$. By the same argument we obtain $C^*(p_n) \geq 1+C^*(p_{n-1},\bar{p}_{n-1}) \geq 1+2(n-1)=2n-1$.

It remains to show $L^*(p_n) \geq 2^n-1$. This follows easily from Algorithm 1 since p_n does not become constant by fixing less than all n variables. Q.E.D.

We have seen that it is rather simple to construct optimal decision trees for p_n and $\bar{p}_n$. In the following we present an efficient algorithm for the construction of an optimal decision tree for any symmetric Boolean function. Such algorithms do not exist for Boolean networks or formulae. In general there are known only few efficient algorithms for the construction of optimal computation schemes. Therefore our result offers the problem of finding more classes of functions where efficient algorithms for the computation of optimal decision trees or *-branching programs exist.

We assume that a symmetric function is represented by its value vector $v(f)=(v_0,\dots,v_n)$ (see Chapter 3). Because of the symmetry of the functions we may assume w.l.o.g. that the nodes of level i are labelled by x_{n+1-i}. The graph structure of a decision tree is determined. Therefore we have to decide only whether we may stop the computation. This is possible iff the partial function which has to be computed at the considered node is constant.

Algorithm 1:

Input: $v(f) \in \{0,1\}^{n+1}$, the value vector of a symmetric function $f: \{0,1\}^n \rightarrow \{0,1\}$.

1: We determine the constant parts of v. If $v_{i-1} \neq v_i = \dots = v_j \neq v_{j+1}$ where $v_{-1} := v_{n+1} := -1$ we store the interval $[i,j]$ together with v_i in an array at place i and at place j. Thus each interval is stored twice if $i \neq j$ and once if $i=j$. At each array place we store at most one interval.

2: Perform procedure $[0,n]$.

We define procedure $[k,\ell]$ for all $0 \leq k \leq \ell \leq n$.

Procedure $[k,\ell]$

1: Check whether some interval $[k',\ell]$ where $k' \leq k$ or $[k,\ell']$ where $\ell \leq \ell'$ is stored. In the positive case go to 2, else go to 3.

2: Label the node by the value stored together with the interval and STOP.

3: Label the node by $x_{\ell-k}$ and construct two direct successors. For the left successor call procedure $[k,\ell-1]$ and for the right successor call procedure $[k+1,\ell]$.

Theorem 3: Algorithm 1 constructs optimal decision trees for symmetric Boolean functions. If f is not constant the size of the running time equals the size of the constructed decision tree and is therefore minimal.

Proof: At first we prove the correctness of the algorithm. It is obvious that on the i-th level we label the nodes by a constant or by x_{n+1-i}. If a node is considered by procedure $[k,\ell]$ the current value vector is $(v_k,\dots,v_\ell)$. The intervals are correctly updated in Step 3. Therefore we can conclude that the algorithm works right if it labels some node by a constant. The length of the intervals is always decreased by one. If we reach for the first time an interval of constant values at least the right or left endpoint of the interval coincides with the right or left endpoint of the proper maximum interval. Therefore we label a node by a constant at the first point of time where this is correct.

Now we consider the running time of the algorithm. Using the obvious procedure we may store the appropriate intervals [i,j] in time O(n). For each node the proper procedure [k,ℓ] has constant running time since the check of Step 1 can be done by two tests. Thus the running time of procedure [0,n] altogether is only by a constant factor larger than the number of nodes of the constructed decision tree. By Lemma 1 we know for all non constant symmetric functions f that $L^*(f) \geq D^*(f)=n$. Thus we get the proposed result for the running time. Q.E.D.

5. AN EFFICIENT ALGORITHM FOR THE CONSTRUCTION OF OPTIMAL *-BRANCHING PROGRAMS FOR SYMMETRIC FUNCTIONS

We like to present an efficient algorithm for the construction of optimal *-branching programs for symmetric Boolean functions.

Lemma 2: For each symmetric Boolean function f there exists an optimal *-branching program which is levelled and where each node on level ℓ is labelled by a constant or by $x_{n+1-\ell}$.

Proof: We consider any optimal *-branching program for f. A linkage node is a node with more than one direct predecessor. Let p_1 and p_2 be two paths which are linked at the linkage node L. We like to prove for linkage nodes L in optimal *-branching programs which are labelled by a variable that the set of labellings is on all paths from the source to L the same. Let us assume on the contrary that p_1 and p_2 are paths from the source to L where some variable x_k is tested on p_1 but not on p_2. Let f' be the function computed by the *-branching program starting at L. By assumption f' is not constant. f' is symmetric on the set of variables which are not tested on p_2. Otherwise we could fix the variables tested on p_2 in such a way that we reach L. f' cannot depend on these variables. If f' is not symmetric on the other variables we have two possibilities of fixing these variables fulfilling the following properties. They do not differ in the number of ones but the value of f' differs. Altogether we get two different possibilities of fixing all variables with the same number of ones and different values for f in contradiction to the symmetry of f.

Thus f' is a non constant, symmetric function on a set of variables containing x_k. But the branching program for f' starting at L cannot test x_k since x_k has been tested on p_1. This contradicts Lemma 1.

Since on all paths from the source to L we have tested the same set of variables and each variable only once all these paths have the same lengths. That means that the underlying graph is levelled.

We fix the graph and rename the labels of the inner nodes. An inner node on level ℓ gets label $x_{n+1-\ell}$. Obviously we again obtain a *-branching program. It remains to show that it computes again f. Let $a \in \{0,1\}^n$ and p be the path we have to follow for input a in the reconstructed program. Let π be a permutation on $\{1,\dots,n\}$ such that for the old program the node on level ℓ on p does not exist or is labelled by $x_{\pi(n+1-\ell)}$. Let $a':=(a_{\sigma(1)},\dots,a_{\sigma(n)})$ for $\sigma:=\pi^{-1}$. Because of the symmetry of f we have f(a)=f(a'). If the input is a', the old program forces us to follow p. Thus the endpoint of p is labelled by f(a'). This label has not been changed during the reconstruction of the program. Thus the new program computes correctly f(a). Q.E.D.

By Lemma 2 we know a lot about the structure of optimal *-branching programs for symmetric Boolean functions f. We start with the source labelled by a constant if f is constant or labelled by x_n otherwise. After having labelled all nodes on level ℓ by appropriate constants or $x_{n+1-\ell}$, the nodes labelled by $x_{n+1-\ell}$ get two direct successors, one for $x_{n+1-\ell}=0$ and one for $x_{n+1-\ell}=1$. At first we decide for each new node whether it may be labelled by a constant. This can be done by the same tests as in Algorithm 1. For the nodes which do not become labelled by constants we decide which nodes may be merged to one node. By Lemma 2 we have to decide this question only for nodes on the same level. For each node N at level $\ell+1$ not labelled by a constant we have to compute the non constant and symmetric function f_N on $\{x_1,\dots,x_{n-\ell}\}$ which results from f by fixing $x_{n-\ell+1},\dots,x_n$ in a way that we reach N. By the proof of Lemma 2 we may merge N and N' iff $f_N=f_{N'}$. The value vectors of f_N and $f_{N'}$ are substrings of v(f), the value vector of f. If we have merged as many nodes as possible, we label all the unlabelled nodes on level $\ell+1$ by $x_{n-\ell}$. Then we go on in the same way until there are no nodes without successors labelled by a variable. This happens on level n+1.

Thus the following algorithm constructs an optimal *-branching program for any symmetric function f.

Algorithm 2:

Input: $v(f) \in \{0,1\}^{n+1}$, the value vector of a symmetric function f: $\{0,1\}^n \to \{0,1\}$.

1: We determine the constant parts of v(f). If $v_{i-1} \neq v_i = \ldots = v_j \neq v_{j+1}$ where $v_{-1} := v_{n+1} := -1$ we store the interval [i,j] together with v_i in an array at place i and at place j.

2: Create a node on level 1, label the node by [0,n], $\ell=0$.

3: $\ell := \ell+1$. For all nodes on level ℓ check whether for its label [i,j] (where $j-i=n+1-\ell$) some interval [i',j] where $i' \leq i$ or [i,j'] where $j \leq j'$ is stored. In the positive case relabel the node by the value stored together with the interval.

4: Stop if $\ell=n+1$.

5: Otherwise perform a maximal merging on the set of nodes on level ℓ labelled by intervals (this step will be explained later in more detail).

6: Consider all nodes on level ℓ labelled by an interval. A node with label [i,j] gets a left successor with label [i,j-1] and a right successor with label [i+1,j]. The node itself is relabelled by $x_{n-\ell+1}$. Go to 3.

If Step 5 would be given for free we again would obtain an algorithm where the size of the running time equals for all non constant symmetric functions the size of the computed *-branching program.

We present two procedures for Step 5. The first one does not increase the size of the running time but we assume that much storage space ($O(2^n)$) is given and that we may handle very large numbers (length O(n)). In this situation we compute for each considered interval [i,j] the number z[i,j] whose binary representation is $(v_i,\ldots,v_j)$. z[0,n] can be computed in linear time. z[i,j-1] and z[i+1,j] have to be computed only in a situation where we know already z[i,j].

$$z[i+1,j] = \begin{cases} z[i,j]/2 & \text{if } z[i,j] \text{ is even} \\ (z[i,j]-1)/2 & \text{if } z[i,j] \text{ is odd} \end{cases}$$

$$z[i,j-1] = \begin{cases} z[i,j] & \text{if } z[i,j] < 2^{j-i} \\ z[i,j]-2^{j-i} & \text{if } z[i,j] \geq 2^{j-i} \end{cases}$$

Thus the computation of the z-values does not increase the size of the running time of the algorithm. We can conclude that two nodes labelled [i,j] and [i',j'] on the same level may be merged iff z[i,j]=z[i',j'].

We may realize Step 5 in the following way. We handle the nodes on level ℓ labelled by intervals in an arbitrary order. We use a second array A of length 2^n. Nothing has to be done for $\ell=1$. If we handle for $\ell > 1$ a node labelled [i,j] we look at A[z[i,j]]. If this place is empty we store there [i,j]. If this place is occupied by [i',j'] we test whether j-i=j'-i'. In the negative case we store [i,j] instead of [i',j']. In this and the preceding case we handle the first node on level ℓ with z-value equal to z[i,j]. If j-i=j'-i' we merge [i,j] and [i',j'] by replacing the edge to [i,j] by an edge to [i',j'].

The procedure is correct. For each node we need only a constant amount of time. For each node of the optimal *-branching program we do not create more than two nodes which may become eliminated (merged) afterwards. Thus by this procedure the size of the running time of our algorithm equals the size of the constructed *-branching program if f is not constant.

This approach may be criticized because of its large amount of storage space and its assumption that we may handle very large numbers very quickly. Therefore we like to present shortly a second realization of Step 5. Here our purpose is to describe briefly an efficient procedure using bit operations rather than looking for optimal procedures.

The binary representations of the values z[i+1,j] and z[i,j-1] are the substrings $(v_{i+1},\dots,v_j)$ and $(v_i,\dots,v_{j-1})$ of v(f). By an easy bucket sort on the left endpoint of the interval labels we may merge all nodes having the same label. Afterwards we consider the strings $z[k,\ell]$ for all nodes for constant ℓ-k. In the first step we divide the set into two subclasses of strings starting with 0 or with 1. These sets are treated one after another (or in parallel). They are divided in further subsets looking at the second, third,... component. Empty sets and sets of one element need not to be examined further. The set of nodes forming one class at the end of this classification is a maximal set for merging. Here we do not create more than ℓ classes on level ℓ since there are not more than ℓ different intervals [i,j] where $j-i=n+1-\ell$. Thus the necessary storage space is largely reduced. The running time is multiplied by not more than n, the length of the substrings. But here we count bit operations. We summarize our results.

<u>Theorem 4:</u> Algorithm 2 constructs optimal *-branching programs for symmetric Boolean functions $f: \{0,1\}^n \to \{0,1\}$ represented by

their value vectors. If we may use a storage space of size $O(2^n)$ and if we may operate on numbers of length $O(n)$ the size of the running time of the algorithm equals the size of the constructed *-branching program. Otherwise the running time is at most by the factor n larger.

Corollary 2: $C^{**}(f) \leq n(n+1)/2=n^2/2+n/2$ for all symmetric $f: \{0,1\}^n \to \{0,1\}$.

At last we present some symmetric Boolean functions f where $C^{**}(f)=\Omega(n^2)$ and even $C^{**}(f)=n^2/2-o(n^2)$ showing that Corollary 2 gives the right size for the most difficult symmetric function. Furthermore we obtain the proposed trade-off result.

Definition 8: The exactly-half-function f equals 1 iff the number of ones is $\lceil (n+1)/2 \rceil$. The majority function g equals 1 iff the number of ones is at least $\lceil (n+1)/2 \rceil$. Let the value vector of h be $(a_0,\ldots,a_n)$ which has ones at the positions $i(i+1)/2-1$.

Theorem 5: The network complexity of f,g and h is linear. The *-branching program complexity of f and g is at least $n^2/8-O(n)$ and of h at least $n^2/2-O(n^{3/2})$.

Proof: All non constant symmetric Boolean functions have linear Boolean network complexity (see Savage (1976)).

In order to prove the lower bounds on the *-branching program complexity we give bounds L_1, L_2, and L_3 such that we need for the computation of f, g, and h on each level $\ell \leq L_i$ exactly ℓ nodes. L_i is a valid bound for f_i iff all L_i substrings of length $n+2-L_i$ are different. By L_i we get the lower bound $L_i(L_i+1)/2$.

$L_1:=L_2:=\lfloor (n+3)/2 \rfloor$. There is only one substring of length $\lceil (n+1)/2 \rceil = n+2-\lfloor (n+3)/2 \rfloor$ without 1, for all other substrings the position of the one / the first one is different.

$L_3:=n-N+1$ where $N:=(8n)^{1/2}$. The length of the largest 0-block is at most N/2. All substrings of length N+1 have two ones. The length and the position of a full 0-block between two ones determine the proper interval. Q.E.D.

6. NEW RESULTS FOR THE CLIQUE FUNCTION

In this last chapter we like to present some results on the complexity of decision trees and one-time-only branching programs for the clique function. We shall prove these results in another paper. Independently Pudlák&Zák (1983) proved other results especially for large cliques.

The k-clique function $f_{k,n}$ is defined on $n(n-1)/2$ variables

x_{ij} $(1 \le i < j \le n)$ and equals 1 iff the graph on $\{1,\ldots,n\}$ specified by the variables contains a k-clique. We are able to prove the following results.

1.) For all Boolean functions the decision tree complexity is not smaller than the number of monoms in its minimal polynomial plus the number of clauses in its minimal conjunctive form.

2.) By the result above we get a lower bound of size $2^{n \log 5}$ for the 3-clique function and of size $(k-1)^{n-k+1}$ for all k.

3.) For large k we can do much better by counting the number of inner nodes near the root. We get for $k(n):=n^{2/3}$ the lower bound $2^{h(n)}$ where $h(n):=(n^{4/3}-n^{2/3})/2$.

4.) The best known decision tree for the 3-clique function has size at most $2^{g(n)}$ where $g(n):=n^2/4+2n+1$.

5.) For fixed k the complexity of one-time-only branching programs for $f_{k,n}$ is at least of size $n^{k(k-1)/2}$. Here again we count the number of inner nodes near the root.

6.) For k dependent on n we again get larger bounds. If for example $k(n):=(n/2)^{1/2}$ the lower bound has size $2^{n/4}$.

REFERENCES

Bollobás,B. (1978). Extremal graph theory.Academic Press.

Borodin,A./Dolev,D./Fich,F.E.&Paul,W. (1983). Bounds for width two branching programs. 15th Ann.Symp.on Theory of Computing,87-93.

Masek,W. (1976). A fast algorithm for the string editing problem and decision graph complexity. M.Sc.Thesis,MIT.

Pudlák,P.&Zák,S. (1983). Space complexity of computations. Preprint, Univ.Prague.

Rivest,R.L.&Vuillemin,J.(1976). On recognizing graph properties from adjacency matrices. Theoretical Computer Science 3, 371-384.

Savage,J.E. (1976). The complexity of computing. John Wiley.

Spira,P.M.(1971). On time-hardware complexity tradeoffs for Boolean functions. Proc.of 4th Hawaii Internat.Symp.on System Sciences, 525-527.